THE
MESSENGER
READER

THE
MESSENGER
READER

Stories, Poetry, and Essays
from The Messenger *Magazine*

S<small>ONDRA</small> K<small>ATHRYN</small> W<small>ILSON,</small>

EDITOR

THE MODERN LIBRARY

NEW YORK

Library of Congress Cataloging-in-Publication Data

The messenger reader : stories, poetry, and essays
from The messenger magazine / Sondra Kathryn Wilson, editor.
p.   cm.
Includes bibliographical references.
ISBN 0-375-75539-X (alk. paper)
1. American literature—Afro-American authors.   2. Afro-Americans—
New York (State)—New York—Literary collections.   3. American
literature—New York (State)—New York.   4. American literature—
20th century.   5. Harlem Renaissance.   I. Wilson, Sondra K.
II. Messenger (New York, N.Y.)
PS508.N3M47 2000
810.8′0896073′09041—dc21   99-39882

Printed in the United States of America

Modern Library website address:
www.modernlibrary.com

2 4 6 8 9 7 5 3 1

THE MESSENGER

Trouncing tyrants and traitors,
Hampering henchmen and haters,
Erecting enlightenment's empire

Messenger of merit and manliness,
Emancipating the enslaved;
Symbol of sane salvation;
Scorning slavish surrender;
Emblazoning economic enlightenment;
Nemesis of a nasty nation;
Grinding the great and the grovelling;
Exacting eternal equality;
Rearing the ramparts of reason.

WALTER EVERETTE HAWKINS
September 1923

ACKNOWLEDGMENTS

I wish to thank Manie Barron of Random House for conceiving the idea of this work and for his invaluable advice and support.

I wish to thank the staff of Schomburg Center for Research in Black Culture, the New York Public Library, for their assistance in processing the material published here.

CONTENTS

PART TWO: FICTION AND PLAYS

PART THREE: BOOK AND THEATER REVIEWS

PART FOUR: ESSAYS

Literary and Cultural Essays

INTRODUCTION

IF WE MUST DIE

If we must die, let it not be like hogs
Hunted and penned in an inglorious spot,
While round us bark the mad and hungry dogs,
Making their mock at our accursed lot.
If we must die, O let us nobly die,
So that our precious blood may not be shed
In vain; then even the monsters we defy
Shall be constrained to honor us though dead!*

In his poem "If We Must Die," Claude McKay embodies the new spirit and new self-confidence that were flourishing among black intellectuals and writers shortly before the advent of the Harlem Renaissance of the 1920s. This newfound intellectual and cultural freedom owed much to the eloquent editorials in *The Messenger.* Founded by A. Philip Randolph and Chandler Owen, the New York–based journal first appeared in 1917 for the express purpose of promoting a socialist movement.

Born in Crescent City, Florida, Randolph moved to New York around 1906. After studying at the City College of New York, he became active in the socialist movement. While he was editor of *The Mes-*

---

*See "If We Must Die," by Claude McKay, in the September 1919 issue of *The Messenger* and on page 36 of *The* Messenger *Reader.*

senger in 1921 he made an unsuccessful bid for the office of secretary of state in New York on the socialist ticket. During *The Messenger*'s final years, he abandoned his militancy and devoted more of his efforts to organizing the Brotherhood of Sleeping Car Porters. *Messenger* cofounder Chandler Owen was born in Warrenton, North Carolina, in 1889. After graduating from Virginia Union University, he moved to New York, where he met A. Philip Randolph, and joined the Socialist Party in 1916. Randolph and Owen were the key figures of *The Messenger*'s editorial team, and their inner circle included W. A. Domingo, George S. Schuyler, Theophilus Lewis, William Colson, and J. A. Rogers.

The Messenger was published sporadically during its early years because of meager funding, the First World War, and printers' strikes. It was not published on a consistent basis until 1921, and in 1928 the magazine folded permanently. During its eleven-year run, the journal boasted of being "the only magazine of scientific radicalism in the world published by Negroes."

———

In this Introduction, I want to explain *The Messenger*'s role in the evolution of the Harlem Renaissance. The magazine's poems, short stories, reviews, and essays presented here illustrate its function as an intellectual and cultural outlet for black artists. These writings resonate with the new type of black militancy *The Messenger* helped to produce. I hope to make evident how this spirit of rebellion helped to engender the Harlem Renaissance.

The noted scholar David Levering Lewis wrote that "The Harlem Renaissance was a somewhat forced phenomenon, a cultural nationalism of the parlor, institutionally encouraged and directed by leaders of the national civil rights establishment for the paramount purpose of improving race relations."[*] Writer Arna Bontemps divided the literary movement into two phases. Phase one (1921 to 1924) was the period of primary black propaganda. *The Crisis, Opportunity,* and *The Messenger* magazines were the most important supporters of phase two (1924 to 1931),[†] which eventually served to connect Harlem writers to the white intelligentsia who had access to establishment publishing entities. This relationship proved essential in promulgating the Harlem

———

[*] David Levering Lewis, *The Portable Harlem Renaissance* (New York: Viking, 1994), p. xv.

[†] Arna Bontemps, ed., *The Harlem Renaissance Remembered* (New York: Dodd Mead, 1972), pp. 272–73.

Renaissance. (*The* Crisis *Reader* and *The* Opportunity *Reader,* two previous volumes in this series, include discussions of those magazines' roles in the development of the Harlem Renaissance.)

After the First World War, gifted black writers such as Arna Bontemps, Langston Hughes, Claude McKay, Wallace Thurman, and Zora Neale Hurston gravitated to Harlem. By this time there were more African-American journalists, dramatists, poets, composers, intellectuals, and actors with international recognition there than in all other American cities combined. In spite of this diverse collection of talent, barriers based on racial prejudice caused black writers to be treated like pariahs in the white publishing world. And, because most white publishers believed that African-American writings were substandard, blacks had often been reduced to publishing either with obscure or dubious publishing outfits or by using their own funds. This opinion, according to David Levering Lewis, was evidenced by the fact that only six significant literary writings by African Americans had been published between 1908 and 1923: Sutton Griggs's *Pointing the Way* (1908), W.E.B. Du Bois's *The Quest of the Silver Fleece* (1911), James Weldon Johnson's critically acclaimed *The Autobiography of an Ex-Colored Man* (1912), Du Bois's *Darkwater* (1920), Claude McKay's *Harlem Shadows* (1922), and Jean Toomer's *Cane* (1923).*

The postwar influx of black intellectuals and artists into Harlem, coupled with a lack of outlets for their work, meant that *The Messenger,* like the *Crisis* and *Opportunity* magazines, became a literary springboard for nascent black writers.

The Messenger's contribution to the development of the Harlem Renaissance is not as obvious as that of the NAACP's *Crisis* magazine and the Urban League's *Opportunity* magazine. This may be because *The Messenger* was not united with a civil-rights organization, but rather was confederated with a political philosophy of resolute socialism. Moreover, *The Messenger* didn't have as strong a literary inclination as did the NAACP's and the Urban League's house organs. At the NAACP, this was evidenced by the literary and intellectual works of four brilliant black writers on staff who shared the strong conviction that the power of literature and art could diminish racial prejudice: James Weldon Johnson, W.E.B. Du Bois, Walter White, and Jessie Fauset. These NAACP officials were already leading literary figures by

---

*David Levering Lewis, *When Harlem Was in Vogue* (New York: Oxford University Press, 1989), p. 86.

the early 1920s. Likewise, the Urban League's director of research, Charles S. Johnson, was also the editor of *Opportunity.* Johnson was "the farsighted manipulative editor ... trained as a sociologist but sensitive to the power of the arts."*

The Crisis and *Opportunity* instituted the famous literary-contest award dinners that offered cash prizes to inspire and encourage cultural and intellectual efforts among black writers. It was these contest ceremonies that worked so successfully to connect the black literati to downtown white patrons and publishers. It is likely that the well-organized stratagems of *The Crisis* and *Opportunity* accounted for these publications' perceived predominance in the promotion of black literature and art. Particularly in its early issues, *The Messenger* unequivocally made socialistic economics and politics a priority over culture. Nonetheless, by the mid-1920s it was devoting considerable space to literary writings. Consequently, *The Messenger* was discontinued in 1928, during the height of the Harlem Renaissance. In spite of its turbulent history, *The Messenger* proffered an essential radical dimension to African-American social and political thought. Moreover, it was the singular black civil-rights journal that could boast having the best black drama critic on staff in Theophilus Lewis.

———

The Messenger called for a brand of socialism that would emancipate the workers of America and institute a just economic system. Randolph and Owen believed that centuries of capitalism had perpetuated the existing system, which disenfranchised both black and white workers, and they conceived the idea of using unions as a means to achieving a smooth and painless socialist revolution. Their goal was to unionize American workers, then entice them to become members of the socialist party.

A look at the journal's advertisement space, which was dominated by powerful socialist groups, reveals its primary funding sources. According to Wallace Thurman, a onetime contributing editor for *The Messenger* in the mid-1920s, these funders may have influenced its philosophy. He noted that the magazine "reflected the policy of whoever paid off best at the time."

Early on, the *Messenger* editors were driven in their competition with *The Crisis* to be the most radical and uncompromising journal for

---

*Arnold Rampersad, *The Life of Langston Hughes, Vol. 1: I, Too, Sing America* (New York: Oxford University Press, 1986), p. 106.

black America. W.E.B. Du Bois, editor of *The Crisis* and the most prominent black intellectual of his time, was acrimoniously pounded by the socialist publication for what the editors believed to be his wrongheaded policies. In their stinging editorials, *The Messenger* accused the NAACP of espousing an inconsistent policy on segregation. Well established as proponents of antisegregation in all phases of American life, the NAACP nevertheless endorsed a policy of segregation for military units during World War I. The leading civil rights organization could not articulate an acceptable rationale for their contradictory support of self-segregation. *The Messenger* made the argument that black participation in the war was too high a price to pay to a racist nation that did not deserve such loyalty. Furthermore, a *Messenger* notice that was unmistakably directed toward the leaders of the NAACP stated: "our aim is to appeal to reason, to lift our pens above the cringing demagogy of the times and above the cheap, peanut politics of the old reactionary Negro leaders."*

The Messenger declared firmly that the "new style Negro" would "no longer turn the other cheek." The publication even applauded the African Americans who had fought back in the nation's capital and in Chicago when racial upheavals had occurred there during 1919. This "new style Negro" was determined to make this nation safe for black people. Under the influence of socialism, W. A. Domingo opined that the "new style Negro" cannot be subdued with political spoils and patronage into a false sense of security. But more than that, race leaders must support a labor party and reject capitalism. Black men must fight back, he argued.† Social essays presented in this volume like "The Failure of Negro Leadership," "Socialism the Negroes' Hope," and " 'If We Must Die' " further delineate *The Messenger*'s concept of "the new style Negro."

When black men returned from the war having participated in its moral crusade for international democracy, they realized that the only way to claim the mantle of freedom for African Americans was to fight back physically, culturally, and intellectually. The war experience proved to be a valuable lesson in democracy, and this indoctrination translated into a new type of militancy in race relations.

The participation of blacks in the war, coupled with *The Messenger*'s

---

* See advertisement in *The Messenger*, September 1919.

† Nathan Irvin Huggins, *Harlem Renaissance* (New York: Oxford University Press, 1971), p. 58.

radicalism, gave many of them a renewed spirit and a feeling of power. This metamorphosis sparked a social and literary upsurge. *The Messenger's* connection to the Harlem Renaissance was not forged systematically but rather was a product of African Americans' response to zealous radical voices crusading for socialism. Though most African Americans rejected the journal's philosophy of socialism, many race leaders accepted the major elements of its message.

In 1925 the philosopher Alain Locke, using the theme "new style Negro" extolled by *The Messenger,* assembled a number of writers to create the critically acclaimed book *The New Negro.* Filled with poems, short stories, essays, and plays, the volume was described by Locke as the first fruits of the Harlem Renaissance. *The New Negro* was "the definitive presentation of the artistic and social goals of the New Negro movement."[*]

The Messenger *Reader* constructs a narrative that illuminates the cultural and intellectual aspects of black life from 1917 to 1928. In assuming the responsibility of promoting African-American literature and art as a means of diminishing racial injustice, novelist and *Messenger* editor Wallace Thurman must be credited for publishing many of the works by Harlem Renaissance authors appearing in this volume: the first short stories by Langston Hughes, a series of sketches by Zora Neale Hurston, a short story by Dorothy West, poems by Georgia Douglas Johnson and Arna Bontemps. Many lesser-known but equally talented writers like Thomas Millard Henry, Irene Gaines, William N. Colson, and Angelina Grimke help to build this story, edifying the black cultural movement of the period. This volume also includes the short stories and dramatic criticisms of the undeservedly little-known Theophilus Lewis—called the "literary brains" of *The Messenger*—who published the most effective and consistent writings on the theater during the Harlem Renaissance.

The Harlem Renaissance of the 1920s symbolizes a flashpoint in American literature. Similar black literary movements, as scholars have predicted, will emerge again and again. This recurrence is significant because with each new play, poem, song, story, and essay by an African American, greater clarity will be given to American culture. This is vitally critical because this nation desperately needs to square itself with its multicultural dilemma, and what better way to accomplish this than through the revelations of great black literature?

[*] See Robert Hayden's Preface to the Antheneum edition of *The New Negro* (New York: Macmillan and Co., 1968).

EDITOR'S NOTE: The contents of this volume have been reproduced largely as they originally appeared in *The Messenger* magazine. Though some obvious typographical and spelling errors have been silently corrected, most idiosyncrasies of spelling, punctuation, and typography have been preserved.

PART ONE

POETRY

Arna Bontemps

Song

Lead me yet another day
By the hand along the way.
Ah, never end the strolling till
The pathway meets the hill.

Never rush an early light.
Never urge away the night.
Seldom wake the sleeping one
Till the dream is done.

Woodnote

Trees
That stand the winter through
And make no sound at all
Do not suffer like the trees
That ache with the laboring wind.
Yet these
Sway so listlessly
You would not think that they
Could be so very sad . . .
You might not think
That hearts like ours
Would beat so wearily.

"Song" and "Woodnote" were published in April 1926.

COUNTEE P. CULLEN

Pagan Prayer

Not for myself I make this prayer,
But for this race of mine
That stretches forth from shadowed places
Dark hands for bread and wine.

For me, my heart is pagan mad,
My feet are never still;
But grant these hearths to keep them warm
In homes high on a hill.

For me, my faith lies fallowing;
I bow not till I see;
But these are humble and believe;
Bless their credulity.

For me, I pay my debts in kind,
And find no better way;
Bless these who turn the other cheek
For love of you, and pray.

Our Father, God; our Brother, Christ;
So are we taught to pray;
Their kinship seems a little thing
Who sorrow all the day.

Our Father, God; our Brother, Christ—
Or are we bastard kin
That to our plaints your ears are closed,
Your doors barred from within?

Our Father, God; our Brother, Christ,
Retrieve my race again;
So shall you compass this black sheep,
This pagan heart. Amen.

"Pagan Prayer" was published in March 1924.

ANGELINA W. GRIMKE

To Miss Harriet E. Riggs

It must be beautiful to be
  Splendidly free;
Yet know the world more fair to see,
  Because of you.

It must be beautiful to know,
  Where'er you go,
· That eyes and hearts will sweeter grow,
  Because of you.

It must be beautiful to hear,
  From far and near,
The many voices lifting clear,
  Because of you.

It must be beautiful to feel,
  The while you kneel,
That lovely prayers will upward steal,
  Because of you.

It must be beautiful, indeed,
  To hold the meed;
Yet leave in hearts a crying need.
  Because of you.

Dear Friend, so much of us is you,
  The fine, the true,
That God a little nearer drew,
  Because of you.

May Loveliness about you press,
  Your heart caress,
And Quietness, and Quietness—
  Because of you.

"To Miss Harriet E. Riggs" was published in February 1923.

ARCHIBALD H. GRIMKE

Her Thirteen Black Soldiers

She hanged them, her thirteen black soldiers,
She hanged them for mutiny and murder,
She hanged them after she had put on them her uniform,
After she had put on them her uniform, the uniform of her soldiers,
She told them they were to be brave, to fight and, if needs be to die
       for her.
This was many years before she hanged them, her thirteen black
       soldiers.
She told them to go there and they went,
To come here and they came, her brave black soldiers.
For her they went without food and water,
For her they suffered cold and heat,
For her they marched by day,
For her they watched by night,
For her in strange lands they stood fearless,
For her in strange lands they watched shelterless,
For her in strange lands they fought,
For her in strange lands they bled,
For her they faced fevers and fierce men,
For her they were always and everywhere ready to die.
And now she has hanged them, her thirteen black soldiers.
For murder and mutiny she hanged them in anger and hate,
Hanged them in secret and dark and disgrace,
In secret and dark she disowned them,
In secret and dark buried them and left them in nameless disgrace.
Why did she hang them, her thirteen black soldiers?
Why did she bury them in nameless disgrace?
They had served her, her faithful black soldiers,
They had served her without flinching,
They had served her in peril, in fever, with wounds.
For her at her bidding they marched ready to die,
For her they gave their bodies to wind and rain and cold,

For her they marched without turning or tiring to face her enemies,
For her they charged them and their cannon,
For her they leaped over danger and breastworks,
For her they clutched out of defeat, victory,
For her they laid their all at her feet, her thirteen black soldiers.
But she hanged them in anger and hate,
And buried them in nameless disgrace.
Yes, why did she hang them, her thirteen black soldiers?
What had they done to merit such fate?
She sent them to Houston, to Houston, in Texas,
She sent them in her uniform to this Southern city,
She sent them her soldiers, her thirteen brave soldiers.
They went at her bidding to Houston,
They went where they were ordered.
They could not choose another place,
For they were soldiers and went where they were ordered.
They marched into Houston not knowing what awaited them.
Insult awaited them and violence.
Insult and violence hissed at them from house windows and struck at
        them in the streets,
American colorphobia hissed and struck at them as they passed by on
        the streets.
In street cars they met discrimination and insult,
"They are not soldiers, they and their uniforms,
They are but common niggers,
They must be treated like common niggers,
They and their uniform."
So hissed colorphobia, indigenous to Texas.
And then it squirted its venom on them,
Squirted its venom on them and on her uniform.
In their black faces the venom splashed,
Into their brave heads colorphobia sunk its fangs,
And covered with foul slime her uniform,
The uniform of thirteen black soldiers.
And what did she do, she who put that uniform on them,
And bade them to do and die if needs be for her?
Did she raise an arm to protect them?
Did she raise her voice to frighten away the reptilian thing?
Did she lift a finger or shy a word of rebuke at it?
Did she do anything in defense of her black soldiers?
She did nothing. She sat complacent, indifferent in her seat of power.

She had eyes but she refused to see what Houston was doing to her
      black soldiers,
She had ears but she stuffed them with cotton,
That she might not hear the murmured rage of her black soldiers.
They suffered alone, they were defenseless against insult and
      violence,
For she would not see them nor hear them nor protect them.
Then in desperation they smote the reptilian thing,
They smote it as they had smitten before her enemies,
For was it not her enemy, the reptilian thing, as well as their own?
They in an hour of madness smote it in battle furiously,
And it shrank back from their blows hysterical,
Terror and fear of death seized it, and it cried unto her for help.
And she, who would not hear her black soldiers in their dire need,
She, who put her uniform on them, heard their enemy.
She flew at its call and hanged her brave black soldiers.
She hanged them for doing for themselves what she ought to have
      done for them,
She hanged them for resenting insult to her uniform,
She hanged them for defending from violence her brave black
      soldiers.
Loyal to the last were they and obedient.
"Attention!" she said to them, her thirteen black soldiers,
And without fear or bravado they marched at her bidding, singing
      their death song,
They marched with the dignity of brave men to the gallows,
With the souls of warriors they marched without a whimper to their
      doom.
And so they were hanged, her thirteen black soldiers,
And so they lie buried in nameless disgrace.

"Her Thirteen Black Soldiers" was published in September 1919.

WALTER EVERETTE HAWKINS

Too Much Religion

There is too much time for doctrine:
Too much talk of church and creeds;
Far too little time for duty,
And to heal some heart that bleeds.
Too much Sunday Church religion,
Too many stale and bookish prayers;
Too many souls are getting ragged,
Watching what their neighbor wears.

There is too much talk of heaven,
Too much talk of golden streets,
When one can't be sympathetic,
When a needy neighbor meets;
Too much talk about the riches
You expect to get "up there."
When one will not do his duty
As a decent Christian here.

And you needn't think the angels
Have no other work to do,
But to stitch on fancy garments
To be packed away for you;
For some people live so crooked
Those robes may refuse to fit:
Let us have less talk of heaven
And do right a little bit.

The Bursting of the Chrysalis

Long, long shut in this dismal shell
I slept, I mused, I dreamed
Of things in brighter worlds that dwell,

No poet ever themed;
I broke from out the prison cell,
And out on wings I beamed.

Here and Hereafter

Now you preach a lot of Heaven,
And you talk a lot of Hell,
But the future never troubles me—
'Tis plain as tongue can tell;
And it's mighty poor religion
That won't keep a man from fear;
For the next place must be Heaven,
Since 'tis Hell I'm having here.

Love's Unchangeableness

The kingdoms of ages have gone,
They crumble and lie with the sod,
Like leaves their rich glories are strewn—
They return to their doom or their God,
And where is the pride of the past.
The glories of earthly domains?
They fall 'neath the withering blast—
And yet, O, yet, Love still remains.

We watch the bright trend of the age,
And gather its wisdom and lore,
Commune with the Savage and Sage,
And snatch from Dame Science her store;
But wealth and all wisdom may fail,
And Want follow fast in their train,
Still over the wreck and the Pale
The emblem of Love will remain.

The Voice in the Wilderness

Deep as God's eternal years,
Sad as Christ's atoning tears,
Dread as heart-strings rent apart,
Are the pangs that thrill and smart

Deep within the black man's heart.
      Years of unrequited toil,
In the mould and mill to moil:
He to bear the lash and load,
Hunger's grip and spoiler's goad;
Toil and grime his lot by day,
Fill the mart where others prey;
He to bear the dust and heat,
Smooth the road for others' feet;
He like patient ox to plod,
Bruised beneath the chastening rod,
Tho the load be crushing hard,
Still forbid to call on God.
He to give his blood and brawn,
And himself another's pawn;
He to die for others' good,
Feed another's soil with blood;
He to ask nor fare, nor fee,
Neither life nor liberty;
He to make the weak man strong,
His reward, abuse and wrong.
      This the recompense they give.
Hounds to hunt the fugitive
Fleeing from the cruel lash,
Where Oppression leaves his gash;
Where the mob doth burn and lynch,
Where his blood their thirst doth quench;
Where, despite the boast of laws,
Men are wronged without a cause.
      This my country? cruel Dame!
O for a mantle to hide her shame!
O for tears to wash her guilt
For the blood her hands have spilt!
This the land my heart must pride
Where my fathers bled and died!
Land that boasts of slavery,
Cruel Hate and tyranny?
Where the poor unheeded die,
Christianity a lie,
Human brotherhood a snare,
Liberty a vague despair;

Where to be with right is wrong,
Where the weak crushed by the strong;
Where to be a man is crime,
Where the worthy dare not climb;
Where the Inquisition's paw
Serves to execute the law;
Where manhood is but a name,
Where the fool is raised to fame,
And is lifted up in song
If his creed should serve the strong;
Where the weak must bend and bleed,
Premium put on lust and greed.

Even in the halls of state
True men dare not advocate
Justice for the poor and weak,
They are doomed if once they speak;
Even they who rule the throne
Help the hellish business on.

Public sentiment will not
Dare forgive the bane and blot
Should, perchance, co-workers meet
To adjust the wrongs of state,
And in mutual friendship feel
That the nation's highest weal,
That the people's greatest good
Demands united brotherhood.

Yet within the dens of vice
All may offer sacrifice;
All may freely enter in
Where the paths lead down to sin.
All in fellowship may blend
Where the lures of lust contend,
Where the harlot spreads her arms,
And where vice displays its charms;
Where the serpent hides his stings,
And upon the victim springs;
Where the biting viper darts,
Where the adder's poison smarts,
All in brotherhood may dwell
On the road that leads to hell.

This the land demands my praise

And the service of my days?
This the "land of liberty"?
This the land that men call "free"?
Free, indeed, if they be strong,
Freer still to do the wrong;
Free to persecute the weak,
Free to doom and damn the meek;
Free to rob and cheat, and lie
With no fear of penalty;
Free to revel in the gain,
Wrung from hearts that plead in vain.
    Raise the drooping heart, O God,
Grant the humble foot of sod
Where the wail of war is o'er,
Where the din is heard no more,
Where from blood men's hands are clean,
Where the spoiler is not seen,
Where his curse no more is heard,
Where men's hate no more is stirred,
Where the fowler's snare is not,
Where men's jealousies forgot,
Where the meek uninjured may
Look unto their God and pray,—
There to spend one hour of peace
Where brute force and lying cease.
From the cruel, crushing blows,
From the blighting, blinding woes,
From the cruel curse of foes,
Grant, O God, a day's repose.

Credo

I am an Iconoclast.
I break the limbs of idols
And smash the traditions of men.

I am an Anarchist.
I believe in war and destruction,—
Not in the killing of men, but
The killing of creed and custom.

I am an Agnostic.
I accept nothing without questioning.

It is my inherent right and duty
To ask the reason why.

To accept without a reason
Is to debase one's humanity
And destroy the fundamental process
In the ascertainment of Truth.

I believe in Justice and Freedom.
To me, Liberty is priestly and kingly.
Freedom is my Bride, Liberty my Angel of Light,
Justice my God.

I am opposed to all laws of state
Or country, all creeds of church and social orders,
All conventionalities of society and system
Which cross the path of the light of Liberty
Or obstruct the reign of Right.

Where Air of Freedom Is

Where air of freedom is,
   I will not yield to men,—
   To narrow caste of men
   Whose hearts are steeped in sin.
   I'd rather sell the king,
   And let his goods be stole,
   Than yield to base control
   Of vile and godless men.

Where air of freedom is,
   I will not yield to men.
   I'd rather choose to die
   Than be a living lie,—
   A lie in all I teach,
   A lie in all I preach,
   While truth within my heart
   Its burning fires dart
   To burn my mask of sin.
   I'd rather victory win
   Thru martyr's death than grin
     At wrongs of godless men.

Where air of freedom is,
    I will not yield to men.
I spurn the alms of men,
The livery of kings,
I own far nobler things.
I'd rather choose to own
The pauper's garb and bone,
The eagle's eye of truth,
The lion's strength of youth,
The liberty of thought,
A free man's right unbought,
A conscience and a soul
Beyond the king's control
Than be the lord of slaves,
Of quaking, aching slaves,
Of senseless, soulless knaves,
Or seek to revel in
His ill-got wealth and fame,
His world-wide name of shame,
His liberty to sin,—
    I will not yield to men!

These poems by Walter Everette Hawkins were published in the following issues of The Messenger: *"Too Much Religion," "The Bursting of the Chrysalis," "Here and Hereafter," "Love's Unchangeableness," November 1917; "The Voice in the Wilderness," January 1918; "Credo," March 1919; and "Where Air of Freedom Is," June 1919.*

THOMAS MILLARD HENRY

Ruthlessville

Their floors are cribs of ants and bugs—
I mean the folks of Ruthlessville—
Beneath each bed are liquor jugs;
Narcotic dirt their corners fill.
I mean the folks of Ruthlessville.

Their cupboards smell of musty foods,
Their wealth leans to a wanton use,
They swell their breasts with heartless moods
And leave the coils of virtue loose.
I mean the folks of Ruthlessville.

They squint an eye at aims sublime,
In blowing bubbles they have push.
A trifle grinds away their time;
They breathe an artificial wish.
I mean the folks of Ruthlessville.

Their mode of life is like the bears'—
Blind to the energy of truth.
Their thumbs are down on him who cares;
They hurt him like an aching tooth.
I mean the folks of Ruthlessville.

The Song of Psyche

Hark this message I bring, in this carol I sing,
From a song that I heard in the park.
'Twasn't trammelled in word, for it came from a bird;
'Twas divined from the notes of a lark.

The Song

"Go abroad and impart to the students of Art
All you learn from the Psyche of Light.
Tell them Art is too long to be traversed for Wrong:—
To the wise it is sacred to write.
They must write to remove worthy thralls from the groove,
And unfetter the joy of the land.
They must all hold the rose to the sinister nose,
And awaken the rude to the grand.
They must lavish their sheen to the shame of the mean,
And the elfs who would sully young souls
They must chide and deride and compel them to hide
From their view like the suppliant moles.
The corrupt they must sift for the sake of their gift
Till the Gods become happy above.
And their works mustn't cease till they bring greater peace,
And have spurned sentimentalized love."

'Twas a message serene from a treetop half green,
Further tinted with touches of gold.
On a bench near by there I sat like a guy
Partly doubting the thing he was told.

Dreams Are the Workman's Friends

Dreams are the workman's friends. Their rapture can
Awake his spirits better than old wines;
To 'waken him to beauty is their plan;
They bring him rubies from remote confines.
    Dreams are the workman's friends.

I daily hang my latchstrings out of doors
For them. They throw conditions to the winds.
They find me lighting lamps or tinting floors;
And yet they greet me like old-fashioned friends.
    Dreams are the workman's friends.

Forsooth, the elves of limbo leave my camp,
They jostle in confusion in retreat.
My rapture drives them onward like a lamp
Drives on the dark before the pilgrim's feet.
    Dreams are the workman's friends.

They bring me mingled rapture o'er the crest,
That once behind horizons hid away.
Their gift of rapture burns within my breast
Like twilight beams that love the dying day.
    Dreams are the workman's friends.

My Motive

Should you who listen to my flute
Conclude 'twere best if I were mute,
Or should you doubt that I have won
The wreath of praise, the glad "well done";
If you some better verse have read,
My soul would still be comforted:—
For though I limitations feel,
Love, strangling judgment, made me kneel,—
Constrained by reverence, not conceit—
To vent my soul at Beauty's feet.

Countee Cullen

On Pegasus you've flown into a sheen—
A glorious passion has possessed your tongue.
You moved old doctors with your lispings, strung
Harplike, awaking melodies serene.
Though in this moon when conscious song seems lean,
And bends to prose, your steed with wings outflung,
Veils the Plebeian quills;—wreath-hemmed while young
As Byron was, or Dunbar, at nineteen.
Your diapasons fill Apollo's skies;
Yet, when his restless Nine encircle you,
For pennyroyal sinks your hooked line,
You tonic us mid pleasure and surprise . . .
So I one of your patients credit you
For songs like meat, like medicine, like wine.

Sphinxes

The somber clouds must leave off weeping,
Fell tears. Jove's wind, the mighty hound

With upcurved neck, their trail is sweeping;
Jove's wind upon their trail is found
Whenever it rains.

The sordid clouds shall dread Wind's coming
With splay feet drumming mile on mole.
Whose flapping wings are thunderhumming,
Who throws dust around him pile on pile,
Because it rains.

The belly-heaving Wind is roaring,
His breath is boring to the ear,
More madly than the deep sea's snoring,
Drab clouds are tremulous with fear,
Whenever it rains.

That Poison, Late Sleep

I can name you one time when my feelings were great,
It was when I was hopped on for sleeping too late.
I slept hard that morning, just like it was night;
(Late sleep will disgrace one, I'm telling you right.
You'll see what I mean in a minute, just wait;
You'll know how it fled me down by-ways of Fate.)

I'd arrang'd for some work with a janitor-boss,
But I got there too late, and it made him all cross.
So, though no more cash for me shot up in sight
Than the pay that I might have been owning by night,
Why, his tongue was so strong, and his tone so irate
That I cursed him right back, and got fir'd out the gate.

And, mind you, my story is only half through:
'Twas the time I was spending my wages on Loue.
'Twas the morn just preceding the night of the dance,
And that poisonous sleep cut me off like a lance,
And next thing a break with my love was my fate,
So today I am getting my cap set for Kate.

O that poison, sweet sleep, surely fixed me that day.
It, in one way, was bully, but Lord! did it pay?
Why the break with my Loue was some blow to my heart.—

My! I dote on my Kate when the wound starts to smart.
Still 'tis part of my function to swell and feel great
Whenever I'm hopped on for sleeping too late.

These poems by Thomas Millard Henry were published in the following issues of The
Messenger: *"Ruthlessville," September 1923; "The Song of Psyche," "Dreams Are the
Workman's Friends," and "My Motive," January 1924; "Countee Cullen," October 1924;
"Sphinxes," July 1925; "That Poison, Late Sleep," September 1925.*

LANGSTON HUGHES

Grant Park

The haunting face of poverty,
The hands of pain,
The rough, gargantuan feet of fate,
The nails of conscience in a soul
That didn't want to do wrong—
You can see what they've done
To brothers of mine
In one back-yard of Fifth Avenue.
You can see what they've done
To brothers of mine—
Sleepers on iron benches
Behind the Library in Grant Park.

Gods

The ivory gods,
And the ebony gods,
And the gods of diamond and jade,
Sit silently on their temple shelves
While the people
Are afraid.
Yet the ivory gods,
And the ebony gods,
And the gods of diamond-jade,
Are only silly puppet gods
That the people themselves
Have made.

Prayer for a Winter Night

O, Great God of Cold and Winter,
Wrap the earth about in an icy blanket

And freeze the poor in their beds.
All those who haven't enough cover
To keep them warm,
Nor food enough to keep them strong—
Freeze, dear God.
Let their limbs grow stiff
And their hearts cease to beat,
Then tomorrow
They'll wake up in some rich kingdom of nowhere
Where nothingness is everything and
Everything is nothingness.

Minnie Sings Her Blues

Cabaret, cabaret!
That's where my man and me go.
Cabaret, cabaret!
That's where we go,—
Leaves de snow outside
And our troubles at de do'.

Jazz band, jazz band!
My man and me dance.
When I cuddles up to him
No other girl's got a chance.

Baby, babe,
I'm midnight mad.
If daddy didn't love me
It sho' would be sad.

If my man didn't love me
I'd go away.
Oh! If he didn't love me
I'd go away
And dig me a grave this very day

Blues . . . blues!
Blue blue-blues!
I'd sho have dem blues.

Formula

Poetry should treat
   Of lofty things
Soaring thoughts
   And birds with wings.

The Muse of Poetry
   Should not know
That roses
   In manure grow.

The Muse of Poetry
   Should not care
That earthly pain
   Is everywhere.

Poetry!
   Treat of lofty things:
Soaring thoughts
   And birds with wings.

Poem for Youth

Raindrops
On the crumbling walls
Of tradition,
Sunlight
Across mouldy pits
Of yesterday.

Oh,
Wise old men,
What do you say
About the fiddles
And the jazz
And the loud Hey! Hey!
About the dancing girls,
And the laughing boys,
And the Brilliant lights,
And the blaring joys,
The firecracker days
And the nights,—
   Love-toys?

Staid old men,
What do you say
About sun-filled rain
Drowning yesterday?

The Naughty Child

The naughty child
Who ventured to go cut flowers,
Fell into the mill-pond
And was drowned.
But the good children all
Are living yet,
Nice folks now
In a very nice town.

Desire

Desire to us
Was like a double death.
Swift dying
Of our mingled breath,
Evaporation
Of an unknown strange perfume
Between us quickly
In a naked room.

These poems by Langston Hughes were published in the following issues of The Messenger: *"Grant Park" and "Gods," March 1924; "Prayer for a Winter Night," April 1924; "Minnie Sings Her Blues," May 1926; "Formula," August 1926; "Poem for Youth" and "The Naughty Child," April 1927; "Desire," May 1927.*

GEORGIA DOUGLAS JOHNSON

To Love

Life's little hour is fleet, so fleet
But love's is fleeter still,
So let us lift the chalice dear
And drink, and drink until
The shadows lengthen to repose
And fierce desires still,
Then may our souls view tranquilly
The low light o'er the hill!

Africa

O what a privilege *to be*—
Breath of The Breath Eternal;
To have the life,
To have the strife
Of that dark mystery
A son of Africa, whose blood
Holds nations all in fee,
Commanding by one sultry drop
The whole identity;
She whispers at the gate of birth
And lo! the rainbow on the earth.

Your Voice Keeps Ringing Down the Day

Your voice keeps ringing down the day
In accents soft and mild
With which you have beguiled
And wooed me as a child.
Your presence bounds me every way
And thrills me in its fold
With phantom hands that hold
Like cherished chains of gold.

Paradox

I know you love me better, cold—
Strange as the pyramids of old,
Responselessly;
But I am frail, am spent and weak
With surging torrents that bespeak
A living fire!
So, like a veil, my poor disguise
Is draped to save me from your eyes'
Deep challenges.
Fain would I fling this robe aside
And from you, in your bosom hide
Eternally!
Alas!
You love me better cold,
Like frozen pyramids of old,
Unyieldingly!

Romance

When I was young I used to say
Romance will come riding by,
And I shall surely smile
And play with him a while.

When I grew older then I said
Romance may come riding by
I wonder shall I smile
And play with him a while?

But now alas, I only say
Romance came not riding by
And I shall never smile,
He has been dead the while!

Promise

If you can laugh along the road,
Altho you bend beneath a load
Of sorrow,

Your hope-lit eyes shall surely see
A rainbow sweep eternity
      Tomorrow.

Toy

You deck my body lavishly,
   I'm sleek and overfed;
And yet my soul is perishing,
   Denied of daily bread.

You make a plaything of my life.
   My every trust betray,
And when I would be penitent,
   You kiss my prayers away.

Prejudice

The world is dark,
I cannot see my way!
Eternal clouds
Obscure the light of day—
I seek a break, a rift, a little space,
There to behold
One God-illumined place!

Crucifixion

Ho! my Brother,
Pass me not by so scornfully,
I'm doing this living of being black,
Perhaps I bear your own life-pack;
And heavy, heavy is the load
That bends my body to the road.
But, I have kept a smile for Fate,
I neither cry, nor cringe, nor hate;
Intrepidly I strive to bear
This handicap: the planets wear
The Maker's imprint, and with mine
I swing into this rhythmic line,

In this guise was I made a man—
The world to conquer—and I can.
So I go forward fearlessly
To LIFE, through DEATH,
On CALVARY!

Appassionata

A wild heart in a wretched frame,
Long welted by the years,
A flame that evermore consumes
The vertiment it bears;
So soon to crumble cold, and still,
Its final flicker fail,
And leave within its fevered wake
An ashen-dusted trail.

Disenthralment

Upon a lonely hill I stand,
    And from its height I see
The secrets of the backward way
    I walked in mystery.

The aura fades about your brow,
    I read the riddle clear,
Your little soul stands bare relieved
    Of all that made your dear.

At last—I see you as you are,
    A creature without charms!
Would I had never climbed the hill
    But perished in your arms!

Loss

So you are back—back at my feet,
A suppliant once more,
But life can never, never be
Just as it was before.

For you have robbed me of a thing
More prized than jewels are—

A thing as vital to my need
As light is to a star.

Uncertain now, I hesitate
In fatal impotence
Since you my prince have faltered,
I have lost my confidence.

Karma

Captive am I to chains that bind my willing heart,
Nor seek release, tho well I know
Within this avenue of dreams grim sorrow waits,
And that some day, beneath its shade,
I shall be led—to Calvary!

These poems by Georgia Douglas Johnson were published in the following issues of The Messenger: *"To Love," January 1923; "Africa," January 1924; "Your Voice Keeps Ringing Down the Day," July 1924; "Paradox," June 1926; "Romance," October 1924; "Promise," "Toy," and "Prejudice," June 1925; "Crucifixion," September 1925; Appassionata," "Disenthralment," "Loss," August 1926; and "Karma," September 1926.*

HELENE JOHNSON

Fiat Lux

Her eyes had caught a bit of loveliness,
A flower blooming in the prison yard;
She ran to it and pressed it to her lips,
This Godsend of a land beyond the walls;
She drank its divine beauty with her kiss.

A guard wrested the flower from her hand—
With awful art her humble back laid bare,
Soft skin and darker than a dreamless night;
He tossed aside the burden of her hair.
"I'll teach you to pick flowers in this yard.
They ain't for niggers." He began to flog.

Her pale palmed hands grasped the thin air in quest
Until, like two antalgic words, they fell
And whispered something to her heaving breast.
Then she forgot the misery of her back.
Somehow she knew that God, her God was there:
That what was pain was but her striped flesh.
Her soul, inviolate, was havened in prayer.
On a cross of bigotry she was crucified
Because she was not white. And like her Father
On the holyrood, whispered "Forgive."
And in her eyes there shone a Candlemas light.

He flung the whip into the flower bed—
He did not even see that she was dead.

Love in Midsummer

Ah love
Is like a throbbing wind,
A lullaby all crooning,
Ah love
Is like a summer sea's soft breast.
Ah love's
A sobbing violin
That naive night is tuning,
Ah love
Is down from off the white moon's nest.

"Fiat Lux" and "Love in Midsummer" were published in September 1926 and October 1926, respectively.

S. Miller Johnson

Variations on a Black Theme

I have seen my little black Nellie gal—all naked!
She was wearing a beach-robe of black and gold over one-piece
       bathing togs of blue and white.
She was strolling and singing and dancing 'long a silver sand-clad
       river bank
Trimmed with budding cane and tiny-leafed drooping willows.

   I saw the tilt of her plump black breast
     Beneath that robe of black and gold
  Would its young beauty stand the test
    Of flames that brown lips hold?

I'd like to take her lithe dark body in my arms
And gently squeeze from it
Rich juices of poetry and song.
For she's a slim gay gal with a heart and a song and a smile,
With a strut and a love for jazz!

As Nellie was singing and strolling and dancing 'long that silver sand-
      clad river bank,
She didn't see me sitting over there behind those drooping willows
      that waved by the silver river.
She didn't know I was feasting on the delicious rhythm of her liquid
      movements. . . .
And the sweet charm of her soft slim body—
Dark as the depths of Bantu-land
And as near the teeming earth where God is.

Nellie thought she was out there by herself . . . nobody peeping.
For she looked as free as the tall slim pines brushing bits of white
      clouds from the sky on the other side of the silver river,
As she skipped along that silver beach,
Her little black feet sinking up to her dancing ankles in silver sand.

Nellie threw back her head and smiled at her lover, the Sun.
She stretched her snake-like body up towards mighty heavens
She relaxed with a sigh in the arms of the sun-glow.
Ah! thought I, with a thrill and a jump.
The dance to the Sun and the Silver River!

She flung off her robe of black and gold
And danced to the Sun and the Silver River
A dance primitive as the earth, mother of gods.
She sang a song as she danced there in the silver sand—
A song ripe with oldness and teeming with newness, like the god-
       bearing earth,
'Neath pillared Angkor's mighty shades
   Her palm-like body sways in dance.
Now slow, now mad. The rhythm fades,
   Dissolves itself in air. By chance

Her flowered tunic falls away,
   (The frantic dance goes on and on)
And shows her flesh in glad array
Adorned with gems from Askalon.

Nellie flung aside her suit of blue and white.
The Sun pretended to hide his face behind a little piece of white
    cloud.
But the sun was just fooling; he looked right through that veil of
    cloud at my Nellie.
I got kind of jealous when the Sun looked at my Nellie with no
    clothes on.

Nellie danced on.
She shook herself,
Like a doe jumping up from good healthful sleep
In shaded woodlands
By singing rivulets
And maiden springs—
Springs that whine like a brown gal longing for loving.

Nellie kept singing and dancing,
Singing a song mellow with many years, and new,—
Like the great god-bearing earth:

She floats in honey-tinted sighs,
    She trips about on wings of song.
Desire beckons her with cries
    Of, "Perfect happiness ere long!"

She's frankincense and myrrh, I ween.
    Her countenance is fair.
Her head the proudest ever seen
    Bedecked with silk-black hair.

Nellie's wild black hair fell loose,
Half veiling her beaming black face
Soft as finest chamois.

She lingered wantonly towards the edge of the silver water.
And placed her slender dark hands on her strong supple hips,
And gazed down upon her unclad self,
Her face aglow with mother-longing,
Like the mighty earth, mother of all the great gods of Black Folk.

With golden bracelets 'round her arm,
    A red rose in her hair,
Her soul is autumn-brown and warm.
    A poet's dream is living there.

Her darting, cutting, dashing eyes
    Half-closed, yet full of fire,
Ope wide, then close with mild surprise,
    To trap some some eager sire.

From side to side she swayed her comely hips,
Palm-like beneath the peeping giggling Sun.
Her step was firm, now weak, now pleading
To the Sun, her lover;
Now defiant, now ranting, now expressive of flight
Before her rival The Silver River.
The muscles of her swift black legs were taut,
Ready to run errands for her lover the Sun.

The soft curves of her neck,
The mellow outlines of her back
Flowed clearly . . . then confusedly,
As the dance got faster and faster.
I saw her dimpled knees, like smiling baby's cheeks.
I saw her tender breasts springing regularly,

Tipped with polished bronze,
Teeming with passion,
Pouting for love.

A drooping willow raised his drooping head
To feast his eyes on my Nellie dancing there naked on silver sand by
      the Silver River for her lover, the Sun.
I started to get kind of sore.
But I knew the old willow was too old to do any harm,
So I chanted:

    Do not disturb my very own.
      I'll let you stand afar and look
    At her whose soul is wine to me,
      A golden book, a soothing tone.

I saw her warm pert, laughing mouth.
I saw her right red lips
Magnetic, honey-dewed, half-parted,
Uncurtain the tips of her white, white teeth—
White like rice in a red-rimmed ebony bowl!
I saw her eyes smiling through her long black hair
Which hung all loose and lustrous in the Sun-glow.
I heard my Nellie say to her lover the Sun:

"Come love me now, come love me long."
And I saw the Sun run off giggling behind the clouds.
Nellie shrugged her shoulders
And thrust her fists in her cynical ribs,
And leaned slightly forward,
And sang with the voice of a low-down hag
The song of the Black Fates:

"Dark gal born
Of a dark, dark woman
Ahey!
Sho' bound to see dark days."

She plunged into the stream and swam against the tide,
While I gazed on, wrapt in celestial bliss, wild-eyed.

"Variations on a Black Theme" was published in March 1927.

Claude McKay

If We Must Die

If we must die, let it not be like hogs
Hunted and penned in an inglorious spot,
While round us bark the mad and hungry dogs,
Making their mock at our accursed lot.
If we must die, O let us nobly die,
So that our precious blood may not be shed
In vain; then even the monsters we defy
Shall be constrained to honor us though dead!

O kinsmen! we must meet the common foe!
Though far outnumbered let us show us brave,
And for their thousand blows deal one deathblow!
What though before us lies the open grave?
Like men we'll face the murderous, cowardly pack,
Pressed to the wall, dying, but fighting back!

Labor's Day

Once poets in their safe and calm retreat
Essayed the singing of the fertile soil,
The workman, bare-armed in the noonday heat,
Happy and grateful at his peaceful toil;
But now their voices hollow sound and cold,
Like imitated music, false and strange,
Or half truths of a day that could not hold
Its own against the eternal tide of change.
For Labor, Lord, himself will limn his life
And sing the modern songs of hope and vision,
And write the inspired tale of long-drawn strife
While mocked the poor blind world in grim derision,
Until she opened wide her eyes in awe
To see a new world under labor's law!

Birds of Prey

Their shadows dim the sunshine of our day
    As they go lumbering across the sky,
Squawking in joy of feeling safe on high,
    Beating their heavy wings of owlish gray.
They scare the singing birds of earth away
    As, greed-impelled, they circle threateningly,
Watching the toilers with malignant eye—
    Birds of the darkness—human birds of prey.

They swoop down upon us in merciless might,
    They fasten in our bleeding flesh their claws
(We may be black or yellow, brown or white)
    And, tugging and tearing without rest or pause,
They flap their hideous wings with wild delight
    And stuff our gory hearts into their maws.

"If We Must Die" and "Labor's Day" were published in September 1919; "Birds of Prey" was published in December 1919.

R. Bruce Nugent

Query

My feet in the night
My head in the day;
How could I know
My feet were but clay.

"Query" was published in April 1926.

WILLIAM PICKENS

Up, Sons of Freedom!

(TUNE: THE MARSEILLAISE—NATIONAL SONG OF FRANCE)

Ye sons of freedom, up, to battle!
We go to war against the wrong;
No longer we th' oppressor's cattle,
We rise as men, ten million strong!
We rise as men, ten million strong!
Shall cowards kill and burn our mothers,
Make bastard-orphans of the young,
And then with threats bestill our tongue,
While life is in our bodies, brothers?

Refrain: Up, up, ye men of bronze!
Breathe now a freeman's breath!
And claim your liberty in life
Or freedom in your death!

With wealth and power the tryants fight us
With laws and mobs and bolts and bars,
But, up! let not these things affright us!
We fight with God and with the stars!
We fight with God and with the stars!
Our pathway may be long and gory—
Precious is freedom, high the price,
Bought ever at a sacrifice—
But at the end we gain the glory!

With ignorance they shall not bind us,
We claim the freedom of the school;
With sophistries they shall not blind us,
We will be men and no man's tool!
We will be men and no man's tool!
We ask not pity, O oppressor,
Justice alone is our demand,

The right to use our brain and hand,
The right to be our soul's possessor!

We fight the fight of all the ages,
And walk the path of all the just;
We hear the voice of all the sages:
We will be free if die we must!
We will be free if die we must!
No tyrant's touch or gun shall turn us,
We fight for mothers, babes and wives,
We die for these, our dearer lives,
Though the oppressor shoot and burn us!

O Freedom! let thy spirit charm us!
Let us not heed the coward's fear:
The hand of death can never harm us,
For freedom is than life more dear!
For freedom is than life more dear!
Jehovah, God of all the races,
Sustain our heart, accept our soul,—
From everywhere to freedom's goal,
Millions of Black Men, turn your faces!

"Up, Sons of Freedom!" was published in September 1924.

Wallace Thurman

Confession

I called you human tumbleweed
And chided you for sowing seed
Of misanthropic malcontent;
Yet I suspect my savage breast
Would never nurture seeds of rest,
Even if you sowed them there.

"Confession" was published in April 1926.

PART TWO

FICTION AND PLAYS

THE UNQUENCHABLE FIRE

Robert W. Bagnall displays his prodigious talent for breathing life into natural, domestic, and social scenes. He is equally adept at plumbing the deep inner workings of human emotions. In this tale, he discloses the unsettling capacity of otherwise beneficent mortals to let strong feelings propel them to demonic and hate-filled actions at a momentary turn of circumstance, particularly when the instance is tainted by a blood-mix among races. This story was published in November 1924.

Three hundred miles of Kentucky roads that day the speedometer had registered. It was cold and my motor coat seemed to be powerless to keep me warm. Chilled to the bone, dog tired, and as hungry as a famished timber wolf, I saw at last a farmhouse in the distance. Houses were few and far between in this region of heavy timber, and night, bleak and black, was rapidly outstriding me. I decided to seek shelter.

As I turned into the long lane leading to the solitary farmhouse, I thought with pleasurable anticipation of the warm fire, the hot food, and the bed, I expected to find. All day the chill wind had been blowing an intermittent gale. Like a banshee or a weir wolf it howled. Ragged clouds raced across a dim moon like witches playing hide and seek. The shadows of the dark woods on either side of the country lane seemed to conceal unwholesome figures that were lurking there, watching for a chance to spring at my throat. Dark, desolate, chill, and cheerless, the night held but two comforting things—the patch of light from the farmhouse window, and the pencil beams of light cast by my motor lamps.

At the end of the lane, a big gate barred the way, and as I climbed from my seat to open this, I was greeted by the hollow and furious baying of two great black hounds which stood with straddled legs on the other side, and bared their fangs, reminding me of the "hound of the Baskervilles."

"Hello! Hello! The house!" I shouted. It seemed an interminable time before there came a response. A chain clanked, there was the sound of bars removed, and *slowly the door opened, the light within rushing out, like an imprisoned fairy.*

In the doorway, outlined by the light within, stood the gigantic figure of a man, whose head nearly touched the lintel. He stood with his hands shading his eyes, peering out of the half opened door.

"Who's that?" he called. "What do ye want?" The voice was that of an old man and it contained a note of fear. It was a monotone—a dead voice, which seemed to belong to one in whom hope had died, and in it was dread. "Shut up, ye varmints," he called to the dogs, and at his voice, with tails between their legs, they slunk to cover.

"I am lost, tired and hungry," I called, "and I want a place to stop tonight."

There was a long pause which startled me, for this was a hospitable country.

At length, the man spoke: "Wal, open the gate and drive in. The dogs won't bother you. I guess I've got to put ye up."

"A boot-legger," I said to myself, "who doesn't relish a possible prohibition officer entertained unawares." I parked my car in front of the house and entered. It was a typical farmhouse into which I came. The lamp failed to light all the big space and the dark shadows caused my eyes, unused to the glare, to be blinded to much of it. But the fireplace held a big, warm blaze which bade me a glowing welcome.

I turned to look at the man of the house and saw a once powerful figure over six feet four, now emaciated and worn. His great gnarled hands showed the strength that had been his. His face was the color of old parchment and seamed with wrinkles. The skin was drawn tight on the cheek bones like a death mask, and his mouth constantly twitched. This spasm and the man's whole appearance revealed that he had suffered some great shock. His hair, snow-white and shaggy, stood up on his head in a most peculiar manner. It seemed to be literally standing up with fright. My gaze would stray to it. But one was most haunted by that man's eyes. They were the eyes of a trapped animal. They were filled with such horror and terror that they chilled my blood. At the slightest sound they would glance here and there like a hunted beast, and glare as if in a frenzy of fear.

"Make yourself at home, stranger," said my host. "My name's Tower." As I told my name and removed my coat, there was the feeling that the name sounded vaguely familiar, but I could not remember where I had heard it.

"I'll see what Mandy can git fer you to eat. Warm yerself." With that he strode out of the room and in the distance I could hear his voice calling: "Mandy! You Mandy!" A dim voice answered—a woman's voice.

What is the matter with this man, I wondered. Some awful tragedy has overshadowed him. Just this way might Oedipus have looked when he learned that he had slain his father and taken his mother to wife.

I walked over to the fireplace and stooped to warm my hands. Suddenly behind me came a woman's voice, tired, hopeless, fearful.

"Did you see him in the lane?"

Startled, I wheeled, for I had thought myself alone in the room. Then I saw her. She sat in a rocker amid the shadows on the other side of the room. Her blue eyes burned with madness as she looked at me. Her face was pitiably thin and pinched. She wore a red calico wrapper which seemed without shape or form. *Her mouth now hung open and I could see she was insane.* Just then the fire flared up and revealed her hair. Masses of dishevelled gold, falling in glistening showers around her, the light from the flames dancing upon its rippling sheen. As she sat, she rocked and rocked without cessation, and her fingers never ended pulling at her locks.

"I saw nobody," I answered, but already her attention was gone, and her wild eyes stared into space.

"What have I come upon, a mad house?" I whispered to myself. "What awful thing has happened here?"

Then the man stood in the door. "Come and git some grub," he said.

The meal was indifferent, but my hunger was a sufficient appetizer. It was served by a middle-aged mulatto woman, who gave evidence of having been very comely. My host stood by the mantle in silence and smoked as I ate. Every little while, the mulatto would glance at him with a concentrated look of hatred. At these times his mouth would twitch more rapidly and with greater violence.

I didn't sleep well, tired as I was. I didn't like the house nor its occupants, and outside the wind howled as if a thousand demons had been let loose out of hell.

It must have been about three o'clock when a wild scream awoke me. It came again and again, the long drawn-out cry of a tortured and anguished soul, and then came that moaning cry: "O pappy, O pappy, why, Oh why did we do it?"

I crept to my door and heard the murmur of voices, and that heart-rending sobbing of a woman, the sobbing of a woman whose heart is broken beyond cure.

At the sound of that sobbing, like a flash came to me the memory which had eluded me all the evening. I knew now who these people were and what was their tragedy. It was a year ago that I had heard their tale, and now for the first time I recognized them as the subjects of the story told me.

Seated in the smoking compartment of a pullman car a year ago, with the hazy outline of the same Kentucky mountains looking like purple shadows against a pale sky, my fellow travelers and I had talked about lynching. It was then that one of them, a gentleman stock breeder said: "Don't imagine that those lynched are the only ones who suffer as the result of it all. Let me tell you that often the white lyncher pays a bigger price than the Negro victim. The black man's torture is soon ended; his life snuffed out in a little while, but often, there's hell to pay for a long time afterwards for the whites who lynch."

Someone started to speak when the stock breader continued: "May I tell you a story of what happened in this section less than a year ago?" He began: "Just twenty miles from my home is the farm of John Tower. Tower was one of the most popular men in this country. The strong man of this region, the champion amateur boxer and wrestler, the jolly spirit at gatherings, his blue eyes crinkling with his sunny smiles, his infectious laugh resounding on every occasion—he was the local hero. His golden hair and huge bulk made him look like one of the old Vikings. Women adored him, but while he had a pleasant word for all, he paid no serious attention to any of them. Tower had lost his wife, and many of the women thought that he needed a mother for his five-year-old girl, a winsome thing with her father's hair and eyes, but he did not seem to agree with them. He was immensely proud of her and while she sat on his knee and rumpled his hair by the hour, his face would light in a wonderful way. Every night, as he drove down the lane, a rare smile of joy would irradiate his countenance as the little girl would run out to the gate, and waving her arms and jumping up and down in glee, would shout, 'Here comes daddy!'

"From some place up the state, Tower had brought a mulatto woman to keep house for him. She was a fine looking woman who had a little son about six years old. The boy had blue eyes and jet black curls and showed little trace of Negro blood. It wasn't long before the gossips were whispering that Mandy was more than a housekeeper and remarking about the boy's eyes resembling Tower's. It may have been a chance resemblance, but the boy did somehow remind one of Tower. At any rate, you know, gentlemen, that the sort of relationship implied is not uncommon here in the South. But whatever Tower and his mulatto housekeeper were to each other, everyone agreed that the boy never dreamed that Tower was his father, although he adored the man.

Wherever Tower went, you would see seated on the wagon beside him the little colored lad and, until she began to get around eleven or twelve, his little girl. The boy showed so little trace of color that strangers thought the children were brother and sister. They were great chums—the two children, and Tower's friends at times warned him that it wasn't well for even the children of the two races to be so intimate.

"The boy had the habit of waiting at the end of that farmhouse lane for Tower when he did not accompany him. He would climb up on to the seat beside Tower and ride down the lane to open the big gate at the end. The lad's affection for Tower seemed to be returned in full measure. He wanted the boy near him, it appeared, and apparently forgot his race.

"I remember an incident when the boy sat on a box in a corner of the store where Tower was chatting with acquaintances. One of these called to the lad, 'Say, little nigger, bring me that bag near you.' The boy's form grew tense but he didn't move. In one stride, Tower stood in front of the man, his fists clenched, his face white with fury. 'Call Jimmie a nigger again,' he said, 'an' I'll knock yer teeth down yer throat.'

"As a result of all this people said Tower was spoiling the boy, and that no good would come from a nigger being taught to forget his place.

"In a little while, the boy and girl had passed childhood. She was as pretty as a sunset, with something of its dazzling effect. The boy now called her Miss Annie and appeared to know his place. He was a huge lad for his twenty years, six feet two, and had the habit of holding high his head and looking you straight in the eyes—a habit that made it hard for you to remember that he was not white.

"It was shortly after this that the thunderbolt fell. Tower's girl had not been well for some time. She grew thin; her color left; she couldn't eat, and she appeared melancholy. Tower wanted to send for a physician, but she persuaded him that soon she would be well again. Mandy it was who told Tower something that caused him to send post-haste for the doctor. When he learned that Annie was to be a mother, he was like one stricken. And then he became furious. He swore that he would wring the neck of the man who had ruined his little girl, and then he began to try to force her secret from her. She had his will, and it wasn't until he reluctantly swore on her mother's Bible to do no harm to her lover that Annie told his name. It was Jimmie, the colored boy, who had grown up with her. They loved each other; they knew it would not be permitted and so they had met secretly for over a year. He had wanted her to go North to marry him but she wouldn't. It was not his fault; she had loved him so much, and she had made him do her will. As she sobbed out her tale, Tower looked at her as if she were a monster. Then, white as salt, without a word, he strode over to the mantel, caught down his rifle, and started for the door. With a wild cry, the girl caught his arm, but with a shrug he flung her to the end of the room where she lay in an unconscious heap.

"The night had just fallen when he left, but the clock had struck midnight when he returned. Warned in some way, Jimmie was gone. Tower's quest had been in vain.

"No one knows what he did to that girl during the night, but in the morning when all the country round belched forth grim-faced white men with guns and dogs, the girl told a different tale. The Negro, Jim, had raped her and threatened her life, if she told; forcing her again and again to do his bidding on pain of death.

"Death was in the air when she finished her story. You could smell its acrid odor, you could taste it, you could see it reflected in the stark gleaming eye-balls of these erstwhile kindly Kentucky farmers. You could hear it in the hoarse growl of their voices—in the sharp baying of their hounds. These men, in a moment, had shed like an irksome garment centuries of civilization. They had become the man beast whose sole lust was to kill—to kill! The blood lust was theirs, and the thrall of that most ancient and exciting of sports—the man hunt.

"It wasn't much of a chase. Two hours had not gone before they found the hapless wretch in the woods near the farm.

"Like a pack of wolves, pulling down their quarry, they were upon him. Down he went under the struggling mass of frenzied men, each seeking to strike, to tear, to destroy him. Tower tore through them, throwing them aside as a hunter scatters a pack of hounds lest they ruin the skin of the kill. The men fell back, and Tower stood face to face with Jimmie. Gripping the boy's shoulders with a grasp that almost crunched the bones, his nostrils dilated, his face contorted into a horrible mask, he glared into the boy's face. The boy's eyes did not sink before his glare. His face white, but his head erect, looking for a moment like Tower's other self, he met look with look, cold blue steel meeting cold blue steel.

"Tower's huge hands reached for the boy's throat and then dropped to his sides. 'Take him!' he growled.

"With a beast-like snarl, the mob was upon him. Ox chains fastened him to a sturdy oak. Leaves and faggots in feverish haste were heaped around him. The blood lust hurried them. The mob had made its preparation. They poured gasoline over the faggots, over his clothing.

"All the while the boy and Tower stared each at the other. Tower's fingers opened and shut like talons—his face a grimace of hate. Whatever the boy had been to him was past. He was now only a nigger who had ruined his daughter, just as he was to the mob—a nigger who had raped a white girl.

"Someone placed a lighted torch in Tower's hand. With a snarling oath, he lighted the faggot. The flames leaped up, but before the smoke blotted out his face, Jimmie looked the last time at Tower—a look not to be forgotten. Higher leaped the flames, thicker swirled the smoke. More fuel! More gasoline! It was over and the boy had not uttered a word or a cry. Unsatisfied, the mob pumped bullets into the charred body until it was literally torn to pieces.

"Things will leak out. The girl went raving mad and babbled the truth. But the mob had no remorse. 'He got what was coming to him,' they said, 'daring to have a white girl for a sweetheart!' They envisioned themselves as heroes, protectors of white womanhood and Anglo-Saxon purity of blood.

"The child came before its time—dead. The girl has never recovered her mind. She believes her Negro lover comes back to reproach her for betraying him. And Tower has become the broken, fearhaunted wretch. The neighbors leave them alone. They dwell there, the man, the girl, and Mandy—the boy's mother. Why this woman stays or why Tower permits her to stay, no one knows. She hates him. Her every gesture shows it, and some think she will yet kill him in revenge.

"Tower, it is said, believes that whenever he drives into that lane, the lad comes as he did in life, climbs to the seat beside him, and at the end, opens the gate. He says that the boy stares at him with his somber blue eyes as he did on the day of the lynching, and it causes his flesh to run cold. Tower will not leave the house after dark—for he says Jimmie is waiting outside for him. Remorse and terror stalk over at his side. The Negro lad's fate was far easier."

The stock breeder ended. There was a silence and then a mining engineer started to make some comment. Just then, the porter called another station stop, and I hurried out to get together my luggage.

All this now came back to me as the echo of that cry of despair rang in my ears, "O pappy, why, O why, did we do it!"

I didn't sleep any more that night, haunted by the thought of the tragedy in that house. When gray dawn was breaking, I dressed and came down stairs, and there in front of the fireplace, with his head in his hands, as if he had not been to bed, sat Tower. In the wan light of the morning he looked more forlorn and distressed than ever.

I greeted him in as bright a manner as possible, but received no reply. Thinking that the old man, weary with his remorse, had at length fallen asleep, I came nearer, when I noticed that his eyes were wide open, a look of stark horror and animal terror in them. The man was dead.

As I turned to call some occupant of the house, I noticed on a table nearby an open Bible, with the words underlined in red ink: "Where the worm dieth not, and the fire is not quenched."

SILK STOCKINGS

Anita Scott Coleman declares her story a "plain tale of plain people." Nevertheless, she builds a narrative that shows how great truths and life's richest rewards are revealed to human beings, whether in a complex manner or by chance. Her main character, Nancy Meade, has a love of silk stockings, symbolizing mere imitations of life. Coleman published this story in August 1926.

This is a plain tale of plain people. Have you ever thought about it.... How the grand, somebody folks are responsible for all the scandal to be found in yellow journals and the poor nobody folks supply the sob-sisters with material for their columns.... But for tragedies from which drama is woven, go to plain everyday folks.... For humor, the essence of comedy, ditto—go to plain folks.... The reason why here in a nutshell, is; because plain folks never stage their acts.... They do not know, so plain are they, that all of tragedy and all of comedy is in each hour of their daily lives....

"There are chords in the human heart, strange varying strings which are only struck by accident." (Accident, no time to stage the effect.) "Which will remain mute and senseless to appeals the most passionate and earnest and respond at last to the slightest casual touch"—(casual, just common, you know.) "In the most insensible or childish minds there is some train of reflection, which art can seldom lead or skill assist; but which will reveal itself, as great truths have done, by chance." There ... you have the gist of this story.... Unless you wish, you need not read on....

Silk stockings are plain things—that is, to some.... And to others, silk stockings belong in the class with grand somebody folks.... And to others; silk stockings are sob-sister material....

To a very young person named Nancy Meade, silk stockings were so plain things they were dove-tailed into her mind as necessities along with bread and meat.

To young strapping John Light silk stockings were—well, his mother never wore them....

To the plain villain in this plain tale silk stockings at so much per, were handy articles for appropriating admiration for oneself or for fanning the flames of adoration, as you like, in another....

Little Nancy earned her living by dancing as it was her only paying asset, its plain enough to anybody, why.... But she had the reputation of being a good little thing. And all the other girls in "Oh, You Chocolate Dolls" the cheap troupe with which she was booked, called her "The kid" and barring the sheerist mite of raillery which being feminine, at times had a "cattish" trend, let her alone.... All the men respected her.... Proving that they did so by their immovable reluctance about footing any little bill she might have incurred at an after-the-show-supper or for an off-stage, in between acts—sandwich.

And Nancy not having the means to foot many extras herself kept dutifully at home—"Home" being any place at which the troupe put-up—and in quite lady-like manner plying her needle. Nancy's dissipation was clothes. Pretty clothes . . . ravishing clothes . . . silken clothes. She adored fine laces and thick plushy velvets and she possessed a ferret's nose for scenting out the most expensive and the most exquisite garments in any man's shop.... So, the clothes she wore were the sort homely women dream about. . . . Clothes that made her coworkers green with envy.... She didn't have money, but she had the knack of putting clothes together with a needle and thread—Her clothes made the chambermaids at the varying hotels pop their eyes and clothes that made women she passed on the street turn about for a second, sometimes even a third, stare....

Nancy was certainly nimble-fingered to a marked degree as well as quick on her toes.... She did a great deal of mending, ripping, letting out, altering and remaking. At times she even dyed and pressed lingerie, blouses and dresses; but silk stockings are peculiar things....

Nancy just couldn't make silk stockings. . . . Nor could she alter them—rip them up and make them over.... Of course, she might have darned them; but who, being a lover of silk hose wishes to darn them? Who versed in the oddities of silk stockings, even wants to darn them? Whatever your arguments, Nancy did not.

She bought silk stockings like a thoroughbred, wore them like a queen, and discarded them, when they threatened a "run" like any other devotee.

Nancy earned all she got. I have told you how. But she did not get much and with a penchant for finery and an especial longing for silken hosiery.... Raise the curtain please ... here comes the villain.

Gerald Lincoln McKay; do not be glad to meet....

Gerald had kept no accurate account of his "scalps," the term he used for his numerous lady-loves with whom he had played around with and discarded. He was actually a connoisseur of ladies ... and just as cold-blooded in his tactics with them as any critical judge of antiques and art. He spoke of the gentler sex as types.... He would say: "That Mrs. West.... Ah, yes.... Your red-hot mamma type.... Little Elfie Sanders ... sure I know her ... real baby type.... Ida Moss.... By the way, there now, is your Kitten type.... He would stroke his long chin and run his eyes over a roomful of girls and comment: "Not an innocent type here—la, la, that kind's passing."

Few men enjoyed his presence. But the devil having engineered his transportation into this realm had seen to it, that he pleased the ladies. His was a long sallow face, ivory-colored.... His was the hair women delight to pass their hands through, soft, and thick, and wavy, and he kept it scented. ... And he possessed that indeterminate orb, which poets call soulful....

Speaking of his eyes.... "There'd come a moment," the girls said.... "When you would be studying 'bout.... Oh, nothing at all and you'd glance up at Gerald"—he was gracefully tall.—"And you'd feel—oh, you couldn't explain it—and the next thing you'd be—according to your type—hugging him or he'd be hugging you ..."

As you might know the innocent type was Gerald's particular prey. ... It did him good. Gave a zest to his life.... Kept him keen for battle. ... Sharpened his weapons.... Appeased his appetite to prove the innocent little things not innocent at all ...

At first sight of Nancy, Gerald girthed himself for battle.

He really had a way with women.... And Nancy was soon glowing and beaming under his expert tutelage.

That love transforms a woman is not altogether true; because a woman can love most earnestly a thousand years; if that were possible, and none would ever know it, so far as any difference it may make in her ability to scintillate and dazzle; but give her a lover, one who feeds her vanity; now then, we have the secret of the transformation.

Nancy was not in love with Gerald, thank heaven. Yet, probably time would have wrought real havoc had not Providence moved John Silas Light straight onto the stage ... when the scene was set for the entrance of the hero.

John Silas Light, a torch-bearer. Perhaps you have never heard of him and have never caught the glimmer of his torch. Often, girls had declared to one another: "They wouldn't have him. He is too slow" . . . but each had locked in the closed chamber of her heart, the fervent hope; that beneath her fiancé's dashing qualities, were hidden and waiting for marriage to reveal them, the sterling attributes of a John Silas Light.

He is likely to be the fellow who goes to work at six o'clock every morning and eats lunch from a tin-pail at noon, finding the cold lumpy food palatable; because "his old gal" prepared it. He goes straight home, when he is off the job and once there, he is apt to become ridiculous while at play with a couple of kids. . . . For strangely enough, considering his length and girth, he can conform his proportions to a ginger-bread-man's or a squealing pig's and he can march and growl like Bruin, the bear. And, too, he is a bit of a bore always annoying the gang with harping about his wife and his wonder-baby; but then, you can borrow a portion of his pay-check and so long as he thinks you "square," he will go hungry before ever asking you to "hand" it back. And without really meaning to, you fall into the habit of letting your troublesome ten-year-old spend his evenings over to his house. . . . Rests you so, to have him some safe place out of the way. . . . Besides, all the other youngsters in the neighborhood are there.

Nancy's John Silas Light revered all women—smile if you want to—because his mother was; as was the Holy Virgin, a woman. He hated to see women carrying bundles or cranking cars, he always wanted to assist them; and, because often, he could not, owing to convention and because of color, made all there was of pathos in his plain existence.

As often as not, he over-stepped convention in a straight-forward, big-hearted way. But he could neither side-step nor over-step color, and to attempt "stepping on it" was like stepping upon a puncture-proof air mattress, it merely bulged in another place. So, he was rapidly becoming soured. The warping things of life often does that to the John Silas Lights; just as time and heat turns sweet milk to clabber.

He was becoming worn as an old shoe is worn and he needed polishing and brightening up. . . . And what better than to have a blithe, pretty creature like Nancy dance right into his heart?

John sat in the front row and watched Nancy's face or perhaps, all of her winsome body, instead of just her legs. . . . He thought her adorable.

And Nancy, strange as it may sound, saw John from across the footlights and straightway forgot to perform for her audience. . . . She began dancing just for him. . . .

Yes.... It was done ... the portrayal of your hero and heroine's love-making; but it takes too fine writing for this plain tale....

Hence:—John and Nancy were married the forthcoming Spring as soon as her contract ended.

And, mind you, John didn't even have the ciphers to a bank account, nor did he give a single fig for silk stockings....

John was a worshipper of women and as most worshippers are, had not the wit to discover why they were so easy to worship. It's a common saying, that when a woman is ugly it is her own fault. A louse can interpret the meaning; but not so John.... Such a cue as the following gave no light to him.... There's a cream for every face.... A style for every figure.... Fabrics to match the style and colors to match complexions.... And where is the leg that is unsightly in a nice silk stocking?

A moral daubed on at the end spoils any good story; but taking it right in the middle hits the nail on the head and it drives in without hurting a thumb. The moral is here, but find it....

John was inordinately happy. He forgot to sulk because the Creator had run into dark colors when he happened along.... In due time, he threw all doubts, all fears, and all precautions to the four winds and became a father.

Blithe Nancy emerged from the ordeal in no wit daunted. She was as girlishly rounded as ever; as nimble upon her toes as ever and far more eager for pretty new clothes....

Many of her prenuptial garments had been cut up and done over into the prettiest, cunningest baby things you ever saw.... You can't blame Nancy for expecting a whole new outfit for herself as soon as this baby-business was over. She did not get it.... She cast subtle hints and talked largely of all her clothes being "rags" and complaining childishly "that she didn't have a thing to wear."... All to no use.

Then, in a desperate moment, she quite matter of factly, asked John to buy her some stockings....

Now, John's mother was a thick stoutish, old-fashioned lady who did not believe silk was silk unless it "rustled," and had all her life encased her legs in cotton. John, manifesting the contrariness of man, immediately, upon hearing Nancy's request, settled his thoughts upon the stockings his mother had worn and never once thought of—he could have looked for that matter—the stockings his wife was wearing.

That evening he gave Nancy the stockings which he had dutifully bought.... Hanging about wistfully to watch her unwrap them, so that he might witness her delight.... But Nancy was yet coy enough not to.

She waited to be alone and one glance at them . . . those awful stockings! made her cry herself to sleep.

Next morning, for the first time since her marriage, Nancy began an appraisal of "This man I now wed." A fatal moment in the lives of married folks. A ripe moment for Love to set his thumb to his nose, spread his wings and fly out of the window to escape Satan, who enters the door. . . .

Completely out of sorts and bitter because of the scurvy trick life had played her. . . . Scurvy? It was worse, if she was never to have any more nice things to wear. Why—what was the use in living?

She put Baby to sleep and ran out to the grocery. One had to go on eating and drinking. . . . Drinking and eating even if they had to wear horrid, horrible stockings. . . . Tears blinded her. She could not see . . . the human fashion-plate that stopped short at sight of her.

"By the Lord, it's Nancy," he exclaimed and set himself to the task, no art, of making her see him. . . .

Angrily, Nancy dashed the tears from her eyes and quickened her pace. . . . She wouldn't be a weeping pillow . . . not for . . . not for twenty Johns. . . . If he wanted her to be old and ugly. . . . If—

"Why, Gerald! . . ."

" 'Lo Nan—Pardon . . . er, ah, er, Mrs.—er, Light."

The name accompanied with a real girlish giggle, supplemented by Nancy.

They entered the Grocer's and Gerald stood by, while she made her purchases. Gerald carried her tiny parcels and walked with her to her gate.

Oh, no, he couldn't possibly "come in." That, he reasoned was too free and above board. . . . And being free and above board is never good diplomacy when you are weighed down with motives that are about fifty leagues under board.

Gerald felt that John had spoiled his fishing, pushed him away from a mighty lovely stream. . . . And if he could sneak back and muddy the stream, he would be willing to call it "quits." As for Nancy, pshaw, her type was usually flighty. He would be careful not to go too far. All he wanted was to make the "old joker" jealous. It would be wise not to start visiting. The old fool would consider the visits to him. He would never suspect a man who came to his home openly.

Gerald laughed in his sleeve at his own imagining of John asking him to "Come in." Welcoming him in his hearty way. . . . Calling to Nancy to fix a bit to eat. . . . Offering him a cigar. . . . Showing him the baby, bragging, like the donkey that he was. He pictured John following him to the door, down the walk, out to the gate and sending his big voice after him far down the street, calling "Come again." . . .

Gerald was a clever craftsman, he manoeuvered adroitly.

Nancy started slipping out to meet him. They would drop into a "movie" while it was dark and steal out again through the throbbing, people-jammed blackness. They would wander about and find a snug seat in the park where the night-scent from flowers and shrubbery pressed upon them while they exchanged confidences. . . .

"Well, you see if you had stuck to me. . . ."

"Oh, Gerald. . . ."

"You couldn't expect a dub—"

"Now don't you dare say a word 'bout John. . . ."

"I wasn't saying nothin' at all 'bout him (damning John under his breath). "I was going to say you couldn't expect a dub like me to win anybody like you—"

"Oh, Gerald," mournfully.

"Ah, yes, it's oh, Gerald, but you keep on sticking to that big st—, er John. . . . Why don't you leave him? Come and go with me. . . . Come on, honey. . . . You're not happy. . . . You couldn't be. . . . Answer me, honey. . . .

There would be a faint sob. . . . Yes, indeed, poor Nancy was unhappy, terribly torn with conflicting emotions. . . . What with actually praying for John to rise up some evening and order her to stay home and see that she obeyed him, instead of saying:—"Don't stay out any later than ten Nannie. . . . At half past ten to the dot, old Sonny-boy wakes up and yells for you. . . . Enjoy yourself but don't forget the time. . . ." And what with being elated at having Gerald make love to her. . . . Why, it actually proved that she didn't look badly, in cheap horrid clothes, after all.

Anyway, John was doing all he could for her and baby and it didn't really matter even if she was "naked." . . . Only Gerald did have such exquisite taste. . . . And John—she fancied she could see him sitting at home, alone, his shoes kicked off and his feet in those thick, ridged, speckled socks he wore. . . . Suddenly she wanted to be there also; but under the circumstances, of course, she couldn't be, so instead, she snuggled ever so slightly towards Gerald.

Ever and ever so slightly; but then Gerald was there, strung like a ukelele, waiting for that very, mouse-like movement. With no further ado, he took her in his arms and held her. Merely laughing at her stifled little "don'ts," and expertly wiping away her tears with kisses.

Afterwards: . . . Nancy slipping, darting, even dodging back home.

Letting herself cautiously into her own house. Resorting to slyness to cover up her entrance. Shivering like a too-daring mouse whilst making ready to get into bed. The thrills of the evening all drowned in a deluge of panic, lest John awaken. . . . Guilty tears dropping silently against the pillow and finally sleep, dreamless and unbroken, until daylight. . . . Awakening in a drowsy contentment, aware that her head is pillowed upon John's curving arm and that he is snoring outrageously. Leaping up, with the knowledge; that drenched her in a pleasurable shower, that she must make ready his breakfast. . . . Altogether pleased with her plain, humdrum duties—happy to be John's wife. . . .

But later in the day thoughts of the night before smudge her pleasure. . . . She insists to herself that she has acted quite alright. Of course, Gerald knew, she didn't mean a thing. Bolstering her wilted convictions with one of Gerald's glib speeches:

"She needn't be a dead one, just 'cause she was married."

It was later than usual. Each time it got later than usual. Long since, John had "turned in" to lie down beside Sonny-boy so that Sonny would hush crying for her and had dropped off himself, into a heavy slumber. The door was unlocked and only the hall-light left burning. Nancy thought of all this and felt sure she hated John. What right had he to give her so much rope. It was his duty to take care of her just as it was hers to care for Sonny-boy. And what care would she be giving Sonny-boy if she never questioned his coming or his going and accepted everything he did, as a matter of course. "It was John's business to guard his own castle." Gerald's eloquence. . . . She actually believed he would not care—didn't care enough about her to even care what she did. Besides, here she was away from home and it was ever so late and he was at home in bed—of course, he didn't care. . . . Of a sudden, she was replying to Gerald's query, and her answer was—yes.

They had a long way to go. Nancy would not take a cab and Gerald assuming precautions he did not feel, led her a roundabout route, turning numerous corners, crossing many streets, traversing block after block. . . . To while away the time, Gerald said sweet things to Nancy and kept squeezing her hand which lay on his arm.

The moon shone brightly, not giving light, as does the sun—for men to behold minutely but only to dazzle man's vision with a radiance.

Even the houses Nancy passed were washed in radiance and sketched into the tapestry of night, beautiful as fairy-places. . . . The tree-leaves were knitted into laces to lay against the silver shine of moon, and all about, was the magic of silver and old lace. . . . A dazzling, light and queer things became discernible.

Nancy was no longer listening to Gerald's silly speeches. She was thinking. . . . She had come upon "Some train of reflection which art can seldom lead or skill assist; but which will reveal itself as great truths have done, by chance." Idly, she began to pick out objects that were distinguishable in the moonlight. It grew fascinating. And she laughed aloud, when the luminous light dazzled her eyes into seeking awry. . . . She sought to share her fun with Gerald, who, somehow—silly little Nancy even remarked:—that Gerald was never good company, unless he was playing at love. . . . He was an adept at oogling and talking baby-talk. . . . But his oogles never included the beggar down on the corner and cause him to drop a coin into the old beggar's hat . . . as did John. . . . Nor did it ever include a wistful child with his face pressed to the window of a candy-shop. Once they had come across the Widow Green's boy, with his face glued to a show-window. She remembered the child's expectant grin when he caught the sound of her voice. . . . How eagerly he had wheeled about, thinking to see John, and his disappointment—that was not allayed—at sight of Gerald.

Nancy was thinking, at last. . . .

Gerald would not join her in the pastime though she went on tripping along beside him, with her hand still lying upon his arm. . . . She saw many, many things, some masquerading in the moonlight so well, until she could not, try as she would, discover what they were: others startlingly distinct.

They were alongside a yard, a homelike yard with a low picket fence, that set jamb-up to the pavement. A paling clamped to the fence, was one of the supports for a clothesline which swung across the yard. A portion of the line was very near the walk and a wash had been left out to sway and flap and swish in the breeze. . . . A pillow slip bulged grotesquely and flapped and popped like a toy-pistol, and swung limply waiting to be charged again with the soft night air.

Nancy's eyes swept the clothes-line, then settled in a fixed stare at something there upon. . . .

At the same moment Gerald belched—he was quite near his destination. . . . "Moonlight is meant for lovers. . . ."

He was surprised out of all his smug niceties by the scream close under his ear that started to be shrill, then choked. . . . Nancy had snatched her hand from within the crook of his arm, before he could collect his scattered wits . . . and was fleeing like a mad thing back down the path they had come. . . . For an instant in his great astonishment, Gerald was struck by the beauty of that flight—a swift shadow vanishing in a silver mist—

But soon he was mumbling to himself, "What did she see? . . ."

"Ugh—," he shuddered. . . . "Ugh," he complained again. He was done with Nancy; wouldn't have no woman who could see things that-a-way. He muttered, stumbled, and continued on his way. . . .

While the night winds swayed the clothesline until it set to jerking, curiously, as if feet were in them kicking, a man's sox, cheap and coarse, even in the moonlight, and beside them dancing—the cream of silk and wool, pink at heel and toe; the finest they could buy—

An infant's tiny stockings. . . .

Indeed. . . . "There are chords in the human heart strange varying strings, which are only struck by accident. . . . Chords, which remain mute and senseless to appeals the most passionate and earnest—that respond at last, to the slightest, casual touch. . . ."

The Young Glory of Him

The crew of the freighter West Illana *and a family of four passengers are the cast of this Langston Hughes story. The narrator, a discerning cabin boy, spotlights for the reader an unfulfilled love aboard the* West Illana. *Daisy Jones, a nondescript passenger, falls deeply in love with Eric Gynt, who she believes is the best-looking sailor on the ship. Unfortunately, he doesn't return her love. This one-sided love leads to tragedy. Hughes published this short story in April 1927.*

She had written in her diary in a thin school-girl's hand: "Oh, the young glory of him! His name is Eric Gynt and he is the handsomest sailor on the ship. I met him yesterday. It was my first time out on deck because I had been seasick for four days since leaving New York. I was sitting in my deck chair reading Browning when all my college class-notes on "The Ring and the Book" blew away. He was going to the bridge, but he ran and caught some of my papers for me. The others went into the sea. I didn't mind the loss of half my notes, though—because I met him. I must have been greatly confused for all I could stammer was, 'Thank you very much.' And he went on up to the bridge. But this morning I met him again and he said, 'Good morning,' and I said, 'Good morning,' too."

We had been at sea ten days when I read this in her diary. Of course, I had no business reading her diary at all, but then I was cabin-boy on the "West Illana," New York to West Africa, and it was my duty to clean the passengers' rooms. But as the "West Illana" was essentially a freight ship, there were only four passengers aboard—a trader, the girl who kept the diary, and her parents—two well-meaning middle-aged New England missionaries. One morning the girl left her diary open on the little desk near her bunk and I read it. There wasn't much because it began with her getting on the ship. And the book was new.

All the boys in the fo'c'sle, though, were already "wise" to her liking Eric. They had for three days now been teasing him about it. But I thought she was, like him, just passing the time away—until I read her diary. There in all seriousness she had written: "I want him to love me. I have been so lonesome all my life." And further down for July 2: "Suppose he really would love me. I always dreamed of being loved by a sailor. And he is truly wonderful! His hair is all golden and curly and he says he never loved any girl before. I told him I had never loved any boy either. And I told him about how I had been in a girls' school (church school, too), where I never saw any men.... I do love him! I do! I do!"

It was my duty to serve the meals to the officers and passengers—nine in all. That evening at dinner the girl wore a stiff white dress and a knitted scarf about her shoulders. Her name was Daisy Jones. With her thin body, sandy hair, dry little freckled face, and the spectacles she wore for reading, she looked thirty although she was only eighteen. At the fifth evening meal served at sea, I heard the two missionaries tell the captain all about their daughter. As I poured water and passed dishes between heads, I listened. For ten years the elderly couple had been stationed in Africa and only once in all this time had they returned to America to see Daisy. Her high school and college years had been spent in a very Christian Methodist Seminary for girls. Now that she was graduated, they had returned for the graduation exercises and to take their daughter back with them. They didn't know her very well, they said. She had always been away from them, but they hoped to make a missionary of her, too. She seemed willing and meek. They smiled at the daughter across the table and she smiled back—a wan, strange little smile. The captain said, "Well, you're doing a good work." The trader agreed. Then the missionaries and the trader began a conversation concerning the necessity for more Christian Protestant missions along the Congo in order to combat the spread of Catholicism. I passed the bread pudding. The "West Illana," the ship in which we all lived, pushed slowly and solemnly through the night. Six bells.

—

Back aft in the sailors' quarters. Twelve days from New York. Double bunks on four sides. A box. Two chairs. Sailors, wipers, oilers, mess-boys amid a confusion of laughter, oaths, and bits of song. The men are "kidding" Eric about Daisy.

"Ain't satisfied with the girls in port. Must be gettin' good an' holy now—makin' love to missionaries' daughters."

"O, you sweet-looking blond boy!"

"Some lady-killer. Even passengers fallin' fer 'im."

"Why don't you take on the old lady, too? She's better lookin' than the daughter. Daisy looks like she's been through the war—all washed out and everything."

"Man, I had a girl in Havre ten times as good looking as she is." And the conversation began to turn, as usual, to the girls of the ports, the merits and defects of those of Havre as compared with those of Barcelona, and to intimate details of nights of love.

"Sure, I've had plenty o' women. And I got something to show for mine," said Eric, the Dane.

"I guess you have," jibed Porto Rico.

"O, not what you mean," said the young sailor. And he pulled out his sea-bag from under a bunk. "I got a box of souvenirs, and letters, and pictures from damn near every girl I ever knew anywhere."

He took up a long card-board box and opened it. "See this little jeweled dagger. I took it away from a girl in San Isidro Street in Havana."

Roars of laughter. Score of vulgar jibes.

"And see this red silk stocking. A burlesque dame in New York found it missing when I left one morning."

Ha! Ha! Ha! Ha! Some lover the boy was!

"My first girl in Copenhagen gave me this bit of hair. I was sixteen then. Just started to sea." And he held up a bunch of flaxen curls tied with a blue ribbon. He had rings, too, and a piece of filmy silk lingerie; and a pack of letters scrawled in badly spelled language; and pictures taken in Yokohama and Seattle and Naples.

He put the box away and began to talk about Daisy. "She's a good kid, but dumb. Gave me a little black Bible the other day and I'm keeping it over my heart." He showed the men the small leather-bound book in the left-hand pocket of his shirt. "She wanted me to kiss her last night, and Christ! you know I wasn't going to refuse." And he acted in pantomime how he had taken her in his arms and crushed her against the bulkhead. "And then she ran away across the deck like she was afraid." It was a joke among the crew for the next two weeks to ask the Dane, "Is she still running away?"

———

Port of Horta in the Azores—toy city on the edge of the sea, lonely. Not much cargo to unload. We stay a half day and sail at midnight. Porto Rico and I, as well as most of the crew, have been ashore buying wine at the wine-shops, ambling up and down the cobblestone streets among ox-carts and peasants, and going after sun-down to promenade on the seawall with the girls of the town who like to walk with young sailors. Now it is growing late. Porto Rico and I return to the ship at ten o'clock. For a quarter each a Portuguese boatman rows us out to the "West Illana" anchored in the harbor. Through a confusion of little boats and barges receiving cargo from the steamer, we reach the ladder and climb aboard.

I went straight to the saloon to close the port-holes and lower the lights for the night. There at the entrance to the corridor stood our youngest passenger, Daisy Jones. I knew she was waiting for Eric. "Good evening," I said and passed on.

Five minutes afterwards I came on deck and stood near the galley door watching the cranes unloading from the midship hatch, swinging over and out, lowering bags of wheat into the little boats below. I had never seen a boat unload at night before. Daisy Jones stood in the corridor of the saloon looking not at the cargo rising out of the hatch and falling toward the sea, but at the gangway up which Eric must come. He came with some fellow seamen, six or eight, laughing and swearing. He had lost his cap and his blond hair was tousled. His blue eyes sparkled and his boy's face flushed with the joy of wine. He saw Daisy. "I'm gonna have some fun," he said. And he went across the deck under the swinging bags of wheat, held out his hand, and spoke to her. Half fascinated by the careless beauty of his face and the blue gaiety of his eyes, yet half afraid, she drew back in the shadow of the dark hall, stood for a moment while he whispered something in her ear, then turned and ran into her room. The sailors standing with me near the galley laughed. Then we all went back aft to our quarters. At one o'clock we sailed.

The next morning at sea when I went in to clean her room I read this in her diary: "Last night he looked like a blond Greek god returning from a festival. O, the young glory of him! . . . And he asked me if I would go ashore with him sometime, too. In Dakar he said. . . . I would like to see an African town at night and I believe he would take care of me. But I don't dare go. I'm afraid."

I laughed because I knew she would go. Her mother and father retired early always. And Eric said no woman refused to do what he asked. Well, it was none of my business. I closed her diary, shut the desk, and began to sweep the rug on the deck.

———

Dakar in Senegal, one of the most fascinating ports in all Africa, and one of the few with dock and harbor facilities. The "West Illana" pushes in to a pier and we look down on a jetty crowded with sweltering humanity. Natives in long Mohammedan robes; French colonial officials; black traders from the desert bartering feathers, statuettes of brass and ivory, dates and strange fruits; women and children; missionaries waiting for papers or news; and those little boy guides one sees in so many sea-towns sent to pick up sailors to bring to the houses of prostitution. Port of Dakar on a day when the sun blazes.

Port of Dakar when the sun has fallen into the sea and darkness comes. The tiny garden cafe in M. Brousard's Grand Hotel de Nice et Lyon. Native music, a fountain, black waiters, smoke, wine, and the stars. A crowd of boisterous seamen about the tables, a dozen little dark girls and a few French women. The fat proprietor rubs his hands well pleased at the business the bar is doing. One of the French girls begins singing "Madelon," but Mike from Newark drowns her out with "Why Should I Cry Over You." The bo's'un has gone to sleep sprawled across a table. Jerry is doing a sailor's hornpipe on the edge of the fountain. A drunken babble of laughter and voices fills the little garden. Through a haze of wine in the brain and smoke in the air, I see Chips coming towards our table.

"Just walked up the street," he said. "And guess who I saw—Eric and the dumb-looking missionary girl by themselves. They was comin' out o' that hotel down the way yonder and she was cryin'. And they was headin' back toward the ship."

"I'll bet he had her where she couldn't run this time," said Porto Rico.

"That boy ain't so pure and innocent," croaked an old oiler. "She'll learn to fool with sailors."

"She'll pray tonight all right."

"She was cryin'," Chips went on. "And him just laughin' at her like he didn't give a damn."

Splash! The sailor who had been dancing the hornpipe fell backwards in the fountain! "Bravo!" yelled the French girls. "Hee! Hee! Hee!" cried the little African ladies. "Hooray!" shouted the drunken seamen. And the noise of falling glasses, laughter, applause, women's voices, ironic music rose to the stars. "Let's get another bottle of cognac," said Porto Rico.

———

The sun is blazing the next day when we leave Dakar. My head aches and I am in no mood for extra work, yet Daisy Jones stays in bed all morning and I must carry a luncheon of soup and toast to her room on a tray.

"She is ill," her mother said. "I tell her about staying up so late of nights reading those books."

I would have laughed but my head throbbed and burned. I went back to the bunk and slept all the afternoon.

That evening at dinner Daisy Jones did not appear. "She has been crying," her mother said. "It must be her nerves."

"Young folks are hard to understand," added the father.

When I knocked on her door to ask if she wished anything, she said, "No, I'm going to get up and sit on deck for a while." So I went away. After I had cleared the table and cleaned the pantry, I went back to her room, got fresh linen from the steward, and made up her bed while she sat on deck between her parents. Then I went into the galley and talked to the cooks for awhile as they peeled potatoes for breakfast. A warm breeze came in the door. The stars seemed near enough to touch. When I returned to lower the lights in the saloon I could see that the missionaries were getting ready for bed. The girl still sat on the deck, but she was alone now.

It must have been near midnight that it happened. I was lying in my berth reading, Porto Rico snoring in the bunk above, when I heard the bells clang in the engine room and felt the ship slow down. Then I heard the shrill blasts of the whistle and jumped up, slid into my pants, and ran out on deck. "Man overboard!" Mates running and shouting. Commands being issued. I saw the sailors lowering a life-boat. Then I knew what happened: Daisy Jones had jumped into the sea.

I ran up the iron stairs to the midship deck, past the galley door, past the covered hatch, through the saloon corridor and into her room. I knew she wasn't there. The lights were burning and the berth was just as I had made it up after dinner. But on the white spread near the pillow lay a note in a sealed envelope addressed to "Father and Mother." On the desk her diary was open. But all she had written that day had been obliterated with heavy pen and ink lines, except for a few words at the bottom of the page: "I thought he loved me, but I know he doesn't. I can't bear it." Tears had fallen, too, on that page.

Slowly I closed the diary, slipped it under my shirt, and went out on deck. When no one was looking I let it fall over the rail into the sea. With all the confusion outside, the two old misionaries had not awakened. Then I remembered how they had slept at Horta and Dakar in spite of the noise of unloading cargo. Ten years of Africa, I thought, makes one want to sleep. But soon the captain came to wake them. The lifeboat still moved about on the quiet moon-washed face of the sea, but there was not a trace of her body. A great sky full of stars looked down quietly and gave no comment.

———

Next morning, of course, Eric felt badly enough. Some of the men were angry with him for having anything to do with the girl at all. Nobody, though, seemed to feel that he in any way had caused her death. Chips said, "Women just can't help it. They go wild over the kid, clean crazy. See what a fool this skirt was." And the captain called him to his room and talked with him after breakfast.

But in a few days the youngster was all right again, laughing, singing, joking and swearing as usual. And the night we docked at Freetown I saw him take the little black Bible that had once belonged to Daisy Jones and put it in his box along with a garter from Horta, a red silk stocking from New York, a jeweled dagger from Havana, and a bunch of flaxen curls that a girl in Copenhagen gave him.

BODIES IN THE MOONLIGHT

Langston Hughes again uses the West Illana *as one of the settings for this tale. The story centers on a crass, rough, and strong seaman, Porto Rico, and a gentle, more romantic, young Hughes-like narrator, both of whom are sexually attracted to the beautiful Nunuma. In coastal West Africa, the two suitors come to blows over their hot-blooded passion for the lovely lass. Hughes published this story in April 1927.*

Sailors call it the Fever Coast—that two or three thousand miles of West Africa from Senegal to Loanda.

For four weeks now our ship had been anchored "in the stream" loading cocoa beans. There had been some mix-up in the schedule and the old man had no orders to move on. Six of our men had been sent ashore with tropic fever to the European Hospital. The potatoes were running out and the captain no longer issued money to his mixed crew. The sun blazed by day and the moon shone at night and more men fell ill with the fever. Or developed venereal diseases. And there our steamer lay tossing wearily in the blue water, a half mile off the coast beyond the beating surf.

At eighteen when one is a rover, the world is wonderful—I was a messboy on my first trip to sea. I had thrown all my school books overboard and for several months I had not written to my parents. People I had known as a boy had not been kind to me, I thought, but now I was free. The sea had taken me like a mother and a freight ship named the "West Illana" had become my home.

The sun was setting, and the sea and sky were all stained with blood. With a wet cloth full of soap powder, I scoured the sink in my mess pantry where I had just finished washing the dinner dishes. Then I went into the saloon and closed the port holes. The water was purple now and the sky blue-violet. The first stars popped out. The chief mate came down looking for his cap. It was on the deck under the table and he stooped to pick it up.

"Christ, mess, I'm tired o' this damn place," he said. Then, "Did ya leave any ginger cakes out for lunch tonight?"

"No," I replied. "The steward didn't gimme any."

"Lousy runt! Food must be gettin' low." I heard the chief mate going up the iron stairs to his room. I threw my white coat in a drawer of the buffet, carefully concealed a flat can of salmon in my shirt, and went on deck. It was dark.

"Goin' ashore?" the young Swede on watch at the gang plank called out.

"Sure," I replied.

"Well, I ain't. Them women over there's got me burnt up. You and Porto Rico better watch out!"

"You the one that oughta been careful," I laughed back. "Jesus, you're dumb! Porto Rico and I are in love."

"Yea, and with the same girl," said the Swede. "*You* had better watch out now."

I went on down the deck past the lighted ports of the engineers' rooms and around to the door of the officers' mess.

"Ain't you through yet?" I said.

"Hell, no! The damn bo's'un was late comin' to eat again but the way I told him about it, he won't be late no more." Porto Rico was washing knives and forks in a very dirty bucket of water. *"Cabrón!"* he said. "Just when I wanted to go ashore!" As though he didn't go ashore every night.

"I'm goin' on back aft. Hurry up and we'll catch the next boat when it comes out. I s'pose you gonna see her, too. . . . What you gonna take her tonight?"

"Hombre!" Then in a whisper, "Couldn't save a damn thing but a hunk o' bread today. Looks like to me in two weeks won't be nothin' to eat on this tank. Ain't much here now—but I got a bar o' soap to give that mutty boatman if he takes us ashore. I'm gonna. . . ."

The conversation died as the steward came down the corridor. He stepped into the galley where the Jamaican cooks were peeling potatoes. I went on back aft. Five bells.

———

For a cake of soap as payment we were paddled ashore. An African in a loincloth at either end, Porto Rico and I in the middle, we sat in a narrow little canoe so deep in water that one momentarily expected it to fill with the sea and sink. Under the stars. The ocean deep and evil. The lights of the "West Illana" at our stern. The palm-fringed line of shore and the boom of surf ahead. Off on the edge of the water the moon rose round, golden, and lazy. The sky seemed heavy with its weight of stars and the sea deep and weary, lipping the sides of the little boat.

"Estoy cansado," said Porto Rico.

"I wish I was back in New York. I swear I do," I said. "Damn Nunuma."

But the excitement of landing in the surf loosened us from our momentary melancholy and we stood on the sand not far from the line of palm trees. The canoe and its two silent natives put to sea again. "Gimme a cigarette." Feet crossing the hard sand. "Gimme a cigarette." We were going to see Nunuma.

Nunuma—because I remember her I write this story. Because of her and the scar across my throat. At eighteen, women are strange bodies, strange, taunting, desirable bodies. Flesh and spirit. And the song is in the flesh even more than in the spirit.

We saw Nunuma the first day my "buddy" and I went ashore at Lonbar. A slender dark young girl, ripe breasts bare, a single strip of cloth about her body, squatted on her heels behind a pile of yams in the public square. There were many old women and young girls in the market place, but none other like Nunuma, delicate and lovely as a jungle flower, beautiful as a poem.

"O, you sweetie," said Porto Rico. "Some broad," said Mike from Newark. And the sailors bought all her yams.

That night when we came ashore again, a little barefoot boy, professional guide, showed Porto Rico and me to Nunuma's house—the usual native hut with its thatched roof and low eaves. She stood in the door-way, bright cloth about her body, face dusk-bronze in the moonlight. O lovely flower growing too near the sea! Sailors must have passed her way before that night, but Nunuma had received none of them. "Me no like white sailor man," she explained later in her West African English. "He rough and mean."

The little boy guide patted off down the grassy road, coin in hand. "Hello, kid." In a few minutes another girl appeared from somewhere, joined us, and we sat down together in front of the hut. We four. The other girl never told her name. She was solid and well-built, but not beautiful like Nunuma. There wasn't much to say. Hands touch. Lips touch. The moon burned. By and by we went into the hut. . . . In the morning Porto Rico and I gave each of the girls two shillings when we left.

———

Wide and white and cool the dawn as the slender native canoe paddled us back to the ship an hour before breakfast. Wide and cool and green the morning sea as the white sun shot up. The "West Illana" lay solemnly at anchor. We paid the boatman and were about to climb the gang-way stairs when a black girl ran down. "Get the hell off here!" It was the third mate's voice. "I should think the men would see enough o' you women on shore without bringing you on the damn ship. Don't lemme catch you here again," and he swore roundly several great sea-man's oaths. The woman was very much frightened. She chattered to the boatmen as they paddled away and her hands trembled. She was fat. Her face was not beautiful like Nunuma's.

That day the sun boiled. The winches rattled with their loads of cocoa beans lifted from native boats. The Kru-boys chipped the deck. And two sailors fell ill with the fever. That night Porto Rico and I went to see Nunuma—and the other girl. Neither one of us cared about the name of the other girl. She was just a body—a used thing of the port towns.

Days, nights. Nights, days. The vast impersonal African sky, now full of stars, now white with sun. The "West Illana" quiet and sober. Cocoa beans all loaded. Six men with fever ashore in the hospital. No orders. The captain impatient. Mahogany logs to load in Gran Basam. Christ, when are we moving on? The chief cook sick with a disease of the whore houses. Steward worried about the food running low. "Nobody but a fool goes to sea anyhow," says the bo's'un.

Porto Rico and I were ashore every night. Almost every afternoon between meals—ashore . . . Nunuma. Nunuma . . . O, mother of God! . . . Sometimes I see her alone. Sometimes she and Porto Rico, I and the other girl are together. Sometimes she and Porto Rico alone are with each other. . . . Nunuma! Nunuma! . . . I have given her the red slippers I bought in Dakar. Porto Rico has given her the Spanish shawl he picked up at Cadiz coming down. And now that we have no money we smuggle her stolen food from the ship's pantries. And Porto Rico gave her a string of beads.

He is my friend but I wish he wouldn't put his hands on Nunuma. Nunuma is beautiful and Porto Rico is not a man to know beauty. Be-sides he is jealous. One morning in the galley he asked me why I didn't fool with the other girl sometimes and leave him Nunuma alone. "You don't own the woman, do you?" I demanded. His large hands slowly clenched to fists and a sneer crossed his face. "Fight!" yelled the second cook. "Hell," I said, "We ain't gonna fight about a port-town girl." "No," he replied, and smiled.

"You bloody young niggers," said the old Jamaican baker.

Nunuma was beautiful. Nunuma's face was like a flower in the moonlight and her body soft and slender. At eighteen one has not known many soft bodies of women. One has not often kissed lips like the petals of pansies—unless one has been a sailor like Porto Rico. Porto Rico, hard, and rough, and strong, with a knowledge of women in half the port towns of the world. Porto Rico, who did not know that Nunuma's face was like a flower in the moonlight. Who did not care that her body was soft and tender. I wanted Porto Rico to keep his hands off Nunuma's body. He shouldn't touch her. He who had known so many dirty women. . . . Yet Porto Rico was my friend. . . . But Nunuma was beautiful. At eighteen one can go mad over the beauty of a woman. And forget a friend. . . . I believe I loved Nunuma.

———

Feet crossing the dry sand. We were going to see her. "Gimme a cigarette," I repeated. Feet crossing the dry sand carrying one to the line of palm trees, carrying one to the grassy roads running between the thatched huts. Native fires gleaming, sailors in white pants drinking palm wine and feeling the breasts of girls, laughing. Africans with bare black feet, single cloths about their bodies, walking under the moon. The ship's carpenter drunk beneath a mango tree.

"Say, mess, did you hear the news?" calls the young wireless-man and the super-cargo who are passing in the road. We stop. "No," says Porto Rico. "What is it?"

"Haul anchor tomorrow for Gran Basam. Old Man's glad as hell," says the wireless.

"Lord knows I am," adds the super-cargo. "Die before I'd make another trip down this coast."

Sailing in the morning. . . . Nunuma. Nunuma. . . . Gran Basam, Accra, Freetown, Cape Verde Islands, New York. . . . Nunuma! Nunuma! . . . Sailing in the morning.

She is standing in her doorway, the Spanish shawl wrapped about her body instead of the customary bright cloth. Her lips are red and her face like a flower, dusk-dark in the moonlight. " 'Lo kid," she smiles.

"You're vamping the boys tonight."

"Look just like Broadway."

"Me no like white sailor man."

Bantering talk.

Grotesque gifts to offer an African flower-girl—Porto Rico undoes his half loaf of bread and extends it awkwardly. I take a flat can of salmon from inside my shirt. We offer them both. She laughs and takes them inside the hut. Silence. When she comes out we sit down on the ground. And she is in the middle between we two men. The other girl is not there. Nunuma's body is slender and brown. She sings a tribal song about the moon. She points to the moon. Hands touch. Lips touch. A dusk-dark girl in the golden night, my buddy and I.

"We're sailing in the morning," I said.

"Yep, we haul anchor," added Porto Rico. "We leave."

"Mornin' go? In mornin' ship he go?" Nunuma's eyes grew wide in the moonlight. "Then you love me tonight," she said. "You love me tonight." And her lips were like flower petals. But she clasped her hands and the dark face looked into the moonlight. Her warm brown body sat between us. Her twin breasts pointed into the moonlight. Her slender feet in red slippers. Her eyes looking at the moon.

"You go back to the ship," said Porto Rico to me, "and get your sleep."

"No," I said.

"Go back to the ship, kid." He and I both rose. One can be a fool over a woman at eighteen.

"I won't go back! You can't make me!" My hand sought the clasp-knife in my pocket.

"*Hijo de la. . . .*" he began an oath in Spanish and his lips trembled.

Like a dart of moonlight, Nunuma ran, without a scream, into her hut.

"Keep your hands off her," I shouted. "Keep your damn dirty hands off her!"

Before my fingers could leave my pocket, something silver flashed in the pale light. A flood of oaths in English and Spanish drenched my ears. And a warm red fluid ran from my throat, stained and spread on the whiteness of my shirt, dripped on my suddenly weak and useless hands.

"Keep your hands . . . off . . . her," I stammered. "Keep your hands off . . . Nunuma." And I fell face forward in the grass and dug my fingers in the earth and cried, "Keep your damn dirty hands off her," until the world lurched and grew dark. And all the stars fell down.

At sea in a bunk with a bandage about my neck. Porto Rico saying, "Jesus, kid, you know I didn't mean to do it. I was crazy, that's all." White caps of waves through the port holes. White blazing sun in the sky. Those things are almost forgotten now—but the scar, and the memory of Nunuma, make me write this story.

THE LITTLE VIRGIN

Langston Hughes tells another story that takes place on the West Illana. *Using the freighter's polyglot crew, Hughes verifies his ingenious capacity to speak and report in the languages of a broad spectrum of cultures, temperaments, and personalities. Little Virgin, a naive and virginal young white man, sheds his docile shell to defend an African woman who has been slapped by one of his shipmates. Hughes published this story in December 1927.*

The "West Illana" dipped slowly through the green water seven days out from the port of New York. But in a week at sea even a crew made up of Greeks, West Indian Negroes, Irish, Portuguese and Americans can become pretty well acquainted. When the weather is warm and sailors lounge on the after-deck of evenings telling stories, men learn to know one another. The sea breeds a strange comradeship, a strict fraternity, and many a time I have seen the most heterogeneous crew imaginable stick together like brothers in a sailors' fight in a foreign port. Nor is there ever any separation in that vast verbal warfare all seamen wage against all chief stewards over the always bad food. The sea is like a wide-armed mother and the humble toilers of the sea, blood brothers.

But sometimes there comes one to whom the ways of the water folk are strange. . . . The sailors called him the Little Virgin because they discovered that he had never known a woman and because of his polite manners. He was a blond boy, sixteen or so, probably a runaway from some neat middle-class home in an inland village. He came looking for adventure at sea. He admitted he had not worked on ship before but he proved an apt apprentice, and soon learned to chip decks and scrub bulkheads with the rest of the ordinaries. But he didn't learn their way of talking so easily and he was very shy. He didn't grab for the potato pan at meals and try to snatch the largest potato. Indeed, if he got no potatoes at all he said nothing.

> "O, give us some time to
> Blow the man down!"

On the hatch in front of the after-deck house in the early evening, dinner over, the talk had been of sailing ships and the old days of the sea. Paddy, in a deep Irish brogue, was telling his wild experiences on whalers. Over against the rail the Swede sang, to himself, a chantey which some of the steamship men had never even heard:

> "What do you think
> We had for breakfast?
> Wey, hey!
> Blow the man down!"

The warm wind came from the South and the faint throb of the engines and the chug, chug, of the propeller accompanied his song:

> "A monkey's heart
> And a donkey's liver.
> Give us some time to
> Blow the man down!"

"Yez," said Paddy, "When the old John Emory went to Rio, them was the days."

> "O, they sailed us down
> The Congo River
> Wey, hey!
> Blow the man down!"

One of the A.B.'s on watch passed with a lighted lantern, went up the iron stairs, and hung it over the stern of the ship. It was getting dark. The blue depths of the sky began to be dotted with stars and the little waves below lapped languidly, one on the other.

> "And O! I'll sail
> The seas forever.
> Give us some time to
> Blow the man down!"

"Say, was everybody in your town as dumb as you?" Eric demanded suddenly of the Little Virgin.

"Heck, no!" the kid answered. "My father—"

"Why don't you say, 'Hell, no,' you pink angel?" Jerry drawled.

"Hell—no," said the boy slowly for he hadn't yet learned to swear with the facility of the sea.

"Women won't think you're a sailor 'less you learn to cuss better 'an that there 'Go! darn' and 'By heck' you got,—like some country hayseed 'stead of a seaman."

"Yes, sir," said the boy.

"Hombre! Who ever says he was a seaman," laughed Porto Rico.

"And we're gonna show you some women in Horta next week. I been there before, Virgin, and I know 'em. They're wild and they'll lead you to slaughter. Show us how you make love, kid."

And then the torture of the self-conscious and embarrassed boy began,—he who was the daily butt of sailors' jibes and vulgar jokes. The men liked him and the cleanness of him, but the fun of seeing him red and confused was too great to resist. So everything the youngster did or said by day became a subject for ribald wit and ridicule at night on the after-hatch. And the lad, who was unable to banter jokes and obscenities, looked lost and alone and very miserable. Everyone seemed his enemy, no one his friend. Words can be terribly cruel when a person does not know how to construct a defense or laugh at a joke.

"I don't know how to make love," the boy said.

"O, you Little Virgin! Mama's nice baby!" Chips sang in falsetto.

"Pretty Percy!"

"What kind a sailor is this?"

> "Now he was all
> Most twenty-three.
> But still sat on
> His mother's knee.
> He'd never . . ."

"Say, kid, tell us . . . ," began one of the Greek firemen.

"Don't tell that Greek nothin', Virgin." It was Mike from Newark speaking. "Get up an' sock him in the eye!"

The absurdity of this command brought a gale of laughter from the men on the hatch. Chips rolled over and over. But for some reason or other it angered the fireman.

"What a hell you tell da kid to hit me for? You would ain't do it yourself," the Greek yelled.

"Stand up an' see if I won't," countered Mike. There hadn't been a fight on board for three days now and the ship plowed slowly and calmly through the water under the starry darkness. Things were dull and quiet like the slow move of the steamer. "I'm tired o' you guys ridin' the Virgin anyhow. You must think he likes it. He's a good kid and he don't bother none o' you."

"He's no you brother," said the Greek. And he made a sudden plunge at Mike from Newark, but in an instant the fireman was going backward toward the bulkhead sent there by a blow from the New Jersey man's fist. Then, before the Greek could recover his balance, the bo'sun sprang between them.

"Stop this fight," he commanded. "You dumb fools!" And two or three sailors grabbed each of the combatants by the arms.

"Damn!" said Eric. "The bo'sun's always stoppin' fights."

"That's dirty," I agreed, because I wanted to see the fight go on, too.

But Mike and the Greek were held apart until, each struggling nobly to get at the other, their vocabulary of insults in both the language of the Hellespont and Newark were exhausted. Then Mike, with a final oath regarding the parentage of all Greeks, turned to the frightened Little Virgin and said, "Come on, kid, let's go inside. I'll teach you to play pinochle." And the two of them left the deck.

"Sure, that's the best you can do is play pinochle," somebody jeered, while the fireman began to talk rapidly to a fellow countryman. An hour later when I passed the mess-room door on my way to bed I saw the Little Virgin and Mike from Newark leaning on the wooden table deep in conversation. And the young boy looked happy for the first time since leaving New York. He had seemingly found a friend.

———

So the days passed filled with sunshine and the slow roll of the little waves. And the nights passed warm and starry as the old freighter steamed unhurriedly through the black waters toward Africa. And the dawns came pink and gold, strangely cool and calm with a magic vastness about them lying softly on the wide circle of the waters. Then the sun would shoot up, disturbing the colorful quiet. And some mornings there would be flying-fish lying on the deck which the third mate, coming down from the bridge, would pick up and take to the galley to have cooked for his breakfast. At eight bells the watch changed and the Little Virgin, along with the rest of the ordinaries, would come out for work.

The Virgin and Mike from Newark were boon companions now. They worked together during the day and played cards or talked at night. From Mike the kid learned how to tie sailors' knots, how to do the least work with the greatest appearance of effort, and how to lower a life boat during fire-drill. He began to learn, too, the vocabulary of the sea, to pick up a varied string of true seamen's oaths, and to acquire an amusing collection of filthy stories. Everything that Mike did, the Little Virgin tried to do, too. Before the village boy this young sailor from Newark seemed a model of all the manly virtues. And Mike had lived a life which the Virgin envied and wished to emulate. He, like the Virgin, had left home without telling anybody and in his three years away from the paternal roof had visited half the ports of the world. Furthermore, to hear Mike talk, there had been many thrilling and dangerous adventures in the strange places he had known. The Little Virgin would sit for hours, with the greatest credulity, listening to the Newark boy's stories. Then he would dream of the things that would happen to himself some day and how he would go back home and tell the fellows in his little village about them while they stood open-mouthed and amazed around this wanderer returned.

So the days passed and the "West Illana" put in at a port in Senegal. That night after dinner almost everybody went ashore. There was good business in the French wine shops where seamen and native women gathered before the night grew late. Porto Rico, Jerry and I were sitting at a little table in the crowded Bar Boudon when we saw Mike, the Virgin, Chips and Paddy enter. They were accompanied by four little dark girls and they all sat down at one table at the far end of the room. Drinks were brought. There was much talking and noise,—a tangle of languages and sounds. A smell of beer, wine and smoke floated under the murky yellow lights. The blue blouses of seamen, the white coats of the native waiters, and the black faces of the little girls spotted the room.

An hour of drinking and laughter must have passed when suddenly there was great turmoil at the other end of the place and somebody yelled, "Fight!" I climbed on a chair just in time to see Mike from Newark strike the Little Virgin full in the face and send him sprawling backwards among the tables and the feet of sailors. Then I saw a black woman spring at Mike, her fingers like claws, and in her turn fall backwards, struck in the face, among the tables and the feet of sailors. Then somebody threw a bottle and the free-for-all began. The lights went out. And I went out, too,—into the cobblestone street and safety from the flying missles. By and by I saw Chips emerge from the mélée and I asked him how the fight started.

"Over nothin'," said Chips. "All them darn fools drunk and one of the girls knocks a glass o' beer over on Mike and gets his pants wet, so he up and slaps her face and she crys. Then the Little Virgin hops up and says no gentleman would hit a woman so Mike up and hits him, too. The kid tries to come back at him but he knocks him sprawlin'. Then the girl tries to come back at Mike and he knocks her sprawlin'. Then somebody throws a bottle and hell breaks loose. And I comes on out.... Paddy is carrying the Little Virgin back to the ship now, and the kid's cryin' like a baby and sayin' over and over, 'No gentleman would hit a woman. No gentleman would hit a woman.' He's drunk. But Jesus! All that fuss over a African gal! And Mike and the Virgin being such good friends, too.... Licker'll cause anything,—the rotten slop.... Let's go down the road and get another drink." And the carpenter took me jovially by the arm.

"No," I said. "I'm going back to the ship. I'm tired o' this stuff." And I went off alone through the quiet street toward the dock where the ship was lying under the stars against the vast blackness of the harbor, infinitely calm and restful.

I met Paddy staggering down the gangplank, returning ashore to join the drunken sailors. I said hello to the man on watch as I went aboard and crossed the deck toward the bunk house. It was very quiet on ship and the seamen's quarters were warmly lighted but empty save for one figure,—the Little Virgin who lay sobbing as though his heart would break, face downward on his dirty pillow. It was strange to see someone crying in that room.

"What's the matter, kid?" I said.

"He oughtn't to hit a woman," sobbed the Virgin. "Mike oughtn't to hit a woman." And the young boy kept repeating the phrase over and over and cursing between sobs, awkwardly like a child. "He oughtn't to hit a woman." His breath smelled of wine and beer and his face was flushed, damp and warm.

"You're drunk," I said. "Go to sleep.... Mike was drunk, too." And I pulled off his clothes, put a blanket over him, and went to my own quarters to bed. But for a long while the sobs of the youngster disturbed the quiet of the empty fo's'cle and I could not close my eyes for strangeness of the sound.

The next day, when we sailed, the Virgin was unable to rise from his bunk. His head ached. His hands were hot and he felt dizzy. That afternoon at sea, he began to sob again deliriously. Someone told the steward that the boy was ill and when the chief mate came back to take his temperature, he pronounced it a severe case of tropic fever and ordered him removed at once to the hospital in the forward part of the boat. As soon as the bunk was ready Mike picked the boy up and carried him there himself. And for three days, during hours off duty, Mike sat near the Virgin as he tossed and moaned, and turned from side to side, or sobbed, or talked aloud when the delirium returned.

Meanwhile the "West Illana" steamed slowly through a tropic sea. On the third morning the ship anchored at Calabar, the French doctor came aboard, and the sick boy was sent ashore to the European hospital. As they carried him down the gangplank in a blanket at high noon while the sun blazed, he kept sobbing over and over in the raucous voice of delirium, "Oughtn't to hit a woman. . . . No, no, no. . . . Mike oughtn't hit a woman. . . . God knows he oughtn't . . . hit . . . a . . . woman." And the blanketed figure trembled with chill in the heat of the African day. And his voice rose shrill against the rattle of the cranes lifting cargo, "He oughtn't hit a woman. . . . Oughtn't . . . never to hit a . . . woman."

THE EATONVILLE ANTHOLOGY

Zora Neale Hurston shows off her talent for blending folklore with fiction. Using her hometown of Eatonville, Florida, as the setting for these thirteen small sketches, she unequivocally proves her storytelling skills. In this anthology, the colorful personalities she creates come to life. The reader has the feeling of actually being in Eatonville and enjoying the fun. This anthology was published in two parts, in September and October 1926.

I
THE PLEADING WOMAN

Mrs. Tony Roberts is the pleading woman. She just loves to ask for things. Her husband gives her all he can rake and scrape, which is considerably more than most wives get for their housekeeping, but she goes from door to door begging for things.

She starts at the store. "Mist' Clarke," she sing-songs in a high keening voice, "gimme lil' piece uh meat tuh boil a pot uh greens wid. Lawd knows me an' mah chillen is SO hongry! Hits uh SHAME! Tony don't fee-ee-eee-ed me!"

Mr. Clarke knows that she has money and that her larder is well stocked, for Tony Roberts is the best provider on his list. But her keening annoys him and he arises heavily. The pleader at this shows all the joy of a starving man being seated at a feast.

"Thass right Mist' Clarke. De Lawd loveth de cheerful giver. Gimme jes' a lil' piece 'bout dis big (indicating the width of her hand) an' de Lawd'll bless yuh."

She follows this angel-on-earth to his meat tub and superintends the cutting, crying out in pain when he refuses to move the knife over just a teeny bit mo'.

Finally, meat in hand, she departs, remarking on the meanness of some people who give a piece of salt meat only two-fingers wide when they were plainly asked for a hand-wide piece. Clarke puts it down to Tony's account and resumes his reading.

With the slab of salt pork as a foundation, she visits various homes until she has collected all she wants for the day. At the Piersons, for instance: "Sister Pierson, plee-ee-ease gimme uh han'ful uh collard greens fuh me an' mah po' chillen! 'Deed, me an' mah chillen is SO hongry. Tony doan' fee-ee-eed me!"

Mrs. Pierson picks a bunch of greens for her, but she springs away from them as if they were poison. "Lawd a mussy, Mis' Pierson, you ain't gonna gimme dat lil' eye-full uh greens fuh me an' mah chillen, is you? Don't be so graspin'; Gawd won't bless yuh. Gimme uh han'full mo'. Lawd, some folks is got everything, an' theys jes' as gripin' an stingy!"

Mrs. Pierson raises the ante, and the pleading woman moves on to the next place, and on and on. The next day, it commences all over.

II
TURPENTINE LOVE

Jim Merchant is always in good humor—even with his wife. He says he fell in love with her at first sight. That was some years ago. She has had all her teeth pulled out, but they still get along splendidly.

He says the first time he called on her he found out that she was subject to fits. This didn't cool his love, however. She had several in his presence.

One Sunday, while he was there, she had one, and her mother tried to give her a dose of turpentine to stop it. Accidently, she spilled it in her eye and it cured her. She never had another fit, so they got married and have kept each other in good humor ever since.

III

Becky Moore has eleven children of assorted colors and sizes. She has never been married, but that is not her fault. She has never stopped any of the fathers of her children from proposing, so if she has no father for her children it's not her fault. The men round about are entirely to blame.

The other mothers of the town are afraid that it is catching. They won't let their children play with hers.

IV
TIPPY

Sykes Jones' family all shoot craps. The most interesting member of the family—also fond of bones, but of another kind—is Tippy, the Jones' dog.

He is so thin, that it amazes one that he lives at all. He sneaks into village kitchens if the housewives are careless about the doors and steals meats, even off the stoves. He also sucks eggs.

For these offenses he has been sentenced to death dozens of times, and the sentences executed upon him, only they didn't work. He has been fed bluestone, strychnine, nux vomica, even an entire Peruna bottle beaten up. It didn't fatten him, but it didn't kill him. So Eatonville has resigned itself to the plague of Tippy, reflecting that it has erred in certain matters and is being chastened.

In spite of all the attempts upon his life, Tippy is still willing to be friendly with anyone who will let him.

V
THE WAY OF A MAN WITH A TRAIN

Old Man Anderson lived seven or eight miles out in the country from Eatonville. Over by Lake Apopka. He raised feed-corn and cassava and went to market with it two or three times a year. He bought all of his victuals wholesale so he wouldn't have to come to town for several months more.

He was different from us citybred folks. He had never seen a train. Everybody laughed at him for even the smallest child in Eatonville had either been to Maitland or Orlando and watched a train go by. On Sunday afternoons all of the young people of the village would go over to Maitland, a mile away, to see Number 35 whizz southward on its way to Tampa and wave at the passengers. So we looked down on him a little. Even we children felt superior in the presence of a person so lacking in worldly knowledge.

The grown-ups kept telling him he ought to go see a train. He always said he didn't have time to wait so long. Only two trains a day passed through Maitland. But patronage and ridicule finally had its effect and Old Man Anderson drove in one morning early. Number 78 went north to Jacksonville at 10:20. He drove his light wagon over in the woods beside the railroad below Maitland, and sat down to wait.

He began to fear that his horse would get frightened and run away with the wagon. So he took him out and led him deeper into the grove and tied him securely. Then he returned to his wagon and waited some more. Then he remembered that some of the train-wise villagers had said the engine belched fire and smoke. He had better move his wagon out of danger. It might catch afire. He climbed down from the seat and placed himself between the shafts to draw it away. Just then 78 came thundering over the trestle spouting smoke, and suddenly began blowing for Maitland. Old Man Anderson became so frightened he ran away with the wagon through the woods and tore it up worse than the horse ever could have done. He doesn't know yet what a train looks like, and says he doesn't care.

VI
COON TAYLOR

Coon Taylor never did any real stealing. Of course, if he saw a chicken or a watermelon or muskmelon or anything like that that he wanted he'd take it. The people used to get mad but they never could catch him. He took so many melons from Joe Clarke that he set up in the melon patch one night with his shotgun loaded with rock salt. He was going to fix Coon. But he was tired. It is hard work being a mayor, postmaster, storekeeper and everything. He dropped asleep sitting on a stump in the middle of the patch. So he didn't see Coon when he came. Coon didn't see him either, that is, not at first. He knew the stump was there, however. He had opened many of Clarke's juicy Florida Favorite on it. He selected his fruit, walked over to the stump and burst the melon on it. That is, he thought it was the stump until it fell over with a yell. Then he knew it was no stump and departed hastily from those parts. He had cleared the fence when Clarke came to, as it were. So the charge of rock salt was wasted on the desert air.

During the sugar-cane season, he found he couldn't resist Clarke's soft green cane, but Clarke did not go to sleep this time. So after he had cut six or eight stalks by the moonlight, Clarke rose up out of the cane strippings with his shotgun and made Coon sit right down and chew up the last one of them on the spot. And the next day he made Coon leave his town for three months.

VII
VILLAGE FICTION

Joe Lindsay is said by Lum Boger to be the largest manufacturer of prevarications in Eatonville; Brazzle (late owner of the world's leanest and meanest mule) contends that his business is the largest in the state and his wife holds that he is the biggest liar in the world.

Exhibit A—He claims that while he was in Orlando one day he saw a doctor cut open a woman, remove everything—liver, lights and heart included—clean each of them separately; the doctor then washed out the empty woman, dried her out neatly with a towel and replaced the organs so expertly that she was up and about her work in a couple of weeks.

VIII

Sewell is a man who lives all to himself. He moves a great deal. So often, that 'Lige Moseley says his chickens are so used to moving that every time he comes out into his backyard the chickens lie down and cross their legs, ready to be tied up again.

He is baldheaded; but he says he doesn't mind that, because he wants as little as possible between him and God.

IX

Mrs. Clarke is Joe Clarke's wife. She is a soft-looking, middle-aged woman, whose bust and stomach are always holding a get-together.

She waits on the store sometimes and cries every time he yells at her which he does every time she makes a mistake, which is quite often. She calls her husband "Jody." They say he used to beat her in the store when he was a young man, but he is not so impatient now. He can wait until he goes home.

She shouts in Church every Sunday and shakes the hand of fellowship with everybody in the Church with her eyes closed, but somehow always misses her husband.

X

Mrs. McDuffy goes to Church every Sunday and always shouts and tells her "determination." Her husband always sits in the back row and beats her as soon as they get home. He says there's no sense in her shouting, as big a devil as she is. She just does it to slur him. Elijah Moseley asked her why she didn't stop shouting, seeing she always got a beating about it. She says she can't "squinch the sperrit." Then Elijah asked Mr. McDuffy to stop beating her, seeing that she was going to shout anyway. He answered that she just did it for spite and that his fist was just as hard as her head. He could last just as long as she. So the village let the matter rest.

XI

DOUBLE-SHUFFLE

Back in the good old days before the World War, things were very simple in Eatonville. People didn't fox-trot. When the town wanted to put on its Sunday clothes and wash behind the ears, it put on a "breakdown." The daring younger set would two-step and waltz, but the good church members and the elders stuck to the grand march. By rural canons dancing is wicked, but one is not held to have danced until the feet have been crossed. Feet don't get crossed when one grand marches.

At elaborate affairs the organ from the Methodist church was moved up to the hall and Lizzimore, the blind man presided. When informal gatherings were held, he merely played his guitar assisted by any volunteer with mouth organs or accordions.

Among white people the march is as mild as if it had been passed on by Volstead. But it still has a kick in Eatonville. Everybody happy, shining eyes, gleaming teeth. Feet dragged 'shhlap, shhlap! to beat out the time. No orchestra needed. Round and round! Back again, parseme-la! shlap! shlap! Strut! Strut! Seaboard! Shlap! Shlap! Tiddy bumm! Mr. Clarke in the lead with Mrs. Mosely.

It's too much for some of the young folks. Double shuffling commences. Buck and wing. Lizzimore about to break his guitar. Accordion doing contortions. People fall back against the walls, and let the soloist have it, shouting as they clap the old, old double shuffle songs.

> 'Me an' mah honey got two mo' days
> Two mo' days tuh do de buck'

Sweating bodies, laughing mouths, grotesque faces, feet drumming fiercely. Deacons clapping as hard as the rest.

"Great big nigger, black as tar
Trying tuh git tuh hebben on uh 'lectric car."

"Some love cabbage, some love kale
But I love a gal wid a short skirt tail."

Long tall angel—steppin' down,
Long white robe an' starry crown.

'Ah would not marry uh black gal (bumm bumm!)
Tell yuh de reason why
Every time she comb her hair
She make de goo-goo eye.

Would not marry a yaller gal (bumm bumm!)
Tell yuh de reason why
Her neck so long an' stringy
Ahm 'fraid she'd never die.

Would not marry uh preacher
Tell yuh de reason why
Every time he comes tuh town
He makes de chicken fly.

When the buck dance was over, the boys would give the floor to the girls and they would parse-me-la with a slye eye out of the corner to see if anybody was looking who might "have them up in church" on conference night. Then there would be more dancing. Then Mr. Clarke would call for everybody's best attention and announce that *'freshments was served! Every gent'man would please take his lady by the arm and scorch her right up to de table fur a treat!*

Then the men would stick their arms out with a flourish and ask their ladies: "You lak chicken? Well, then, take a wing." And the ladies would take the proffered "wings" and parade up to the long table and be served. Of course most of them had brought baskets in which were heaps of jointed and fried chicken, two or three kinds of pies, cakes, potato pone and chicken purlo. The hall would separate into happy groups about the baskets until time for more dancing.

But the boys and girls got scattered about during the war, and now they dance the fox-trot by a brand new piano. They do waltz and two-step still, but no one now considers it good form to lock his chin over his partner's shoulder and stick out behind. One night just for fun and to humor the old folks, they danced, that is, they grand marched, but everyone picked up their feet. *Bah!!*

XII

THE HEAD OF THE NAIL

Daisy Taylor was the town vamp. Not that she was pretty. But sirens were all but non-existent in the town. Perhaps she was forced to it by circumstances. She was quite dark, with little brushy patches of hair squatting over her head. These were held down by shingle-nails often. No one knows whether she did this for artistic effect or for lack of hair-pins, but there they were shining in the little patches of hair when she got all dressed for the afternoon and came up to Clarke's store to see if there was any mail for her.

It was seldom that anyone wrote to Daisy, but she knew that the men of the town would be assembled there by five o'clock, and some one could usually be induced to buy her some soda water or peanuts.

Daisy flirted with married men. There were only two single men in town. Lum Boger, who was engaged to the assistant school-teacher, and Hiram Lester, who had been off to school at Tuskegee and wouldn't look at a person like Daisy. In addition to other drawbacks, she was pigeon-toed and her petticoat was always showing so perhaps he was justified. There was nothing else to do except flirt with married men.

This went on for a long time. First one wife then another complained of her, or drove her from the preserves by threat.

But the affair with Crooms was the most prolonged and serious. He was even known to have bought her a pair of shoes.

Mrs. Laura Crooms was a meek little woman who took all of her troubles crying, and talked a great deal of leaving things in the hands of God.

The affair came to a head one night in orange picking time. Crooms was over at Oneido picking oranges. Many fruit pickers move from one town to the other during the season.

The *town* was collected at the store-postoffice as is customary on Saturday nights. The *town* has had its bath and with its week's pay in pocket fares forth to be merry. The men tell stories and treat the ladies to soda water, peanuts and peppermint candy.

Daisy was trying to get treats, but the porch was cold to her that night.

"Ah don't keer if you don't treat me. What's a dirty lil nickel?" She flung this at Walter Thomas. "The everloving Mister Crooms will gimme anything atall Ah wants."

"You better shet up yo' mouf talking 'bout Albert Crooms. Heah his wife comes right now."

Daisy went akimbo. "Who? Me? Ah don't keer whut Laura Crooms think. If she ain't a heavy hip-ted Mama enough to keep him, she don't need to come crying to me."

She stood making goo-goo eyes as Mrs. Crooms walked upon the porch. Daisy laughed loud, made several references to Albert Crooms, and when she saw the mail-bag come in from Maitland she said, "Ah better go in an' see if Ah ain't got a letter from Oneido."

The more Daisy played the game of getting Mrs. Crooms' goat, the better she liked it. She ran in and out of the store laughing until she could scarcely stand. Some of the people present began to talk to Mrs. Crooms—to egg her on to halt Daisy's boasting, but she was for leaving it all in the hands of God. Walter Thomas kept on after Mrs. Crooms until she stiffened and resolved to fight. Daisy was inside when she came to this resolve and never dreamed anything of the kind could happen. She had gotten hold of an envelope and came laughing and shouting, "Oh, Ah can't stand to see Oneido lose!"

There was a box of ax-handles on display on the porch, propped up against the door jamb. As Daisy stepped upon the porch, Mrs. Crooms leaned the heavy end of one of those handles heavily upon her head. She staggered from the porch to the ground and the timid Laura, fearful of a counter-attack, struck again and Daisy toppled into the town ditch. There was not enough water in there to do more than muss her up. Every time she tried to rise, down would come that ax-handle again. Laura was fighting a scared fight. With Daisy thoroughly licked, she retired to the store porch and left her fallen enemy in the ditch. None of the men helped Daisy—even to get out of the ditch. But Elijah Moseley, who was some distance down the street when the trouble began arrived as the victor was withdrawing. He rushed up and picked Daisy out of the mud and began feeling her head.

"Is she hurt much?" Joe Clarke asked from the doorway.

"I don't know," Elijah answered, "I was just looking to see if Laura had been lucky enough to hit one of those nails on the head and drive it in."

Before a week was up, Daisy moved to Orlando. There in a wider sphere, perhaps, her talents as a vamp were appreciated.

XIII
PANTS AND CAL'LINE

Sister Cal'line Potts was a silent woman. Did all of her laughing down inside, but did the thing that kept the town in an uproar of laughter. It was the general opinion of the village that Cal'line would do anything she had a mind to. And she had a mind to do several things.

Mitchell Potts, her husband, had a weakness for women. No one ever believed that she was jealous. She did things to the women, surely. But most any townsman would have said that she did them because she liked the novel situation and the queer things she could bring out of it.

Once he took up with Delphine—called Mis' Pheeny by the town. She lived on the outskirts on the edge of the piney woods. The town winked and talked. People don't make secrets of such things in villages. Cal'line went about her business with her thin black lips pursed tight as ever, and her shiny black eyes unchanged.

"Dat devil of a Cal'line's got somethin' up her sleeve!" The town smiled in anticipation.

"Delphine is too big a cigar for her to smoke. She ain't crazy," said some as the weeks went on and nothing happened. Even Pheeny herself would give an extra flirt to her over-starched petticoats as she rustled into church past her of Sundays.

Mitch Potts said furthermore, that he was tired of Cal'line's foolishness. She had to stay where he put her. His African soup-bone (arm) was too strong to let a woman run over him. 'Nough was 'nough. And he did some fancy cussing, and he was the fanciest cusser in the county.

So the town waited and the longer it waited, the odds changed slowly from the wife to the husband.

One Saturday, Mitch knocked off work at two o'clock and went over to Maitland. He came back with a rectangular box under his arm and kept straight on out to the barn and put it away. He ducked around the corner of the house quickly, but even so, his wife glimpsed the package. Very much like a shoe-box. So!

He put on the kettle and took a bath. She stood in her bare feet at the ironing board and kept on ironing. He dressed. It was about five o'clock but still very light. He fiddled around outside. She kept on with her ironing. As soon as the sun got red, he sauntered out to the barn, got the parcel and walked away down the road, past the store and out into the piney woods. As soon as he left the house, Cal'line slipped on her shoes without taking time to don stockings, put on one of her husband's old Stetsons, worn and floppy, slung the axe over her shoulder and followed in his wake. He was hailed cheerily as he passed the sitters on the store porch and answered smiling sheepishly and passed on. Two minutes later passed his wife, silently, unsmilingly, and set the porch to giggling and betting.

An hour passed perhaps. It was dark. Clarke had long ago lighted the swinging kerosene lamp inside.

SEVEN YEARS FOR RACHEL

In this rich and well-crafted tale, Theophilus Lewis makes a strong case for the avoidance of forbidden love. Lewis tells the story of Sam Jones, a married man who falls in love with the virtuous and much younger Rachel Pettus. Lewis's grasp of the mental machinations of love and passion and the high price one pays for illicit love is graphic and insightful. This story was published in three parts: November 1923 and January and February 1924.

The row Sam Jones started with his wife, to provide himself with a pretext for storming out of the house in a huff, turned out to be a howling success, as the vernacular has it. The howling was contributed by Sam himself when, at the moment of his exit, a teacup splintered itself against his skull with disastrous consequences to his feelings and dignity. He made a mental note to avenge himself in an appropriate manner sometime in the future, but for the present—well, he was out of the house and that was all he wanted.

He passed through the little front yard and slammed the picket gate behind him, then walked rapidly toward Randall Avenue, feigning great haste in order to avoid returning the salutations of neighbors sitting out on their porches enjoying the cool of the evening.

When he turned the corner he reduced his pace and composed himself. He was a superb buck of a man with a skin of shining black, a massive frame and powerful elastic gait. The serious expression of his countenance marked him as the possessor of considerable force of character. In a company of black troopers he would have been made a sergeant; from amongst the members of a section gang he would have been selected for a straw boss; in his community he held a position of respect and in his church he had risen to the rank of deacon. The scene of household strife he had just escaped from was a new experience to him. He realized that the blame was his own, however, and as he sauntered along Randall Avenue he abandoned the plans for revenge he had formed a few minutes earlier.

Randall Avenue was that part of the county pike which passed through the heart of Upper Calvert, a hustling little village of Southern Maryland. It boasted of two blocks of cement sidewalk, a dozen stores, a motion picture theatre and two short rows of gas lamps. The lamps were burning now and shafts of light streamed through the store windows, streaking the grey obscurity of dusk with a weak, yellowish radiance. To Sam, who had never traveled more than twenty miles from the cabin he was born in, the street with its array of tawdry shops and vague lights presented the glamorous aspect of a metropolitan boulevard.

A few minutes walk brought him to the corner of Troy Street, which, like Jay Street where Sam lived, was merely a nondescript village lane inhabited by negroes. All the other half dozen streets in Upper Calvert were of the same type, except that white people lived in them. At the corner of Troy Street he hesitated, as if unable to decide whether to turn back or go on. He remembered that earlier in the evening he had spent an hour strolling up and down the street, and not a glimpse of Rachel Pettus had rewarded him. Had he seen her, he would have exchanged the time of day with her and made some random comments on the weather; perhaps, he would have inquired about her parents' health. Then he would have continued on his way, the music of her voice still singing in his soul, his bosom flooded with a great happiness the existence of which she would not suspect.

At present, however, Sam was trying to frame a plausible pretext for going direct to the house. He was not a rapid thinker, and several minutes passed before he hit upon the simple expedient of pretending to want to borrow a small sum of money from Rachel's father. The plan was an excellent one, as the return of the money would give him another opportunity to visit the house. He was on the verge of putting the plan into effect when he saw Rachel and one of the village swains coming toward the corner.

Sam felt a sudden pang of jealousy; nevertheless, he returned their greeting affably enough. "Where you all goin'?" he asked, affecting the air of benign maturity patronizing youth without regard to sex.

"We's jes' takin' er little stroll," Rachel replied, in a dulcet alto drawl.

"Hit's pretty hot ter-night," Sam observed. "Wouldn't you all like er ice-cream soda?"

Rachel glanced at her escort, then accepted the invitation for both. A few minutes later they entered the ice-cream emporium in Randall

Avenue and took seats in the section reserved for colored customers in the rear end of the store.

In the brilliant interior of the refectory it could be seen that Rachel was a comely young woman in the early twenties, with a slender sylph-like figure as fragile as a flower, a complexion of unblemished black and skin as smooth and glossy as celestial silk. She possessed a languorous grace of form and movement, enhanced by the ineffable charm of youth, and her countenance bore the stamp of a lively intelligence. It was plain that Sam's passion for her was not inspired by her physical charm, however, for she was not nearly so attractive as his wife. Had Amelia Jones been a widow or a frivolous wife, she could have counted twenty discerning admirers to Rachel's one. But love, while it can be readily analyzed in the abstract, is in the concrete, more often than not, unexplainable: and Sam's affection for Rachel must remain as incomprehensible to us as it was to him.

It was while they were sipping their sodas that he discovered that she was not indifferent to him. He noticed that her sweetest smiles and softest glances were not for her youthful companion, but furtively bent in his direction. Hitherto, he had believed himself the possessor of an affection which was unrequited and unsuspected and which must always remain so; and he had resigned himself to his fate. The most he had ever hoped for was to see her and hear the melody of her voice and bask in the radiance of her presence as often as he could. Even now her reciprocal glances did not embolden him beyond the point of broaching a vague hint or two.

He was still preserving his pose of genial middle-age, with no ulterior motive in view, entertaining youth for the sheer fun of it. "I's glad I met you young folks," he declared, paternally. "I likes ter see young folks enjoy demselves." He paused; perhaps, to emphasize a phrase he did not wish to stress with his voice. "I walks down dis way ever' night—ter sorter shake my supper down. But I never got dis much pleasure f'om de stroll befo'."

About the same hour the following evening Sam again sauntered down Randall Avenue. In his bosom was the fervent hope that Rachel had picked up his hint and would come out to meet him. If she did not, he intended to employ his money borrowing ruse and visit her home. But the ruse was not required. When he reached the corner of Troy Street he found Rachel standing in a shadowed spot waiting for him.

He was too delighted to speak; and surprised too, for he had hoped rather than expected to find her there.

"You didn't spec ter fin' me here, did you?" she asked, in a caressing murmur. Her dulcet voice seemed to be refined to a soft soprano, and its tenderness intensified his ecstasy. It further astonished him too, for it informed him that he was her accepted lover.

In his delight, he could not think coherently at once; the simple reply to her question did not occur to him. Not quite relevantly, he suggested, "Let's go in de movin' pictures." "No," she objected, discreetly. "Let's jes' walk—out dis way." And she gestured away from the center of the village, where the radiance of the gas lamps and the lighted shop windows cast the glare of publicity on an attenuated throng of rustic boulevardiers. "All right," Sam consented, deriving a subtly sensuous joy from resigning himself to her wish. They turned their backs to the village and faced the open country where Randall Avenue became the Nottingham Pike and wound in crazy convolutions through an idyllic undulating landscape now reposing in the tranquil solitude of night. The moon had risen just high enough to touch the rounded hilltops with a silvery lustre, leaving the low places of the earth swathed in mysterious shadows. A few scraps of cloud moved slowly and lazily across the sky from south to north, like floating islands in a sable sea. The stars looked down austerely. Multitudes of crickets, like lost souls ignorant of their damnation, rejoiced in the nether darkness of the undergrowth, while from shadowy copses came the ululations of owls and the weird melody of whip-poor-wills. A profusion of spicy and fragrant odors embalmed the air and the soft south wind was as caressing as a virgin's kiss.

For a while the lovers were spellbound by the enchanting loveliness of the night and the indescribable sweetness of their contact. Sam's fingers sought Rachel's hand and she surrendered it to him. Thus they walked along in silence, speaking no syllable, but holding rapturous discourse in passion's inarticulate language which endows the pressure of hand upon hand with an eloquence transcending the power of words. They had gone a mile, perhaps, when Rachel softly sighed. It was the first sound she had uttered since leaving the village. Sam sighed too, he could not help it. Then, instinctively, they both halted.

"I ain't comin' out ter meet you no more," she said, with mingled tenderness and sadness.

Sam sighed again. "Hit's wrong, I specs," he mumbled.

"I wouldn't er come dis time, only I knowed you loved me an' I wanted you ter know I loves you. I jes' had ter tell you, jes' once." She paused and sighed and added, "But hit's sinful."

"Yes, hit's sinful," he echoed.

Here, in the minds of both, conviction sharply clashed with feeling.

Sam was a deacon in Zion Hill Baptist church in Upper Calvert. Rachel was a Methodist, and every Sunday, when the weather was not violent, she made the three-mile journey to Nottingham to teach a Sunday school class in Little Bethel. Steeped in the traditional beliefs of the pious peasant community, they could not nor would not attempt to justify their passion. They believed they were sinning. But under that virtuous belief was the half-conscious but poignant feeling that the celestial and mundane powers which outlawed their love were neither moral nor just but oppressive. Had the feeling reached the plane of conscious thought they would have rebelled against the conventions. But it did not and they submitted to having their affections throttled.

Their sensual African natures would not permit the complete immolation of the hour, however, and as they returned toward the village they chatted brightly, mostly of themselves. "How long has you loved me, Sam?" Rachel asked, at one point of the homeward journey.

"I don't know," he replied. "Hit's been er long time though." He paused a second, then went on, reminiscently, "I was er man when you was bo'n; an' married when you was er little tot"; he reflected bitterly. "I watched you grow up, an' hit 'peared like you was dif'rent f'om other chillun. 'Member how I used ter pick you out f'om de res' an' buy you er ginger cake?"

For affirmative answer, she drew closer to him, so that her warm breath, like a sweet, infinitesimal sirocco, fanned his cheek for an instant.

"Specs I must er loved you den," he declared, "but I didn't know hit."

Then they became silent again and remained so until they reached a bend of the road which brought them in sight of the village. There they halted, both stopping at the same instant as if inspired by the same thought.

"I aint comin' out ter see you no more," Rachel declared again. "An' I don't want you ter try ter see me."

"Hit won't be no harm fo' us ter jes' see each other," Sam protested.

"De flesh is weak," she reminded him sagely. " 'Pears like hit aint de Lawd's will fo' hit ter be so we could marry. Hit aint his will fo' us ter lover each other neither, but we can't help dat. But I'll be jes' de same as ef I was married ter you, Sam—I means I won't never love no other man."

"An' I'll be jes' de same as ef I was single, Rachel. I swears hit ter de Lawd."

"Den, kiss me, Sam," she murmured tenderly.

And he kissed her.

During the fortnight following the renunciation Sam suffered intensely. The desire to see Rachel would not be suppressed; and as he did not yield to it, feeling that to do so would be a breach of faith, it tormented him incessantly. His days became periods of wretchedness, and his nights were filled with terrifying dreams in which he saw Rachel spurning his love or married to another man or dead. Unceasing torture inevitably altered his disposition. A chronic grouch replaced his whilom constant cheerfulness. In his home he became an irascible despot whose petty tyrannies provoked incessant household insurrections. At last his wretchedness became unbearable and he determined to consult one of the local conjurers.

Most of the spell weavers and root doctors who infested the countryside were Christians as well as voodooists, and professed to exercise their craft for benevolent purposes only—that is, they claimed to be willing to put evil spells on none but sinners. One Zeb Hicks, however, was an exception. Zeb was a malformed homunculus with a wizened body and a club foot. His head was of enormous size, and his black face, with its innumerable wrinkles, crevices, cracks, creases and folds resembled a huge dried prune. In this sooty mask were set eyes of a very light hazel color, which at times glowed with a greenish cast, investing him with the monstrous aspect of a Caucasian spirit imprisoned in the mummified carcass of a Nubian. It was well known that if he put a bad mouth on one, one would straightway start running through the woods barking like a dog, or swell up with some incurable dropsy, or die vomiting frogs or provoke God and be brained with a thunderbolt. It was to Zeb that Sam appealed for advice.

After listening to Sam's disclosure, the witch man shook his head solemnly and declared the case too difficult for his resources. "I kin make er gal love you," Zeb declared. "But you don't want dat, 'cause she loves you already. Or I kin move another pusson outer de way, but you don't want dat neither, so I don't see what I kin do fo' you." He paused, thoughtfully, while Sam sat drooped in the silence of despair. Presently, the witch man suggested, "You mout try sellin' yo' soul ter de Devil. You has ter do dat fo' yo' self though. I can't do hit fo' you."

"How does you do hit?" Sam inquired. At that time he had formed no conscious resolve to go to that extreme. He was instinctively grasping at the straw of hope thrown out to him.

"You jes' walks ter de fo'k of de road seven mawnin's runnin', an' spresses yo' 'tention ter sell yo' soul an wishes fo' what you wants," Zeb informed him. "On de seventh mawnin' de Devil mout 'pear ter you, mebbe he won't. But he'll give you what you wants anyhow, an' yo' soul b'longs ter him fo' seven years. An' ef you dies in dat time you goes ter hell."

———

Sam did not follow this advice immediately; but after another fortnight of wretchedness his intense desire for Rachel overcame all restraint, and he made the seven pilgrimages to the fork of the road. The Devil did not appear on the seventh morning—for which non-appearance Sam was mighty grateful—and as he noticed no change in his feelings he decided that, after all, the whole business was probably bunk. But when a motor truck barely missed running him down a few minutes later he experienced an awful nausea in the region of his navel.

Several uneventful days of wretchedness had passed when, in a late watch of the night, Amelia roused him from a reposeful slumber. "Sam! Sam! Wake up!" she was calling.

"What you want?" he growled angrily. It happened that she had disturbed the first restful sleep he had enjoyed for several nights.

"I's sick an' I wants er doctor," Amelia replied.

"Can't get no doctor dis time of night," he fumed; and prepared to go to sleep again.

Amelia said no more, but Sam, who found he could not go to sleep again, heard her utter a gasp or a weak moan now and then, as if in great pain. Finally he raised up on his elbow and asked what hurt her.

"Hit's my heart, I wants er doctor," she said. Her gasps were becoming more frequent and Sam became concerned.

" 'Taint nothin' 'cept heart-bu'n. I'll get de arrermatic spirits of ammonia." And, suiting the action to the word, he got out of bed and lit the lamp.

The room was crowded with shabby furniture and the walls were littered with lithographs, pennants from county fairs, framed mottos and tintypes of friends and relatives long departed and turned to clods. Sam paid no attention to these familiar objects but went straight to a shelf which was crowded with a dusty accumulation of phials, pill boxes, cartons and packages containing drugs. He did not find the bottle he was seeking at once, and turned about to ask Amelia where it was.

Her expression frightened him. It was an expression of intense suffering blended with a heroic resolution to bear it with fortitude. Instantly, every aspect of his bargain with Satan flashed to Sam's mind. The phosphorescent haze of mystery was cleared away and he saw the pact in its stark reality. It was being carried out in that merciless, dispassionately efficient manner with which super-mortal agencies proceed to accomplish their ends. Sam shuddered and a cold sweat popped out all over him. He had hoped that his union with Rachel would be brought about in some mysterious way which would cause Amelia some inconvenience, perhaps, but no serious harm. He had never thought of this extreme method of getting her out of the way. But what could one expect of the Devil? At that moment he would have gladly withdrawn from the bargain. That was not possible, however, so he did the next best thing; he decided to fetch a doctor.

"I can't fin' de arrermatic spirits of ammonia," he said, to soothe her and cover his own fright. "Specs I'll have ter get de doctor after all."

He slipped on his pants and shoes and called his eldest boy and instructed him to stay with his mother until he returned. Then he hastened out of the house. He had only to go to Randall Avenue, and soon returned with a physician.

Medical aid was unavailing, however; and a few minutes after the physician's arrival Amelia died in a very prosaic manner—that is, all her breath gushed out in one deep sigh and her half-closed eyelids flew wide open, exposing irises fixed in a ludicrous stare which seemed more insane than lifeless. She passed out without bequeathing the customary blessing on her children, without reproaches for her erring husband.

Sam, with a feeling of augmented guilt, was of the opinion that she was cut off in her sins; but the women who shrouded her the next morning declared she had gone straight to Heaven, so serene was the expression of her countenance after her eyelids had been weighted down with pennies. The doctor said she had died of acute indigestion. He should have been called in sooner.

Neither the asseverations of the housewives nor the opinion of the man of science could allay Sam's remorse. At the instant of his wife's death, the conviction that he was an active accessory to her murder lodged in his bosom and continued to dwell there and torment him ever after.

Followed the briefest period of formal bereavement rustic propriety would permit. Four months after Amelia's burial, Sam and Rachel were married in the little Methodist parsonage in Nottingham. After the ceremony the newlyweds walked back to Upper Calvert along the Nottingham Pike.

It was a glorious afternoon in October. The country was resplendent in its autumnal finery of russet and gold and yellowish green, and the beautiful Indian Summer haze, almost as ponderable as mist, hovered over the landscape like a luminous fog. If ever Rachel appeared to be a regnant creature, it was that afternoon, when her features, radiant as they were with joyous passion, were touched with fire by the declining sun's horizontal rays, which made topaz transparencies of her nostrils and eyelids and turned her dull black hair to burnished bronze.

The transcendent loveliness with which the happiness of the hour endowed her did not exceed her exaltation of mind. The blissful consummation of her love had appeared so remote a few months earlier that it now seemed to her that nothing less miraculous and benevolent than a visitation of Providence had brought it to pass.

"Hit's been mos' six months since de night we came out dis way, aint hit?" she observed, reminiscently, as they drew near Upper Calvert.

"Yes, 'bout dat long," her husband replied.

"Hit 'peared like our love was hopeless den," she continued. Her voice trembled slightly, as if, for the moment, the pathos of the memory outweighed the happiness of the present. "But here hit is fulfilled. Hit shows how hit pays ter do what's right an' put yo' trust in de Lawd. Ef we had yielded ter temptation an' vi'lated de Seventh Commandment He would er frowned on us. But we 'frained from sinning, an' in His own time an' way de Lawd has rewarded us."

The unintended irony of her sentiments caused Sam to flinch. His felony had never seemed so black as at that moment, when suddenly contrasted with his bride's innocence. Her expression of her naïve belief that he had pursued a virtuous *laissez faire* course of action and her gratitude to heaven for what he believed was the gift of Satan brought to a focus certain diffused misgivings which had been augmenting his remorse ever since Amelia's death. He could no longer avoid the realization that in making his treaty with the Infernal he had not only sinned against Heaven and his first wife but had perpetrated a fraud on Rachel as well. At present his betrayal of her trust and reverence seemed the most serious of his crimes. He had deprived her of the upright, God fearing man she loved and foisted on her the sin-crusted hypocrite who she did not yet know existed. With the deception between them, they could never share that unreserved intimacy of thought and feeling without which their married life would be something base, in a way—something carnal and incomplete and clouded with the same insincerity which had bedeviled the latter years of his union with his first wife.

During the past fortnight Sam had frequently suspected but had never admitted that such a situation would arise as a result of his covenant. The issue had crystallized now, however, and he perceived that iniquities of all sorts must flow from such an evil bargain as inevitably as a stink rises from a rotting carcass. It was only natural, he now saw, that a soul in bondage to the Devil must be a wellspring of wickedness to the last day of its servitude. Too late he perceived, as has many another man who has presumed to dicker with powers too strong and too clever for the sons of Adam, that his impatient attempt to tinker with the plan of Providence had not resulted in any amelioration of his wretchedness.

In even the meanest of men, however, there is often a leaven of stoicism which makes them face crises nobly. Sam had no thought of self pity. Instead he heroically resolved to prevent Rachel from sharing his own inevitable fate. He decided to tell her how their marriage had been made possible, feeling certain that she would recoil from him in pious horror. Then she could return to her people and he alone would bear the punishment for his crime.

They were nearing the place where, that bland summer night months ago, they had made their first renunciation. There was a touch of dramatic intensity, as well as poetic justice, in the play of circumstances which was compelling him to make a greater renunciation on the same spot. Suddenly he halted and cleared his throat to speak.

"Ah! You 'members de place!" Rachel murmured, as she stopped too, at the same instant, as if her body were synchronized with his and one mind governed both.

"H'm," Sam faltered, trying to begin his confession. But while he remained inarticulate Rachel continued fluently: "Here's where we had our fust kiss an' thought hit would be de las' one. De Lawd sho has 'nointed us with his blessin'." As she spoke her grasp on his arm became firmer and more caressing, her voice was fraught with infinite tenderness, and her eyes were luminous with love and filled with tears of happiness. To confess to her then, while her happiness was at the flood, and change her ecstasy to woe was more than Sam could force himself to do. It would be kinder to gash her flesh with a razor, he felt, and decided to put off his confession until her passion had subsided somewhat. Some might condemn him for his lack of manliness and moral courage. Still, if it was a noble impulse that prompted his confession, it was a compassionate one that forbade it. And compassion, perhaps, is the one virtue which makes man morally superior to the immortals.

"Why don't you say something, Sam?" Rachel asked at last, marking his silence and abstraction. "You looks like yo' min' was far erway." She sighed and concluded, "Well, I specs I can't have you all ter myself jes' yet. Amelia's been gone sich er sho't time."

" 'Taint dat. Specs I's jes too happy fo' wo'ds," he lied. Then they continued on their way to the village.

A period of unruffled felicity followed. Their happiness was unalloyed—so far as that term can be correctly employed to describe any condition in this life of constant changes and compromises. Rachel was an affectionate wife to Sam and a devoted and, considering her youth and their lusty adolescence, an efficient step-mother to his boys. So beatific was the atmosphere in the little home that Sam was loath to mar it by revealing his secret. As months passed without any new complication arising, he at length decided it would not be necessary to tell her at all. He would serve his period of bondage in secret and her peace of mind need never be disturbed. This state of millennial serenity endured six months.

Then, by almost imperceptible degrees, at first, a change in Rachel's constitution manifested itself. It first appeared in the form of demonstrations of excessive affection for her husband. Then her physical vigor showed a gradual decline, the seductive languor of her person becoming a settled lassitude, while her usual comeliness at times seemed refined to a rare and exquisite beauty. In the afternoon her eyes shone with an excessive brilliance and a hectic flush glowed through the translucent ebony of her cheeks, as though her light of life were shining exceedingly bright and beautiful, like a scarlet cathedral lamp beaming through a pane of polished jet.

—

He avoided the bright lights of Randall Avenue, and tramped through various dark streets until he reached a fringe of forest which bordered one side of the village. The gloom and silence of the place at once soothed and stimulated his mind. For a few minutes he leaned against one of the tall trees and mused on the elusiveness of human happiness and its incompleteness and instability when secured for a brief moment. But his mind did not soar among generalities long. His thoughts soon descended to the consideration of his present dilemma.

The thought of coming down with consumption while the Infernal held a lien on his soul filled him with terror. To knowingly place himself in danger of infection, he reasoned, would be tantamount to self-murder, which, according to local tradition, was one of the unforgivable sins.

Still, to safeguard his own health he would have to sacrifice Rachel's. To refuse to sleep with her without telling her why would leave her mind the victim of its present false impression; to tell her why would grieve her even more. In either case the doctor's "no worry" dictum would have to be violated, which would aggravate her disease and perhaps hasten her death. Already guilty of complicity in the murder of one wife, he was loath to add another blood crime to his growing list of iniquities.

"Shucks! I oughter tol' her when we was fust married," he soliloquized. "Den she would er left me an' I wouldn't be in dis fix now." Then he heeled the tree trunk viciously, and fumed in disgust, "Doggone hit! 'Pears like I's jes' got to figger ever'thing out wrong."

A fit of desperation seized him then, and he decided to make himself the he-goat of sacrifice, feeling that after all it did not matter much, as either alternative he chose was almost certain to be the wrong one. When he lay down beside Rachel that night his heart was heavy with the conviction that he was turning his back on salvation. But he knew it would have felt no lighter if he had made the opposite choice. As it was, the consciousness of noble self-sacrifice consoled him and, in a way, compensated him for the increased peril of his soul.

Rachel's consumption grew worse—rapidly. Time came when she realized that her days on earth were numbered. She was not terrified at all, for she knew that long, long ago, her Saviour had gone to prepare a place for her; and she even began to anticipate the inevitable with a mild impatience, certain that crossing Jordan would be but a blissful moment of passing from this world of sighs and sorrows to a land of everlasting joy and light.

As the end drew nearer, these anticipations of celestial bliss were communicated to Sam, mainly in the form of nocturnal discourses after he had gone to bed. At times, in long monologues rich with phrases from Holy Writ and embellished with quotations from Wesleyan hymns, she would dwell on the ecstasy that would be hers when she met her Saviour face to face, to praise Him and glorify Him for ten thousand times ten thousand years. At other times, she seemed fascinated by the prospect of eternal felicity awaiting her and Sam and Amelia in the Aiden where human passions and jealousies are not and they neither marry nor are given in marriage.

"I's happier ever' day 'cause we didn't anger de Lawd by breakin de Seventh Commandment," she frequently declared, with monotonous reiteration. "Now we kin meet Amelia in Heaven 'thout nothin' ter be 'shamed of. C'ose she'd er forgive us anyhow, even ef we had sinned. But hit's so much better not ter need no forgivin'."

Those were days that flayed Sam's soul. Daily he was confronted with the treasure he had exchanged Salvation for wasting away to an ashy skeleton with cloudy eyes, sunken cheeks and lips parched and shriveled like dead leaves the Autumn winds pluck from maples; while his nightly repose was disturbed by the cracked voice, no longer sweet, ironically forecasting joys he would never know. Anon, these nocturnal monologues became sources of terror to him. In the darkened room, when he could not see her face, her weak voice seemed to come from a vast distance, as if from beyond the grave. It was as if the croak of some invisible spirit were taunting him with his folly. Some nights this creepy feeling became so vivid that he would get up and light the lamp, to assure himself that Rachel was still alive and talking.

Sam's wretchedness was ameliorated, however, by the knowledge that it was partly voluntary. That he was doomed to perdition he was quite convinced. Still, he could have cut loose and gone to hell a-galloping. He had heard of others doing so and enjoying a world of fun on the way. But he preferred to continue his gentle ministrations to his wife, religiously adhering to his determination not to cause her the slightest worry, just as religiously concealing from her the haunting fears and chronic despair which tormented him incessantly. That was a labor of love, and it was not relinquished until, in the exhaustion that followed a hemorrhage, Rachel dozed off in the long, long sleep that lasts forever.

The day set for Rachel's burial began with a raw, murky morning filled with an impenetrable fog. As the hours advanced the fog changed to a fine rain which descended without sound but with such persistence and in such volumes that the landscape was soon saturated. When the little cortege started for the Methodist church the roads were immaculately clean and fresh in appearance and uncomfortably soggy in condition, while the darker surfaces of the landscape, sheathed in myriads of needle points of water, wore the warlike lustre of burnished iron. The weather had not perceptibly changed when the procession left the church for the cemetery. But before the interment was completed the prevailing east wind became violent, suddenly smote the earth with a terrific force that stripped the trees of their glistening mail, and swept a deluge inland from the coast.

Most of the mourners sought the shelter of their vehicles, which was none too ample, as most of the conveyances were buggies and buckboards. Sam declined even this slight protection from the fury of the storm. With a few faithful sympathizers, he stood bareheaded in the downpour until the last spadeful of earth was placed on the mound over that parcel of dearer earth which had been to him all the Heaven he would ever know. Ever devoted to her while she lived, he gave the last full measure of tenderness to her memory. He wanted people to say, "She must have been a good woman, because her husband loved her so and grieved so hard when she died."

He was soaked to the skin when he reached home, and cold to the bone. After changing to dry clothes, he started a roaring fire in the kitchen range and sat close beside it. As he absently added fuel from time to time he was vaguely conscious that he seemed unable to get warm. What he was vividly aware of was the spectral stillness and loneliness of the house—an unearthly stillness it was, which the hiss and crackle of the fire and the occasional scampering of a mouse over the floor made to seem more oppressive. And the loneliness was as persistent as the silence. Not even the fact of his boys being in the room relieved his utter desolation. His feeling of isolation triumphed over their presence just as the implacable stillness of the room prevailed over their low, furtively cheerful conversation.

While he sat huddled over the stove, unable to get warm and shrinking from the spectral silence, there came to him, like a sunbeam suddenly shining through a rift in a thundercloud, one of those cheering thoughts which often come to comfort men in their most despondent moods. It occurred to him that perhaps the taking off of Rachel was Heaven's way of releasing him from his servitude to Satan. When the thought first came it struck him with the force of Gospel truth, and his heart filled and overflowed with thanksgiving. Then came a moment of doubt. What had he done to deserve Heaven's reprieve? He had not even prayed for it. Had such mites of virtue as his contrition after Amelia's death and his daily sacrifices during the long illness of Rachel earned clemency for him, even though, like the publican, he had not presumed to lift his eyes toward Zion? He feared to answer these questions, lest hope mislead rather than discretion guide his judgment. Still, he would not wilfully turn his back on the ray of hope, the act might be an unintentional spurning of Heaven's proffer of peace. The only escape from this new quandary was to consult a mind abler or, at least, less perplexed than his own. Although it meant divulging his secret to the world, he determined to seek enlightenment of his quondam pastor on the morrow.

But the fire . . . Why did it not heat the room? He stirred the blazing fagots in the stove, threw in fresh wood and wrapped himself in a blanket. But even then he could not get warm.

The next day he was unable to carry out his determination to consult the parson. Pains in the head, chest and limbs, accompanied by a high fever and a racking cough, kept him confined to the house. Late in the afternoon a neighboring housewife came in and administered hot toddy and quinine and advised him to go to bed. "Dat's er grave-yard cough," she warned him. "You kotched hit when you got wet in de buryin' groun'. You better be careful with hit."

Sam was careful with his cold. A fortnight passed before he ventured outdoors. The pain had gone and the fever was not perceptible then, but the cough was as bad as ever, and he had lost an alarming amount of strength and weight. He was so weak that the light overcoat which the bright, cold weather of early winter required was a considerable burden. He left home with the intention of making his deferred visit to the parsonage, and had gone about half the distance when he met the homunculus Zeb hobbling through the village.

Sam's first impulse was to shun the conjurer, who, in a way, was the author of all his woe; but a swift second thought suggested that he might glean from him the information he was going to seek at the parsonage. As they drew near each other, the witch man seemed to eye the wasted frame and feeble steps of the whilom stalwart Sam with malevolent satisfaction.

"Did you hear I los' my wife?" Sam asked, when they came within conversing distance.

"I didn't hear 'bout hit, but I knows hit jes' de same," Zeb replied.

"Well den, bein's I los' her befo' de seven years was up, specs de Devil ain't got no mo' claim on my soul," Sam observed, in the most offhand manner he could affect.

"How come you specs dat?" Zeb demanded. "Didn't you get de gal yo' heart was sot on?"

"Sho I did," Sam admitted.

"Did you ast ter keep her seven years when you make de bargain?"

"I didn't think of hit den," Sam replied, truthfully.

"Den, ef you only ast ter *get* de gal an' didn't ast ter *keep* her, hit 'pears ter me like de Devil has kep' his part of de bargain, an' you has got ter keep yo' part," Zeb declared. And without further ado he hobbled on his way.

To Sam, Zeb's opinion seemed an undue stressing of the letter of the law at the expense of its spirit; nevertheless, it was an extremely sad sick man who appeared at the parsonage a few minutes later.

"I ain't seen you in chu'ch fo' er mighty long time," the preacher observed as he admitted his visitor. "Specs you's become er backslider."

"I *has* sorter fell f'om grace," Sam confessed. "Dat's what I's come ter 'sult you 'bout."

"Hit's er step in de right direction," the preacher commended him. The preacher was a venerable cotton-headed patriarch of the old school—that is to say, he was a morally upright man whose theology was a quaint mixture of local superstition, hangovers from African fetichism and the Bible taken literally. He gave a patient hearing to Sam's story of his dealings with the Devil and the resultant complications. Then, although awestruck by the revelation of greater depravity than he had suspected, he preserved an aloof and severe ecclesiastical poise while he delivered his opinion of the case.

"Hit 'pears ter me dat sellin' yo' soul ter de Devil was 'quivalent ter sinnin' 'gainst de Holy Ghost?" the parson declared. "An' dat's er unfo'givable sin. I don't say fo' certain, but hit 'pears like dat ter me."

Sam's hope, which had been buoyed up by the preacher's patient listening to his story, fell to zero again. "I thought mebbe de Lawd was punishin' me when he took Rachel," he said, "an' at de same time deliverin' me f'om Satan." The probability that Heaven had annulled his covenant with the Infernal by depriving him of the emolument he had received was his last hope and he clung to it desperately.

"Hit don't 'pear like dat ter me," the preacher rebutted. "Yo' sins is too many. When you lusted after Rachel while you' fust wife was livin' you broke de Seventh Commandment by committin' 'dultery in yo' heart. Den you's guilty of 'plicity in Amelia's murder. Wust of all, you sol' yo' soul ter de Devil. Has you any right ter spec de Lawd ter f'give you fo' all dat?"

"Den dere's no hope fo' me?" Sam cried.

"I don't say dat," the preacher extemporized, in gentler tones. "De mercy of de Lawd is infinite. But I don't see how you kin offer him yo' soul when hit b'longs ter de Devil. Mebbe when de seven years is up you kin be saved, but dat's between you an' yo' God." He went on in this manner nearly an hour longer, doing what he could to console Sam but holding out no definite hope.

A Deserter from Armageddon

In this tale, Theophilus Lewis's colorful descriptions place the reader inside the scenes. His main character, Roscoe, foresees a tragedy that he believes will be caused by the devil. Nevertheless, his love, jealousy, and cowardice unite and prevent him from staving off the devil's actions. Lewis published this story in two parts, in March and April 1924.

Early one summer evening, in a beautiful old-fashioned garden where lilacs, magnolias and rambler roses bloomed in prodigal profusion, filling the air with their rich fragrance, while a glory of phlox, cannæ, nasturtiums and asters was promised for later in the season, the stooping figure of a Negro laborer could have been seen and the metallic snip, snip, snip of a pair of gardener's shears could have been heard as the toiler trimmed the grass under hedgery, around borders and in out-of-the-way corners where the lawn mower had failed to reach. It was that indefinite hour of the day which can be called either sunset or dusk, according to whether one faces the west or east. Had the toiler scanned the west, where a bank of luminous cloud filled that half of the firmament with a rosy light, he would have been tempted to stand up and rest his back a bit, feeling assured of another hour of daylight; had he looked toward the east, from whence an ever-widening segment of darkness expanded upward toward the zenith, he would have decided to speed up his work, lest night overtake him with his task unfinished. He did not look up at all, however, but kept his eyes and attention fixed on his work with the commendable concentration of a worthy craftsman. He completed his task while there was still considerable light in the sky, and when he had finished he stood up and stretched himself to relieve the cricks in his back and legs and meanwhile surveyed the job with merited satisfaction.

He was a strapping young fellow, in the late twenties, with a complexion approximating the color of cedar bark, patient eyes and a serious but not over firm expression about the mouth and jaw. After a rapid inspection of his work, he thrust the shears, points upward, in the hip pocket of his overalls, and walked to where a lawn mower stood with a rake lying on the ground beside it. Then, carrying the rake under one arm and pushing the lawn mower ahead of him, he followed a gravel path which curved around the house and led to a barn in the rear. When he had put the tools away he crossed the space between the barn and the kitchen and tapped lightly on the screen door.

A neat, silver-haired white woman came to the door in response to the knock. "Have you finished the lawn, Roscoe?" she asked. Her voice was superlatively soft and sweet, the gift of the climate, perhaps, or an heritage of a by-gone culture.

"Yes'm, Miss Warren," Roscoe replied. "It's got ever'thing done fust class."

"Did you trim under the hedges and around the borders?"

"Yes'm, and in de co'ners too."

"And did you rake the lawn *thoroughly?*"

"Yes'm," he declared, and added, conscientiously, " 'ceptin' in er few co'ners."

"That won't matter much," Mrs. Warren observed, indulgently. "Here's seventy-five cents for you," she concluded, taking the money from her apron pocket.

"Thank you, Miss Warren," Roscoe bowed, grinning happily. "Specs I'll be goin' home now."

"All right, Roscoe. Good-bye."

"Good-bye, Miss Warren."

A few minutes later he had reached the county road and was striding along at a pace which rapidly put distance between himself and Mrs. Warren's pretty house and beautiful garden. Mrs. Warren's house stood in picturesque isolation about a mile from the tiny village of Rosaryville. Roscoe's little cottage stood about the same distance on the other side of the hamlet. He covered the distance quickly that evening, spurred on, perhaps, by the anticipation of a savory supper and the affectionate greeting of his wife, of whom he was extravagantly fond. He wondered what Rosalie would have for supper. Spare rib stew with rich creamy gravy perhaps; or ham and cabbage with tender young corn. It was Saturday, and those were the dishes his wife was partial to for the week-end. And hot biscuits and buttermilk.

These cheerful speculations suddenly ceased, however, when he came in sight of his cottage. Instead of the light which usually shone from the kitchen window when he worked late, gleaming through the twilight or night like a friendly beacon, he saw the house looming dark and cheerless in the evening murk with the forlorn aspect of a forsaken place. His heart sank with misgiving when he noticed the absence of the light, for finding the house deserted thus, though not a frequent occurrence, was no new experience to him; it had happened before. It meant that he would find no wife to welcome him in that dark house; perhaps a cold supper, perhaps no supper, according to Rosalie's whim before she had gone out. His pace slackened and his steps became heavy, and the fatigue of the day's toil, which he had not noticed before, seemed suddenly to descend on him. When he reached the house he was in the grip of that poignant depression which inevitably appals one when disappointment is met where one expected to find affection and cheer.

Indoors, a deeper gloom than the outside twilight prevailed, and Roscoe, bearing in mind his wife's aptitude for leaving such objects as brooms and chairs in inappropriate places, groped his way to the shelf where the matches were kept with extreme caution. When he struck a light, the dingy little kitchen with its shabby furniture leaped suddenly into view, like a tawdry little world coming into being at the command of a minor god. It was an unstable world for a few seconds though, for, as the weak little flame guttered feebly, the gloom alternately receded from and resurged upon the inconstant circle of radiance, causing the objects in the room to emerge suddenly into light and existence and as suddenly vanish in night and nothingness. Not till the flame was applied to the bracket lamp which hung over the shelf was darkness definitely vanquished and the reign of light assured, establishing an orderly array of surfaces, outlines, angles, nuances and masses where all had been black chaos.

The light, which in an instant transferred the commonplace furniture and utensils from the realm of the invisible and ideal to the world of the tangible and real, disclosed an ordinary little kitchen in an indifferent state of cleanliness. The floor had been swept clean, but the dustpan containing the sweepings had been carelessly left lying on a chair. There were no dirty dishes in sight, but a dingy dishrag lay drying on the table beside some wasted sugar which was exciting a lively competition between flies and some enterprising ants.

Near the center of the table was a scrap of paper weighted down with a salt cellar. Roscoe saw the note as soon as he lit the lamp and picked it up and read its message. "I has gone to Calvert to dance," the note ran. "You can come for me if you want to. Your supper is in the stove. Rosalie."

"Doggone hit! She oughtn't ter run off like dis," Roscoe fumed, disappointment having now changed to vexation. "Hard as I wo'ks ter keep er roof over her haid. She ain't treatin' me right." Roscoe, like many Negro peasants, had the habit of expressing his thoughts aloud—an evidence of excessive carnality, perhaps; thought in such persons being almost unable to proceed without the physical assistance of the vocal organs. While transferring his supper from the oven to the table, he continued his soliloquy, interrogating himself and answering his own questions with such animation that a pedestrian passing outside the house would have concluded that two persons were quarreling within.

The supper was cold—it was spare rib stew—the gravy in cooling had become a viscous, unpalatable jelly which adhered to the meat and made it unpalatable also. The biscuits were cold. Preceded by no hot solids to create the proper thirst, the buttermilk tasted flat and was without tang. The whole meal was a failure.

" 'Taint fit ter eat!" he fumed, pushing his plate away in disgust after a few mouthfuls. Peevishness rather than the condition of the food had killed his appetite; and peevishness continued to inspire him as he went on: "Doggone hit! She gets mo' no 'count ever' day."

"You kin com fo' me ef you wants ter," he continued, derisively repeating a sentence of Rosalie's note; and, of course, translating it into dialect. "Huh! Devil fetch her! Let her get home de bes' way she kin. I ain't goin' ter lose my res' 'bout her."

It then occurred to him that while he was fretting in the lonely house angry and miserable, his wife was enjoying herself at the dance. And there would be no dearth of swains willing to see her home. The thought was unendurable. It did not seem just that he who had been wronged should suffer while she who had wronged him should enjoy the sweets of the situation. He suddenly reversed his decision.

"Dern hit! I's stood fo' her galavantin' roun' long enough. I's goin' ter make her come erway f'om dat dance right erway. I's done reasoned with her an' prayed for her, an' hit ain't done no good. Now I's goin' ter show her who's de boss in dis house."

He turned the light down low and left the house. It was then about nine o'clock. The moon had not yet appeared but the night was clear and cloudless, and the benign southern sky, magnificently spangled with stars, was like an immense masterpiece of wakasa inlaid with fragments of pearl. There being no light, the world of color was not; the masses of the landscape loomed in the enveloping night like grotesque black shadows on a dark background, assuming strange shapes and fantastic outlines and fretting the skyline with exquisite lace-like filigrees worthy to enhance the sombre splendor of a temple in Tartarus. A more poetic soul than Roscoe would have reveled in the night's uncanny beauty, while a more timorous man would have been terrified by the sinister aspect of its impenetrable gloom. But the stolid peasant was too unimaginative to lodge the finer feeling and at present too preoccupied to feel fear without special cause. He plodded along as indifferent to his surroundings as he was to the distance between Bagdad and Damascus. When he reached Calvert he could have described the scenes he had passed no more accurately than he could have told how many crickets he had heard fiddling amongst the herbs or the number of steps required to bring him to his journey's end.

Upper Calvert—the Calvert of Rosalie's note—was the focus of the social activity of the county's colored population. The Baptist church was there, also the district school for colored children and the Odd Fellows' hall. Odd Fellows' hall was a modest dwelling house with the partitions of the lower floor knocked out to make a place for dancing. Roscoe knew he would find his wife there.

It happened that he entered the hall during an intermission. Most of the women were sitting on benches ranged along the walls and most of the men were standing, as there were not enough seats to go around. Everybody was talking or giggling at something somebody else was saying and a formidable Babel rose from the assemblage which made the sound of the musicians tuning their instruments almost inaudible.

Rosalie was one of the few women standing. She was a comely young woman, slightly under medium height, with a deliciously buxom figure, flashing black eyes and skin as smooth as silk and the precise color of a ripe persimmon. Roscoe saw her the moment he entered the hall and made his way to where she stood.

"You come on home!" he commanded in his very sternest voice and manner.

" 'Tain't time ter go home yet," Rosalie countered blandly, pretending to mistake his meaning.

"Don't make no diffunce 'bout de time!" he exploded. "You come on home. Think I's goin' ter 'low you ter neglect me an' de house an' go galavantin' 'roun with er passel or no 'count niggers? How you get that way?"

"Man, you talks like er frazzlin' fool!" his wife flared hotly. "Didn't I keep supper waitin' er whole hour an' er half 'thout you showin' up? An' didn't I leave hit in de stove where hit would keep warm fo' you? Didn't I? Well, you didn't come home till you got good an' ready, an' I ain't goin' ter leave here till I's er mind ter." She placed her arms akimbo, as she concluded, and stood before him defiantly. She was more hot tempered than her husband and she was not very much afraid of him. Besides, she had just adroitly executed the feminine maneuver of putting the male on the defensive.

"You knows I'd er been home ef I didn't have ter wo'k late," Roscoe contended, in a much milder voice.

"Huh! You gets off f'om de store at six o'clock, an' I kep supper waitin' till half-pas' seven. *Dat's* what I knows."

"I mowed Miss Warren's lawn after I got off f'om de store," he explained. "An' I didn't finish hit till mos' nigh eight o'clock."

"Dat's what *you* say," Rosalie sneered, incredulously. "Specs you was somewheres chewin' de rag with some of yo' nasty-nice chu'ch sisters."

"I wasn't neither. I was mowin' Miss Warren's lawn. I kin prove hit by Miss Warren."

They were beginning to attract attention, but at this point the musicians struck up the eccentric strains of "Turkey in the Straw." Eager couples stepped out on the floor and began to dance, while other revelers, taken unawares, hastily sought their partners. A strange young man appeared at Rosalie's side and proffered his arm in a courtly manner. He did not *come* to her side, Roscoe did not see him approaching from any direction. He simply appeared—so suddenly that Roscoe, with subsequent events in mind, afterward swore that he had materialized in an instant out of the invisible.

He was a distinguished looking personage, with a great bank of glossy black hair, smooth coppery skin like an Indian's, fiery eyes and a handsome moustache. His raiment was costly, and he stood out in the assemblage of coarsely clad peasants like a prince among paupers. A jewel glittered in his tie, his collar was white as snow and his fine clothes reeked with the odor of wet matches. All this Roscoe perceived in an instant. The next moment the dandy took Rosalie's hand with an air of authority and whirled her into the midst of the eddying mass of dancers.

Roscoe was too astonished by the fellow's effrontery to take the action the situation demanded. Several seconds passed before he realized the significance of the incident and felt resentment. Then he decided it would be better to wait till the end of the dance before reproving the fellow.

While waiting for the next intermission he sat down on one of the benches and watched the dancers. With few exceptions, he knew everybody in the hall. Most of the men were frankly members of the rustic Bohemia—pilgarlics who loafed the whole year except during the Spring planting and Fall harvesting; tellers of tales and singers of songs they were, and connoisseurs of mead and cider and authorities on rabbit hunting and coon treeing; picturesque mendicants who invited themselves to a cottage at meal-time, ate a bellyful and paid for it with a ghost story or a bit of scandal from the next hamlet; or, if the conversation took a high turn, held their own in a serious discussion of Holy Writ.

Most of the women were of a more stable element of society—servant girls and field women who could be seen in church every Sunday morning. A few frivolous wives were there, and a few dusky Magdalenes; but these last were very discreet and a stranger could not have distinguished them from the rest.

The female contingent being slightly in excess of the number of men in the hall, a few of the young women were unable to obtain partners for every dance. Among the temporary wall flowers looking on impatiently was a hoidenish young widow with a superb Brunhildean figure and a fetching way with the men. In times past it had been bruited about the countryside that she cherished a tender feeling for Roscoe: and perhaps a spark of the old fire still smoldered in the depths of her voluptuous bosom. She made her way to where he was sitting and seated herself beside him.

"You look worried, Mr. Joyful," she said, her rich alto voice striking a note of profound sympathy.

Roscoe regarded her with grateful eyes. "Who's dat smart dude dancin' with my wife, Sarah?" he asked, huskily.

"I don't know," Sarah replied. "I ain't never seen him befo', an' he ain't danced with nobody else ternight."

Roscoe sighed.

"I ain't one ter interfere between man an' wife," Sarah observed, cautiously. "But I swears ter de Lawd Rosalie ain't treatin' you right. I seen her go out early dis evenin' an' leave de house dark as de tomb. And I says—'Dere now, Mister Joyful ain't goin' ter fin' no supper when he comes home f'om wo'k ter-night. 'Tain't right,' I says, 'hard as he wo'ks ter keep er roof over her haid an' bread in her mouf. 'Tain't right, I don't care ef hit was my own dear sister what done hit.' "

Roscoe tried to speak but the words stuck in his throat. His was one of those deeply emotional natures easily moved by an expression of sympathy. He could hardly keep from melting down in tears at the contemplation of his wrongs so vividly visualized by a sympathetic soul.

Sarah perceived his embarrassment and continued: "An' I says, 'I'll save some of my supper an' keep hit hot fo' Mister Joyful, ef he ain't too late gettin' home,' 'cause I knowed you'd 'preciate hit."

"I sho would er," Roscoe managed to say.

"I knows you would. I had some gran' giblet stew an' hot biskits. Specs you didn't get home till late though, 'cause I watched yo' house till mos' nigh eight o'clock."

"I got home 'bout dat time," Roscoe said. "But yo' house was dark too."

"Specs I'd jes' left," the widow surmised.

Just then the music stopped with a fancy flourish, and the swirling mass of dancers disintegrated into chattering groups, cooing couples and smiling individuals. Rosalie did not return to where her husband was sitting. The gallant stranger led her to a seat across the hall, and from where Roscoe sat it seemed that they fell easily into intimate conversation. Her face was flushed and radiant. Roscoe sensed that she was receiving pretty compliments and replying with animated sallies of her own.

"Jes' look at dat!" Sarah exclaimed. "Ain't dat brazen?"

"Doggone ef I's goin ter stan' fo' hit," Roscoe vowed, wrath at last overcoming restraint. He rose and started across the hall to his wife.

For some reason the stranger at that moment left Rosalie's side and moved off toward Roscoe's right. Roscoe halted, hesitating between the desire to upbraid his wife and an impulse to pursue the stranger and punish him; meanwhile his eyes followed the young man. After taking a few steps, the stranger halted, too, then quickly turned about so that Roscoe saw him standing in profile while his head and torso cast an enormous shadow on the opposite wall. The moment the movement was executed the shadow became more vivid than the body casting it, owing to its greater size perhaps, and attracted the focus of Roscoe's gaze. A cold shiver ran down Roscoe's back, his mouth flew open and his eyes popped out till they hurt, for it was not the shadow of a man he saw, but as perfect a silhouette of Satan as he had ever seen pictured on a Sunday School lesson card. The sharp chin, the high cheek bone and the accipitrine nose were all faithfully outlined on the white surface of the wall. Not only that, but Roscoe was certain that he saw the outline of a stubby horn, slightly curved forward, protruding above the rounded pompadour. He could not see the far horn, but that was because it was directly in line with its twin, and so not visible.

The stranger held the pose only a moment. Then he turned around again and the sinister aspect of the shadow vanished. He sauntered toward the door in a leisurely manner, meanwhile carefully smoothing the silky locks of his pompadour—to conceal the presence of the horns, Roscoe thought.

Roscoe continued across the hall to his wife. He was no longer angry with her now; instead he was filled with solicitude for her safety. His intention to censure her had changed to a resolve to warn her.

"You better not dance with dat man no mo'," he began.

"Den you come on dance with me," Rosalie flashed, roguishly.

This unexpected sortie caused the speech of warning he was going to make to leave his head completely. "You knows I don't dance," he protested.

"Well, den, don't be interferin' with me," she demanded. "I's got ter have *somebody* ter dance with."

"Why don't you dance with somebody you knows," Roscoe asked, unconsciously giving more ground.

"Beggars can't be choosers," she parried. "I's got ter dance with somebody what's willin' ter dance with me, ain't I?"

The brief intermission came to an end. The ancient piano trebled the opening strains of the Cake Walk and the banjo and two guitars chimed in hastily. Shouts of delight hailed the music from every quarter, eager couples flew to each other's arms and glided into the mazes of the dance. The rhythm of shuffling feet blended with the harmony of the tune while the swaying of supple bodies synchronized with its melody—became as it were melody made visible.

"Come on home," Roscoe urged. "Hit mus' be mos' midnight now."

Rosalie did not answer. She did not hear him. She was under the spell of the music, and anxiously looked about for her partner. Like the matron of Sodom, she was fascinated by the view of the plain and deaf to the warnings of her husband. The stranger appeared in the same silent, sudden manner as before and presented his arm. Rosalie took it and they gayly joined the dance.

This second display of cheek convinced Roscoe that there was something unnatural about the man. Roscoe was as strong as a bull and looked it; he knew no mere *roué* would so contemptuously affront him. Besides, Rosalie's mind was obviously under some strange influence. Frivolous she ever was; recalcitrant she had been before; but she had never been openly contumacious. Roscoe suspected that the stranger had cast a spell on her. If that were so, there was nothing he could do except abandon her to her fate. Trying further to warn her would be futile, for his human persuasion could not prevail against the supernatural. The fear which had been growing on him since he had seen the apparition on the wall became unruly terror with this thought, and a wild impulse to rush out of the house seized him. However, he quickly reflected that in the hall were light and a multitude while outdoors darkness and loneliness reigned. Still, this crowd of sinners might be doomed to speedy destruction for all he knew, and in that case safety lay where they were not. Perhaps it was Heaven's will for them to remain blissfully ignorant of the presence of evil while his guardian angel had warned him by showing him the sinister shadow on the wall. He pondered this matter a few minutes, then drew from his pocket a small Bible he always carried with him. He opened the book at one of the psalms he had committed to memory and quietly left the hall.

He marked the page with his finger until he reached the outskirts of the village; then he opened the book and held it up before him as if to read. The moon had risen now, spreading its tranquil light as a covering over the landscape, as if to conceal from the Seraphim the revolting carnage taking place in the quiet wheatfields and hen houses where field mice were ravaging the tender stalks and owls were murdering field mice while weasels were sucking the blood of pullets that had feasted all day on worms. The moonlight was not bright enough to read by, but Roscoe, as he strode along, continued to hold the book up in front of him while he repeated the psalm from memory: "P'serve me, O God: for in thee do I put my trust." . . . wilt not leave my soul in hell. . . . Thou wilt show me the path of life." . . . And when he reached the end of the chapter he began again at the beginning: "P'serve me, O God: for in thee do I put my trust." . . .

Chanting scripture allayed but did not dispel Roscoe's terror. When he arrived home he turned the light up as bright as he could get it, and bolted the kitchen door and braced it by tilting a chair under the knob. Then he went into the gaudy little parlor and secured the front door in the same manner. When he returned to the kitchen he laid the open Bible on the table and seated himself so he could keep one hand on the holy book constantly. Quietude, light and a feeling of comparative safety combined to relieve the intensity of his fear still further; but fear diminished, it seemed, only to give place to those ironical second thoughts which inevitably come to mock all human action.

In his peculiar manner of soliloquizing aloud, he reviewed the incidents of the night from the moment he had beheld the infernal shadow to his arrival home. It now occurred to him that he had displayed very little virtue and courage in his precipitate flight from the dance hall. No evil could have harmed him with the Bible in his hand, he reflected, and he should have included his wife under its protection.

BONG!!!

Roscoe jumped up. He gripped his Bible instinctively, and his heart palpitated wildly. A moment of intense fright paralyzed him.

Then he realized that the startling sound was only the eight-day clock striking one. He sat down and tried to laugh away his fright, but his brow was already glistening with a cold sweat and several minutes passed before he could compose himself.

He should have warned Sarah Ganaway, too, he thought, when calmness returned. And with that thought came a pang of remorse. A few seconds later he remembered that he had often heard of Christians compelling evil spirits to disappear by touching them with the Bible. If he had done that instead of running away, perhaps he could have saved all those sinners. In recognition of such an exploit, his church brethren would make him a deacon and the recording angel would put another star in his crown. Instead of the reward of the valorous Christian soldier, however, all he had was the memory of an inglorious retreat. "Phoo!" It was like a bad taste in the mouth.

His regrets and cogitations were suddenly interrupted by somebody trying the kitchen door.

"Who's dat?" Roscoe cried, clutching his Bible.

"Open de door, fool!" replied an angry voice, instantly followed by a vicious kick.

Roscoe recognized Rosalie's voice and let her in.

"How come de door all barred up?" she demanded. "Must be 'fraid of burglars or somethin'. Huh! Big hulkin' nigger like you all barred an' bolted up like he was somethin' precious." Her voice rang with wrath and her face was flushed with anger or excitement.

Her husband ignored her caustic remarks. "Fine time ter be comin' home f'om er dance," he observed, as he bolted the door again. "Mos' two o'clock Sunday mawnin'. De Lawd sho is merciful ter 'low some sinners ter live."

"Man! Don't come preachin' ter me, much pain as I's in!" Rosalie screamed. "Jes' save yo' little tissue paper Jesus an' yo' co'nstalk God till you goes ter chu'ch to-day. 'Cause I don't want ter hear nothin' 'bout 'em."

This was not an expression of skepticism, but, rather, a petulant outburst of irreligion. Among the Southern peasantry negro skeptics are as rare as white blackbirds but unconsciously irreligious blacks are almost as common as superstitious ones.

Roscoe gazed at his wife in pious horror. "Where does you spec ter spen' eternity?" he asked, solemnly. Rosalie did not answer, but sank down in the chair in which she sat and leaned forward and let her head rest on the table. A few stifled gasps escaped her, and Roscoe saw she was sick, grief-stricken or excessively angry.

"What's de matter?" he asked.

"Can't you see I's in misery?" she snapped.

"What's de matter with you?" he asked again. A sympathetic concern made his voice tremble a little, and he placed his hand on her shoulder tenderly.

"I's all shook up inside," she said, sitting up straight. "I's lucky ter be here alive."

She paused and frowned, as if a sharp pain had stabbed her. Then she continued: "We was right in de middle of de Virginia Reel when de floor broke down all of er sudden an' ever'body foun' deyself scramblin' roun' in de celler. I knowed dat floor was rotten, but nobody thought hit was so weak dat hit would break through all at once. An' den, somehow de house cotched on fire, an' dere we was. How I got out of dat cellar through all dat fire an' smoke de Lawd only knows. Hit was black as pitch in dat hole, an' you could hear de niggers yellin' an' smell 'em frizzlin' and feel 'em swinging' on ter you an' holdin' you back when you was tryin' ter climb out, but you couldn't see yo' han' befo' you, hit was so black. When I got out of dere at las', all de white folks in Calve't was throwin' water on de fire an' all de niggers what wasn't at de dance was wringin' dey han's an' cryin' an' prayin'. Hit was awful. Dere ain't been nothin' like hit since de fall of Sodom an' Gomorrer an' dere won't be nothin' like hit no mo' till de las' Judgment Day."

She seemed to forget her pain while she talked, but when she finished her narrative her brow contracted suddenly and she laid her head on the table again for relief.

Roscoe listened to her tale with bated breath, and while he listened the conviction grew on him that had he shown a little courage and presence of mind he could have prevented the holocaust. "How many was bu'nt up?" he asked, when she concluded.

"How does I know? I didn't count 'em." Rosalie snapped, straightening up again. The question seemed silly to her and she was peeved again. "All of 'em I specs; mos' of 'em, anyway."

It is probable that Rosalie magnified the seriousness of the disaster. She was excited and of a race notoriously prone to exaggerate. But her husband, even more emotional than she was, imagined the holocaust even more tragic than she described it.

"Lawd! Lawd! Lawd!" he mumbled hysterically. Then he remembered Sarah Ganaway and inquired if she had been saved.

"I don't know nothin' 'bout dat nigger wench. An' I cares less," Rosalie flared, jealousy flashing through her suffering like lightning splitting a thundercloud.

"An' where's de fine young man you danced with all night?"

"Bu'nt up, I specs," she surmised.

Roscoe saw a way to mitigate the remorse that had begun to torment him. The opportunity to garner a great harvest for the Master had slipped away, but there still remained a chance to salvage one soul from gleanings. And one sinner saved, he had culled from Holy Writ, causes great rejoicing among the angels.

"Dis ought ter be er pow'ful warnin' ter you," he declared, solemnly preparing to impress a great moral lesson on his wife.

"I's done tol' you I don't want ter hear no preachin'," Rosalie retorted.

"You better want ter lis'n ter some preachin'," her husband insisted, gravely. "Ef you knowed who dat young man you was dancin' with was, you'd be down on yo' knees prayin' right now."

Rosalie became apprehensive. "Who was he?" she asked, curiously.

"Hit was de Devil hisself," Roscoe declared. "An' he went dere 'spressly ter visit death and destruction on dat crowd of sinners."

Rosalie started. "Go on," she sniffed, "you's always got some sich crazy notion in dat addled haid of yourn."

"Call me crazy ef you wants ter," Roscoe rejoined, "but I knows what I's talkin' 'bout." He then narrated how he had observed what others in the dance hall, being sinners under the spell of Lucifer, had failed to see. He described the ominous shadow with intense vividness, elaborating on the incident to the extent of declaring that, afterward, he had actually seen horns protruding through the stranger's massive pompadour. This was not wilful deception on his part, but merely an instance of the common propensity of an uncritical mind to confuse experiences with suspicions and so delude itself with its own fantasies. Having established the stranger's identity, Roscoe's next endeavor was to explain the connection between his appearance and the disastrous end of the dance. Nor did he fail to emphasize the great lesson to be derived from the calamity by the lucky ones who had escaped destruction.

"Well, I d'clare! You's de doggondest fool I's ever seen!" was Rosalie's sarcastic comment when he had concluded his moralizing. "Come on, let's go ter bed." Her airy unconcern was wholly affected, however, as a keener observer than her husband would have readily perceived. But

Roscoe believed he had utterly failed to impress her. He took the lamp down from its bracket and gloomily led the way to the bedroom.

Roscoe had not been asleep long—it seemed to him that he had just dozed off—when he was aroused by Rosalie screaming and clinging to him in frantic terror. "Wake up! Wake up!" he called, thinking she had a nightmare. Then he saw that she was already fully awake. "What's de matter?" he asked.

"Hit's dat man!" she cried. "He's in dis here room!"

"What man?" Roscoe asked, in a complex of wonder and incipient fright.

"Dat man what was at de dance," she answered. "Can't you *see* him?" Her eyes and nostrils were dilated and her body trembled as if stricken with palsy.

The lamp stood on the bureau burning dimly. Roscoe could see every piece of furniture in the room; he could even see such small objects as the soap receiver on the washstand and the daguerreotypes on the mantelpiece; but he could not see the man his wife saw. The thought of a spirit in the room visible to Rosalie but invisible to him, coming after his experiences earlier in the night, filled him with a terror as intense as that of his wife. And his extreme fear was not at all mitigated by the fact that his Bible was downstairs in the kitchen, hence, for the instant, out of reach.

"Shucks! You's been dreamin'," he declared, with a dry, mirthless chuckle. This was to allay his own fear rather than to comfort his wife.

" 'Tain't no dream neither," Rosalie insisted. "He's standin' dere right now—right by de foot of de bed."

"You's talkin' out'n yo' haid. You mus' have er fever," Roscoe scoffed. He attempted to laugh again, but only achieved a guttural cackle. "Specs I'd better get de doctor fo' you," he added.

He started to get out of bed then, but Rosalie, thrown into a paroxysm of horror by the thought of being left alone, clung to him with the tenacity of a fury. "No! No! No!" she protested. "I don't need no doctor!"

The idea of getting out of the house on any pretext, once it had occurred to him, mastered Roscoe's mind completely. He disengaged his wife's arms with force, and she, prostrated by exertion and terror, sank back on the bed in a swoon.

He did not stop to dress himself, but scooped up his pants and shoes with a single sweep of the arm. Then he picked up the lamp and hurried downstairs to the kitchen. He found his Bible still lying where he had left it, and hastily turned to his memorized psalm and flattened the book out so it would remain open while he put on his clothes. When he got his pants and shoes on, he discovered that he had left his shirt upstairs in the bedroom. He did not consider going back for it a moment, but put on his jumper over his undershirt and picked up his Bible and left the house.

The nearest doctor lived in Rosaryville, a mile away; but Roscoe's mind was so stupefied with fear when he left the house that he set out toward Upper Calvert, which was three miles distant. He had gone a quarter of a mile or more before he discovered that he was going in the wrong direction and retraced his steps. Going back toward Rosaryville, he had to pass Sarah Ganaway's cottage which stood a stone's throw from his own house. As he approached the dwelling, he decided to stop there and inquire if Sarah had been injured in the dance hall disaster. If she were not hurt seriously, he would ask her to run over and stay with Rosalie until he returned with the doctor. He pounded on the door lustily for several minutes before getting any response from within the house, and was about to go away when Sarah raised her bedroom window and looked out.

"Who's dat?" she called.

"Hit's me, Roscoe. Was you hurt much when de dance hall c'lapsed and cotched on fire?"

"No, Roscoe, I wasn't hurt at all. 'Pears like de Lawd mus' er warned me, 'cause I left de hall jes' 'bout five minutes befo' de floor fell in."

"I's mighty glad you 'scaped," Roscoe assured her. "Rosalie was shook up pretty bad. I's goin' for er doctor fo' her now. Kin you go over an' stay with her till I gets back?"

"Sho, Roscoe. I's always willin' ter do er favor fo' *you*," Sarah replied, with a tender inflection of the "you."

"Thanks," said Roscoe, "I'll get back jes' as quick as I kin."

Roscoe, for all his faults—if shortcomings chargeable to one's limitations can be called faults—was essentially an honest fellow who could not deliberately dissemble, not even with himself. He was inclined toward self analysis, too, so far as his powers would permit, ever reviewing his conduct and judging himself severely if not sagely. His terror, which reached its flood while he was in the bedroom, had begun to ebb as soon as he got outdoors. The brief conversation with Sarah had sobered him still more, and when he left her cottage his thought-paralyzing fear had been reduced to a mild timorousness which did not preclude reflection.

His real motive for leaving the house, he admitted to himself, was not to fetch a doctor but to escape the evil spirit that terrified his wife. Immediately he perceived the futility of trying to evade the supernatural, for the Infernal could intercept him here on the road as easily as he had appeared to him in the dance hall and to Rosalie in their bedroom. He might have well stayed at home and faced his doom like a man.

He had an impulse to return home, and only the fact that he had told Sarah he was going for the doctor prevented him. No son of Adam is without his modicum of vanity; certainly no Negro is. Admitting his cowardice to himself was one thing; revealing it to the world was something else again; so he pressed on toward Rosaryville, determined to keep up the pretense for the present, although he no longer had any heart in it.

Then came the second thoughts, those incorrigible mockers of all human decisions and conduct, convincing him that his cowardice had cost him another opportunity to vanquish the Power of Darkness. Instead of fleeing the house, he reflected, he ought to have secured his Bible and returned to the bedroom and exorcised the spirit, commanding it, seen or unseen, to depart from the room. It would have been a brilliant victory which, in a way, would have offset his defeat earlier in the night. But no. His reason overwhelmed in an orgasm of fear, he had forgotten Heaven's power to protect him and had lost his head and his faith and deserted the post of duty. No doubt, the recording angel was thoroughly disgusted with him. If Heaven would only give him another chance, however—. But Heaven did not, reserving its opportunities for valor for some soul capable of making better use of them.

When Roscoe returned with the doctor they found Sarah pacing to and fro along the road in front of the house. "She's dead," she said, when they drew near. She tried to simulate a sympathetic sadness, but there was a distinct note of triumph in her voice.

"Lawd! Don't tell me dat!" Roscoe cried. He halted in his tracks, suddenly, and his body relaxed in a curious manner, so that his head wobbled unsteadily like something balanced on a loose swivel, while his arms dangled at his sides in an odd way as if attached to his shoulders by strings about to break.

"Yes, she's dead," Sarah repeated. "An' sich er time I had. When I got here she was in er faint. I put er wet towel on her haid ter revive her, an' de fust thing she done when I brung her to was to start hollerin' dere was some man in de room. I tried ter pacify her, 'cause I couldn't see er blessed thing. But she jes' kept tryin' ter get out'n de bed, cryin' 'Lemme go! Don't let him cotch me!' "

"I's er bigger woman den Rosalie, an' I's er pow'ful lot stronger, but hit was all I could do ter hol' her in de bed. An' at las' she gives er awful scream an' wrapped her arms 'roun' my neck fit ter choke me. When I got myself loose she was dead."

Sarah paused for breath. Before either Roscoe or the doctor could speak, she commenced again. "When she was screamin' an' carryin' on, I thought she was out'n her haid. But now I knows dere was sho nuff some ghost or mebbe de Devil hisself in dere. 'Cause when I laid her back on de bed, her nightgown sorter fell open like, an' bless my soul! ef dere wasn't er black spot on her left side bu'nt ter er cinder! Specs dat's where de Devil took her soul out'n her body; 'cause Rosalie wasn't saved an' died in her sins."

Roscoe said nothing. His face assumed a limp, flaccid expression and he stared straight in front of him, which happened to be toward the east where the first milky promise of dawn had appeared.

"This woman is excited, or crazy," the doctor scoffed. "Let's investigate this." He started toward the house and the others followed at his heels. The doctor was an old school Southerner whose ministrations among the Negroes were, in the main, enterprises of charity. He had a brusk way of speaking to them, but the recipients of his beneficence knew very well that his stern manner was superficial.

In the bedroom, he drew back the sheet Sarah had covered Rosalie with and opened her nightgown, revealing the perfectly formed torso of a buxom woman, not yet cold and not yet pallid with the bloodless hue of death. Roscoe stood a pace behind the doctor, looking on, and Sarah stood a step behind Roscoe, clinging to his arm. But not all the pressure of her fingers on his biceps was inspired by her interest in the autopsy. True enough, on the flesh over the left floating rib was an ugly blue-black splotch, about the size and with the irregular shape of an oak leaf, vividly contrasting with the apricot color of the surrounding skin. The doctor felt the livid scar and around it, then closed the bosom of the dead woman's nightgown and re-covered her with the sheet.

"Why it's only a———" He paused, abruptly. His face assumed a whimsical expression for a moment, then affected seriousness again. "It's a curious case," he said. "But we'll say she died of internal injuries. Come to my office after awhile and I'll give you the death certificate." Then he left the room, furtively chuckling in his goatee, after the manner of a man privy to some Celestial prank and amused by his fellow mortals taking the matter seriously.

Roscoe and Sarah followed him downstairs. Perhaps the former expected to receive some further directions. If so, he was disappointed, for the doctor left the house instantly without saying another word.

After his departure a brief spell of silence intervened. Roscoe sat down and covered his face with his hands while Sarah, her arms folded on her bosom, leaned against the wall and regarded him tenderly. Presently, a terrific dry sob convulsed his powerful shoulders.

"Don't take hit so hard," Sarah soothed. "You done all you could do."

"No I didn't," Roscoe cried, dropping his hands and raising his eyes to meet hers. "Dat's what makes hit hurt so. Hit's all my fault. Hit's my fault dat all dem souls was los' in de dance hall too. 'Cause I seen de Devil dere with my own two eyes, jes' as plain as I sees you right now. An' 'stead of warnin' you all, I run erway an' come 'long home. Now all dem souls is los' an' Rosalie's los', an' hit's all 'cause I didn't make de good fight fo' de Lawd."

Sarah was profoundly impressed by this, and the words of consolation with which she saw fit to comfort him, for reasons of her own, were not prompted by the deep rooted fatalism they seemed to imply. "Don't let dat fret you," she counseled. "What was ter be had ter be. Hit mus' er been ordained dat dem souls was ter go dat way, an' nothin' you could do would er stopped hit."

When she concluded she went to the stove and lifted a lid. The fire was out. Her face assumed the expression of affectionate contempt for masculine incompetence which only a woman who has been a wife can feel. "Here, you go lie down an' res' while I makes er fire an' heats er pot of coffee," she suggested. "Hit'll be light by dat time, an' you kin go fetch de undertaker. An' on yo' way ter Nottingham, stop at Sister Greentree's an' ask her ter come an' help me lay Rosalie out."

Brief Biography of

Fletcher J. Mosely

Here, Theophilus Lewis tells the story of Fletcher J. Mosely, brilliantly using the themes of superstition and magical thinking. Tragically, a conjured prophecy becomes the main character's fate. The story was published in July 1924.

Fletcher Josephus Mosely was born with a mole on his neck, and the officiating midwife, who was as well versed in occult matters as she was in obstetrics, prophesied that he would be hanged. Folks were careful to keep the baleful knowledge from the family's ears, however, and the brown-skin baby grew up and reached manhood without ever becoming aware of the doom hanging over him.

The summer of his thirty-first year found him making a living as an itinerant waiter at the Prince George House, a resort hotel situated about midway between Nottingham and Upper Calvert, two unimportant villages in southern Maryland. He was a burnt out specimen of manhood then, growing senile before time, with an insatiable thirst for hard liquor and suffering from various manifestations of the old rale. Still, he had enough vital force left in him to fall in love with Miranda Minatree.

Miranda was a buxom, comely young woman with happy eyes and skin smooth as satin and the color of a roasted coffee bean; and she had the refreshing seductiveness of something tender and green and vigorous growing in the earth. She was one of the dishwashers at the hotel and the only native of the countryside employed there. The other colored help, waiters and chambermaids, had been recruited from the black belts of Baltimore and Washington, and the white kitchen crew had been imported from various slums of middle Europe. It was Miranda's conspicuous freshness, contrasted with the run down appearance of this motley array of rotting men and stale women, that caught Mosely's eye and won his heart.

Mosely's sentiment was not unobserved, of course, and at least one pair of eyes looked on with approval. They were the eyes of the boss, Mr. Ringold. The proprietor was glad to see Mosely's affection turning in Miranda's direction because in quondam days he had marked the waiter paying too much attention to Anna Weitzel, the checker; and Anna was a blond girl whose native village was hidden away in some obscure Bavarian valley. Now, hot Scotch-Irish blood ran in Mr. Ringold's veins, the militant puritanism of the Presbyterian faith burned in his soul, and the major element of his temperament was the Southern tradition of truculence and white holiness. He was a ponderous man, physically, towering every inch of six feet above the floor, with an enormous paunch hung onto him, and a head like a huge lump of dough. Whenever he saw Mosely and Anna talking together intimately, little carmine spots would flash out on his paste colored cheeks and his belly would begin to quiver violently, as if agitated by some inner mechanism. But he could never catch the waiter red-handed enough to reprimand him. Mosely and Anna would always divert their conversation to dining-room matter before he could get near enough to hear what they really were talking about. Miranda's coming changed all that; hence Mr. Ringold's great joy when, the day after he hired her, the mecca of Mosely's interest shifted from the checker's desk to the china rack.

At first it was a solo courtship that Mosely carried on, with Miranda not even bothering to repulse his sentimental sallies. She seemed even too unresponsive to ignore him. She just gazed blankly at his sugary smiles and significant glances as if too thick to understand their meaning. During her first week in the pantry the only talk that passed between them was an exchange of matutinal greetings.

"Hello!" Mosely would sing-song. Striving to throw irresistible melifluence into his voice, he actually achieved something of the attenuated falsetto of a saxophone playing in high key.

"Good mawnin'," Miranda would reply, in a voice naturally fresh and sweet, but utterly void of sentimental response.

Discouraged, Mosely would spend the rest of the day bombarding her with soft smiles and ineffectual glances from a distance.

But as time wore on he inevitably grew bolder. One morning he was held in the kitchen waiting for a delayed order of poached eggs. The kitchen and pantry were in one large room divided by an imaginary line. Mosely preferred to wait near the china rack rather than by the steam table.

"Awful dull in this hole," he observed, alluding to the hotel and its environs.

Miranda did not answer.

"Ain't there no dancing or nothing 'round here?" he continued, after a second or so. "Nowheres where you can have some fun?"

"Dere's dancin' in Calve't ever' Saturday night," Miranda informed him.

Mosely smiled, wistfully, as if the inutility of the information had dawned on him the moment he received it. "Guess it don't do me no good to know," he sighed. "Ain't got nobody to go with."

"Dat's too bad."

"Suppose you and me take a night off some Saturday," he suggested, hopefully.

"I don't dance," Miranda replied. "I b'longs ter chu'ch."

"Take away your poached eggs!" the fry cook shouted. And Mosely was heartily glad of the chance to walk away from her with a semblance of dignity.

Another day another try.

"Ain't there no movies 'round here?" he asked her one afternoon.

"Sure. Dere's movies in Calve't ever' night and er show in Not'nham ever' Thu'sday an' Saturday night," she replied.

"Which is the best?"

"De show in Calve't."

"Do you like movies?"

"Sometimes."

"Then let's take in a show some night?"

But Miranda declined.

Pretty soon he had used up his entire bag of tricks without making any impression on her. He became discouraged. Then, when he lost his amorous bravado, the scrap of sincerity left in him got a chance to reveal itself, and lame speeches and a halting manner won a response where fluent flatteries had failed. Miranda was affected by his presence to such an extent that she had to feign preoccupation when he approached her. Several times he turned about suddenly and discovered her looking at him with a glow of intense interest in her eyes.

Then came the lucky night when an over friendly rat frightened her and Mosely ran to her succor and shooed the beast off. In the warmth generated by his chivalry and her gratitude the feeling of restraint that existed between them evaporated. Miranda was giving the last licks to the supper dishes at the time, and Mosely stayed to help her finish up. Then they went outdoors for a walk.

It was a fine night. The black sky was inlaid with stars and the yellow moon lay flat on its surface like some queer curio of old ivory lying on a panel of wakasa. It was hard to believe that the pearl light that filled space and shone on the contours of the earth came from that frigid disk which seemed so worn and ancient. It seemed, rather, that that frail radiance was but the visible quality of the currents of soft air gently sweeping across the landscape.

There was passion in the air!

On the lawn back of the hotel, where Mr. Ringold permitted the help to recreate themselves so long as they did not talk too loud, Anna Weitzel was luxuriating in the caresses of the Slovene fry cook and a waiter and a chambermaid were enacting the prologue of a Rabelaisian love story. Mosely and Miranda did not tarry there, but instinctively sought the drive and followed it till it joined the public highway. At the junction of the roads they stopped, at the same instant, as if inspired by a mutual impulse.

"What fo' we come dis way?" Miranda asked, as they halted.

"I came 'cause you did," he answered.

Then it dawned on them that neither knew why they had come that way. The discovery tickled them. Their blended laughter rang out for a moment and in the warmth of their mirth the last remnant of reserve melted away.

For a few minutes they stood motionless and silent; unreserved, candid; a bit awed by their new relationship.

Then Miranda tilted her head and sniffed at a fragrant breeze. "I smells sweet-briar," she said. "Ain't hit go'geous!"

Mosely did not hear. At that instant he was all eye, enchanted by the sensuous appeal of the firm lines of her profile and the robust curve of her bosom. She looked like a dark dryad growing out of the ground she stood on and while he gazed at her the immemorial satyr stirred in him. He took her in his arms and she yielded her strong, soft body to him and gave him her lips.

Then they moved over to the side of the road and sat down and began to talk of post-nuptial matters as if they had come there with that express end in view. They would get married at the end of the summer, they decided; then they would go on a several years' junket, working together in other hotels in other climes, and between seasons having a good time in many strange cities. And when they had been everywhere and seen everything and saved money enough they would come back to Nottingham and settle down and live quietly and happy to the end of their days.

The next day Mosely made a flying trip to Baltimore and bought the engagement ring. A fortnight later he was sorry he had done it. His fibre did not contain enough moral tungsten to carry the incandescence of a pure passion longer than a week, and at the end of that period his ardor cooled to a formal philandering that puzzled Miranda but did not deceive her. Finally he decided to call the business off and asked her to return his ring.

Miranda refused, taking a moral stand. She had grown up seeing betrothal and marriage occur with almost the exactitude and finality of pollenization. According to local ideology, for a lover to alter his attitude after choosing his mate was almost as much against nature as it would be for a grain of tassel dust to welch after marrying a strand of maize silk. Such perverseness was always the work of evil forces. To yield in the matter would be abetting sin.

Miranda believed Mosely had been conjured. When a nightmare began to disturb her sleep every night belief became conviction. Accordingly, she took an afternoon off and visited Granny Smallwood, the most famed of the local hoodoo specialists, and told her the whole story of Mosely's persistent wooing and described the subsequent rapid refrigeration of his passion.

"Does you have bad dreams?" Granny asked her.

"Yes, Granny. I was comin' ter dat." Miranda replied. "Mos' ever' night er witch rides me. An' I wakes up mos' scared ter death! With my hea't mos' leapin' out'n my mouth. I's dat scared!"

"Specs hit's you what's conjured 'stead o' him," the seeress observed. "You's been bewitched so's you's no longer pleasin' ter him."

"Lawd! Granny, what'll I do?" Miranda cried.

"Now, now, chile, don't fret," the wise woman said, soothingly. "I'll fix ever'thing all right." She paused then and lapsed into a spell of profound reflection.

After a minute or so Granny went to her cupboard and took down a little jar labeled CLOVES. She was an unbelievably massive woman with almost the girth of a tobacco hogshead. Moving her enormous body was such a laborious task that she usually eschewed talking when not at rest. She forbore talking now until she had sat down again and mopped her shining black face with a bandanna. Then she delivered her instructions.

"You take dis here powder I's gwine ter give you, an' mix hit with er tablespoon o' salt an' two tablespoons o' pepper, an' wrop hit up in er hank'rchief an' put hit under yo' piller when you goes ter bed. Er witch allus has ter get out'n her skin when she rides you, an' leave hit standin' som'ers in de room. Nex' time she bothers you, shake her off'n you quick as you kin, den, de minute you wakes up, th'ow de powder all 'roun' de room so some of hit'll get inter her hide befo' she kin jump inter hit herself. Hit'll bu'n her up so she'll have ter get out'n her skin soon as she gets home an' stay out'n hit two or three days. I 'low she'll never come back ter pester you no mo'."

Miranda thanked her and paid her, then returned to the hotel and carried out her instructions so far as preparation was concerned. That same night she had another squabble with Mosely over the ring.

"Why don't you be reasonable?" he demanded, after he had argued in vain for ten minutes. "You ought to be glad we're lucky enough to see our mistake before it's too late."

"I ain't made no mistake." Miranda declared. "I said I loved you, an' I did. An' I still loves you. An' you loves me too, only you don't know hit."

"What're you tryin' to do? Make a fool out of me?"

"You knows I ain't," she replied, trying to propitiate him. "I means you only thinks you don't love me no mo' 'cause I's bewitched."

"You're crazy!"

"No, I ain't," she answered. "I only seems dat way ter you 'cause I's been conjured by somebody what's jealous of us. But de spell'll be off'n me soon, an' you'll love me jes de same as you did at fust."

This pathetic attempt to propitiate him only served to increase Mosely's scorn. In the course of knocking about city slums and pleasure resorts he had lost his own grosser superstitions along with his dialect and to about the same extent. After his passion had cooled he looked upon those crudities in Miranda as marks of inferiority. He wondered how he ever could have been under the delusion that he loved her.

"Aw, we can't make it, sis," he declared, with unemotional finality. "We might as well cut it—right now!"

Miranda did not blame him for his coldness. How could he love a woman who was unattractive to him because she was conjured? But his hard words hurt her nevertheless, and she turned away from him and fled to her room to cry.

Mosely was exasperated. He had half a notion to run after her and tear the ring off her finger; perhaps tear the finger off too. But a sage second thought warned him that such a move would be temerarious and foolish. He might make a disturbance and fail to recover the ring.

Then the other waiters would razz the life out of him; not for the attempt but for the failure.

He was bound to get the ring, though; self-respect demanded it. If he let Miranda get away with keeping his ring he would be almost as much of a sucker as he would be if he let her make him marry her against his will. Then the material consideration was not to be overlooked. Another day might bring another romance and a solitaire as good as new would come in handy. Since persuasion had failed and force would be risky he decided to try strategy.

Half an hour later, by means of propitious window peeping, he discovered where Miranda put the ring when she went to bed. The rest was easy. The help's quarters were in the basement of the hotel, with the rooms grouped in patriarchial fashion around Mr. Ringold's apartment. It was against Mr. Ringold's orders for any door to be locked at any time, the proprietor being of the opinion that immoralities might take place behind barred doors that the inmates of a room would be loath to indulge in if they knew the door likely to be yanked open from the outside at any moment. Thus, all Mosely had to do was to wait till everybody was asleep and then creep into Miranda's room and recover his ring.

But the thing did not work out as well in practice as it appeared in theory. Either by strange coincidence or occult arrangement, Mosely attempted his entry into Miranda's room at the same instant the witch began to ride her. He eased the door open just as Miranda succeeded in shaking the witch off, and stuck his head in for a preliminary peep a moment before she flung her magic powder in the air, aiming at the hag's hide. It seems that all the pepper in the mixture, by a special magic of its own, separated itself from the other ingredients and lodged in Mosely's eyes.

For a minute he could not do a thing but stand stock still and make some queer guttural noises like the squeaks of a half-killed rat. Miranda thought the uncanny sounds came from the witch, and she let out a yell that roused the house.

Mosely realized that he had better beat it back to the waiters' quarters instanter or he would find himself in an awful jam. But he was half blind and still too confused to know what he was doing, and in his haste to make it back to his room before being discovered he opened the wrong door and went in Anna Weitzel's room by mistake.

Anna had been roused by Miranda's scream. She was half scared already, and when she saw Mosely's vague bulk lurch in the door her first thought was that her room was being invaded by some monstrous poltergeist. She had an impulse to scream and she did so with huge success. Her next thought was to escape from the room, but there she fizzled.

She sprang out of bed and bolted for the door. But as she rushed past Mosely their feet became entangled and they tripped each other and fell. Naturally, both tried to get up at the same time, and in their excitement each impeded the other so that neither could rise. They were still scrambling about on the floor, Anna's screams mingling with Mosely's blasphemies, when light suddenly flooded the room, revealing Mr. Ringold, with a cluster of curious faces at his back, standing in the door.

The proprietor took the situation in at a glance. At the same instant its full meaning flashed on Mosely. But the waiter was not in a position to act as his interests prompted while the fat proprietor was free to avenge the affront to his lily-white puritanism as he saw fit. He clutched Mosely by the collar with one powerful paw and drew him up out of the tangle of arms and legs while belting him with sweeping open-hand swings of the other palm.

"You dirty rascal!" he snarled. "I'll kill you! I'll kill you!"

Rage reduced his voice to a hiss and the little red daubs that appeared on his cheeks in moments of ordinary anger now spread over his entire face.

Mosely had no physical fear of the proprietor but he understood only too well what might be the consequences of his annihilating wrath. Hence he did not resist him till he felt his feet free and firm on the floor. Then he shook himself loose from Mr. Ringold's grasp and gave him a push in the belly that sent him sprawling on the floor in a most undignified position, seeing that he had no clothes on except his nightshirt. Mosely then ducked out of the window and disappeared in the darkness.

How it fared with Mosely in the woods that night is wrapped up in mystery and will never be known. But whatever dangers menaced him out there were certainly less than the perils he would have had to face in the excited scene he left behind him.

Mr. Ringold got up spouting orders. "Get lanterns! Get pistols! Get bloodhounds! Don't let him get away!"

The foreign kitchen crew had caught the local meaning of the affair now and they jumped to carry out the boss' orders. The colored help obeyed with even more alacrity. They had seen the thing from Mr.

Ringold's angle from the first and felt that Mosely had humiliated them. Besides, as they were somewhat cowed by the southern tradition, flaunting their resentment helped them to conceal their fear.

The running about of menials did not accomplish anything, however, and pretty soon it had to be called off. Guests began to come down from upstairs to see what the racket was about and the denizens of the lower quarters had to put some clothes on.

After he had pulled his pants on over his nightshirt and explained to the guests that a rape had been committed, or attempted, Mr. Ringold was in a cooler but not less vindictive frame of mind. He got the sheriff on the telephone and gave him the case; then called up all the station agents in the vicinity and warned them to be on the lookout for a strange Negro who might try to buy a ticket, also suggesting that they have all conductors passing through inspect their trains. His final move was to phone the news to every conspicuous white resident of the neighborhood. In an hour he had the countryside pretty well stirred up and a loose but constantly tightening dragnet spread.

Along about daybreak groups of farmers began to arrive in flivvers and automobiles. A few came in ancient buckboards, too, and still fewer, who did not live far enough away to bother about a lift, straggled up afoot. In varying moods they listened to Mr. Ringold's story of the affair which always ended with, "I got to her room just in the nick of time. If I had been a little later God only knows what would have happened." Then he would give Anna a chance to tell her side of it.

"Tell them just how it was, dear," he would say, paternally. "In your own words, in your own simple way."

And Anna would. By now she was fully convinced that Mosely had intended to attack her. She was still terrified by the imaginary danger she had escaped and full of self pity and running over with tears. Besides, when she found herself raised to the rank of a tragic figure receiving the chivalrous concern of the local knighthood, it gave her such a good feeling that she just had to yield to the womanly weakness of luxuriating in distress. Her story was an improvement on Mr. Ringold's version in every respect, especially where she enlarged on the clawing and garroting in a manner that gave the affair a sadistic flavor. Her hard tale would have inclined many a man less fiery than the least adventurous in her audience to go out and break a lance for her.

When some twenty-odd men had arrived on the scene somebody suggested that it would be a good idea to beat through the bottom along the railroad. The others took to the idea at once and they began to move off.

"I wish I could go with you," Mr. Ringold remarked, with feeling. "But I guess I better stay here till the sheriff comes."

"Yeah, reckon you better," one of the posse replied. "Tell him which way we went. No use him going over the same ground we're covering."

"Guess you'll find him down there all right," Mr. Ringold observed. "He can't get away. I got all the station agents on the lookout."

"Aw, he wouldn't try to buy a ticket," a voice from the crowd declared. "It's the freight trains we got to watch."

Men kept coming all the morning, and before the sheriff came, along about eleven o'clock, three parties were out scouring the country on their own. After he got the details of the case the sheriff deputized three or four late stragglers who happened to be hanging about and the search for the fugitive began.

The turmoil had subsided by this hour, but things were still in a pretty unsettled state at the hotel, with the kitchen crew constantly agitated and the waiters and chambermaids half scared to death; with Anna breaking out in sporadic bursts of hysteria; with Mr. Ringold fervently praying to God that Mosely would be caught; with Miranda fervently praying to God that he would not.

Indeed, Miranda alone perceived the true nature of the affair—that it had occurred under supernatural auspices. She spent the day performing sundry rites while continually consulting the heavens for a sign.

She was not surprised when, an hour or so later, the sheriff came back to the hotel with baleful news. He had found Mosely in the bottom by the railroad, strung up by the neck, with his body stripped to the waist and his chest riddled with bullets. He had no idea who had killed him. His official report would read, "Killed by persons unknown while a fugitive from justice."

"Hit was de witch," Miranda said to herself. "She put er spell on him an' made him go in de white gal's room—ter get even with me."

She was not quite right in this; unless the same witch had been a member of the occult council that in the beginning caused Mosely to be born with a mole on his neck.

The Bird in the Bush

Theophilus Lewis introduces his story's main character, Marie Steele, and provides a peek inside her hungry psyche. This new Harlemite is faced with a choice between holding on to what is real—a true commitment from a boring man who loves her—or pursuing the elusive, an exciting, tempestuous man. This story was published in January 1926.

The bell rang. Robert's eager feet pattered down the hall. A brief dialogue at the door, between the child and a low masculine voice. Then Robert's call that vibrated all through the flat.

"Somebody to see Miss Steele!"

Robert's mother chimed in, "*Maree!* somebody to *see* you!" She sang it; like it was a line of comic opera libretto.

They always announced the lodgers' visitors just that way, without ever dropping a word or changing an inflection, so you would think they were rehearsing a play or something and the prompter would give them a call if they left out anything.

"Show him in front," Marie directed. Then she pushed her door shut. The hall led past her room and she didn't want the man to look in. That too was a piece of drama. She knew it was nobody but Bascom. In a few minutes he would be in the room. But closing the door produced a certain effect. It reminded him their intimacy was not yet complete.

She kept him waiting a few minutes, also for effect. In the meantime she dabbed some highbrown face powder in the meshes of tiny crows' feet which fretted the corners of her eyes and gave herself a final looking over in the mirror. Not bad. Only another woman would guess she was twenty-nine. No man, thanks to her bobbed hair and slender figure, would take her for older than twenty-six. Bascom thought she was about twenty-four. "You never can tell though," he would have said.

"Women are so deceiving. She might be twenty-five." But Bascom was now past the stage where age mattered. That was the consoling thought she dwelt on while looking over the room before going out. She didn't expect to find anything out of place and there wasn't, but it's better to be on the safe side. Sometimes you drop a handkerchief or stocking without noticing it.

According to the ritual of the house, Marie and her caller had to spend the first quarter of an hour or so in the living room—"in front", they called it. But there was no privacy in there, what with little Robert tumbling on the floor, the man lodger wanting to play the victrola while he practised a new dance step, and the other girl lodger coming in every few minutes to look out the window to see if her sheik was coming—and incidentally to give Bascom a glad look out of the tail of her eye. In a few minutes the landlady would finish up in the kitchen and come in to read the magazines and make silly comments. And the landlady's husband, Robert, Sr., would drag in after her, with his abominable pipe, crusty jokes and stale smelling feet. Well, in only a few days now Bascom would deliver her from this nest of petty annoyances and disgusts. When she thought of it she could hardly restrain herself from smothering him with kisses. But she did not give way to that pagan impulse. She just continued their unemotional conversation about the weather, about her brother and his brother, until, according to the usage of the house, it was proper to take him to her room.

When they were alone Bascom kissed her, awkwardly, with boyish eagerness held in restraint by boyish timorousness. Then he dropped his heavy hulk in the rocking chair. Marie sat on the side of the bed.

"I ain't got long to stay tonight," he said. "Got to get this insurance fixed up. Brought it round here for you to sign."

Again she felt a gust of tenderness sweep over her. "You darling!" she wanted to cry. And give him a hug that would choke him. Discretion told her she had better not do that. Not that the pet name would alarm him. But if she called him that now she would reveal such a typhoon of feeling he would be scared to death. Instead she scanned his sleek brown countenance with all the indifference she could affect.

"Can't you let it go till later on?" she asked.

"Nope. Ought to have it all over with right now," he declared. "But somehow it slipped my mind, we've been so busy picking out the furniture and looking for a flat." He had the paper out now, and unfolded. His fountain pen was ready. "Sign right there," he instructed her. "Where it says 'beneficiary's signature.' "

Marie signed. Bascom put the paper back in his pocket and looked at his watch. "Got to meet the agent at nine o'clock," he said. "It's half past eight now."

They spent the next few minutes talking about their wedding trip. They were going to see Bascom's folks in South Carolina. If he could find a dependable man to leave in charge of his barbershop they would also visit Marie's people in the West Indies. Bascom had his eye on a man. He was going to have a talk with him tonight, after he had finished his business with the insurance agent.

But they had talked about all that before—all except the insurance and the man he had in mind to take charge of his shop. Marie wondered what interest he found in going over it all again, sitting there stolidly indifferent to the door ajar in front of him and the window on the area way open at his back. . . . The door ajar and the window open. . . . It was like he wasn't planning to get married to a woman at all. A dressmaker's form would do just as well.

"How did he get that way?" she wondered, as he continued as wood to the feverish medley of sounds from the flats below, above, across the way, drifting in the window.

A baritone voice, rising louder than the metallic ring of a cheap piano, was singing:

> Yaller gal sleeps in a rosewood bed,
> Brown skin gal the same.
> Old black gal sleeps on a pallet on the floor,
> But she's got a man just the same.
> All night long, all night long.

An interlude of silence. A child began to squall. A milk bottle fell off a window still and crashed down in the court with an explosion like a dynamite blast. The child stopped crying. The sizzle and smell of frying bacon. Another quiet moment.

"What's that!" Marie and Bascom cried together, as they rushed to the window and looked out.

A woman screamed. A man struck her. She kept on shrieking and the man kept on hitting her and heads popped out the area way windows to see what flat it was in. "I told you to keep away from that nigger!" the man raged. You imagined he must be frothing at the mouth. "I told you if I seen you with him again I'd kill you!" You could hear his blows falling on the woman faster than she could cry out and he kept it up till she stopped screaming and begged him not to hit her any more. After he left off beating her they began to quarrel; the man's voice sullen, half remorseful; the woman's resentful, then conciliatory—moving toward making it up.

"It's a dirty shame the way some men treat women," Bascom observed, as they left the window.

Marie agreed with him. It *was* a shame. Still, there was something in the sound of the blows mingling with the woman's screams that made her breath come faster. She wished Bascom would kiss her. But he was not stirred by the turbulent rhythm of life throbbing about him. His good-night kiss was the same timid, tepid caress it had always been.

The minute the door was shut behind Bascom her thoughts turned to the nights about this time last summer when Lester was coming to see her. Those were radiant nights! And here she was at the nadir of that sparkling season with a fit of blues coming on.

She tried to think of something else, of some period of her past which would show up the present in a less depressing light. Period was good. As if there had ever been a time when she had found life easy. Truth was, her adulthood, as well as her latter adolescence, had been a continuous grind to feed herself, pay her own roomrent, keep up the installments on her clothes and meet her church dues. Only uninterrupted good health had enabled her to keep about even with the game. There had never been a time when two weeks sickness would not have swept her over the margin of respectability. Even her chances to get married had been neglible. She was a Catholic and Bascom was the first worthwhile man she had attracted who had not balked at going to see the priest. Now that she was on the threshold of security, with a home and children and everything almost within her grasp, she ought to be happy.

But her thoughts were rebels. A mob milling in the streets crying out for Barabbas. Last summer! Last summer! Lester! Lester! Unruly thoughts she could neither club into submission nor persuade to disperse.

The night she first met Lester. It wasn't night yet, however, but along about sunset of a sizzling hot day at the beginning of June. About half-past seven. A soft nacre radiance filled the sky, and its loveliness rained down and splashed odd cornices and window sills and the rivers of people in the streets with the gilt and gaudiness of an oriental bazaar. Bronze boys and girls were promenading Lenox Avenue strumming ukeleles and softly singing of Gulf Coast nostalgia. Folks coming home from work did not look tired. Animation, eagerness, avidity for life, shone on the faces converging on the movie theatres. Black satin faces window-shopping; faces blocked out of teakwood, just strolling. Carnival in the air.

Marie was going to the movies. A little distance from the theatre she stopped to look at a child dancing. Twenty-odd passers-by had stopped to look on and inside the circle of grownups half a dozen children were clapping their hands and chanting a rhythm:

> Go on Sam!
> Go on Sam!
> Sam ain't got no bones in his belly.
> Go on Sam!

The dance was a spirited piece of footwork that had migrated up here from Charleston or Beal Street, or some other pagan paradise in the sticks, and while he danced the kid put something of the passion of a dervish into it. The crowd got thicker, shifting, applauding, craning; those in the rear tiptoeing or peering between heads in front. Later that evening Marie remembered she first saw Lester standing in the opposite arc of the circle. She kept her gaze fixed on him a few seconds, for he had an attractive and striking countenance—the face of an athlete with just enough woman in him to make him lose a race. The skin was fine too, almost feminine in its softness, and the color of a chestnut.

A burst of applause brought Marie's attention back to the dancer. The boy was cutting a fancy step that was a knockout and the crowd could not hold in its enthusiasm. She did not notice Lester any more till as a result of the constant seething of the crowd she found herself right at his elbow.

"Queer how we gravitated toward each other, isn't it?" he observed.

Ordinarily she would have pretended she didn't hear him. But there was an undisguised eagerness in his voice and manner which quickened a responsive feeling in her, and before she could check it she had answered him.

"Yes, it is," she said.

After that it was easy for them to fall into conversation, and, when the little dancer had played himself out in a final frenzy, to go on to the movies together. No, not easy; inevitable. That was the way Lester put it.

"It's destiny," he declared. "Either that or chemistry. Depending on whether you're old-fashioned or modern."

They were in the theatre then, and in the dim light of the place

Marie could see his face glowing with a boyish—no, an explorer's curiosity, as if their meeting were an important and puzzling matter and chock full of interest. She felt like she was setting out on an argosy with a man with a plume in his hat.

"I incline to chemistry," he continued. "I believe the world is a retort quite small enough for atoms with an affinity for each other to move together. That accounts for it being so easy for me to talk to you. I don't get on fast with women as a rule, not even when I meet them in the usual way—at a party or through friends. They think I'm bashful, but it ain't that. I just can't think of anything to say and they hardly ever say anything that interests me."

He spoke with a light air and frequent pauses, and something like a roisterer's smile continually playing about his mouth warned Marie he did not really believe in this talk about chemistry and what-not. He didn't any more than half believe it anyway. It was only by-play to entertain and beguile her. She didn't like him any less for that.

"But it was just as easy for me to speak to you," he declared. "It didn't seem like an act of will at all. The words came right out with my breath, and . . ."

"I felt just the same way!" Marie cut in.

"You did!" he exclaimed. "Well, what do you know about that?" Then he picked up where he had left off. "And look at the way I'm talking now! Rattling away like a Philadelphia lawyer. It must be because there's something in you my mind has needed all along to make it function right . . . But I'm keeping your mind off the pictures."

When he saw her home after the show he kissed her. They were standing at the door to her apartment, she was just about to slip her key in the latch, when he cracked a banal joke about her being a high liver because her room was on the fifth floor. He had the knack of making even an old wheeze seem funny and she laughed. While she was off her guard he caught her in his arms so she was helpless. For a moment she felt a tremor of anger—at the low cunning of it. Disarming her with an imbecile joke, and then . . . and then her thoughts just melted away and her head began to swim and she felt herself getting weak, as if all the life and breath in her were throbbing from her body into his . . . If he had not released her the instant he did she would have died. She had to clutch the doorknob, when he let her go, to keep from falling. She was that limp and weak.

"Who told you you could kiss me?" she asked when her breath came back. She was not pretending offended modesty, but frank curiosity. She was smiling.

"I didn't have to be told," Lester replied. "I am bigger and stronger than you are and I wanted to kiss you." Then he left her.

She never quite lost her head in such unwomanlike madness again. But mad enough. The entire episode, she now realized, had been nothing more than a delightful excursion into madness. Well, she was sane enough now. The evidences of sanity were all around her. There was the smell of Bascom's brand of tobacco still lingering in the room, and the aroma of his barbershop, which always accompanied him like his aura and remained after him like his ghost; and there was his fountain pen he had forgot to put back in his pocket lying on the bureau. Oh yes, she was all wrapped up in sanity. There, in the bureau drawer, were a receipt for three months' rent on a flat and various receipts from furniture stores and a receipt for a deposit paid to the gas company. And a life insurance policy made out in her favor was coming, and a marriage license, and Bascom, and security, and stodgyness, and she could write back to her people in the West Indies and tell them she had done well in America.

Still, she wondered if she would not be willing to sacrifice all this comfort and security and go back to the daily grind in the sweatshop, on condition that she could recapture Lester and the lyric nights they had spent together. She knew she would. But there was no use thinking about it. It was out of the question. She borrowed a magazine from the landlady and tried to read. But it was no use. A player-piano in one of the flats opening on the area way began to reel off the "Breakdown Blues" and the syncopation carried her mind back to the night when Lester had conceived the piece.

Lester was a journeyman piano player and he worked about four nights a week relieving the regular pianists of several cabaret orchestras. He regarded himself as a sort of jazz Moussorgowski distilling blues songs from the tumult and humors of the streets, and when he was not working he used to ramble around Harlem for hours; looking for themes. Marie often went with him, foolishly tramping herself footsore after pedaling a sewing machine all day. Such queer things make people happy.

She would never forget the night he got the idea for the "Breakdown Blues" because there was an adventure attached to it. They were gazing in a window at a rent party, an economic evolution of the Dixie breakdown, when the people inside got mad and doused them with a pitcher of water. Marie's West Indian temper flared up in an instant and she was hot for bawling them out, but Lester saw the incident as a rich if somewhat crude and raucus joke. "Make a note of that," he laughed, when they had turned the next corner and Marie had cooled down a bit. "So my biographer can write 'Breakdown Blues cost him three weeks in bed with pneumonia'." The pneumonia, of course, did not materialize but the "Breakdown Blues" did. Coon shouters were moaning it in the theatres now and every night an increasing number of player-pianos proclaimed its waxing popularity.

No doubt other syncopated ululations of his were on the way. There ought to be, she reasoned, for she had watched him begin their brewing. One, while he stood fascinated by the lyric of a boy and girl walking locked arms; another, while reflecting on the poignancy of a man and woman scrapping over a third party. And others ... Many others.

The magazine she had started to read slipped from her lap and fell to the floor. The sound vexed her, as if its interruption of her reverie were an impertinence. She picked the magazine up and was on the point of throwing it out the window when she caught herself and laughed at her silliness. It would be more sensible to throw herself out the window, she reflected. And still more sensible, if she had a stick of dynamite and a place to stand, to blow the whole God damn world to atoms. A cardinal sin. But she didn't feel a bit pentinent and that was another. How would Father Neuman feel, she wondered, waxing rebellious, if life offered him a choice like the one it was offering her? Marry an ox or keep on fighting the subway rush and sweating at the sewing machine. Well, if she could have Lester and his passion and tenderness and humor along with it, she would choose the drudgery. That meant good-bye comfort, security, and perhaps, confessional.

She decided to go to see Lester and talk the whole thing over with him in the old candid, intimate way they used to talk before they had quarreled. He wasn't taking the quarrel seriously; she knew that. He was vain and willful and waiting for her to give in. She was ready to do that, for the truth was she was at fault. Perhaps her surrender would put him in a pliant mood.

It would not be the first time she had sounded him on the marriage question. The other time was the latter part of last summer; no, the middle of the fall, just before she met Bascom. The idea had popped into her head and she had come right out with it, in the midst of a petting bout.

"Don't you think we ought to get married?" she asked, suddenly. "You know ..." She interpolated a pat on the cheek and a kiss. ... "Well ... Well, we *ought* to!"

"Now I'll tell one!" Lester scoffed. Then his mood became such an odd blend of mockery and intensity she couldn't tell whether he was still joking or dead in earnest. "Getting married is for timid men," he declared. "When a fellow feels lacking in manhood he likes to think he has the white folks' judges and police and army and navy to help him hold his woman in case a stronger man comes along. I don't feel that way. I don't think there's a man in the world that could steal you away from me."

Then he pressed her head down on his shoulder and kissed her hair. A moment later she felt his torso quivering. "Vanity of vanities," he chuckled. And squeezed her hand.

For the time being Marie was disarmed, as she always was by his quaint humors and exaggerations, and before she got around to the idea again they had quarreled and she had taken up with Bascom as a sort of consolation. She now saw that she ought to have pressed her point. But it was no use lingering on that. The important thing was to make her present attack effective.

She hoped she would find Lester home. If he wasn't she would wait for him. In the meantime she took off her white stockings and put on a black pair, and exchanged her summery voile dress for a frock of black silk with red piping and a line of tiny red buttons. When she looked at herself in the mirror her reflection pleased her. She looked fit. Her eyes and teeth were bright, and her skin, fired by her inner animation, shone with the luster of translucent copper. She liked the martial tilt of her head too, and the rhythm and strength she could see latent in her immobile body. Her lips were a trifle faded though, and she touched them with a lipstick. "War paint," she laughed, as she turned away from the glass.

Now—Where the mischief were her keys? While she was looking for them the phone rang. A moment later the landlady's falsetto, "Miss *Steele*! This is for you."

It was Bascom. He had finished his business earlier than he had expected, and wanted to know if it was too late for him to come up a little while. "If your landlady won't mind," he added, apologetically.

Marie had an impulse to hang up the receiver. But when you fight poverty for years you develop an instinctive ability to choke impulses. No use letting go the bird in her hand, she thought. She could see Lester tomorrow.

"Oh! She won't mind," she told Bascom. "Come right up." Then she remembered she had changed her dress. "No, don't come up," she called. "I think I'd rather take a walk first. Wait for me at the door."

When she returned to her room Marie sat down a few minutes so

Bascom would think she was changing her dress. He had never wanted to come back after leaving her before. Perhaps he was coming to life. It was a hopeful sign anyway. After they were married and she didn't have to hold her feelings in restraint any longer, maybe she could kindle him with some of her own fire; so he would show some of the warmth of a human being. But even if she couldn't get a good man, a good husband wasn't to be sniffed at. This thing of getting up at six o'clock every morning was no joke.

The Golden Penknife

In this strange tale, S. Miller Johnson trots out his insight into the cultural affectations and uncommon natures of two immigrant Slavic families in early Detroit (Hamtramck). In strong and circuitous fashion, a golden penknife, alcohol, and the intrusion of a mysterious dark sheik effectively destroy all hope of the two families uniting according to old-country tradition. This story was published in August 1925.

Now Anna was a pretty little devil. Her lips, pursed as if to invite a kiss, were red enough without rouge; and so were her cheeks. Her eyes, clear and light and roaming, fairly beamed with loveliness that clamored for wholesome expression. Anna's life, however, was sadly unguided. She walked spritely as if she were tipping up on something. Sometimes she gasped a little when she talked, but that slight defect added to her attractiveness. This girl was unique in her sphere; she didn't want her golden curls bobbed. Nor did she smoke cigarettes. Nor did she drink—though her dad operated a restaurant and maintained, besides, a flourishing bootlegging business.

At one time Anna had attended church regularly, said her confessions—which were innocent enough when she was a child—observed mass, and Y. W. C. A., and read the *Free Press* and conformed outwardly to its stupid Rotarian philosophy. And yet, she remembered, that ever since the age of puberty, she had suffered as most normal girls suffer during that period; there was the enormous struggle between inward natural desires and conventional morality. Like a father's true daughter, Anna had tried to conform to her father's and her lover's idea of what a good woman should be.

She first told her troubles to the priest, who gave her the conventional advice:

"After you are married you'll be all right."

So Anna went home and waited. She wasn't old enough to marry, she thought, and she wouldn't marry if she were old enough. She therefore reacted on the advice of the priest without obtaining any satisfactory results.

And so Anna Paul went again to confer with the good Father Raski. The stupid and pious Father was puzzled to see the shivering figure of the pretty creature standing before him, seeking something spiritual that would calm her raging insides. Only a Freud could have analyzed the thoughts of the good Father that day. Raski prescribed tennis and basket ball and swimming, and wholesome reading and prayer, the Virgin and a lot of other rigamarole. All these Anna tried and found wanting. Why, the idea! Even mother had offered these same remedies once.

The restless girl now started reading in order to find out for herself. After making several excursions into the field of modern literature on sex, freedom of women, ethics, etc., Anna made a final pilgrimage to the venerable Raski.

"You are a fake!" she shouted in the Father's face.

Then she whirled around and rushed from the sanctum sanctorum. This, indeed, ended Anna's relation with Holy Church. From that time on Anna read everything on sex she could get her hands on. Novels, plays, poetry, Freud, Jung, Mencken, Ellis, Nietzsche, et al. She subscribed for the *Smart Set*, ransacked the libraries, haunted bookshops, searched book lists; bought, borrowed and stole books. 'Tis a wonder she didn't develop into a rank sensualist or a Socialist—or even a Bolsheviki, for that matter.

Anna kept her head, however. The more she read, the tamer she became. Even Boccaccio, Balzac, and Casanova didn't upset her. To discover that she had been living a world of lies and lies and lies, sickened and disgusted her. As she saw the clay feet of her idols dissolving, the idols themselves falling and smashing, she grew morose; she wished that she herself could dissolve into nothingness. Unlike many of her more modern sisters under similar conditions. Anna didn't wish to see solace in mere sensuality; she sought peace of soul and body, she yearned for some one who shared her views, and who would give her sympathy.

Anna was in love with Fred Soskii. Now Fred was of Russian extraction. In him, as in a great many descendants of Russian peasants, East and West had met. And there was a mighty conflict of differing natures—a conflict of the dreamer, the nihilist, and the blood-loving vandal. At present the dreamer was predominating, expressing itself in Babbitism. The other opposing temperaments were not altogether dormant. Anna and Fred were in love.

Their parents had left the land of the Volga and come to live in Detroit, where they hoped to amass a fortune in the grocery business. Fred's folks continued in the food game and achieved considerable financial distinction. They now owned a car and several grocery stores—two in Hamtramck and one in 31st Street in Detroit. The Pauls owned a car too. But they had only one daughter, Anna, once vivacious, pretty and intriguing, now reserved, stern, cynical, truly "anti." The Pauls possessed no grocery stores now. The stimulus given to bootlegging by the passage of the Volstead Act had led the Pauls into a flourishing and respectable liquor business. They went to mass regularly, sold their whiskey and groceries. They were becoming beautifully Americanized.

Fred was the most American of them all, in spite of his Catholicism. He successfully managed his father's grocery stores. In theory he believed he should sacrifice the normal pleasures of youth to business success, and after achieving that success, Fred thought the proper thing to do was to cast aside all liaisons, marry a chaste, pretty woman and settle down, have one or two kids—let the pretty chaste woman nurse his gray hairs—take out insurance, join the Rotarians, denounce lawbreakers, boost the Y, be patriotic, etc., etc., etc.

Indeed Fred was a steady lad. He knew the value of putting business before pleasure. His parents liked that in him. Others also liked that in him. But there were other likable qualities and features in and about Fred. His pink cheeks flushed as he smiled good naturedly to the customers who came to his store to purchase a bunch of lettuce, a dozen eggs, or a can or two of pork and beans. With Fred the smile and the ruddy cheeks were natural. But as he dealt with the buyers and sellers about town, he had learned to capitalize his sunny disposition. In other words, this embryo go-getter was developing the traits that distinguishes the self-made American business man in the making.

When he left the market in the morning, smiling inwardly because he had made a good bargain with those elderly fellows there, he could hear at his back muttering appreciations of his ability as a buyer.

"There's Fred Soskii."

"That boy's gonna make something of himself."

"Knows how to buy all right."

"His old man's coining dough too!"

"Bet he is; has a Studebaker for himself and a Buick roadster for his wife."

"Say," drawled one of the salesmen, as he covered the top of a crate of bad tomatoes with some others that were better and redder. "Say, the boy's sweet on Old Paul's daughter, isn't he?"

"What Paul?"

"Aw, you know Paul—Paul's Cafe up on Chene Street?"

"O, yes." Then under his breath, "Sells some mighty fine stuff up there."

"Damn if he didn't. Where's he get it, I wonder?"

"Scotland by way of Canada. He's in the ring. Cars leave Canada destined for Mexico—side tracked here—goods sent to Paul's and to hotels and Grosse Point, Boston Boulevard—same old tale. Fine thing, I calls it."

And he then threw out his well chewed cud of Brown's Mule and spat dignifiedly.

And another spoke: "That's a humdinger, this Paul girl. She *is a peach*! She's sometimes at the cafe. You'd think she's a nun. Old man uses her for a drawing card, I suppose."

"Maybe. But she hasn't been 'round there much this winter. I'm in there pretty often. Never seen her yet. About three months ago or something thereabouts, I saw her in there one night. Think she's kinder tamed down now. Soskii, the younger—she's got her eye on the youngster, you see."

"Oh, I see, Ray. I really *do* see. Been seeing her goin' 'round with a stranger lookin' like a wop lately."

———

Fred had had an unusually good day. And to-night as he drove towards Anna Paul's, his heart leapt up in him when he contemplated the joy that would be his when they got together. He visualized Anna. The image of her life-giving personality; her smiling face; her soft, whispering child voice; her warm tender body throbbing against his; her langourous kisses that clung to his lips and flavored deliciously his memories of her! If she'd only lay off reading those silly novels and things! They'd turn her head one of these days.

Soskii could hardly wait until June. He and Anna were to be married then. Six months hence! Damn long time he thought.

A traffic cop blew his whistle. Fred brought his machine to a slow stop.

"Cussed policemen. Holding up time unnecessarily. If I were closer to that guy, I'd bargain with him. Bargain with him by George. That's what I'd do. Hellish cops."

Snow fell fast and thick, frosting his wind shield. Yet Broadway at Gratiot was congested. Cars. Pedestrians. Electric lights glaring out of a gray mist. Newsies running to and fro, yelling, "*Times*! Sunday *Star*!" Autos and pedestrians swarming, police whistles shrilling. What means this hurry? What means this shocking bustle? Nothing—nothing—meaningless——

Again the traffic cop's whistle sounded. Fred stepped on his gas. And off he went spinning towards Anna, his mind completely taken up with his loved one.

What was Anna thinking, he wondered. Her chest was heaving for him, maybe. She was sighing for her Fred perhaps. She wanted to talk to her Freddy. Funny how he kept thinking about Anna in this way. Anna—he hadn't seen her in three weeks. He had called. She had never been there to answer the phone. Anna hadn't *always* been out like those high fliers. Heavens, no! She was the kind of girl he wanted for a wife. He had been busy indeed the last three weeks—saving his father's business—He would tell Anna about that. She would laugh softly and tell him how proud she was of him—Vanity? Well, no——

He swung his car out of Grand Boulevard west into Buchanan. Anna's!

Fred rang the bell and Anna met him at the door. She held in her hand a translated copy of *Madame Bovary*—unabridged. Anna's pale, uncertain look frightened him. She didn't seem so glad he had come. Why had she called him? Had she called him? Hers was just a momentary coldness, perhaps, that would wear off as soon as he got her in his arms.

"There's my little lady bird!"

Anna looked down at Fred's wet shoes and up again into his capitalized face. A sleeping odor of digested garlic. A vague feeling of disgust mingled with pity flitted through her little body.

Only a little momentary coldness that——

"Hello, Freddy! So glad you came—at last. Mother and father are out. Went to see the Moscow Art Players. The plays are done in Russian, you know. You know our passion for things Russian. Dad and I have had great fun trying to translate Tolstoi's Anna. I'm going to make dad teach me more about Russian. Mother's Polish, and dad taught her to speak the Russian."

And somehow Fred sensed that Anna's good humor was feigned. Of course she didn't want him to know she wasn't well.

They sat down together. Fred took the girl's hand.

"Anna, my love, you aren't well. Can't I do something for you?" he said warmly, gazing into her mysterious eyes, that held both a coldness and a warmth—a coldness for something near and a warmth for something far away and unattainable.

"No, there's nothing." Then, as if in after thought, "It's been three weeks since you were here yet."

"Yes, dear, and it seems like a year. I've been very busy. Business at a low ebb those three weeks. It took all my time right on the job, keeping things on the go. Thought about you all the time yet."

She turned slightly away, feeling grossly neglected.

"A strange love that can live on mere thoughts of the loved one."

"A great love, you mean, my dear."

"Yes—I—yes——"

Hesitation.

"Let's just sit here in silence a while," Anna said.

She didn't want to tell him that she wanted time to think. He felt that something was in the air. Why was she so cold toward Fred Soskii to-night? Well, she wasn't feeling well. She hadn't felt well since she accidently met Alex Tervanovitch a few months ago. . . . Tervanovitch, dark and thoughtful and mystical. Anna had met him in the basement of an old book shop on Grand River Avenue. She didn't think then that the meeting would lead to romance. And the incident hadn't led to romance in the sentimental sense.

Continued silence between Fred and Anna. Anna, kittenlike, rested her head on Fred's shoulder. Anna thought back.

Her meeting with Tervanovitch had happened rather strangely. She had been prowling through the bookshelves in the dimly lighted basement of the bookshop, when suddenly, like a flash, a multitude of expressions, all compressed into one face, stared at her out of the dimness. She was both repelled and attracted by this face which reminded her of the Sphinx, as mysterious as life itself. She wanted to run away, yet she stayed there looking at the man. The owner of the face looked at the same time annoyed, interested and pleased. Anna stammered a meaningless, "Good evening," and then wondered why she had spoken at all. The fellow didn't notice her. He turned expressionlessly and began again peering into a stack of musty, dusty old books that filled the basement with a fog as he moved them about. His back was now turned towards Anna.

She wanted to see that face again. She would move slowly along the shelves until she could get in front of that interesting being. There he sat on a high stool, peering calmly over the books. Occasionally he smiled enigmatically to himself—like an Oriental, somewhat. When he grinned thus, she fidgeted; yet she continued to move toward the figure—like a child who is both frightened and curious in the face of what might be dangerous. Finally she edged around in front of the gentleman, keeping her back to him. She fumbled with books on the shelf and wondered how she could look around without seeming too bold, without embarrassing him or herself. She stood there nervously fumbling the old books, standing there in the dimly lighted basement of downtown bookshop and wondering how she could get a glimpse of a strange face without embarrassing anybody. She grew more and more afraid. Anna moved on, step by step, until she was some distance from the man. Then she ran upstairs and out into the street. Still scared, she jumped into her car and whizzed home, as if she were being pursued by bandits or cannibals——

And then, the very next day—— —— —— ——— —— —

"Anna, my love——" Fred's voice awoke her from a sort of lethargy. "Anna, are you better now? Just think! Six months from now we'll be married, and then——"

"Oh, Fred, don't mention it."

Now wasn't that just like Anna? She had such naive ways of expressing her unbounded joy.

"Can't I do something for you, Anna?"

"Yes, Freddy old dear; please leave me alone to-night. I'm not well. My head aches terribly—I'll call you tomorrow and let you know how I'm feeling."

"But, Anna——"

"No questions now, Fred——"

"But remember I haven't seen you in three weeks, Anna, and——"

"You love, Freddy?"

"How could you ask that now, Anna?"

"Three weeks," under her breath. Louder, "Well, if you love me, have consideration for my health—Shall I say good night?"

"All right, Anna, my little Anna, I was wrong to insist. Hope you'll feel better to-morrow."

She got his hat and coat and showed him the door. She kissed him rather coldly and turned him out into the cold night.

It all happened so damned quickly. What made Anna act like that? She hadn't done that way before. What could be eating her? As suddenly as a storm comes up over a big lake, something had come between them and sent him out into the night. And it was Anna's—Well,

Anna didn't look so well. And yet his experience with women in love had taught him that when a Jane is really sick, she is not so quick to get rid of one who might give her a little sympathy and petting. But there were exceptions. In this case, perhaps. Anna wouldn't do a thing like that. He knew Anna that well. But something was happening, though. Something had happened. What was it? If she hadn't been so clever—so ill—they would have quarreled to-night, you bet.

Aw, well, women were strange things, anyhow, thought Soskii. He decided to drown his troubles in wine. He'd decided to lay off fast women. Fred would stop at Paul's Cafe and have a drink with the boys before turning in. Must get a long rest to-night. Busy day to-morrow. Carload of oranges from California. Beginning to do things now in a big way. Hooray for the business game!

At the restaurant. Paul's Cafe decorated with red berried holly, palms, ferns, red and green crepe paper. Evergreen. Dancers. Laughter. Jazz. Wine. Laughter, chatter, dancing, wine, song. Women. Sprigs of cedar. Boys. Girls. An added attraction to-night. Dancers whose lithe bodies swayed and bubbled, bubbled and swayed. Snake-like, lithe and rhythmical. Drinks. Laughs. People dancing. Dancing old people. Young people shimmying. Elders outshimmying the wild young generation. Grocer clerks, druggists, restaurant owners, cafe managers, bootleggers. Lively fellows seated at tables and drinking bootleg wine. At other tables—journalists, men high up in the auto and education business, chorus girls, bankers, small store keepers, young dentists, doctors, shop girls, prostitutes, vaudevillians, male and female revellers, etc., etc. Musicians; Jews, Russians, Poles, Italians, Americans—all out for a few hours of innocent gaiety.

Fred Soskii was seated with a gang of lively fellows. Supple bodies swaying—undulating. Fred trying to forget that Anna had stopped loving him. Had she stopped loving him? A woman he knew sat opposite him. He was also trying to forget and ignore her steady dark eyes that were watching him, searching him, questioning him through a cluster of palm leaves. The possessor of those eyes! A sensible looking creature plainly but attractively dressed in a becoming black and gold something consisting of nearly all fringe, ostensibly arranged to show men how far her flesh-colored hose extended above her knees. She wore a black band about her blackhaired head and gold bracelets on her wrists. Her black pumps with gold braid carried gilded buckles. Apparently, she was one of the dancers employed at Pauls to-night. Fred sat restless under her gaze. The dancer had been drinking, but now, her sweet legs carelessly and freely crossed, she was smoking a cigarette. She tapped a leg of her table with the tip of her small black satin pump. She eyed Fred constantly.

This woman wore for a locket a tiny gold penknife fastened to an almost invisible golden chain. When she was not smoking her Chesterfield, she kept the gold penknife between her lips—as some women suck the pendants of their lavallieres.

Stanisky—one of Kroger's managers and Fred's buddy—was talking and fumbling in his pocket for smokes. He found none. He beckoned for a waiter. The waiter glided towards him.

"Cigarettes, please," Stanisky demanded.

Then he nodded for one of the dancers. The one eyeing Fred didn't move a peg. But another, more frolicsome and more artificially made up than the one in black fringe, writhed up to him, pitching her hips from side to side, and smiling through her rouge and powder. She danced before the two friends. Fred looked on, his head in a whirl. The liquor and the dancer were responsible for his whirling head. The whiskey, the noise of the orchestra, Anna, the eyes of that woman across the table. God! How could he stand it all?

The frolicsome dancer was a wow! A scarce brassiere she wore. Very scarce, indeed. The nipples of her bubbies were covered with little tips of semi-transparent shiny fabric. Tight tights. A pair of tiny silvery wings, her dark, bewitching eyes, her hair done up in Spanish style with a large fan-like comb, set with sparkling imitation diamonds, her small head thrown back—this gave her the appearance of an artist's interpretation of "The mountain-nymph, sweet Liberty." An almost completely nude dancer dressed scantily in faded pinks and lively lavenders and gliding about under a spot light that gave new and varied colors to everything its beams touched. The effect of rich lavender trimmed with ermine and gold dipped in a mixture of sunset and rainbow lying on white clouds wrapped in azure silken swaddling clothes. A riot of color gyrating about a dancer whose movements bore a close relation to those violent wrigglings made by the earliest dancers, when dancing was intentionally a means of attracting one sex to the other.

The sprite advanced, her body tense, her arms thrust limpidly forward in the manner of the girl in Rodin's Youth. She remained thus for a moment, still advancing. Then she stopped suddenly without changing her posture. Rising abruptly on her toes, she leapt wantonly backward, whirled around and then tripped slowly toward Fred Soskii and Stanisky. Standing on the toes of her left foot, she sent the other flying into the air. She looked at the two men out of the corners of her eyes. Around and around! She shimmyed violently and ended with a long audible sigh that caused her breasts to rise and fall, her chest to heave turbulently. So much emotional depth, so much powerful expression for such a small slender body! The dancer darted off towards an alcove separated from the revellers by a yellow curtain decorated with black and red cubist-impressionistic figures.

The waiter brought the cigarettes and went back to his stand.

"Know her?" asked Stanisky.

The woman in black fringe was still watching Fred.

"Who?"

"The dancer that just left us."

"No, you?"

"No. Call her."

And so the dancer was called. She curtsied and laughed after the manner of some movie actress she had carefully imitated. She accepted a seat between the two men. She accepted also their wine and their smoke. She laughed and shrugged and shrugged and laughed. And as she did so; her tiny silver wings opened and closed like those of a butterfly. The tips of those silvery wings, still under the changing colors of the spot lights, touched her glittering headdress, as she threw back her head and laughed softly, jocundly.

The dancer in black kept her warm cutting eyes on Fred, luciferous eyes—like those of a woman cheated in love. Once more Fred fidgeted under her gripping stare.

Two policemen sauntered in the cafe, grinning. They touched their caps to the manager. Several Y workers, a couple of ministers, a member of the Board of Recreation and Detective-Lieutenant Daskill—a group detailed by the Department of Uplift to investigate such places as Paul's Cafe—were seated at neighboring tables in a rather dark corner. They were drinking, chattering and flirting with some rather flashy dames whose naked backs fairly glared. When the uplifters saw the cops enter, they hid their whiskey and tried to assume a pious attitude. The policemen looked around casually, smiled, shook their heads helplessly and passed out.

"Say, girl," Fred was saying to the gay dancer at his side. "Think I'll just hire you to dance before me all day long—hic—like to see you trying to kick the moon with your sputtering heels."

The dancer laughed kittenishly.

Stanisky spoke: "What you got in your legs to—hic—to make 'em so kickable—hic—limber?"

They all laughed foolishly. Stanisky ran his hand delicately along the dancer's soft, warm, well-tapered legs, as if he could tell by feeling her flesh wherein lay the flexibility of her members. She continued to laugh and drink the wine offered her. She felt a hand, hidden by the table cover, gently gripping and stroking the tenderness of her sensitive thighs. She leaned towards Stanisky, her quivering lips close to his cheek, her body dilating against his shoulder. Just as he turned, she sprang from the table and glided across the room, whirling and contorting petulantly, like a leaf caught up in a whirlwind. She smiled back at the boys, both of whom wanted to grab the dancer and squeeze from her the delicious essences of love.

The boys drank more wine. They could forget their troubles in this sparkling Canadian wine. The woman in black and gold fringe looked daggers at Fred.

"Well, Fred," said Stanisky, "you'd better make the best of these days; you'll be married soon, won't you? Suppose we take these dames out sometimes. They're easy pickins. Aristocrats of their kind yet . . . You used to kinder knock around the one in black over there looking at you so hard, didn't you?"

"Pshaw! Lately, every time I see a woman like that, the more I love Anna. I'm not in for this wild life any more, Stan. Going to settle down—hic—yet."

"Hypocrite! Fred, you make me sick with your one-woman mania." (The liquor had broken down barriers of restraint, modesty, et cetera.) "As a friend, Fred, are you blind and crazy? Why do you let a woman put anything over on you? Listen. Hic. You've been engaged to Anna a long time. She's a woman. Hic. You are a man." (He was talking with his hands.) "You have been seeing and enjoying life—its bitterness— its sweetness. You know of the pleasures and honeys a live woman can give. And yet because you think Anna has denied herself much of what you've enjoyed, you call her innocent, pure, virtuous, and what not." (The jazz band shook the structure. Rock, church, rock. Revellers dancing on dimes.) "That's why you take pride in her. I'll bet she hates you for what you expect of her. And in a year or two after you are married—or before you get married, maybe—she'll be a talking about intellectual companionship, soul-mates, comraderie. Anna's just that kind. She reads everything. She's ahead of you there—hic—yet."

Silence.

The trombones in the jazz orchestra bellowed softly, the violins whined and moaned, the snare drum crackled convulsively, the cornets and clarinets neighed and neighed, the bodies of the dancers swayed and bubbled and bubbled and swayed. Saxophones tooted madly. Fiddlers on top of the piano. Clarinet player sitting flat on the floor. Snare drummer going through the antics of an African witch doctor. Other performers stamping, kicking, and shouting like Negroes at a camp meeting in Louisiana.

"Stan," Fred replied, "you are crazy. You can't mean that——"

"If you'll hear me out, I'll tell you a few things. I've seen Anna in questionable places with strangers and——"

"Strangers to you, perhaps, but not to Anna. Anna out with strangers. You make me laugh. That girl is pure gold, my friend!"

And yet he couldn't give a satisfactory explanation of Anna's actions lately.

"The case is closed, old boy. She'll be your pure gold whatever I tell you about her. Let's turn in. See the dancers some other time by myself."

"So."

As they arose to go, the dancer in black walked in the direction of their table. They were now at the door. This same dancer accosted Soskii.

"Fred?" she queried.

"Oh. Hello Natalie."

"Going *so* soon?"

"And why not? Hic."

"No reason. Won't you stay a *little* longer?"

"Listen, Nat, I've told you I'm through. Why keep on after me?"

"Because I love. You loved me—you said."

"Aw, forget it. I'm sleepy—hic—old kid. See you some other time."

Fred was in an embarrassing position, with a pretty danseuse, love and madness in her eyes, barring his exit.

"I will dance for you soon. You say you like my dance once."

Stanisky smiled and shook his head. People at other tables became curious. Fred was further embarrassed. He tried to force his way past the woman. He essayed to thrust her aside.

"One question, Fred, please. Just one. Will you, please, my—my—I mean, Fred—just Fred like always? One question?" (She wept bitterly almost choking.)

"Providing you let me by. Damn it!"

"Now. You are not going to—quit your Nat, are you, Fred? You will not marry, no?" as she held the lapels of his coat, her face near his, her eyes searching—searching.

Fred did not know she held open in her hand the gold penknife she once wore as a locket.

Fred was drunk and puzzled. He waited.

"You not marry? No?"

She feared the answer would be "yes."

"Why, yes. I thought you knew it."

The girl grew frightened, mad, wild, ravenous, quiet, beautiful, sour, hurt, pitiable, hateful, satanic all in a moment.

"You joking? No."

"Not joking! Leave me. I'm through, I tell you."

She weakened—then strengthened—turned tigerlike. Amid her tears and grating teeth, she raised her knife.

"You will marry her, hein? Pas du tout!"

Fred caught her arm and twisted the knife out of her hand. It fell to the floor. Tapity-tap. Natalie stood black and blue before him, sobbing, tearing away fitfully at his chest, striking his face with her little fists. Fred pushed her aside and picked up the knife.

"I'll keep this as a souvenir," with a sneer and a shrug.

—

Stanisky and Soskii were driving leisurely out Chene Street. Fred's mind was a whirl with thoughts of Anna—Anna—Anna—— Was she really sick or did she just want to get rid of him that night? Which? He looked at his watch. Eleven o'clock. Just then a familiar car swept past his. A woman at the wheel. . . . A glimpse of a dark man in the rear seat. . . . Anna Paul's car? Anna—the dark man. Impossible! Did Stanisky tell the truth that night at the cafe?

—

The next morning Anna left word with her mother that she would be out all day looking for an old book. That was sufficient. Anna went again to the dimly lighted basement of the book shop on Grand River Avenue. Why did she want to go there just to feel the mysterious presence of that stranger with the hard eyes and puzzled face? She would get a good look at his face this time, even if he stabbed her. Pooh. Stab! Who would think of stabbing her?

After that first experience at the old book shop, Anna had returned there almost daily. Most every time she came, she found that same fellow there searching through the old German, French, Greek, Latin and Russian books. Perhaps he had permission of the owner of the store to roam over this pile of apparently useless rubbish. Or he might be hired as janitor. The person, excluding his face, certainly looked like a janitor. Gray unpressed suit, hair unkempt, black and bushy. He needed a shave—a scholar? His heavy eyebrows overhung his slowly blinking eyes. Was he always soused in deep thought? Did he know a lot? His long, thin dark hands cadaverously turned the pages of the books. The man was hardly twenty-five, Anna thought. Was he a sheik? He and Anna were becoming silent friends who met without speaking nearly every day. Later one began to nod as the other entered. Then one day Anna spilled the beans by stammering, "I'd begun to think you weren't coming to-day." The stranger acted as if he hadn't heard the remark.

Later. "You are a book lover, I see." He glanced at *Thus Spake Zarathustra* Anna carried under her arm.

She imagined the fellow knew much; she even suspected now that he was a scholar. She found herself, more now than ever, wanting to pour out her heart to this stranger. His face emitted a calm sympathetic glow closely akin to that given out by Murillo's St. Francis.

Anna answered with a note of fear in her voice, "No, I can't say I'm such a book lover. I'm just a lost little thing with nothing to hold to."

Silence. Like a child, the fellow sat there gazing at the girl's face. He had met many of her type before, perhaps—"Lost little things holding on to nothing."

"Ah, well, you are not alone; this world is full of lost little things holding on to nothing."

"Not everybody?"

"Almost everybody. The farce of it is that the majority fool themselves by making believe they have found eternal verities; *the* right, *the* wrong, *the* beautiful, *the* truth, and on ad infinitum. There are no such things; 'tis the quality of ignorance that informs thus to their eyes."

The stranger had not raised his head during this recitation.

"You confuse me," Anna said with her head thrown to one side, expressing the profound curiosity of a child.

He went on in a sort of incantation.

"Chastity is right in the sight of God, they tell us; yet it is a matter of common knowledge that this same "God," expressing himself through Nature, plants in every normal human being the arch enemy of chasity. They tell us that God is good, and yet the wicked prosper. They tell us that God is just; while the poor, the weak are so because of what is commonly known as injustice meted out by those whom this same God has permitted to prosper. To me it is a joke, this God-ology. Organized guessing I call it. I should like to live in a world with people who dare to act on convictions and conclusions arrived at through their own individual thinking."

Anna gave him a credulous look.

The stranger continued: "Such people would certainly not gouge out one another's guts with cold steel in the name of democracy, a degenerate theory of government by the weak, for the weak, and of the incompetent."

"What do you mean?" Anna asked.

"I don't know. I'm lost too; I've nothing to cling to."

"Like me."

"And a lot of others."

They looked at each other thoughtfully. Anna looked sad and lost. The stranger was sympathetic.

Anna cried: "I meet so many lies, lies, lies, I don't know what course to take. I don't know what to do or believe. Everybody suffers and suffers, and so unnecessarily, it seems. I'm lost."

"It has always been so. You must'nt cry over the world's suffering. The man who did the most of that died at the age of thirty-three yet—was crucified, you know. You want to live longer than that."

> " 'Ah, my beloved, fill the cup that clears
> To-day of past regrets and future fears:
>   *To-morrow!*—Why, to-morrow I may be
> Myself with yesterday's sev'n thousand years.' "

"Yes. That's beautiful. But I'm so helpless and unhappy since I started looking through so much dastardly deceitfulness. I've discovered that many of the things I once held most dear and sacred aren't worth talking about yet."

"That's true of most everybody else too. But listen:

> 'Ah Love! Could you and I with Him conspire
> To grasp this sorry Scheme of Things Entire,
>   Would not we shatter it to bits—and then
> Remold it nearer to the Heart's desire!' "

There was a peculiar inter-attraction. Anna fell sobbing on the stranger's shoulder. His tears fell hot on her neck and rolled warm down her back and into her bosom. She realized the position she was in, and wanted to move her head. And she didn't want to leave one who she thought felt and thought as she did. They cried there like two old friends meeting after a long separation.

"I'm feeling much better now. I'm going now," Anna whined. "Friday?"

"Any time."

"Friday, then."

———

Anna reached home and rushed for the telephone.

"Hello ... Mr. Soskii ... Yes ... Mr. Soskii? ... Fred ... Feel so much better to-day. Can't you come over to-night. . . . Yes, about eight. . . . News for you. . . . Busy? . . . No. . . . All right at eight. . . . So long."

Eight o'clock. Fred. Faint smell of onions. Anxious. Wondering. Fred Soskii rushing towards his fiancee who he felt had thought her way out of his love. Out of the snow and biting cold Fred Soskii came, shivering, go-gettish. Ready to bargain. Ready to praise purity, Blue Belle canned peaches, Horlick's malted milk, etc., etc. Fresh country eggs.

Fred entered. Some cold-warm-far-off look in Anna's eyes. "Hello, lady bird." "Hello, Fred." Strangeness pervading the room. Fred feeling scared and foolish, as if he had lost a chance to make a good buy. They were seated. Fred took her hands. He tried to kiss her. Anna was neutral, impassive.

"Fred, I can't marry you; I don't love you—any more."

"Anna——"

And yet he had felt this coming all along. He knew she was telling the truth. He knew Anna that well. She meant just what she was saying.

"Anna, you're joking?"

"No."

"But what's the trouble, Anna?"

"You expect what I can't give. I'm not the woman you think you know. I'm wild, ravenous, promiscuous, romantic. Marriage no longer has any fascination for me. I haven't yet had time to express myself. To-day I wept on a stranger's shoulder—a stranger I wanted to rape— though I didn't have the courage. Think I shall rape him one of these days. There are too many lies in the world for you to think of marrying yourself to one of them. I myself am a lie, Fred."

"Anna, you're crazy!"

"I know it. Another reason why you shouldn't marry me."

She baffled him. He wanted to hit her, but dared not.

Anna went on, "I've talked it over with father and mother. They say I am crazy too. That means that none of you understand me. I'm sorry for you—not because of any harm I might be causing, but because you are all so stupid."

"Anna—Anna! You'll ruin me!"

"Quiet, Fred. You'll get over it soon. Just think of all the women you had before you met me."

"Anna, I know I've not been straight as I ought to have been, but I want to be; that's why I want you."

"I've decided not to be straight; in fact, I haven't been at heart. I don't like it. Nor do many others. You especially."

Fred dumbfounded.

"Now run along home and begin learning how to forget about it. Go by dad's and tell Basky to give you that quart of port I left there for you."

And again he was shoved out into the cold, cold snowing snow— flakish, sickly snow that looked like Fred felt. He couldn't believe it. Anna had thrown him over. Anna hadn't thrown him over. Anna *had* thrown him over, *jilted* him. Heavens! Heavens!!

Of late Anna's parents grew inquisitive concerning their daughter's whereabouts. In a way they didn't want to keep her from going out. They were frightened with various reports that came to their ears. Late hours driving alone through the city with a dark man in her car. Some said the man was a Chinaman, some a Jap. Others claimed the stranger was a Philipino, or a Bolsheviki. Or a colored man; a Negro! Great God! Or were these all different men. At the Capitol Theatre, at the New Detroit Opera House. Garrick. Other public places. At the Palms. All this threw the Pauls into a panic. Their daughter was going to elope with a Turk, an Indian. The reports conflicted. Some were stupidly jumbled.

And this was not all. Everybody was trying to find out who Anna's new associate was. Some one had seen them kissing in Palmer Park under the cover of night. Another had seen her driving madly down Brush Street. Still another had seen them enter the Crisis Cafe, a passable eating place frequented by the more decent element among the Detroit Negroes. King Wah Ling's. Statler. The Sindadus Grill Room. Her conduct was pronounced disgraceful. Her father could bear it no longer. His business would certainly be seriously affected by her defiant antics. She must stop.

"Anna, won't you have consideration for your father, yet."

"Father, won't you have more consideration for your Anna, yet."

"But, my girlie, Fred's furious, dangerous because you've thrown him over like this, and turned out so——"

"So bad. Exactly. I'm as happy as I have been before—happier. It's none of Fred's business. I don't love him now. I'm not harming anybody."

"Anna—your father——" The old man angered, as his glistening ball spot indicated. "You mind or you get out. There."

"I can certainly go. Thanks for the invitation."

Old Paul's threat didn't work.

———

They had met again at the book store, Anna and her friend. They embraced calmly, profoundly. She could never remember when he began embracing her. His full lips covered hers. There was a mutual exchange of sweetness, memories of nights and evenings they had spent together in various out-of-the-way rendezvous—all this lingered in their lingering kisses.

"I love you," she was saying. "What is your name? Where do you come from? Why do I love you so? It's going to kill me to love you like this."

"Tervanovitch—Askof Tervanovitch. But what's in a name?" he replied, drawing her close to him. "Your lips are honey dripping from the comb."

A book clerk coughed in a far corner of the basement. This ended their meeting for that day.

———

When Anna first got rid of Fred, he was all shaken up; he groped about trying to forget. He refused to have anything more to do with Natalie. Then one evening he saw Anna and her friend dining at the Sindadus Grill Room on Broadway.

"Look Stanisky! There's Anna! Well, damn. Is that why she threw me over? For that damn thing. She can't love him. I won't let her!"

He ordered drinks. The dancing began. Tervanovitch was toasting:

> "For 'Is' and 'Is-Not' though with rule and line,
> And 'Up-and-Down' by logic I define,
> Of all that one should care to fathom, I
> Was never deep in anything but—*Wine!*"

The orchestra struck up a waltz. Anna and her sheik arose and went gliding over the floor. Fred drank heavily. He'd have a talk with Anna. So it's as he had heard. Anna had thrown him aside for that black dog. (The man was no darker than some Italians.)

Anna's partner wore his evening clothes with a certain Latin dignity.

He was helping Anna to her seat. His old world manners attracted the attention of many other women.

"A sheik!"

"Who is he?"

"He doesn't notice anybody else here."

"Why should he?"

Several dissatisfied wives, whose husbands were either elsewhere with their mistresses or attending clubs, tried to catch the stranger's eye by exhibiting vast expanses of their silk-stockinged legs, portions of their bare shoulders, and their girlish smiles. One lady, who had once been Anna's teacher, actually came up and spoke to Anna, with the hope of getting introduced. Nothing doing.

Anna and her partner were now dancing near Fred's table. He could hear the man saying, "This town needs fewer uplifters and more little theatres, my little snow flower." Anna was smiling dreamily under the somnolent influence of the waltz. The orchestra was playing "Moonlight Memories." Her cheek was near her partner's. He could feel her breath against his neck. It is doubtful whether Anna heard what he had said. They graced along as if soaring towards the land of Nirvana on a magic carpet of rose petals.

Stanisky said knowingly, "Fred, that's a colored man yet."

"Impossible. They aren't ever found here."

"Some niggers are mighty light, Fred."

Fred Soskii had become almost Americanized. He bowed his head and sobbed.

"Don't take it so hard, Fred."

"Can't help it, Stan. I love Anna," as he emptied his glass.

Anna saw Fred's face. Nervously to her escort, "Let's go."

Stanisky: "They are leaving. Let's follow."

"I am above that, Stan."

"Fool! Revenge!"

Fred turned blank and white. He unfastened a pen knife from his watch charm. He ran his thumb over the keen edge of the blade. They got up and followed.

Outside the snow was falling rapidly. A sharp wind off the lakes swept over lower Detroit and modulated with the voices of yelling newsboys. The Saturday traffic was heavy, in spite of the fast falling flakes. The wind whipped around corners of buildings and lashed—and lashed—and lashed.

"It's no use starting anything, buddy. She don't love me. I tell you."

He stopped his car. "Here's where you live. Jump out and turn in. I'll drive back home. Heavy day to-morrow. Car load of oranges—twenty barrels of sugar—perishables by the car load—a dispatchment of potatoes—market's good now, too."

Stanisky hesitated.

"Come along now," Fred urged. "Snap it up. Can't let one woman break up my business. We'll pick up the dancers later this week."

"Atterboy! You're getting more sense every day. Guess you're right. Good night."

Fred drove slowly towards his home for a block or two. Then he turned suddenly and beat it for Anna's dwelling place. As quietly as possible, he drove his car to the door of Old Paul's garage, stopped the machine and waited. He took out his watch. He looked at it closely. Eleven forty-five. He pretended there was something wrong with his tires. He walked around his machine three times. He counted the number of times. He felt his feet getting cold. The coldness passed. Like the whiskey he had been drinking, the cold helped to numb him. He laughed expressionately, noiselessly. A whispering laugh. He looked at his watch again. He rubbed his hands. He blew his breath on them. Where were his gloves, he wondered? In the car perhaps. He'd get them later. The drink burnt his stomach. He looked at Anna Paul's house. A dim little framed two-story cozyness, like Anna used to be. The Pauls were in bed, doubtless. That was funny, the Pauls being in bed. No. It was late enough for that. Surely. Fred looked up at the room Anna told him was hers. How many times she had pointed it out to him! He heard the familiar humming of a motor. Anna's car. He walked around his car twice more. He looked at his watch again. Eleven fifty. What a long five minutes. The car he had heard turned the corner and its lights flashed down upon him. Fred felt in his vest pocket for his penknife. The approaching machine slowed down. Fred was concealed behind his car. He opened his penknife. Again his thumb gently ran over the keen edge of its blade. The whiskey dizzied him. Something else deadened his senses. Anna's Buick rolled up. The car near her father's garage caused her no alarm. It belonged to one of the neighbors, or to one of the neighbors' visitors. She jumped out to open the garage door.

Fred stepped from behind his car. Anna started to scream when she saw him. She didn't know who he was.

"Sh-sh-sh—— A friend. Don't scream. Only Fred."

"Fred Soskii! I've a good mind to call father."

"Please don't. Just answer one question and I'll be gone forever. Will you, Anna?"

"Well, what is it?"

He came closer to her meekly. White as the snow under his feet and as cold and as uncontrollable. Anna was steaming and red with anger, which beautified her beaming face, lifted her out of the real and into the ideal.

"Hurry, Mr. Soskii."

"Did you know that fellow's colored you were with to-night?"

"No, I don't know that. Nor do you." She bit her lip. She wanted to hurt. "That's none of your business, anyhow." She wanted to wound him mortally. "What if he is? I *love* him. So there!"

Fred was close to Anna now. She could see his white distorted face. He remembered his golden penknife. He looked straight into Anna's eyes and shook his head slowly. Somehow she couldn't keep her eyes out of his. He raised his hand towards her throat. She thought he was trying to kiss her. Of course she couldn't afford to let him know she was afraid. She threw back her head in scorn.

With a swish and a click, the keen-edged blade lashed her throat. There was a gush of blood, a little hicking, gasping sound. Then faintly from beyond the grave:

"Fred, how could you? My—book—store—man—is——"

Anna staggered and sank.

The snow about her melted, and where her head struck, the snow crimsoned and melted. Fred stood there until the body began to stiffen. He looked at the corpse. He looked at his watch. Twelve o'clock. He looked at his bloody golden penknife. A souvenir. Natalie. He turned Anna's body over with his foot. A milky mist arose from the little pool of steaming blood in which Anna's golden hair lay. Fred Soskii shrugged his shoulders, spat, and turned to go. He felt numb.

The wind off the lakes whipped through the streets, chilling everything it touched. An arc light at the corner sputtered and flared.

Fred Soskii walked calmly towards his machine.

THE SPRING OF '65

Author William Moore has created a gripping tale that casts the tragic fate of a biracial young beauty in counterpoint to the historic assassination of a legendary and beloved national figure. An abiding, passionate love and a tenacious hatred, combined with a mystery, build a thrilling narrative. This story was published in February 1925.

William Moore is a highland African Negro who boasts of a lineage "unclouded by white blood" and got his first glimpses of life in the East End of the Greenwich Village section of New York City a little longer than a half century ago. He received his earlier training in the New York Negro public schools of forty-odd years back, at the College of the City of New York, and later in a course of Belle Lettres at Columbia University. He is ranked among the first flight of American Negro writers and is well known in the literary circles of Chicago and New York. [*Messenger* introduction, Feb. 1925]

Anyone who can bring to mind the 12th of April, 1865, in the City of New York will remember that the day was cloudy and that at night the streets were flooded with a downpour of heavy rain.

If by any chance one had been standing at the corner of Broadway and Prince Street at about 11 o'clock that blustery night he would have been startled by the hurried clatter of a horse's hoofs coming out of the south and a few moments later he would have seen a swift moving hack emerge out of the mist and shadow and madly dash around the corner of Prince Street and a few moments after rush north into Crosby Street.

On the east side of Crosby Street, beginning at the northeast of Prince Street, there stood a row of red brick two story and a half, basement, gable roof houses that ran north to within two houses of the corner of Jersey Street, a short thoroughfare which went east plump into the back of the old St. Patrick Cathedral.

The hack stopped at the curb directly in front of the fourth house from the corner of Jersey Street. At that moment lights on the second floor of the building suddenly flashed out. The driver jumped down from his seat and opened the door of his hack from which a tall, heavy cloaked figure of a man stepped out onto the sidewalk immediately followed by an equally tall and slender formed woman who stepped across the wet walk and ran lightly to the top of the stone steps of the stoop.

"How much do I owe?" the man asked in a pleasant toned baritone voice of the hackman.

"Two dollars and a half, Sir," respectfully answered the hackman.

"You made a good, quick drive of it," said the passenger as he turned and made a quick ascent of the stone steps to the side of the impatiently waiting woman.

"My heavens, how it rains, Dick," lowly spoke the woman as the man gave two sharp, nervous pulls of the door bell.

He made no answer to her comment but as the door opened cautiously and but part way, he said, "It's Dick," and pushed himself into the dark hallway with the woman following close on his heels.

Shutting the door softly, the stout, stockily built man who had answered the summons of the door bell, asked in gruff, though low tones, "Who's with you?"

"Josephine," whispered Dick.

"Hell? what for?" came the startled reply of the questioner. "Yer frien's won't like that, Dick."

At that instant a voice came from the head of the second floor stairway sounding the inquiry, "Who's that, Charlie?"

"It's me, Andrew. Dick—Dick Jackson—me and Josephine."

By this time Charlie had shuffled somewhere off to the rear of the hallway disappearing through a doorway that was but dimly visible in the deepened shadow of that portion of the first floor of the house.

"Did the trunks come?" continued Dick. "We're wet to the skin and need some dry clothes."

"Yes, yesterday," replied Andrew, coming partly down the stairway. "Come on up, they are in the back room up here on the second floor," and turning he led the way showing Dick and his companion the door of a room that opened on the second landing. Neither Andrew nor the woman spoke to the other.

They entered the room and the man, glancing about at its appointments, shut the door and turned the key in the lock. Up to this moment the woman had been strangely silent, keeping her head turned away from the men and held low as though in a studied effort to keep her face hidden from their sight.

With the click of the lock she reached up and turned the half-hearted light to a full brightness. This done, she lifted the low crowned hat from her shapely head and revealed a face rapturously refined and beautiful. Dick stepped to her side and lifted a long cape-like cloak from her shoulders and her tall, slender figure silhouetted against the yellow-grey background of the farther end of the high ceilinged, square room—a sheer revelation of supernal loveliness.

Placing her shapely hands on either shoulder of her companion she reached forward and placing a full, passionate kiss on his clearcut mouth, said: "Dick I wish you were out of this awful mess."

A frown that vanished ere it was full born fluttered across his strong lined face and in its place there came a slight, pale smile as he replied, "O, quit, Joe, nothing's going to happen to bring us trouble. Our cause is a sacred one and we can't stop now—we have no right to stop." His voice quavered a bit and then halted as he caught the muffled hum of a number of voices which seemed to come through a door that must have opened on a room to the front of the one they were in.

The woman's face blanched. Dick gave her a reassuring look and enfolded her in his arms. A low knock sounded on the door that opened on the hallway. Josephine broke from his embrace and walked quickly over to the bed, sat down on its side and buried her face in one of its pillows.

Dick went to the door, and putting his ear close to one of the panels asked, in a jerky, low voice, "Who's there?"

"Charlie. The committee's waitin' on yer."

"All right," he answered, "tell them I'll be with 'em in a few minutes."

Walking over to the bed he sat by the side of the highly agitated woman, and putting his arm around her waist, he raised her to a sitting posture as he caressingly whispered, "It's all right, honey, we're going back home Sunday. This matter'll be settled day after tomorrow, an' then everything will be happy for both of us."

"Let's go tonight, Dick," she appealed, "they'll catch you sure if you don't stop now. An' it's all wrong, Dick, it's all wrong."

Gently putting his hand over her mouth he motioned her not to talk. She fell back on the pillow as the sound of a light tapping came from the hall door.

Dick arose with a quick, angry gesture, went to the door taking the key out of the lock as he opened and stepped lightly into the hallway inserting the key in the other side as he softly closed the door behind him. The woman, hearing the key turn, raised herself on one hand with a startled look in her haunting eyes and then as suddenly sank back on the pillow and again buried her face in its sympathetic softness.

"A woman will hang you yet, an' the rest of us, if you don't quit your foolin' with 'em," angrily protested the man who was only known to Dick as "Charlie," as he led the way through the dark hallway.

"You never mind the woman," replied Dick rather heatedly, "get me out of this damned dark hall to where Andrew and the rest of the boys are and keep your mouth closed."

Charlie ventured no reply to this sally of the younger man except to express his disapprobation in a grunt which voiced volumes of dissent as he turned a knob and opened a door that revealed a room thick with tobacco smoke, and the sickly flare of a small kerosene lamp standing on the top of an old square piano and the expectant presence of five men grimly and indistinctly outlined, in the uncertain light, in different postures here and there about the place.

"What kept you so long, Dick?" questioned one of the men whom Dick recognized as Andrew Pinkney, an old-time friend, "we've got to get down to business in a hurry."

"I know," replied Dick as he took a seat in a chair that his friend motioned to near the piano, "but I had to give the girl some attention— she's nervous and frightened an' wants me to quit."

"Whyin the hell didn't you leave her in Washington then?" angrily retorted one of the men.

"Hello there, George Johnston, is that you? I couldn't make you out in this rotten, poor light. Now don't you go back on me."

Then turning and peering into the faces of the other three men present, he arose from his seat and greeted them heartily and separately with, "Well, well, how are you Jim Scott? And John Blair, as I live! And Arthur Bragg, as gay looking as ever! This is really a treat—a sure 'nough treat. This damned lamp don't give as much light as a tallow candle."

"O, never mind the lamp, what's the news from Washington? When's the gun to be pulled? That's what we want to know," questioned Andrew Pinkney with an impatient gesture.

"Day after tomorrow night, as I get it," replied Dick. "Three or four of 'em. If everything goes all right there'll be hell to pay in Washington an' everywheres else. Maybe it will turn things so upside down it will help us to win, though it looks mighty dark right now."

At this juncture Charlie, who had stepped out of the room during the greeting period, re-entered carrying a good sized tray on which was placed a bottle of whiskey, a pitcher of water and several small glasses. Setting the tray and its burden on the small, marble top center table that stood quite in the middle of the room, he walked out of the room pulling the door noiselessly behind him.

"I am going to drink to the success of the cause," declared Jim Scott, and suiting the action to the word, he stepped to the table, took the bottle in his left hand and poured a good sized portion of its contents into one of the glasses.

"Suppose we have some more light on the subject," laughingly suggested Dick, "it's too damned dark in here to suit me."

"No more light," interposed Andrew Pinkney, "it's too late, police is mighty suspicious of lights these days an' we can't afford to take any more chances than we really have to."

"You don't rec' on we're bein' watched, do you Andy?" interjected Jim Scott.

"You can't tell about it. Charlie told me he saw what looked like two plain clothes men standing over across the street by Niblo's stage door talkin' an' pointing at this house day before yesterday. You can't be too careful. I reckon we can see good 'nough by the lamp to take a drink," laughingly retorted Andrew.

Andrew then proceeded to pour the whiskey into each of the glasses and taking them from the tray one by one handed them around to his companions who now had gathered about him and the center table.

"To the cause!" he said. "To the cause!" they responded in a low toned chorus, and in the stifling quiet of the moment they raised the glasses to their lips and drank in silence—"to the cause."

Silence is never golden when passion is holding men's souls in its deadly grip. Never was it touched by a stronger passion than when this small group of earnest men, standing in the oppressive quiet of this dimly lighted, sparsely furnished room, drank "to the cause" in language unspoken yet couched in the terms of emotions that burned as deep as the depths of a sea whose bottom had never been reached.

Pinkney was the first to speak. "Be seated, fellows, we haven't lost yet. If the plans of the central committee go through all right, why the whole North will be stunned by the blow and barely able to move. That'll be our chance and, perhaps," his voice quavered a bit at this point, "perhaps our forces in the field can be shaped for a fresh start."

Putting their emptied glasses on the tray, each man went to his chair, all save Dick Jackson. He stood as though riveted to the floor, his face ashen with a pallor that had the very touch of death in it. His eyes, however, flashed fire—the fire of a defiance of sinister design.

"I am going back to Washington. They might miss him. I know every hole and corner in the White House and if they don't get him at the theatre, I'll get him there."

The words fell from the young man's lips with a melodramatic distinctness which cut hard and clear into the consciousness of the other members of the party. Each gave a quick, startled look at the other and for a brief moment it seemed as though the shadow of a frightful disaster pervaded the smoke-laden room.

The door opening on the hallway swung suddenly and wide open and in the bare space there stood the tall, frail figure of Josephine, her eyes half shut, her slender arms outstretched reaching for support as she fell in a limp heap across the threshold into the room.

Dick stepped briskly to where she lay and kneeling turned her over on her side and lifting her tenderly in his arms kissed her as he murmured, "What's the matter, honey, get frightened?"

She opened her eyes, clutched him feverishly around the neck and moaned, "You shan't go back, Dick, I won't let you. I'll tell all first!"

"W'at t'hell, we'll have to kill that black wench," exclaimed Jim Scott, as he pulled a handsomely mounted derringer pistol from his left-hand hip pocket and levelled it with the evident intention of firing a bullet into the slight form Dick was holding tightly in his arms, as he appealingly looked up at his highly agitated companion in conspiracy.

But Andrew Pinkney, leaping forward, slapped the pistol out of Scott's hand and in a rasping, excitable tone of voice hissed, "You damned fool, do you want to bring the police in on us with that sort of foolishness? We'll take care of the woman. Keep your shirt on or I'll choke the breath out of you. Take the girl and put her to bed, Dick, she'll be all right in the morning."

Scott with an angry gleam in his eyes walked to the piano and sat on the stool at its front. Charlie coming from somewhere out of the darkness in the hallway stooped, raised the slight body of the unconscious woman and carried her into the rear room, Dick dejectedly following him.

Pinkney stood near the doorway, his face blanched to a cold whiteness and his powerful frame shaking with a suppressed and strongly agitated emotion. He gave a swift glance around the room, closed the door and then walked to the center table from which he took the bottle of whiskey off the tray and pouring a good, big drink lifted the glass and with one gulp swallowed its contents.

"Don't be so damned handy with your pistol, Jim Scott. We'd be in a devil of a fix with the police—itching for a chance to see the inside of this house—coming in on us because some fool among the crowd started a shooting scrap." "W'at did Dick bring that damned black wench up here with him for?" sullenly responded Scott, "She's dangerous."

"I suppose it isn't dangerous shooting off pistols at this time of night," tartly retorted Andrew.

"Aw, call in Dick an' let's get down to business," impatiently suggested George Johnston, "we're wasting a lot of valuable time."

Dick, however, did not wait to be called. He opened the door and entered the room just as Johnston's suggestion faded from that worthy's lips. Aside from a slight paleness he showed no traces of the agitation that had so violently shaken the group a short while before.

"I feel like another drink of the stuff that cheers would do us a world of good just at this time. What do you say about it, Andy, don't you think 'twould help us some?" he said, walking toward the table and its burden of drink and glasses as he spoke.

"Well, a drink it is, Dick," returned Andrew. "Come on, Jim Scott, an' join us. Don't be such a damned, morose fool about something that can't be helped. A man's a man, an' a woman's a woman, even if she is black."

Scott arose from the piano stool, walked over to where the others had gathered and silently watched Dick pour varying portions of whiskey into the several glasses.

Again they drank in silence "to the cause." In a few minutes they were talking in subdued tones concerning the matters which lay close to their hearts. At odd moments the high spots of the conference would rise audibly clear out of the droning hum of low toned but nevertheless intensely agitated concern of each of the men.

"Washington." "You can't trust him now." "What about the woman?" "S'pose he misses, the nigger-loving devil?" "How'll he get out of the theater?" "In H Street." "They'll get all of 'em." And thus it went on until the grey light of the early morning crept into the room through the spaces at either side of the drawn curtains.

Even then they were loath to quit, and only did so upon the suggestion of Andrew Pinkney who opined that, "We'd get a little sleep while Charlie is getting us up some breakfast."

The breakfast time was an occasion shrouded in gloom. True, although the storm of the night before had betaken itself to other parts and the sunlight reflected from the dark brown brick wall that constituted the rear of the old Niblo's shot back a comfortable portion of warmth and light through the shuttered windows of the rather dingy basement dining room, the gloom around the breakfast table was actually thick enough to cut with a dull knife.

"Lee had surrendered!" The morning Herald announced the catastrophe in big, black headlines. Andrew Pinkney held a copy of the paper that Charlie had laid on the table at his place a short while before they had come down to eat, in a nerveless, yet tightly clenched grip of his right hand. Jim Scott scowled and his deep sunken, heavy lidded black eyes glistened in an agony of bitterest despair and hate. And the others, save Dick Jackson, who had not answered yet the summons to breakfast, sat and stood about in a stupor of suspended determination.

The spell of utter helplessness remained unbroken until the door opened and Dick Jackson stood on its threshold transfixed by the throbbings of a sudden born fear as he looked from one to the other with a mute inquiry for the reason for the despondency that showed so plainly in the face of each one of his friends.

"What's the matter, Andy?" he huskily queried as he almost ran to the side of his closest friend, "what's happened?"

"Lee's surrendered," scowled Pinkney, as he halfheartedly gave to Dick the paper containing the announcement of the turn for the worse in the fortunes of the "cause."

"The hell you say!" retorted Dick. "Don't mind that, fellows, we'll win yet," he continued, "we're right and God's with us. Wait 'till the blow hits 'em tomorrow night, then the boot will be on the other foot."

"Damn the luck," almost shouted Jim Scott, "what'll we do now?"

"I'll go back to Washington today," replied Dick, "an' by the eternal right of the 'cause' you'll hear from me. Take care of Joe, Andy, 'till you hear from me, I'm going upstairs to pack up." He rushed out of the room and vanished up the stairway.

All that day and the day following the shutters were pulled close on the Crosby Street house. The city at large, however, bore a holiday look. The war was about to end. Lee had surrendered and the scattered elements of what was left of the Confederate army were in sore and desperate situations. Knots of agitated men were standing on the corners of the heaviest crowded streets earnestly and loudly discussing the final outcome of the war.

That night the police raided the Crosby Street house to discover that it was bare of furniture and that the "birds had flown," as the officer in charge of the raid operations tersely expressed it.

The next morning the city was in a panic. If one had found himself standing at the corner of Crosby and Prince Streets on that fateful night he more than likely would have been one of a number of others who would have been listening to a man reading: "THE PRESIDENT SHOT; ASSASSIN ESCAPED." If he had taken the paper from the reader and looked over into the right-hand corner of the page he could have read, "The body of an unknown, handsome woman about twenty-five years old was found floating in the East River at the foot of Catharine Street early this morning."

SNAKES

Eric D. Walrond's curiously winding roundelay of Caribbean whimsy whisks the reader from the "big island" through the back sides of London to the dark hills of Haiti, only to land in Harlem—there to sample the mystical vagaries of an exacting and exaggerated Providence. This story was published in February 1924.

Lloyd is a West Indian. I say this because it is vital if I am to get over the idea of this sketch. I remember the hot tawny days when he used to do reportorial chores on the *Jamaica Gleaner.* Chores that led him to Raccoon or down to that blistering spot, West Street, on a bullish scent for a "big tree" owlman. Then the war came. And Jamaica sent its black sons to France and Mesopotamia. There he also went. Gory tales drifted back to this isle. One I remember clearly. It had to do with a fur-lough party from the B.W.I. Regiment and some white American troops bivouacked in London. How true it is I do not know. Some English Red Cross lady, I think, started it. On the breast of one of the black soldiers was V.C. . . . and . . . well, but those were emotional days and under such conditions a woman is likely to do almost anything. So before you knew it there was a bunch of cockneys making an idol out of this black boy. Soon there was a snort of disgust, a commotion in the rear and somebody—several of them—let it be known that there was "goin' to be some bustin' done." Of course it really did not come off; it simmered down to an affair of scalps, and after that one was never asked whether Negro colonials were wards of civilization.

"I wonder where I can borrow some money," Lloyd whispered to me. "Gee, I'm up against it."

I always shake my head and smile at the absurd goatee that adorns the tip of his otherwise cleanly shaved chin. Of a rich bronze tint is the color in his face. Smoking one of those grotesque corkscrew pipes, he likes to draw his straw hat, with the Oxford band around it, down so that it looks as if it were grazing the upper edges of his shaggy black eyebrows. Add to that a pair of large, keen, searching, almost searing eyes of the richest sparkling emerald. A stubby, neatly trimmed mustache, very black, decorates thin tightly compressed lips.

In addition to a Lord Mayor of London stride, a freely gargled throat, tweed jacket and the white flannels, there is a walking stick, picked up on the banks of the Orinoco, that exaggerates to a highly envious point, to me, at any rate, the ancestral heritage of my mulatto overlord.

We were going up on the Riviera of Little Africa, Lloyd and I, one hot summer's night. In the wringing tropic months Harlem is exotic. Out of darkly deserted flats comely black and yellow girls tread the teeming polyglot streets. Up to the roof to bask in the syphilitic glow of moonlight or to send forth shadows, echoes, yawns, golden, mystic, languorous, from the guts and crevices of goat alley.

"I like fat women," he would puff over to me. "I hate scraggly, scrawny wenches."

By us the resistless tide of black folk—consumed by feverish longings—ebbs and flows. Examine their comely upturned faces. Salt tear stains; centuries of toil and drudgery obliterated magically. Tomorrow at sunrise as they bolt like herded cattle for the subway—plenty of time for that.

Now is night. And night is everything in the life of a Black Belt.

Again I am being fed on cockney tongue twistings. The nuances of speech are a great study to him. I am sure if I stick around him long enough I will soon be a past master in the dialectic arts of Essex, Lancaster, Surrey, Soho.

"Gee! I must get some dough——"

Near us is a crowd around a little bow-legged black girl doing the "Charleston"—a weird twisting outward of the heels and toes to the weird strumming of palms and ukeleles. On we pass.

We were about to turn a corner, Lloyd and I, when a man, a large black man, with huge, dragging feet, white, rolling eyes, swung around the corner.

"Oh, *maca fu' te*," he cried, falling about Lloyd's knees, and hugging them, "Oh, I know you'd come."

I side-stepped. I think I saw Lloyd's brows corrugate. In his eyes came that sharp, piercing, skeptical look that I knew so well.

"Get up, what's the matter with you, crazy?"

"Oh," bawled the man, loud as a bull, "Oh, the snakes! The snakes in me belly!"

Gnawing at the very oxygen, rending his clothes, the man undid his vest, savagely tore away his lavender silk shirt, and showed us his black, whirling belly. The frosty rays of the street lamp made it possible for us to see the very hair stalking out of his navel.

"Oh, mista, charge me anyt'ing you like. Only cure me! Cure me! Charge me anyt'ing you like. Only take the snakes out o' me belly."

"Here," he said, putting his hand into his pocket and taking out a roll of bills, "Here, mista, take it. Two hundred dollars! Tak' de snakes out o' me belly."

Grotesque phantoms danced and leaped out of the night, smiting our consciousness as his face wizened at the imaginary (?) pain caused by the wriggling snakes in his belly.

"I go tell you," he said, looking at Lloyd, sweat streaming down his black, black face. "I was in Haiti, *oui*. I was a road maker, me and Napoleon Francois. I live wit' 'im, I eat wit' 'im. I lov' Napoleon Francois. Then I go to the mountains and leav' Napoleon Francois wit' my red-headed woman. I lef' 'im wit' her. In my hut I had under the floor—under the boards, you know—over $30,000 in bright gold pieces. Three big canisters full, *oui*. I made that gold in San' Domingo. I leav' Napoleon Francois wit' my red-headed woman. In three months time I come back. I come back and I find no money. I look, I ass my woman, I ass Napoleon Francois. They say I crazy. I had no money. I say, 'What, I crazy? I no have no money? After the six year' I spent in San' Domingo? I have no money? I crazy?' They laugh at me and say I crazy.

"Now I t'ink Napoleon Francois is crook. I no want fight wit' him for he is big man. I leav' my wife and I go to nedder hut. I no slep' mo' wit' my red-headed woman. *I hate him!* I go to some house in the woods. Night time I feel somet'ing crawlin' on me. I look. I look at my foot. *He grow big! Big foot! Sacre gache!* I see three million shining snakes! Snakes in my bed. You know? I sleep on snakes!

"Napoleon Francois—I scream—I run—I try fo' run! I no can run! I no can run! They come in my belly—the snakes—feel—put yo' hand, feel I say, put yo' hand. Feel the snakes in my belly—feel I say—"

And, to my astonishment, Lloyd, taking the corkscrew pipe out of his mouth and frowning with the air of a physician diagnosing a hopeless case put his hand on the man's belly and felt it. He kept it there for a minute, took out his watch, finally shaking his head in despair.

"You can't cure, my friend?" cried the man eagerly. "You can't—"

"How much money have you got?" Lloyd asked, frowningly.

"Oh, I have plenty money. Here, you tak'! Two hundred dollars!"

After making sure that the bills were genuine Lloyd put them in his pocket, scribbled something on a bit of paper, and bade the man go to a West Indian apothecary's on Lenox Avenue.

"That," he puffed over to me as we resumed our walk up the avenue, "is a prescription for ten cents' worth of aloes and scrutcheoneel—it ought to do the bastard some good."

HANNAH BYDE

*In the following story, Dorothy West lays bare Hannah Byde, the bitter
product of excessive self-involvement and misplaced feelings of entitle-
ment. West deftly shows how Hannah Byde manipulates her husband and
others by playing a cruel death game. West published this story in June
1926.*

One comes upon Hannah in her usual attitude of bitter resignation,
gazing listlessly out of the window of her small, conventionally,
cheaply furnished parlor. Hannah, a gentle woman crushed by environment, looking dully down the stretch of drab tomorrows littered
with the ruins of shattered dreams.

She had got to the point, in these last few weeks, when the touch of
her husband's hand on hers, the inevitable proximity in a four-room
flat, the very sound of his breathing swept a sudden wave of nausea
through her body, sickened her, soul and body and mind.

There were moments—frightful even to her—when she pictured
her husband's dead body, and herself, in hypocritical black, weeping by
his bier; or she saw her own repellent corpse swirling in a turgid pool
and laughed a little madly at the image.

But there were times, too—when she took up her unfinished sack
for the Joneses new baby—when a fierce, strange pain would rack
her, and she, breath coming in little gasps, would sink to the floor,
clutching at the tiny garment, and, somehow, soothed, would be a little girl again with plaited hair, a little eager, visioning girl—"Mama,
don't cry! Some day I'll be rich an' ev'rything. You'll see, mama!"—
instead of a spiritless woman of thirty who, having neither the
courage nor strength to struggle out of the mire of mediocrity, had
married, at twenty, George Byde, simply because the enticing hon-
eymoon to Niagara would mark the first break in the uneventful circle of her life.

Holiday crowds hurrying in the street .... bits of gay banter floating up to her.... George noisily reading his paper.... Wreaths in the
shop window across the street.... a proud black family in a new red car
.... George uttering intermittent, expressive little grunts.... A blind
beggar finding a lost dollar bill.... a bullying policeman running in a
drunk .... George, in reflective mood, beating a pencil against his
teeth—

With a sharp intake of breath she turned on him fiercely, her voice
trembling with stifled rage, angry tears filming her eyes.

"For God's sake, stop! You'll drive me mad!"

He dropped his paper. His mouth fell open. He got to his feet, a
great, coarse, not unkindly, startled giant. "Hannah, I ain't—What
under the sun's the matter with you?"

She struggled for composure. "It's nothing. I'm sorry. Sorry,
George." But her eyes filled with pain.

He started toward her and stopped as he saw her stiffen. He said
quietly, "Hannah, you ain't well. You ain't never bin like this."

She was suddenly forced into the open. "No," she said clearly. "I'm
not well. I'm sick—sick to death of you, and your flat, and your cheap
little friends. Oh," she said, her voice choked with passion, "I'd like to
throw myself out of this window. Anything—anything to get away! I
hate you!"

She swayed like some yellow flower in the wind, and for a moment
there was the dreadful silence of partial revelation.

He fumbled, "No, no, hon. You're jes' nervous. I know you women.
Jes' you set down. I'll go see if Doc's home."

She gave a deep sigh. Habitual apathy dulled her tone. "Please don't
bother. I'm all right. It's nerves, I guess. Sometimes the emptiness of
my life frightens me."

A slow anger crept over him. His lips seemed to thicken. "Look here,
Hannah. I'm tiahed of your foolishness. There's limits to what a man
will stand. Guess I give you ev'rything anybody else's got. You never
have nothing much to do here. Y' got a phonygraph—and all them new
records. Y' got a piano. I give you money las' week to buy a new dress.
And yisterday y' got new shoes. I ain't no millionaire, Hannah. Ain't no
man livin' c'n do better'n his best."

She made a restless, weary little gesture. She began to loathe him.
She felt an almost insane desire to hurt him deeply, cruelly. She was
like a taunting mother goading her child to tears.

"Of course I appreciate your sacrifice." Her voice shook a little with
rising hysteria. "You're being perfectly splendid. You feed me. You

clothe me. You've bought me a player piano which I loathe—flaunting emblem of middle-class existence—Oh, don't go to the trouble of trying to understand that—And a stupid victrola stocked with the dreadful noises of your incomparable Mamie Waters. Oh, I'm a happy, contented woman! 'There never is anything to do here.' " She mocked in a shrill, choked voice. "Why, what in God's name is there to do in a dark, badly furnished, four-room flat? Oh, if I weren't such a cowardly fool, I'd find a way out of all this!"

The look of a dangerous, savage beast dominated his face. He stood, in this moment, revealed. Every vestige of civilization had fled. One saw then the flatness of his close-cropped head, the thick, bull-like shortness of his neck, the heavy nose spreading now in a fierce gust of uncontrollable anger, the beads of perspiration that had sprung out on his upper lip, one wondered then how the gentle woman Hannah could have married him. Shut her eyes against his brutal coarseness, his unredeemed ignorance—here no occasional, illiterate appreciation of the beautiful—his lack of spiritual needs, his bodily wants.

And yet one sees them daily, these sensitive, spiritless Negro women caught fast in the tentacles of awful despair. Almost, it seems, they shut their eyes and make a blind plunge, inevitably to be sucked down, down into the depths of dreadful existence.

He started toward her, and she watched his approach with controlled interest. She had long ago ceased to fear his anger and had learned to whip him out of a mood with a flick of her scathing tongue. And now she waited unmoving for the miracle of his heavy hand to end her weary life.

His eyes were black with rage. "By God, you drive me mad! If I was any less of a man I'd beat you till you ran blood. I must have been crazy to marry you. You—you—!"

There was a sharp rapping at the door, drowning his crazy words. Hannah smiled faintly, almost compassionately.

"The psychological moment. What a pity. George."

She crossed the floor, staggering for an instant with a sudden, sharp pain. She opened the door and unconsciously caught her lip in vexation as she admitted her visitor.

"Do come in," she said, almost dryly.

Tillie entered. Tillie, the very recent, very pretty, very silly wife of Doctor Hill: a newly wed popular girl finding matrimony just a big cramping.

She entered boldly, anticipating and ignoring the palpative annoyance in the stern set of Hannah's face. She even shrugged a little, a kind of wriggling that her friends undoubtedly called "cute." She spoke in the unmistakable tone of the middle-class Negro.

"Hello, you! And big boy George! I heard you all walking about downstairs, so I came on up. I bin sittin' by myself all evenin'. Even the gas went out. Here it's New Year's eve, I'm all dolled up, got an invite to a swell shebang sittin' pretty on my dresser—and my sweet daddy walks out on a case! Say, wouldn't that make you leave your happy home?"

George enjoyed it. He grinned sympathetically. Here was a congenial, jazz-loving soul, and, child-like, he promptly shelved his present grievance. He wanted to show off. He wanted, a little pathetically, to blot out the hovering bitterness of Hannah in the gay comraderie of Tillie.

He said eagerly, "Got some new records, Tillie."

She was instantly delighted. "Yeh? Run 'em round the green."

She settled herself in a comfortable chair and crossed her slim legs. Hannah went to the window in customary isolation.

George made a vain search of the cabinet. "Where're them records, Hannah?" he asked.

"On the table ledge," she murmured fretfully.

He struggled to his feet and shuffled over to the table. "Lord," he grumbled, "you ain't undone 'em yet?"

"I've been too tired," she answered wearily.

He and Tillie exchanged mocking glances. He sighed expressively, and Tillie snickered audibly. But their malicious little shafts fell short of the unheeding woman who was beating a sharp, impatient tattoo on the window pane.

George swore softly.

"Whassa matter?" asked Tillie. "Knot?"

He jerked at it furiously. "This devilish string."

"Will do," she asserted companionably. "Got a knife?"

"Yep." He fished in his pocket, produced it. "Here we go." The razor-sharp knife split the twine. "All set." He flung the knife, still open, on the table.

The raucous notes of a jazz singer filled the room. The awful blare of a frenzied colored orchestra, the woman's strident voice swelling, a great deal of "high brown baby" and "low down papa" to offend sensitive ears, and Tillie saying admiringly, "Ain't that the monkey's itch?"

From below came the faint sound of someone clumping, a heavy man stamping snow from his boots. Tillie sprang up, fluttered toward George.

"Jim, I'll bet. Back. You come down with me, G. B., and maybe you c'n coax him to come on up. I got a bottle of somethin' good. We'll watch the new year in and drink its health."

George obediently followed after. "Not so worse. And there oughta be plenty o' stuff in our ice-box. Scare up a little somethin', Hannah. We'll be right back."

As the door banged noisily, Hannah, with a dreadful rush of suppressed sobs, swiftly crossed the carpeted floor, cut short the fearful din of the record, and stood, for a trembling moment, with her hands pressed against her eyes.

Presently her sobs quieted, and she moaned a little, whimpering, too, like a fretful child. She began to walk restlessly up and down, whispering crazily to herself. Sometimes she beat her doubled fists against her head, and ugly words befouled her twisted lips. Sometimes she fell upon her knees, face buried in her outflung arms, and cried aloud to God.

Once, in her mad, sick circle of the room, she staggered against the table, and the hand that went out to steady her closed on a bit of sharp steel. For a moment she stood quite still. Then she opened her eyes, blinking them free of tears. She stared fixedly at the knife in her hand. She noted it for the first time: initialed, heavy, black, four blades, the open one broken off at the point. She ran her fingers along its edge. A drop of blood spurted and dripped from the tip of her finger. It fascinated her. She began to think: this is the tide of my life ebbing out. And suddenly she wanted to see it run swiftly. She wanted terribly to be drained dry of life. She wanted to feel the outgoing tide of existence.

She flung back her head. Her voice rang out in a strange, wild cry of freedom.

But in the instant when she would have freed her soul, darkness swirled down upon her. Wave upon wave of impenetrable blackness in a mad surge. The knife fell away. Her groping hands were like bits of aimless driftwood. She could not fight her way through to consciousness. She plunged deeply into the terrible vastness that roared about her ears.

And almost in awful mockery the bells burst into sound, ushering out the old, heralding the new: for Hannah, only a long, grey twelve month of pain-filled, soul-starved days.

As the last, loud note died away, Tillie burst into the room, followed by George and her husband, voluble in noisy badinage. Instantly she saw the prostrate figure of Hannah and uttered a piercing shriek of terror.

"Oh, my God! Jim!" she cried, and cowered fearfully against the wall, peering through the lattice of her fingers.

George, too, stood quite still, an half empty bottle clutched in his hand, his eyes bulging grotesquely, his mouth falling open, his lips ashen. Instinctively although the knife lay hidden in the folds of her dress, he felt that she was dead. Her every prophetic, fevered word leaped to his suddenly sharpened brain. He wanted to run away and hide. It wasn't fair of Hannah to be lying there mockingly dead. His mind raced ahead to the dreadful details of inquest and burial, and a great resentment welled in his heart. He began to hate the woman he thought lay dead.

Doctor Hill, puffing a little, bent expertly over Hannah. His eye caught the gleam of steel. Surreptitiously he pocketed the knife and sighed. He was a kindly, fat, little bald man with an exhaustless fund of sympathy. Immediately he had understood. That was the way with morbid, self-centered women like Hannah.

He raised himself. "Poor girl, she's fainted. Help me with her, you all."

When they had laid her on the couch, the gay, frayed, red couch with the ugly rent in the centre Hannah's nerve-tipped fingers had torn, Jim sent them into the kitchen.

"I want to talk to her alone. She'll come around in a minute."

He stood above her, looking down at her with incurious pity. The great black circles under her eyes enhanced the sad dark beauty of her face. He knew suddenly, with a tinge of pain, how different would have been her life, how wide the avenues of achievement, how eager the acclaiming crowd, how soft her bed of ease, had this gloriously golden woman been born white. But there was little bitterness in his thoughts. He did not resignedly accept the black man's unequal struggle, but he philosophically foresaw the eventual crashing down of all unjust barriers.

Hannah stirred, moaned a little, opened her eyes, in a quick flash of realization stifled a cry with her hand fiercely pressed to her lips. Doctor Hill bent over her, and suddenly she began to laugh, ending it dreadfully in a sob.

"Hello, Jim," she said, "I'm not dead, am I? I wanted so badly to die."

Weakly she tried to rise, but he forced her down with a gentle hand. "Lie quiet, Hannah," he said.

Obediently she lay back on the cushion, and he sat beside her, letting her hot hand grip his own. She smiled, a wistful, tragic, little smile.

"I had planned it all so nicely, Jim. George was to stumble upon my dead body—his own knife buried in my throat—and grovel beside me in fear and self-reproach. And Tillie, of course, would begin extolling my virtues, while you—Now it's all spoilt!"

He released her hand and patted it gently. He got to his feet. "You must never do this again, Hannah."

She shook her head like a wilful child. "I shan't promise."

His near-sighted, kindly eyes bored into hers. "There is a reason why you must, my dear."

For a long moment she stared questioningly at him, and the words of refutation that leaped to her lips died of despairing certainty at the answer in his eyes.

She rose, swaying, and steadied herself by her feverish grip on his arms. "No," she wailed, "no! no! no!!"

He put an arm about her. "Steady, dear."

She jerked herself free, and flung herself on the couch, burying her stricken face in her hands.

"Jim, I can't! I can't! Don't you see how it is with me?"

He told her seriously, "You must be very careful, Hannah."

Her eyes were tearless, wild. "But, Jim, you know— You've watched me. Jim! I hate my husband. I can't breathe when he's near. He—stifles me. I can't go through with it. I can't! Oh, why couldn't I have died?"

He took both her hands in his and sat beside her, waiting until his quiet presence should soothe her. Finally she gave a great, quivering sigh and was still.

"Listen, Hannah," he began, "you are nervous and distraught. After all, a natural state for a woman of your temperament. But you do not want to die. You want to live. Because you must, my dear. There is a life within you demanding birth. If you seek your life again, your child dies, too. I am quite sure you could not be a murderer.

"You must listen very closely and remember all I say. For with this new year—a new beginning, Hannah—you must see things clearly and rationally, and build your strength against your hour of delivery."

Slowly she raised her eyes to his. She shook her head dumbly. "There's no way out. My hands are tied. Life itself has beaten me."

"Hannah?"

"No. I understand Jim. I see."

"Right," he said, rising cheerfully. "Just you think it all over." He crossed to the door and called, "George! Tillie! You all can come in now."

They entered timorously, and Doctor Hill smiled reassuringly at them. He took his wife's hand and led her to the outer door.

"Out with you and me, my dear. We'll drink the health of the new year downstairs. Mrs. Byde has something very important to say to Mr. Byde. Night, G. B. Be very gentle with Hannah."

George shut the door behind them and went to Hannah. He stood before her, embarrassed, mumbling inaudibly.

"There's going to be a child," she said dully.

She paled before the instant gleam in his eyes.

"You're—glad?"

There was a swell of passion in his voice. "Hannah!" He caught her up in his arms.

"Don't," she cried, her hands a shield against him, "you're—stifling me."

He pressed his mouth to hers and awkwardly released her.

She brushed her hands across her lips, "You've been drinking. I can't bear it."

He was humble. "Just to steady myself. In the kitchen. Me and Tillie."

She was suddenly almost sorry for him. "It's all right, George. It doesn't matter. It's—nothing."

Timidly he put his hand on her shoulder. "You're shivering. Lemme get you a shawl."

"No." She fought against hysteria. "I'm all right, George. It's only that I'm tired. . . . tired." She went unsteadily to her bedroom door, and her groping hand closed on the knob. "You—you'll sleep on the couch tonight? I—I just want to be alone. Good night, George. I shall be all right. Good night."

He stood alone, at a loss, his hands going out to the closed door in clumsy sympathy. He thought: I'll play a piece while she's gettin' undressed. A little jazz'll do her good.

He crossed to the phonograph, his shoes squeaking fearfully. There was something pathetic in his awkward attempt to walk lightly. He started the record where Hannah had cut it short, grinning delightedly as it began to whir.

The jazz notes burst on the air, filled the narrow room, crowded out.

And the woman behind the closed door flung herself across the bed and laughed and laughed and laughed.

THE YELLOW PERIL: A ONE-ACT PLAY

Using Harlem as a setting, George S. Schuyler rushes out his main character, "the Girl," an octoroon who is fair enough to pass for white. An unsophisticated, self-absorbed woman, she believes her fair complexion gives her an advantage over the darker-complexioned women of Harlem. From her apartment she hustles well-to-do Harlem men for money, jewelry, furs, and other expensive items. Schuyler depicts her comeuppance brilliantly. He published this play in January 1925.

SCENE 1: The parlor of a Seventh Avenue apartment, North Harlem, New York City.
    Time: All the time.

CHARACTERS:

The Girl	
Martha	the Maid
Johnnie	the Rent Man
George	the Shoe Man
Frank	the Coat Man
Sammy	the Dress Man
Henry	the Hat Man
Charlie	the Jewelry Man
Phyllis	the Dog

It is about 7:00 p.m. The room is done in bright red. There are two windows backstage with lace curtains and green shades. Between them is a player piano with a neat pile of music rolls atop of it. A long bench is placed before it. On the left are two doors: the nearest to the audience leading into a hall, the other leading into the bathroom. Between these two doors is a library table covered with an imitation animal skin. On the table are several books and popular magazines. On the right are also two doors exactly opposite those on the left. The one nearest the audience leads into the kitchen, while the other leads into a bedroom. Between the two doors is a writing desk. There is a chair on each side of the piano, before the writing desk and alongside the library table. There is a telephone on the library table behind an artistic screen. In the center of the room downstage there is a day bed. The head is nearest the kitchen door. Near the bed is a smoking cabinet. One of its doors are open, and inside can be glimpsed a quart bottle of a shape familiar before Prohibition, and several whiskey glasses. Behind the bed is a floor lamp.

On this day bed reclines an octoroon who could easily pass for white. She possesses lustrous black hair; a chubby, painted baby face; delicate hands and very shapely limbs. She is garbed in pink silk pajamas with baby blue ribbons. On her feet are a dainty pair of house slippers of the same color. She is reading a magazine of the "snappy" variety, and taking occasional puffs from a gold-tipped cigarette. A gold watch encircles her wrist. Asleep on a blue sofa pillow at the foot of the bed is a fluffy white poodle dog. There is no light except that from the floor lamp. After the curtain rises she glances at her watch, and noting the time, rises, casts the cigarette into the receiver, tosses the magazine onto the table, and yawns and stretches lazily.

THE GIRL: Ho hum!... Martha! (*Calling*)

MARTHA: (*Opening the kitchen door*) Yes, Ma'am! (*She is a dark brown girl with rigidly straightened black hair. She wears the apron and cap of a maid*)

THE GIRL: Suppose you run over to the delicatessen store and get me a quart of rye—we're almost out of stuff. You'll find some money on my bureau. I may have some company tonight.

MARTHA: Yes, Ma'am.

THE GIRL: You'd better dust up the parlor a bit too, before you go. And don't forget to take Phyllis out for an airing.... Let's have some light here.

MARTHA: Yes, Ma'am! (*She switches on the lights and disappears into the kitchen*)

THE GIRL: (*Suddenly starting*) Oh! the rent. I almost forgot it! (*She goes over to the telephone*) Give me Bradhurst 00077. No! Not Rhinelander—Bradhurst! Bradhurst 00077! Yes, that's the number I gave—Bradhurst 00077! Hello! Is Mr. Russell in? (*Very sweetly*) May I speak to him, please? (*Martha re-enters with a duster and begins tidying up the room. She looks at the Girl, shakes her head and laughs knowingly*) Oh, Hello Johnnie!—Oh! I'm feelin' kinda bad tonight, sweetheart—no, nothing serious. Say, daddy, send me over fifty right away, please. Yes, for the rent—certainly—tomorrow's the fifteenth, ain't it? Now looka here, Johnnie, I don't want all that who—struck—John—I want that fifty dollars—now you're talking business—oh, I'm awfully sorry, Johnnie, but you can't come over tonight—my husband's coming in—no! I wouldn't dare take a chance—that's a good boy—Friday night, then—good bye, dearest. (*She kisses noisily into the mouthpiece, hangs up, and sighs heavily*) Well, Martha, that's settled. It takes me to make these men toe the mark. He tried to stall me for the rent. Can you beat that? Imagine tryin' to stall *me*!

MARTHA: You're a wonder alright. How do you do it? Don't they ever get wise, or anything?

THE GIRL: (*Dropping into the chair near the library table*) Not a chance in the world. It's easy to handle men because they're *all* saps. All you gotta do is to treat 'em as if they were about ten years old. It's easy as rollin' off a log.

MARTHA: Well, you certainly know these Harlem men, alright. I wonder how you manage to get such big bugs: lawyers, ministers, newspaper men, and that bunch. (*She tidies the day-bed*)

THE GIRL: Oh, there's not much to know about them, except that they are the biggest boobs in New York—and that's saying a lot, too. Of course, the married ones are the worst of the lot; especially the so-called society leaders and business men. Once in a while a fellow gets rambunctious on my hands, but I know how to handle 'em. (*She laughs*)

MARTHA: (*Going into the kitchen*) Well, I'd better get the liquor. (*Calling from the kitchen*) Do you want anything from the delicatessen?

THE GIRL: No, the booze is enough. Musn't give these johns too much—it spoils 'em. "Treat 'em rough" is my motto.

MARTHA: (*Appearing at the kitchen door dressed for the street*) Well, you can get away with it; you're a high yaller. I wish I was your color. I've used everything advertised in the Chicago *Defender*, but I'm just as black as I was when I came from Jamaica two years ago. Have you ever tried to "pass"? You could get by easy, anywhere. (*The girl goes into the bedroom*)

THE GIRL: (*Returning with a blue dressing gown which she lazily dons*) Sure. I lived downtown for a year or two; but there's better pickings up here. Downtown, I was only another white girl. Up here I am worshipped by all the successful business men, professional fellows and society swells, because I am a high yaller. Yes, it's lots easier up here because there's a less competition. These college graduates and swell dames don't stand no chance with me, even if I didn't finish grammar school. All I've got to do is to wink and I can have a hundred black men running after me.

MARTHA: Well, I can't understand it myself!

THE GIRL: Oh, it's easy to understand. You see, all these darkies are crazy about white women, but when they get prominent and up in the world, and all that, they don't dare let the shines know it, and they're ashamed to let the white folks know it. So they kinda compromise and get the whitest colored woman they can find. Of course, they won't admit that, but you can judge by their actions. I know 'em from A to Z. (*She opens the smoking cabinet, pours out a drink and swallows it, lights a cigarette, and then reclines luxuriously on the day bed. The maid chuckles and enters the bedroom*)

MARTHA: (*Coming out of the bedroom*) Come, Phyllis! (*She fastens the lead string on the dog and goes out by the hall door*)

THE GIRL: (*meditatively*) Now, if I can only get a new outfit for that party next week, I'll be sitting pretty. If that darky just brings that fur coat, I'll knock 'em dead. Put on airs with me, will they? I'll make all the dickties look like rag bags. (*The telephone rings. She answers it*) Hello! Hello! Mr. Russel! (*in surprise*) Alright, tell him to come up. (*Hangs up the receiver*) Hell! I told him not to come up here tonight. Damn fool! (*She paces back and forth angrily. The door bell rings. She admits a well dressed, shrewd-looking, sleek, black fellow*) Oh, Hello, Johnnie!

JOHNNIE: (*Kissing her*) Hello, sweetheart!

THE GIRL: (*Shaking her finger reproachfully at him*) I thought I told you not to come up tonight? You're always doing something to jam me!

JOHNNIE: (*apologetically*) Well, I had to come, darling. You know I couldn't trust anybody in Harlem with that amount of money. And I didn't dare send one of my kids with it. Here! (*Handing her several bills. He sits on the day bed.*)

THE GIRL: (*Counting the money*) Well, you could have sent a messenger boy with it. You're the dumbest real estate man I ever saw. You never think of my welfare at all. Here! what does this mean? You're five dollars short.

JOHNNIE: Well, you see honey, I . . .

THE GIRL: Aw, shut up! What do you mean; trying to hold out on me? I told you I wanted fifty dollars. Now if you can't give me what I need I'll get it somewhere else. You're not the only nigger in Harlem that wants a good looking mama! Put that in your pipe and smoke it. There's plenty of men who'll be glad to take your place. (*She throws the money on the library table*) If you're that cheap, I'll quit!

JOHNNIE: (*Thoroughly alarmed, drops to his knees in front of her*) Oh, honey! you wouldn't quit me, would you? I wouldn't have anyone but my wife, then.

THE GIRL: (*Pushing him aside, as she moves to the other side of the room*)

Well, it would serve you right. (*The telephone rings. The girl answers it*) Hello! Hello—Who?—Put him on the wire—Oh, hello! I wasn't expecting you tonight—Well—I suppose I can spare you a minute—Yes, come on up. (*She rings off*) See, (*Turning to Johnnie*) I told you the old man would be here tonight. Come on, beat it! (*Johnnie jumps up and looks around wildly for a place to hide, finally he makes for the hall door*) Come back here, you damn fool! He's coming that way. I told you he was coming but you *would* stick around. (*She glances wildly around the room. The door bell rings*) Quick! go in the kitchen and lock the door! Quick! (*Exit Johnnie into the kitchen. The door bell rings again*) In a minute! (*sweetly. The girl snatches his hat off the day-bed and throws it into the kitchen after Johnnie*) Keep still in there now, you big sap! And lock that door! (*Johnnie locks the door. The bell rings again*)

VOICE IN THE HALL: What's the matter in there? Open the door!

THE GIRL: Just a minute, dear! (*She admits a tall brown-skin man dressed as a clergyman and carrying a brief case. He looks around suspiciously*) Well, why don't you kiss me! (*Putting her arms around his neck*) Ain't you my little reverend?

THE MAN: Ss-h! not so loud. I don't want anybody to know I am here. I'm awfully glad to see you, honey! (*He embraces her*)

THE GIRL: Well, what did you bring me, Georgie, dear?

GEORGE: (*Reaching into the brief case and extracting a bottle of liquor*) Look at this pre-war stuff, will you?

THE GIRL: (*Putting the bottle in the smoking cabinet*) Is *that* all you brought? Where are the shoes I asked you for?

GEORGE: Now, now, don't be so quick to get on your high horse. (*He reaches into the brief case and brings out a pair of expensive shoes*) Here's your shoes.

THE GIRL: (*Embracing him*) Oh, George! you're so good to me! You're worth a hundred of these other men!

GEORGE: That's the talk, honey! (*He starts to take off his coat*)

THE GIRL: Oh, George! I'm sorry, but you can't stay. You know my husband's coming tonight and you don't want to jam me, do you?

GEORGE: (*Reluctantly rising*) Well, alright, but it seems like you're always hustling me off.

THE GIRL: Aw, quit cryin'! You make me sick. A whole lot you care about me. You wouldn't care if my husband cut my throat . . . you and your cheap shoes!

GEORGE: (*aroused*) Cheap shoes! What do you mean; cheap shoes? Them shoes cost me fifteen dollars!

THE GIRL: Well, what of it? Do you think this is a charitable institution? Come on, beat it! (*The telephone rings*) Good God! There he is now. (*She answers the telephone*) Hello! Hello!—Yes—Yes. Well, come on. Where are you now?—In about five minutes—yes—alright then. (*She hangs up the receiver and turns on George excitedly*) Come on—quick! I told you to get out of here. Go in the bedroom! Hurry up!

GEORGE: (*Also excited*) Alright. Hurry up and get rid of him. I've got to attend prayer meeting tonight! (*Exit George into the bedroom*)

JOHNNIE: (*Opening the kitchen door*) Is it alright now?

THE GIRL: (*savagely*) Shut that door, and lock it! (*Exit Johnnie. The door bell rings. She admits a small black fellow who carries a large bundle*)

THE NEWCOMER: Evening, old dear! (*Embracing her*) Look what I brought you?

THE GIRL: Oh you dear! What is it?

THE NEWCOMER: (*Unwrapping the bundle and displaying a long fur coat*) How do you like that, sweetie?

THE GIRL: Oh, Frank! You're worth a hundred of these other men! You're so good to me. How much did it cost?

FRANK: (*dramatically*) Six hundred berries!

THE GIRL: (*Much impressed*) Nothing cheap about you! You must have made a touch.

FRANK: Well, I'm not treasurer of my lodge for nothing, you know. I handle all the funds, and I might as well spend it on you as to have them throwing it away on monkey uniforms and conventions.

THE GIRL: (*hopefully*) Have you got a meeting tonight, Frankie?

FRANK: Nope. I'm gonna stay right here with you.

THE GIRL: Oh! you can't, not tonight. My husband's coming home tonight. You'd better leave now. You don't want to jam me, do you?

FRANK: I don't see why I should run as soon as I get here. I ain't goin' nowhere!

THE GIRL: (*tearfully*) Oh, Frankie, you must! (*The telephone rings*)

FRANK: Naw I won't. I ain't spendin' six hundred iron men for nothin'. I wouldn't run for nobody!

THE GIRL: (*Answering the telephone*) Hello! Hello! Yes, it's me—no, don't come up for a while yet—well—alright then.

FRANK: (*alarmed*) Who's that?

THE GIRL: Why it's my husband. I told you he was coming. Come on, beat it!

FRANK: (*Racing around the room*) Where shall I hide? Where shall I hide? (*He tries the kitchen and bedroom doors and finding them locked, opens the window on the right and steps out on the fire escape. The girl rushes after him, pulls down the sash and lowers the shade*)

THE GIRL: Oh, my God! what a mess! If I ever get out of this . . . (*The doorbell rings. She rushes to the door and admits a gigantic black fellow with a bundle under his arm.*) Oh, you dear boy! I wasn't expecting you so soon. I'm not even dressed yet. (*They embrace*) What have you got there, Sammy?

SAMMY: (*Grinning*) Oh, I've got just what you want. (*He unwraps the bundle and displays a new dress*) Not so bad for seventy-five dollars, eh?

THE GIRL: (*rapturously*) Oh it's so beautiful! You're worth a hundred of these other Harlem men, Sammy. Just what I wanted, too. Oh, you're a darling. (*She kisses him*)

SAMMY: (*Boasting*) Oh, that's nuthin'. I can get a girl like you anything you want.

THE GIRL: Can you, dear?

SAMMY: I'll say I can! . . . Got anything to drink?

THE GIRL: Sure. Did you ever know me when I didn't have anything to drink! (*She pours both a drink*) I'm sorry you can't stay, Sammy. You see, my husband's coming in tonight.

SAMMY: (*huffily*) Say! what do you think I am? What do you think I'm buyin' this stuff for? I had to borrow twenty bucks off my old lady to help pay for that (*Pointing to the gown*).

THE GIRL: Now, Sammy, be nice! I can't help it 'cause he's coming in tonight. I didn't know it until this morning. You wouldn't jam me, would you? (*She looks fearfully at the doors and the right hand window*)

SAMMY: (*suspiciously*) I ain't gonna move a step. So that's that. (*The doorbell rings. He glances wildly about*) Where'll I go?

THE GIRL: Oh God! Go somewhere. (*He rushes around to the doors*) Go out on the fire escape until I get rid of him! (*Pointing to the left-hand window*)

SAMMY: (*Making a dive for the window*) Alright! Alright! (*He starts to raise the window, but it sticks*) What the hell's the matter with this damn window? (*The door bell rings again*)

THE GIRL: Quick! Quick! (*She helps him raise the window and pushes him out, lowering the sash and the shade. The bell rings again, supplemented by a kick at the door*)

A VOICE: Open up there!

THE GIRL: (*Rushing to the door*) Alright, dear! (*She opens the door and admits a small, slender brown-skin man. His hair is slicked down, he sports a deep red necktie and wears a wrist watch. He has a soprano voice and a mincing walk. He carries a hat box*) Hello! What you doing up here tonight? Why didn't you telephone?

THE SLENDER ONE: I just thought I'd surprise you, dearie. (*He drops the hatbox and embraces her*)

THE GIRL: Kiss me on the cheek, dear. You know what I've always told you. . . . What have you got there; something for me?

THE SLENDER ONE: Oh, you know I have, sugar lump! (*He opens the box and brings forth a gorgeous hat*) Isn't it just perfectly beautiful?

THE GIRL: Oh, Henry! It's just what I wanted. You're worth a hundred of these *men* in Harlem. (*She embraces him, turning her head aside*) On the cheek, dear!

HENRY: Now we're going to have a perfectly lovely time, aren't we, darling? You see, I've worn a soft collar—I'm always looking out for you.

THE GIRL: Now, Henry, you can't stay.

HENRY: (*Alarmed*) Oh, Honey! I got off from the "Y" early tonight especially for you. Won't you let me stay? (*He drops to his knees and placing his arms around her, pulls her toward him. She pushes him aside*)

THE GIRL: No, you can't stay! I'm not going to have my husband come in here and catch anything like you around!

HENRY: (*Jumping up*) Now dear, that's terribly mean of you. I would almost say it's downright despicable, the way you treat me. I would, I would, I would. You have no idea what I went through in order to get the twenty dollars for that hat! (*He buries his face in his arms and sobs with much heaving of shoulders*) You treat me abominably, that's what you do. You're mean, mean, mean to me!

THE GIRL: (*Revolted*) Come on, snap out of it, you little sissy! Get on back to your Y.M.C.A. before my husband gets here. Beat it!

HENRY: (*Indignantly, hands on hips*) So that's the way you treat me, eh? I've a good mind never to come here again!

THE GIRL: Well, I've been expecting you to pull something like that. That's why I had you to get the dog for me. (*The door bell rings and Henry jumps in alarm, glances wildly about*) Quick! Under the bed! That's him now. (*Henry dives under the bed. His feet tap the floor in fright*) Keep your feet still, you little fool. (*The bell rings again*) Alright (*loudly*), just a minute. (*She opens the door and admits a big black man in policeman's uniform*) Hello, dear! I've been so lonesome here without you.

THE POLICEMAN: (*Kissing her*) I know you have, honey. (*He has a booming bass voice*)

THE GIRL: Why didn't you 'phone, Charlie? (*He sits in the large chair by the library table and tosses his hat aside. She sits on his knee*)

CHARLIE: I wanted to surprise my little girl.

THE GIRL: Well, you certainly did. I didn't expect you tonight. (*Henry, under the day-bed, can't make his feet behave. Charlie and the girl both hear the tapping*) That's them kids upstairs, honey bunch. (*Embracing him*)

CHARLIE: Oh! I was wondering . . . I see you gotta lotta new stuff. (*Glancing at the coat, hat and gown*)

THE GIRL: Yes, I was downtown shopping today.

CHARLIE: Well, I was shopping too. How do you like that? *(He produces a diamond ring from its box)* Ain't it a beauty?

THE GIRL: (*Slipping the ring on her finger*) Oh, Charlie! You're such a *wonderful* daddy. You're worth a hundred of these other Harlem men! (*She holds her hand up to the light. The ring sparkles*)

CHARLIE: (*Kissing her*) I sure had to shake down the bootleggers to get enough to buy that!

THE GIRL: Won't you have a drink before you go, Charlie?

CHARLIE: Waddaya mean; go? I'm stayin' right here, babe. (*Producing a big flask*) Try some of this Scotch. I got it off that druggist on 135th Street. It's good stuff. (*The girl pours both of them a stiff drink*)

CHARLIE: Well, here's excitin' times!

THE GIRL: They're exciting enough for me right now! (*They drink. Henry's feet misbehave again. The cop listens*)

CHARLIE: What's that?

THE GIRL: Oh, that's them kids upstairs, honey!

CHARLIE: Oh! I forgot. (*The door bell rings. The girl starts*)

THE GIRL: That must be Martha. (*She opens the door and Martha enters with a package and Phyllis*)

MARTHA: (*Glancing at Charlie and handing the package to the Girl*) There's the stuff.

CHARLIE: More hooch, eh? Atta baby!

MARTHA: Yessir, more stuff. (*She unleashes the dog, who immediately makes for Henry's feet. Martha starts for the kitchen*)

THE GIRL: (*quickly*) Martha, play a roll for us, won't you? Just put your things on the piano, or a chair.

MARTHA: (*wonderingly*) Yes, Ma'am! (*She walks to the piano. The telephone rings. Charlie and the Girl reach for it simultaneously. Charlie, being nearest, reaches it first. He answers. Martha takes off her things*)

CHARLIE: Hello! (*Henry's feet misbehave and Phyllis sniffs around him*) Yes—What's that?—On the fire escape! (*The Girl starts*) Alright, I'll fix 'em! (*He replaces the receiver*)

THE GIRL: What is it? (*She is quite agitated*)

CHARLIE: (*Reaching for his gun*) Two crooks on your fire escape, the janitor says. (*Martha runs to first the kitchen door and then the bedroom door. Charlie rushes to the window on the left and shouts out*) Come in here, you! (*The Girl sinks weakly into the chair. Sammy raises the window and crawls into the room*) Put 'em up! Come out o' there, you other guy! (*Frank raises the other window and enters, ranging himself alongside Sammy, with hands pawing the air. The Girl tries to dart out the hall door*) Where you goin', Corinne? Come back here! I can handle these bums. (*Keeping the two men covered, he grasps her robe*)

THE GIRL: (*Sinking back into the chair*) Oh, my God! Oh, my God!

MARTHA: These doors are locked from the inside; I can't open them! (*Henry kicks at the dog. Charlie sees the kick*)

CHARLIE: Uh-huh! I thought there was something crooked here. Come out from under there! (*Henry emerges*) Why, you dirty sissy! What are *you* doing here?

MARTHA: I can't get in the kitchen or bedroom.

CHARLIE: Come out o' them rooms or I'll shoot! (*The two doors open and Johnnie and George emerge with their hats on and hands elevated. The cop motions them over toward the piano*)

MARTHA: (*Rushing over to the girl, who has fainted across the table*) She's fainted! Call the doctor! (*She tries to revive her*)

CHARLIE: What are you guys doin' here?

THE MEN: (*In a chorus*) We came to see Corinne!

CHARLIE: (*Turning to Corinne*) Ah, hah! So! *Five* timing me, eh? (*Corinne, revived by Martha's ministrations, jumps up wildly*)

CORINNE: I don't know them, Charlie. Honest I don't. I never saw 'em before. (*Becoming hysterical*) Really, I'm a good little girl. (*She drops on the day bed, wringing her hands and sobbing*)

THE OTHER MEN: (*In a chorus*) She's a liar; she's my gal! (*They point at her accusingly. Martha grabs her things and runs out the hall door*)

JOHNNIE: I pay her rent!

GEORGE: I buy her shoes!

FRANK: I buy her coats!

SAMMY: I buy her dresses!

HENRY: (*In his soprano*) I also purchase her millinery and I also gave her that dog to remind her of me. (*He places one hand on his hip and smooths his hair with the other. They all make a belligerent motion toward him, and glare. He wilts*) Now, now, gentlemen! Be yourselves, be yourselves!

CHARLIE: (*Stuffing his gun in his pocket and reaching for his cap*) Well, I guess we're all a bunch o' saps. I'd wear this club out on her head, but my wife would hear about it.

JOHNNIE ⎫
GEORGE   ⎬   Mine, too!
FRANK   ⎮
SAMMY   ⎭

HENRY: And I would just be *ruined;* positively *ruined.* (*They all make a belligerent motion toward him, and glare. He wilts again*) Tutt! Tutt! I mean no harm, gentlemen. I mean no harm!

CHARLIE: Well, let's get our stuff off her. I guess we're monkey men, like the rest of the guys in Harlem. (*They all rush for their things. Corinne sits up dejectedly*)

JOHNNIE: (*Sweeping his money off the table and rushing out*) My money!

GEORGE: (*Following him, waving the shoes*) My shoes!

FRANK: (*Following him, waving the coat*) My coat!

SAMMY: (*Following him with the dress*) My dress!

HENRY: (*Picking up Phyllis and the hat, and skipping out the door*) My hat! My dog!

CHARLIE: (*Snatching the ring off Corinne's finger and swaggering out*) My ring!

CORINNE: My God!

CURTAIN

At the Coffee House

In this one-act play set in Greenwich Village, George S. Schuyler creates a story about writers of questionable talent and publishers who seek profit from black stereotypes. This play was published in June 1925.

SCENE—A cellar in Greenwich Village. A few chairs and tables, weird and grotesque paintings and sketches on the walls, a battered upright piano in one corner and windows curtained with batik, complete the picture. A shabbily dressed man and woman are chatting at one of the tables. In the corner a waitress in Russian village costume sits reading a copy of the Dial.

THE MAN: Yes, I'm up against it. Looks like the publishers are in a conspiracy against me for some reason or other. I am certainly getting sick of the whole writing game.

THE WOMAN: What have you been writing?

THE MAN: Oh, poetry, short stories, fantasies, criticism—about everything. I guess I've got a trunk crammed with manuscripts. I can't seem to write anything that will satisfy the publishers. I must get some money from somewhere or I don't know what I'll do. My landlady is getting mighty nasty—I'm three weeks behind, you know.

THE WOMAN: Why don't you try to think of something very unusual to write about. Something about Indians, the South Seas or life in the jungle?

THE MAN: But my dear girl! I don't know anything about those subjects.

THE WOMAN: Why you silly boy! Where did you ever get the idea that you have to know anything much about anything to be a literary success nowadays? A day or two at the public library will furnish you with all the information you need. You have the same false idea that hampers all the other unsuccessful writers. You imagine one has to know a subject from first hand in order to make a living writing about it.

THE MAN: Well, I guess you're right.

THE WOMAN: I know I am! Look at Octavus Cohen, Hugh Wiley, Irvin Cobb, and a whole lot of others. Do you imagine there are any darkies in existence like those in their stories?

THE MAN: If there are, I've never met them. By the way, that gives me an idea! I could write something about the Negroes! Of course, I don't know anything about them except what I've read in the newspapers and magazines, but, as you say, that doesn't matter.

THE WOMAN: Not at all. The average person who reads your stuff— even the publishers—know as little about it as you do. As long as it is funny or very grotesque and creepy, it will make a hit.

THE MAN: But somehow, I rather hate to write on a subject on which I am so ignorant. Besides the poor shines have such a hard time that I hate to do them an injustice.

THE WOMAN: Humph! No wonder you haven't made anything at the writing game! If all the writers waited until they were familiar with their subjects, American literary output would dwindle to almost nothing.

THE MAN: Yes, I suppose so—judging by the stuff that gets into print. By the way, you used to be a reporter. You ought to be able to give me some tips on this matter. You've written news reports on Negroes, haven't you?

THE WOMAN: Lots of them—I used to be court reporter. Its the easiest kind of writing. If you want to write something funny do it in dialect and throw in plenty of references to chicken, watermelon, razors, gin, singing mammies, and all that sort of thing. As for the weird stuff; that's even easier yet.

THE MAN: How so?

THE WOMAN: Well, you've read the Russians, haven't you?

THE MAN: Of course. Who hasn't read the Russians?

THE WOMAN: And you've read Freud?

THE MAN: Yes. I'm a regular Greenwich Villager.

THE WOMAN: Well, write something about the shines in the stark Russian manner. Sketch in an African background with the throb of tom-toms, the medley of jungle noises, the muttering and incantations of the witch doctor, the swish of javelins and the last lunge of a wounded rhinocerous. You've been in the Village long enough to know how to do this. It's a part of racial memory foundation, you know. Then show the thin veneer of white civilization crumbling off the educated darky and revealing the savage underneath.

THE MAN: Capital! You're a genius. I might even bring in a white woman—all the popular writers on the Negro do, you know. I could have the educated shine groveling at her feet begging for forgiveness and then going insane with rage when she scorns him and calls him "Nigger."

THE WOMAN: Fine! Right there would be a good place to strip off the thin veneer of culture and education, and reveal the Negro underneath.

THE MAN: That would give me an excellent opportunity to philosophize to the extent of several pages on the inability of the Negro to adapt himself to our civilization. Suppose we collaborate on this—you need money, too.

THE WOMAN: You bet I need money. I'll take you up on that. You outline the story tonight and I'll go over it with you at my house.

THE MAN: Alright then! I'll go right to work on it (rising). Which way are you going; up or down?

THE WOMAN: (Also rising)—I'm going down.... Wish I was going your way. (They walk toward the door.)

THE WAITRESS: Fifty cents, please! (Speaking to the man.)

THE WOMAN: That's alright, I'll pay it! Here! (Handing her the money.)

THE WAITRESS: Thanks! (She resumes her reading.)

THE MAN: Well, good night!

THE WOMAN: Good night! (Exit both.)

THE WAITRESS (CONTEMPTUOUSLY): Tramps!

(Three months later)

SCENE—The same Coffee House. The place is now disguised as a native hut in the South Sea Islands. Papier mache spears and war clubs adorn the straw-covered walls. There is a new grand piano, new chairs and new tables, but the batik curtains have disappeared. Just outside each window is a futurist painting supposed to represent Polynesian scenes. Each painting is indirectly lighted so as to give the effect of looking out into a tropical world. The same waitress is there dressed as a hula-hula dancer. She is reading a copy of the New Republic. The same man and woman, now faultlessly dressed, are enjoying a bottle of post-Volstead beverage at one of the tables.

THE MAN: So I told him I would give him three thousand dollars for the place; but not a cent more. After a little haggling he gave in.

THE WOMAN: Well, it certainly looks fine in here. You've fixed things up wonderfully. You know I'm living on Long Island now! Cozy little place, too. Only paid fifteen thousand for it. We can look right out on the Sound.

THE MAN: That's fine! Who looks out for the place while you're away?

THE WOMAN: Oh, I've got a swell butler—a colored fellow. He appears to be unusually intelligent. He tells me he used to write about Negroes, too, but the publishers wouldn't give him a look in. Too serious, I suppose.

THE MAN: Yes, I guess so—Have you heard the latest from our publisher?

THE WOMAN: No, what's up?

THE MAN: Oh, nothing much. He's just bringing out the twenty-fifth edition of our book, that's all. We'll get another big check soon.

THE WOMAN: Can you beat it? After all, literature does pay.

THE MAN: Yes, especially stuff about Negroes.

PART THREE

BOOK AND THEATER
REVIEWS

SHODDYISM CALLED HISTORY

In the following essay, William N. Colson reviews three books published in 1919: The American Negro in the Great War *by W. Allison Sweeney,* The American Negro in the World War *by Emmett J. Scott, and* The World War for Human Rights *by Kelly Miller.*

History at best is a fallacy. It is a record of only the most exceptional of human phenomena. A history true in every sense is not to be found on the shelves. Those who have written history have sought almost always to justify a stirring belief, or to subserve a sentimental interest in behalf of some antecedent impression or current conviction. The record of history, the lesson of human experience, can be written only by those who have no interest to subserve except the truth. They must possess absolutely no desire to justify a previous belief. The historical method is one of the most serious imperfections of human reasoning.

The subjects of this review by no means, however, merit such an introductory criticism, since they are not, in fact, histories at all. They are picture books, containing rambling narratives of some of the principle experiences of the Negro in the great war, at home and abroad, arranged according to topics. The materials are drawn from military orders, personal observations, but generally from newspapers. It is, therefore, often inaccurate. Each of the three books is written in easy style, though Kelly Miller and Sweeney often burst into affected rhetorical persiflage. The three authors are one in their praise of the loyalty of the Negro, whatever the attitude of the government. They jointly commit the fallacy of assuming that liberty and freedom are the inevitable rewards of bearing arms in war time.

Emmett J. Scott was a special assistant to the Secretary of War, during the participation of the United States in the conflict. As a matter of fact he was little more than a "morale officer," a special office designed to keep the Negro people contented and fooled about the real issues of the conflict with respect to themselves. Mr. Scott had first hand access to the sources of material. He has selected by no means all the matter available from the War Department, however, nor has he treated the material selected with success. The outstanding purpose of the book seems to be a vindication of Scott himself. W. Allison Sweeney is the contributing Editor of the *Chicago Defender*. His chief source of material was the newspapers and the views of personal correspondents. Kelly Miller was the Dean of the College of Arts and Sciences of Howard University when his book was written. Neither one of these works is a credit to scholarship. They are designed, apparently, to cater to the great mass of half educated Negroes, whose racial consciousness would impel them to buy "Negro Histories," whatever the merits of the matter between the covers.

Mr. Sweeney's book treats of the strength of German militarism; America's entrance into the war; the ready response of the Negro to the draft; previous wars in which the Negro figured; unqualified loyalty of the black man; the Negro fighting units, the 92d Division, the 369th, 370th, 371st and 372d Infantries; the Service of Supply; the war welfare agencies and the Negro; and reconstruction and the new Negro. Most of the discussion is either sentimental, controversial or hyperbolic. Of the twenty-three chapters, as a sample of the subject matter, one contains a roster of Negro officers commissioned at Des Moines, while another full chapter is in the form of a newspaper account, taken from the New York *World*. The best piece of work in Mr. Sweeney's book is a report of the operations of the 8th Illinois Infantry, contributed by Captain John H. Patton. Much of the value of the book is lessened when the author seeks to engage in controversy and blind prophecy. Mr. Sweeney has no conception whatever of reconstruction and the new Negro. He abounds in his praise of such lovers of Negro ignorance as Colonel William Haywood, and of such hypocrites as Woodrow Wilson. Mr. Sweeney ends his book by voicing the delusion that out of war a new nation has emerged.

Emmett J. Scott, in seeking to vindicate himself, has exhibited his own servility—how he was recommended for his position by the basest of Negro traitors, Robert Russa Moton, and how acceptable he was to the reactionary forces of the nation. Mr. Scott's treatment and subject matter are not much different from that of Mr. Sweeney, but Mr. Scott is less controversial. Most of his matter, as does that of Mr. Sweeney, belongs in the appendix rather than in the body of the work. Again, Mr. Scott often arrogates to himself more credit than he is due. He leads the reader to believe that he was responsible in large measure for the fact of Negro officers, see page 62. Mr. Scott also perpetrates the lie in the form of a War Department Bulletin that the Negro was not discriminated against in the draft. He cites many injustices towards the black soldiers but seldom tells what he did to correct them, other than answer letters stating that "requests for investigations will be cheerfully complied with." Scott's correspondence is of little value. The natural inference is that he would be holding his position, even today, whatever unjust policy the War Department might have practiced toward the Negro. The book is written in simple style, but the author often digresses from the conventional third person to emphasize a statement by using the first. Lieutenant T. T. Thompson has contributed material of value to this work. Where the author indulges in opinion, he reflects the most reactionary attitude. He accepts and praises the doctrine that "rights and privileges" are dependent upon the "duties and responsibilities" of citizenship. He does not fathom the biological analogy that a child race, like the human child, possesses "rights, privileges, powers, and immunities" long before it is able to bear the burden of "duties and responsibilities"; that biologically "duties and responsibilities" are dependent upon "rights and privileges." Mr. Scott also fails to state that the Negro soldier is in a worse plight at the end of the war than when the author took up his position as special assistant to Secretary Baker.

Kelly Miller devotes twenty-two chapters of his work to general aspects of the war, without references to the Negro. He adds a chapter, however, on "The Negro in the World War" and "The Disgrace of Democracy," an open letter to Woodrow Wilson. The author is guilty of a rather bold piece of trickery when he places on the back cover of his book the title: "Negro Soldier in Our War." This is an unpardonable piece of criminal camouflage, because only the merest fraction of his book is devoted to the Negro. Kelly Miller's treatment of general aspects of the war reads like the column of a magazine section of a Sunday newspaper. But a return to the Negro question finds him controversial, militant and committing the usual fallacy of history. His treatment abounds in error, both as to fact and opinion. In speaking of the Des Moines camp and colored officers, Mr. Miller says that the camp was an "honor." Provision for the Des Moines camp was made in May, 1917. In placing credit for the camp, the author says: "It is probable that the honor belongs as much to Henry Johnson and Needham Roberts as to anyone else." Then follows a reference to the citation of these two men for gallantry. The writer then adds, see page 458:

"Whether this citation arrived on May 19th, 1917 by design or by accident, it served the purpose of dissolving completely all opposition to the idea of training Negroes to halt the Hun. Immediately thereafter, the War Department created a training camp for educated Negroes at Fort Des Moines, Iowa." *As a matter of fact, the exploit of these two heroes took place a year later than the above date and nearly a year after the Des Moines camp became a so-called "honor" to the Negro.* Dean Miller has done his fast waning reputation great harm in his latest publication.

Neither of these works can be recommended for either information or presentation. They are neither scientific nor scholarly. They leave untold the bitter, but whole truth, about what the soldiers suffered and endured in the great conflict. They picture the Negro as one loyal and willing to fight, because he owes much to a great country. They omit to state the fact that over one hundred thousand of the three hundred and fifty thousand black conscripts were illiterate, because their country denies them opportunity. But illiterate men make slavish soldiers, and slavish soldiers are the best soldiers. A history of the Negro in the recent war is yet to be written.

PHASES OF DU BOIS

William N. Colson reviews Darkwater, *W.E.B. Du Bois's collection of essays, poems, critiques, and short stories, which was published in 1920.*

"The Souls of Black Folk" (1903) states the problem of which "Darkwater" is the tragedy. "Darkwater" could emerge only out of the historic background of "The Souls of Black Folk." Though Mr. Du Bois falsely assumed in 1903 that the problem of the twentieth century was the problem of the color line, he gave genuine expression to the spiritual strivings of those who lived within the Veil. The double point of view, one for "mine own people," and one for those of the skin *blanc*, which all black men in a white world possess, is the ever-existent fact. Emancipation was a strange dream and then a poignant disillusionment. Booker T. Washington meant opportunism and expediency rather than principle and justice. There was need for a lofty vision in the land of the new slavery. Then "The Wings of Atalanta" began to whir in the darkness, and education was spelled. Alexander Crummel became "perfect by suffering," but "The Coming of John" was tragic. From this strange mixture of hope and hopelessness sprang the roots of racial culture. There was an abiding faith in the fathers—in their ultimate achievement of freedom. It was a struggle between good and evil, with evil on the successful offensive. But resolutely, "Wed with truth, I dwell above the Veil," was the new hope.

"Darkwater" (1920) is hope deferred. A contemporaneous literary autobiography, it definitely marks Mr. Du Bois as a *poet* rather than a thinker. The essays, sketches, poems, prose-poetry, critiques and short stories therein contained are but reflections of the *artist* himself. "Vates," says Carlyle, "means both prophet and poet"; *vates* stresses

212 · *The* Messenger *Reader*

the moral and the esthetic in the light of originality, sincerity and genius. These characteristics Mr. Du Bois embodies, but often to the
detriment of the scientific and radical. "Darkwater" is a despairing *cri
de coeur;* an irrefutable fact of agony. However, Mr. Du Bois is a ro-
manticist of a high order. Mystic, passionate, free spirited, even his
more serious essays are never mere prose. They are prayers and pan-
egyrics, strangely wild and picturesque, imaginative, satiric and expressive of heavy feeling. In them is the vigor of Victor Hugo and the
sensuousness of Dumas, the elder. Yet Mr. Du Bois is never to be commonly classified after the manner of the old criticism. A shade or two
more of bald reality would make his style comparable to the natural-
ism of Zola. A lyric outburst breaks in to recall the stimulated on-
slaught of De Quincey; even over ugliness, lynching and death the
prose-poet waxes into song. His use of the themes of death and
beauty is mildly suggestive of Edgar Allan Poe, of the arabesque and
of grotesqueness. Finally, Mr. Du Bois has *taste,* the power to express
the lives of others by the *genius* of his own self-expression.

The creation of life over again is the aim of the *artist.* "Darkwater"
comes within Hegel's conception of literature as "an expression of
race, age and environment." Because Mr. Du Bois has recreated for us
the story of his life from Fisk to Germany, and from Wilberforce to
"The Crisis," and made us feel again the joys and sorrows of "The
Shadow of Years," he has done what he has set out to do. Yet he has not
gone by any means to the uttermost depths. He of the "Talented
Tenth" has not always comprehended the mind and aspirations of the
man farthest down. And with it all there is too much of reliance on
American and European standards of abstract justice rather than on
the standards of right, regardless of race, age and environment. The
book contains more of rich social experience and impression than solution of social problems. Though the life of the author reacted might-
ily at the clash of the War for Gold, this reaction failed to provoke a
plan of constructiveness. This review follows in general the plan which
the author has laid down for himself.

Du Bois, as *idealist,* in his suppressed and poignant "Shadow of
Years," was possessed of will and ability. Early discovering the existence of the Veil, it was his boyish delight to excel his white fellows in
order to prove the fatuity, the *betise* of that Veil. Then, paradoxically, he
was sent away from Massachusetts down to a light in the darkness of
the South, to Fisk. "Marvelously inspired and deeply depressed,"
learning meant more learning. Then came trips within and without the

Veil—to Harvard and prize and honor, to Berlin, to Paris, to Rome—will and ability plus luck, alysium, but lo, back to "the land of the free" once more. Then came the vexed problem of life, bread and butter versus ideals—Wilberforce at $750 per year, the Philadelphia Negro, Atlanta University and dreams. Some force must rise to rend away the Veil! Booming, flooding Niagara was the first step, and then, martyred ground, Harper's Ferry. Men began to listen. Black men wanted a leader chosen by themselves, an interpreter between two worlds. Thus the National Association for the Advancement of Colored People was born.

"A Litany at Atlanta" is the bitter cry of a sensitive soul. There is Du Bois, as *suppliant*.

To picture the mind of your overlord is a most difficult task. Mr. Du Bois, in "The Souls of White Folk," straightway challenges the assumption by white men of the title to the universe "*for them and their heirs forever.*" "What is the black man but America's Belgium?" he cries. "Blackness condemns, and not crime." "White Christianity is a miserable failure." "The real soul of white culture is war and rapine." "Dividends," says he, "are the tests of success," as "the world today is trade." In this last sentence the learned author apparently gives up his former *idee fixe* that the problem of the twentieth century is the problem of the color line. He affirms the fact that race prejudice pays and that the war was fought for the wealth and toil of Africa. There is nothing new in this delineation of the author, but Mr. Du Bois has a penchant for delving into ancient history to vindicate the Negro's right to civilization by showing what the Negro has contributed. It is contended, however, that such a brief is unnecessary. We care little about where the Negro came from or what he brought. What we want to know is where he is going and by what way.

"The Riddle of the Sphinx," old as Africa, is a poem of freedom. Du Bois is *seer* and *prophet*.

As *historian*, Du Bois is one of the leading students of African history in the world today. In "The Hands of Ethiopia" he proudly calls for self-determination for Africa, and Africa for Africans as the only goal. It may be submitted in contradiction, however, that no one can subscribe to Africa for Africans any more than he can subscribe for France for Frenchmen or America for Americans. Every internationalist must favor free intercommunication and the basing of citizenship on merit, rather than on race or nationality. The author often falls into inconsistency by slighting the interplay of social forces. He says: "Only faith in humanity will lead the world to rise above its present color prejudice." He should have said, as he implied before, "only when color prejudice ceases to be profitable will it be extinguished."

Du Bois, as the *hopeless,* now writes "The Princess of the Hither Isles" on the poetical theme of love and death, a beautiful white woman and a black man within the Veil.

The standard for the pedagogy of the economics and sociology of the Negro problem was set by Du Bois, as *teacher of men,* at Atlanta University. With America in microcosm at East St. Louis, he justly describes distribution as the problem of the present world. To be sure, he often mistakes the effect for the cause, as he does when he lays the ground for the new order on the basis of a moral system. It may be said, however, that ethical principles are merely outgrowths of a social system. They are the products of the socio-economic order and never the causes of it.

As *moralist* and *mystic,* Du Bois has conceived in three short stories in "Darkwater" very striking and startling imaginative effects, containing much fantastic suggestion and melodramatic incident. Theophile Gautier has not written a much better ghost story than "The Comet." And "The Second Coming" and "Jesus Christ in Texas," Flaubertian dream literature, are only a little less intense.

Sensitive soul, the ideal of "The Servant in the House," is service without servants. Menial service is the foe of progress.

As a *Socialist* of the Russell-Walling-Spargo point of view, Mr. Du Bois becomes more rational in "The Rulings of Men" than in any other part of his book. Here again he places more faith in the ethical than the economic. Life to him is a spirit—"The Will to Human Brotherhood of All Colors, Races and Creeds." But the creed of Du Bois is static, rarely ever dynamic.

"The Call" is a prose-poem of resolution. "Children of the Moon" is a lyric of aspiration and freedom.

The *panegyrist* now writes on "The Damnation of Women." No finer tribute has been paid to the women of any race! The examples of Harriet Tubman, of Sojourner Truth, of Kate Ferguson, of Mary Shadd and of Louise De Mortie are the rich legacies bequeathed to the women of all the world. Our women are not free. They must be emancipated.

Du Bois is seen as the *hopeful* in "The Immortal Child," the education of whom is the problem of problems. Suppose Coleridge-Taylor had been born in Georgia or Du Bois in Waco. Life is full of the accident of opportunity. The *hopeful* believes in preserving the race by giving abundant birth to children. "Immortality is the present child."

Du Bois is a *wanderer,* a *Bedouin* bent on the Eternal Quest, as he sings of Beauty and Death. A sojourn at Bar Harbor, Jim Crow travel in the South, 1917 and the war, Houston, East St. Louis, impressions of the Grand Canyon, France and Freedom, Toul, Paris and back to America and the Veil—these are the windows of his soul.

"Almighty Death" is a song of life dedicated to Joseph Pulitzer. "The Prayers of God" are the prayers of men. The holy of holies is human beings, intelligence, love and freedom. "A Hymn to the Peoples" is a stirring ode to humanity.

"Darkwater" is primarily a work of *art.* It is the "Black Talented Tenth" in microcosm. There is through it all the expression of pride and faith in race, but in the last analysis the tragic fate of being black in a white world. Based on feeling, but tempered with reason, it must be acknowledged that Mr. Du Bois has performed his function and performed it admirably. It was upon the foundation of *liberalism* created by Mr. Du Bois' personality that the awakening of "The New Negro" had its genesis. But high and far above that necessary foundation is the new thought, the destroying but creating thought. It knows only truth. Freedom will come only when there are no races, no classes, no creeds. The distribution of wealth and knowledge is the problem of the twentieth century. As some one has said: "The hope of peace has passed from liberalism to labor." *Labor* will create a new world, and in that new scheme the Negro must take his place, not as a Negro, but as an equal sharer of all opportunity among equal men.

THE BRASS CHECK

A REVIEW

W. A. Domingo reviews Upton Sinclair's The Brass Check. *The book was published in 1920.*

The Brass Check is a new book by Upton Sinclair, famous as the author of The Jungle. It contains 448 pages and is published at Pasadena, Cal., by the author at 50c. per copy.

In the Jungle, Sinclair, according to his own statement, "aimed at the public's heart but hit its stomach." In the Brass Check if he aimed at the public's brains he has struck the bull's eye. There is not a dull line in the book. It is as thrilling as a romance and as exciting as a baseball game when there is a tie. The reader reads every page with cumulative interest. Perhaps the one fault of the interesting volume is that the author devotes too much space—one half of the book—to his experiences with the Great Incubator of Lies—the Press. The subtitle of the Brass Check is, "A study in journalism," and an illuminating study it is. In clear, terse English, like a skilled surgeon with a scalpel, Upton Sinclair lays bare the soul—if soul they have—of the New York *Times, World* and nearly every important daily, weekly or monthly published in the United States. He calls names, challenges the publishers and editors and does more—gives the proofs.

The Associated Press he excoriates unmercifully. He shows how the news is colored and the people fed with vicious propaganda favorable to Big Business. Indeed, it is the thesis of the book that the press functions in the interest of predatory privilege. He piles the evidence on thick. The death of the great muck-raking magazines—Hampton's, 20th Century, Pearson's—is told with pitiless, merciless attention to detail. How other muckraking magazines, like the Metropolitan and

Everybody's, came to change their policies and become respectable, is exposed. The author has made a definite contribution to truth by muckraking the Press, the Mother of Lies.

However, in showing the groups that have suffered from the lying propaganda of the press he fails to mention Negroes. No group has suffered more from the misrepresentation of the press than the millions of black toilers of this country. What a study Sinclair could have made of say—lynching!

Despite this omission the book is an aid to clear thinking on public questions; it is a guide for those who would properly evaluate current events.

It is a book that every sensible person should read. It will amply repay for the money spent and the time consumed.

THE BOOK OF

AMERICAN NEGRO POETRY

Floyd J. Calvin reviews James Weldon Johnson's anthology The Book of American Negro Poetry. *This review was published in October 1922.*

The chief worth of Mr. Johnson's Book of American Negro Poetry lies in his essay on the Negro's Creative Genius. This is both illuminating and masterful. It is primarily defensive because of the tendency of the great "I Ams" to subtract credit from us the minute our even smutty tunes are popularized with different words. Thus we find the author laboriously proving that we are the originators of jazz, the blues, and other such syncopation and accompanying dances that have the populace in their grip today. We are proud of this painstaking presentation however, for although we are ashamed of some of the themes ourselves, still the tunes are great and when the credit is handed out free of charge we want our share.

But of more potential importance is the narrative of Phillis Wheatley. The author quite feasibly suggests she was first to hail General Washington as "First in peace." This shows careful research. He also remarks:

"Phillis Wheatley has never been given her rightful place in American literature. By some sort of conspiracy she is kept out of most of the books, especially the textbooks on literature used in the schools. Of course, she is not a great American poet—and in her day there were no great American poets—but she is an important American poet. Her importance, if for no other reason, rests on the fact that, save one, she is the first in order of time of all the women poets of America. And she is among the first of all American poets to issue a volume."

And substantial proof follows the assertion.

Foreign poets come in for a generous appraisal. They were of Latin countries where prejudice was less strong, hence they were not forced to be intensely racial. Many were real National poets, such as has been the hopeless dream of some American Negroes. For that reason Mr. Johnson thinks the greatest poets of the race have come from the Latins and will continue to do so for many years.

In looking forward the author strikes a new note.

"The Negro in the United States has achieved or been placed in a certain artistic niche. When he is thought of artistically, it is as a happy-go-lucky, singing, shuffling, banjo-picking being or as a more or less pathetic figure. The picture of him is in a log cabin amid fields of cotton or along the levees. Negro dialect is naturally and by long association the exact instrument for voicing this phase of Negro life; and by that very exactness it is an instrument with two full stops, humor and pathos. So even when he confines himself to purely racial themes, the Aframerican poet realizes that there are phases of Negro life in the United States which cannot be treated in the dialect either adequately or artistically. Take, for example, the phases rising out of life in Harlem, that most wonderful Negro city in the world. I do not deny that a Negro in a log cabin is more picturesque than a Negro in a Harlem flat, but the Negro in the Harlem flat is here, and he is but part of a group growing everywhere in the country, a group whose ideals are becoming increasingly more vital than of the traditionally artistic group even if its members are less picturesque.

"What the colored poet in the United States needs to do is something like what Synge did for the Irish; he needs to find a form that will express the racial spirit by symbols from within rather than by symbols from without, such as the mere mutilation of English spelling and pronunciation. He needs a form that is freer and larger than dialect, but which will still hold the racial flavor; a form expressing the imaginary, the idioms, the peculiar turns of thought, and the distinctive humor and pathos, too, of the Negro, but which will also be capable of voicing the deepest and highest emotions and aspirations, and allow of the widest range of subjects and the widest scope of treatment. . . .

"In stating the need for Aframerican poets in the United States to work out a new and distinctive form of expression I do not wish to be understood to hold any theory that they should limit themselves to Negro poetry, to racial themes; the sooner they are able to write American poetry spontaneously, the better. Nevertheless, I believe that the richest contribution the Negro poet can make to American literature of the future will be the fusion into it of his own individual artistic gifts."

("Aframerican" is a word of the author's own make. We are not asked to adopt it.)

The book is well edited by a distinguished poet and scholar and should be found in every poet-lover's library.

HARLEM SHADOWS

Harlem Shadows, *a collection of poems by Claude McKay published in*
1922, is reviewed by Georgia Douglas Johnson.

This sketch is not an attempt at authentic and prolonged criticism of
Claude McKay's delightful "Harlem Shadows"—only a reaction, im-
pulsive and personal.

Read "The Harlem Dancer":

> "Applauding youths laughed with young prostitutes
> And watched her perfect, half-clothed body sway;
> Her voice was like the sound of blended flutes
> Blown by black players on a picnic day.
> She sang and danced on, gracefully and calm,
> The light gauze hanging loose about her form;
> To me she seemed a proudly-swaying palm
> Grown lovlier for passing through a storm.
> Upon her swarthy neck black shiny curls
> Luxuriant fell; and tossing coins in praise,
> The wine flushed, bold-eyed boys and even the girls,
> Devoured her shape with eager passionate gaze;
> But looking at her falsely-smiling face,
> I knew her self was not in that strange place."

Unfadingly canvassed are the lines: "To me she seemed a proudly
swaying palm," etc., and, "her voice was like the sound of blended
flutes," one can hear the magic tones. This picture of the lovely
Harlem Dancer is as vividly painted on my mind as is the Mona Liza.

Vital and living is "Harlem Shadows":

> "I hear the halting footsteps of a lass
>   In Negro Harlem when the night lets fall
> Its veil. I see the shapes of girls who pass
>   To bend and barter at desires call.
> Ah, little dark girls who in slippered feet
>   Go prowling through the night from street to street!"

The flame-shod feet of "the little dark girls" pass over my heart, and I feel that touch of anguish that was the author's own when he wrote these lines.

The prophecy in the last four lines of "America" is significant:

> "Darkly I gaze into the days ahead,
>   And see her might and granite wonders there,
> Beneath the touch of Time's unerring hand
> Like priceless treasures sinking in the sand."

It is the unmistakable writing on the wall, and yet what tender compassion pervades the author, who continues:

> "I stand within her walls with not a shred
>   Of terror, malice, not a word of jeer."

CHORDS AND DISCHORDS

Chords and Dischords, *published in 1922, is a collection of poems by Walter Everette Hawkins. It is reviewed here by Countee Cullen.*

In the preface to his poems, Mr. Hawkins says, "These verses just wrote themselves. I have merely been the instrument through which some peculiar unknown something has been speaking since childhood.... My greatest reward lies in the hope that some Chords herein struck may be the inspiration of some into whose hands they may come, and set into motion a stream of fellow-feeling, of friendship and love flowing from me to them, thence to all the hearts that throb and thrill with the joy that makes kings and queens of this our common clay." If we had not read one poem by Mr. Hawkins we would know by the expression of this extract from his preface that he has the soul of a poet.

We read this book of poems with the appreciation that is bound to be experienced in the reading of a sincere and honest piece of literature. The author has realized his own limitations and has not attempted to stray from the confines of his own domain. He has not attempted the sublime, probably realizing how fine a line tells its demarcation from the ridiculous. His subjects are simple as are his technical methods of treatment. It does our heart good in these days to notice and commend the earnestness with which he has endeavored to keep his metrical and rhythmical technique flawless.

The lyric quality of his poetry is worthy of commendation. He strikes a high lyric note in "The Recompense," from which we quote the following lines:

> One but to bloom, one bird to sing,
> One star to shine, one harp to ring,
> One smile to gleam between a tear,
> Is all we need to cheer us here.

And these lines from "Ask Me Why I Love You" are their own excuse for being:

> Ask me why I love you, dear,
> And I will ask the vine
> Why its tendrils trustingly
> Round the oak entwine;
> Why you love the mignonette
> Better than the rue,—
> If you will but answer me,
> I will answer you.

In "In Spite of Death," he voices a universal thought in excellent lyric style and has hit upon a title which is itself enviable. The following lines are exhilarating:

> The jonquils ope their petals sweet,
> The poppies dance around my feet:
> In spite of winter and of death,
> The spring is in the zephyr's breath.

To his glory, Mr. Hawkins has not attempted to be a propagandist in his poetry. He probably realizes that we have men, and to spare, for that, and that each Jack does best at his own trade. Between the author and those who read his work with a view to entering into an understanding of his moods, this little book is destined to form a link of friendship and mutual appreciation. Mr. Hawkins has certainly given evidence of potentialities, and we look forward with much interest to his next contribution.

CERTAIN PEOPLE OF IMPORTANCE

Nella Larsen Imes reviews Certain People of Importance *by Kathleen Norris for the May 1923 issue.*

San Francisco and vicinity is the setting of this well put together story of the Crabtree and Brewer families. The title is inappropriate. Yet, speaking truly, that is about the only fault to be found with it. "Certain People of Importance" is a work of extraordinary strength and feeling. Mrs. Norris has peopled her stage with characters that are powerfully human and satisfyingly authentic. Attention and favor are caught at first by the directness of the style; then by the subtle composite of sympathy and irony that goes into the development of individuals, and finally by the sweep and range of the author's narrative power.

The material is certainly ordinary, both in people and in their environment, but Mrs. Norris plays with lively zest over the fatuity and commonplaceness of the situation. This ability to transform the commonplace, rendering it amusing or thrilling, is, however, not the chief distinction of the story. There is a difference of aim and method between it and her earlier novels. This time she interprets her characters and breathes the breath of life into them. We are made to feel their atmosphere, their interests, what makes them go. This is perhaps because the writer has put into them the richness of her own personality. The charm is remarkable. It surrounds Victoria Brewer like an aura so that one loves her. It enmeshes Aunt Fan so that one likes her and stands in somewhat childlike awe of her, despite one's perception of her very human limitations. It gives a mellowness even to the parental officiousness of Pa and Ma Brewer so that one sympathizes with them.

Surely this is Mrs. Norris' best novel. It rings true from beginning to end. I recommend this book, which will in all probability be among those considered for the year's Pulitzer prize, to all readers who care for conscientious work.

FIRE IN THE FLINT

Robert Bagnall reviews Walter F. White's The Fire in the Flint, *published in 1924.*

If H. L. Mencken, the brilliant American critic and author, had a feather in his hat for every writer he has found and inspired his headdress would look like an Arapahoe Indian adorned for the war dance.

What has this got to do with "The Fire in the Flint?" Hereby hangs an interesting tale. Writing to Walter White, who is one of his most ardent devotees, Mencken in commenting on a novel of Negro life in the South by a Southern white man, stated that he had not read the book, but was suspicious of anything from the pen of a southerner on this theme. He continued: "Why don't you do a novel on this subject? You could do a fine job and I would make it a sensation."

Now Walter White, the author of this new book, "The Fire in the Flint," had done very little creative writing. However, he had written many magazine and newspaper articles, and knows the Negro question as few men do, having made in person twenty-seven lynching and riot investigations. There were some who smiled when Walter White decided to take Mencken at his word, for familiar with the style of his articles—a style as bald as the man in Pinaud's eau de Quinine Advertisement—they did not believe that he could do creative writing of any value. But the laugh is now on them, for White has done an exceptionally fine piece of work in "The Fire in the Flint." He has produced real literature, an artistic work sustained throughout, a production that invites the use of superlatives.

The story of "The Fire in the Flint" was in the author's "inwards," ready to spring to birth as is evidenced in the remarkable fact that Walter White wrote the whole thing in two weeks—over seventy thousand words in two weeks!

Of course, he worked it over again and again as to style and characterization, but his story is in all essentials as it was born. And be it said—White is no slouch when it comes to hard work. Like Paddock doing a hundred meters, he studied with the keenest avidity the best masters in style, characterization, and plot, making fine use of expert counsel.

The surprising thing about the book is that White has the full story of the South in the book—a wonderful mine of information, absolutely true and faithful; lynching, peonage, the Klan, the exploitation of Negro women, the terrorization of Negro men, the limitation of friendly, liberal southern whites; the stultification of all real culture among the whites there; the brutal and sordid callousness; and yet his book is not propaganda. It is all woven into a tale that is as thrilling as a drive through Bear Creek Canyon, on a slushy spring day, without chains, with a drunken driver at the wheel. There is one class of people I must warn against reading the book—those with serious heart disease.

The book steadily advances to a climax, without any let down in any part. Not one of his characters is a lay figure; they are all human beings. Some of them are types you know well.

Kenneth, his principal character, is faithfully drawn in his development and relations. Only once is he out of character. When the author makes him take Jane in his arms and stoop to kiss her ten minutes after he has met her for the first time since she was a little girl, his action is not in keeping with the man inexperienced and timid in love affairs that he is pictured as being. It is more like what one would expect our Harlem love pirates to do. In fact, the love story is the one unsatisfactory part of the book, but yet it does not mar it at all.

The character one likes best is Bob, the young spirited brother of Kenneth, resentful of the injustices against his race, coming to a tragic end on the very eve of living a real life. His is a fine bit of character drawing.

Jane is a likeable type and Mamie a wistful character, but a bit shadowy. The Parker Brothers, Stewart, Henry Lane, Roy Ewing and his wife, are all well drawn. Judge Stevenson is a perfect type, drawn with the sharpness of an etching; the Reverend Wilson, and the fat, oily, unctuous, envious, servile Dr. Williams one continually meets when in the South.

The picture of a Southern town is as well drawn as anything of its kind in literature. If you know the South—you know Central City.

In the chapter telling of the death of Bob, the author has done as fine a piece of writing as it has been my pleasure to read in many a day. You cannot read it without the tears coming, or without your jaws setting and your fists clenching. Starting off with the atmosphere of calm and peace, Bob packing for school, it sweeps on from tragedy to stark tragedy which causes the heart to race and one to gasp for breath. It reminds me—in its sheer realism and poignant intensity—of nothing so much as that incomparable "Fight on the Stairhead," in "The Cloister and the Hearth." It is more dramatic than "the attack on the Mill," in Zola's "The Red Mill." Its staccatto style is a perfect medium for its matter and is used with the finest effect.

The dramatic story of the end of Kenneth is also breath-catching, and exceedingly well done. Some may criticise the book because it gives the impression that the situation in the South is hopeless. What other impression would any true picture give? As Judge Stevenson says: "What are we going to do? God knows—I don't. Maybe the lid will blow off some day—then there would be Hell to pay. One thing's going to help and that's Negroes pulling up stakes and going North." That last seems to be the only hope.

The book is infinitely superior to "Birthright," "White and Black," and "Nigger." It is sure to create much comment. It is a tale that you cannot afford not to read. It is melodramatic but true; bitter but fair; and it hasn't a bit of clap-trap nor a cheap line from cover to cover.

As they say in Harlem, Mencken certainly knew his stuff when he bade Walter White write a race novel.

A Stranger at the Gates:

A Review of *Nigger Heaven*

Wallace Thurman reviews Carl Van Vechten's controversial 1926 book, Nigger Heaven.

When I first heard of the author's proposed novel of Negro life in Harlem I immediately conjectured that while the whites would relish it, especially since the current faddistic interest in things Negroid was still a flourishing reality, that Negroes themselves would anathematize both the book and its author. I predicated this conjecture on the fact that most colored people with whom I came into contact bristled belligerently at mention of the title. And some of those who had been most active in showing the author the sights of Harlem crowed about ingratitude, Nordic duplicity, et cetera, as long as the object of their wrath remained downtown, and promptly forgot it when he was uptown, which gave me a chance to speculate upon African duplicity. However, since reading the volume I find myself forced to cancel my first conjecture and come forward with another, which is, that whites may find it a trifle tedious at times, but that Negroes will accept it so warmly that even the detested "Nigger" in the title will be forgotten, and, I would not be surprised should some of our uplift organizations and neighborhood clubs plan to erect a latter-day abolitionist statue to Carl Van Vechten on the corner of 135th Street and Seventh Avenue, for the author has been most fair, and most sympathetic in his treatment of a long mistreated group of subjects. True, some of his individual characters may seem tarnished, but the race as a whole emerges as a group of long suffering martyrs, deservant of a better fate. No one in Harlem could have presented their case more eloquently and with more finesse. Truly, Gareth Johns, you deserve an especial Spingarn medal.

Yet once the characters cease discussing the "Negro problem," once they cease spouting racial equality epigrams, and anti-racial discrimination platitudes, the novel begins to move—begins to pulsate with some genuine rhythms peculiar (objections from Geo. S. Schuyler) to Harlem alone, and, thereupon holds the reader rapt until he reaches the dramatic climax.

Mr. Van Vechten seems at his best in the cabaret scenes, the charity ball, and the Black Mass (and let me insert a question here—where, oh where is this Black Mass in Harlem, for it is too good to be merely a figment of the writer's imagination—I mean too good in the sense that it should not be such a selfish, subjective creation, I, for one, would love to see).

> "An invisible band, silent at the moment they had entered this deserted room, now began to perform wild music, music that moaned and lacerated one's breast with brazen claws of tone, shrieking, tortured music from the depths of hell. And now the hall became peopled, as dancers slipped through the folds of the hangings, men and women with weary faces, faces tired of passion and pleasure. Were these the faces of dead prostitutes and murderers? Pleasure seekers from the cold slabs of the morgue?
>
> "Dance! cried Laska. Dance! She flung herself in his arms and they joined this witches sabbath."

This all occurs in "a circular hall entirely hung in vermillion velvet" ... with ... "a flavor of translucent glass" through which flows "a cloud of light—now orange, now deep purple, now flaming like molten lava, now rolling sea waves of green."

And the two cabaret scenes surpass even the above in their realistic evocation of an individualistic setting, surging with soul shreaving individualistic rhythms.

I shall not dwell upon the chronicle of events that compromise the main motif of the novel proper. I found the trimmings and trappings more genuine and more gracefully done than the thesis. The affair between Mary Love and Byron Kasson struck me as rather puerile. Show me any normal pair of even cultured lovers in Harlem skipping down bridle paths in a park, and show me any girl in Mary's milieu who is as simple as Mary in the matters of an affair du coeur. The tragedy of the myopic Byron who wished to write but could find nothing to write about the while a veritable ocean of material was swirling about him, and his passionate plunge with the fiery and exotic Laska Sartoris into a pool of physical debauch is of sterner stuff and much more calculated to draw the reader back to the volume for a second reading.

"Nigger Heaven" will also provide high Harlem with a new indoor sport, namely, the ascertaining which persons in real life the various characters were drawn from. Speculations are already rampant even before a general circulation of the book, and I have heard from various persons whom each character represents with far more assurance than the author himself could muster.

All in all "Nigger Heaven" should have a wide appeal and gain much favorable notice. As I say, some "ofays" may find arid stretches in it, especially where they are being lampooned in good old N.A.A.C.P. fashion, but the pregnant picturization of certain facets of Negro life in Harlem will serve to make at least partial amends for that Mr. Van Vechten has done what Russett Durwood, in the novel, predicts to Byron someone would do—*i.e.,* beat the Negro litterateurs to a vibrant source pot of literary material which they for the most part have glossed over. And he has done it so well in places that despite the allegation of certain Manhattan sophisticates that he wrote the book merely to prove that there are Negroes who read Paul Morand, Jean Cocteau, Edmond Gosse, Louis Broomfield and Cabell, and who can feel at home in sumptuous settings of tiger-skin covered beds, magenta and silver cushions, taffeta canopied dressing tables, Sevres china, and furniture which is a "Bavarian version of Empire," he has also laid himself liable to being referred to, in the provinces, as another Negro writer.

A Thrush at Eve with an
Atavistic Wound

Wallace Thurman reviews Walter White's book Flight, *published in 1926.*

I do not know which is considered the greater literary criminal, he who writes or rather tries to write without first having suitable material or he who has the suitable material and fails to do it justice. In my opinion it is the latter who is the more oafish offender, for it is surely he who is the most inconsiderate of his expectant audiences, and the most persistent prostitutor of his art.

Now: the Negro is supposedly experiencing a cultural and spiritual renaissance, supposedly emerging from restricted zones to air himself in the more exclusive, the more esoteric ateliers. He is supposed to be developing a new type, which type is in turn destined to be a serious contender in the universal race struggle for supremacy. All of this is very well, very interesting, and very necessary, I suppose, to the scheme of things, and it has all been accomplished by a salient use of a salient weapon—*i. e.,* propaganda.

Mr. White is one of the most salient users of this salient weapon, and it is partly because of his strenuous efforts that the alleged inferior Negro has been pushed from the unnoticed back ranks of the national chorus to a principal position on the polyglot American stage. This, remember, has already been done, and the propagandist school to which Mr. White belongs hopes to accomplish much more with this same efficient weapon. I have no quarrel with them on that score, even if I do doubt the continued potency of their weapon, and even if it does seem to me that it is about time for the next step, about time for the bally-hooing to cease and for the genuine performance to begin. However, my only quarrel with this school is that they are wont to consider their written propaganda as literary art. All art no doubt is propaganda, but all propaganda is most certainly not art. And a novel must, to earn the name, be more than a mere social service report, more than a thinly disguised dissertation on racial relationships and racial maladjustments.

Mimi Daquin, the central figure in Mr. White's latest lucubration, should have been an intense, vibrant personality instead of the outlined verbal puppet that she is. She could have been an individual instead of a general type; as it is Mimi is never more than an alphabetic doll regaled in cliche phrases, too wordy sentences, and paragraphs pregnant with frustrated eloquence. When one thinks of the psychological possibilities of such a theme as the author had to work with, one is almost appalled by the superficial and inadequate treatment that the theme receives. As a novelist Mr. White seems somewhat myopic, and it is this narrow vision that keeps his propaganda just outside the gates of literature-land. Mimi, with her complex racial heritage, her complex and heterogenous social milieu, and her duo-racial urge, could have been as complete and as great a literary creation as, say, Emma Bovary, Nana, Candida or the more contemporaneous, if less great, Clara Barron.

But there is no need to continue this tearful jeremiad, for by this time everyone knows that in my opinion Walter White is primarily a propagandist, an earnest one at that, burning up with the desire to show that his people are not inferior merely because their skins are dark, and consumed by the hope that his social service reports will not only assist in the fruition of this desire, but that they will also perchance become staunch literary survivors instead of ephemeral firecrackers. As a premier writer of propaganda, Mr. White deserves a gilt-edged palm, but as a writer of literature he is still the propagandist distinguished only because it is a new departure for an American Negro to brazenly throw lighted Roman candles into the public market places.

However, I recommend that "Flight" be read by all Nordics, all near Nordics, and all non-Nordics, and that it be read frankly as one-sided propaganda. It will irritate the Nordics, induce thought and provide argumentative material for the near Nordics, and salve the aching stings of the non-Nordics. It will also be of inspirative value to ambitious blacks and keep the talented Negro to the forefront, unless the saturation point has already been reached.

And now I hear that inevitable question: "What more could 'Flight' have done if it had been one of your so-called works of art?" Which question I refuse to answer in so short a space.

BLACK HARVEST

Ida Alexa Ross Wylie's Black Harvest *is reviewed by Wallace Thurman.*

I.A.R. Wylie is at once observant and anticipatory. She has seized upon the pregnant spectacle offered by the savage black legions which the civilized European powers utilized in their late war to end war, and has limned an interesting and ingenious tale.

Every time a white novelist undertakes to write of Negro characters that novelist is immediately accused of not having written understandingly of his black subjects. At times this criticism seems indeed justified, and at other times it seems like mere petulant quibbling. Any novelist, *i.e.,* any sincere novelist treats all subjects whether they be white or black, in the light of his experience. It is the insincere novelist that sees his subjects in patterns, and it is he who should be ignored. Then too, no race of people is exactly what it believes itself to be any more than the southern Negro is what either Octavius Roy Cohen or the latter day abolitionists would have you believe him to be. It takes a brave writer indeed in this day and time to attempt to write about any race save the one to which he belongs, and that writer who will not only write contemporaneously about some other race, but will also write speculatively about the future of that race deserves a croix-de-guerre for braving fire, for to fire he will most certainly be subjected.

The present author centers her tale about a "Jung Seigfried," a black product of a rape committed by a Sengalese soldier under the French flag upon a German prostitute. This mullato Messiah has gained the support of Negroes both in America and Africa, and, at a word from him the entire black population of this world is prepared to march to the tune of "Die Wacht und der Rhine." By this grand gesture I gather that both the now conquered Germans and the now dominated blacks will achieve freedom.

However, "Jung Seigfried" is as we know, a black man, and his white conspirators are the conventional type of whites, which means that they are as fully aware of his color as they are aware of his power and ability. They realize that without him theirs is a lost cause, yet it seems that they prefer to remain subjugated rather than admit this man to be their equal.

All of this wrecks havoc upon the nerves of our slightly hysterical Hans Felde, especially when his desire for a woman—a white woman—becomes pitifully potent.

It is to this that our fellow Negroes will object, and mutter the accusation that these terrible white novelists just wont write truthfully about Negroes. Well, what if they don't, as long as Negroes won't write truthfully about themselves or won't recognize themselves when they are presented truthfully?

Hans Felde is not a far-fetched figure. Born, reared and subtly frustrated in and by the milieu the author creates he could not have acted or reacted any differently towards his environmental stimulus. As a character in "Black Harvest," Hans Felde is a truthful one, and that is all that is necessary, for why should he be a general concoction of what Negroes believe to be Negroid virtues?

Yet this novel is far from satisfying or complete. As entertainment or as controversial stimuli it is indeed good, but one expects a little more from a volume so ambitious in theme and so bristling with positive character electrons. Thus "Black Harvest" remains one of those books that everyone should read, speculate upon, discuss, and then forget.

THE WEARY BLUES

The Weary Blues, *a collection of poems by Langston Hughes, is reviewed here by Theophilus Lewis. This review was published in March 1926.*

Lyric poetry—and I am almost persuaded to Edgar Allan Poe's opinion that there is no other kind of poetry—springs from the core of the mind where the emotional kinship of races is close enough to make the imagery of each intelligible to all. It sprouts from the youth of humanity, the race or the poet and, as youth is parent to maturity, it reveals the mold or pattern from which the more spiritual and intellectual arts will later develop. While the bard whose songs flow unalloyed from the universal human emotions usually wins quicker recognition, he will, unless he is a master of musical speech, inevitably be surpassed by the vigor and arresting originality of the poet bearing the unmistakable mark of his race. If anybody asserts this is simply an expression of my well-known chauvinism, I reply "Bushwah!" Differentiation is always a step forward in the process of evolution.

The "Blues" poems which make up the first part of the book, "The Weary Blues," reveal Langston Hughes as a poet of the latter type. On second thought I see no valid reason why the "Blues" should be distinguished from the earlier poems. They are merely an emphatic expression of the mood discernible in his work from the beginning. To people who think a poet is a man who repeats in verse what he reads in books or newspapers, these poems, all of them, will appear either gauche monstrosities or clever innovations, happily or lamentably, according to whether one likes them or not, destined to live no longer than the current cabaret vogue. Which view marks the failure, or perhaps the inability, to understand the function of an artist.

Langston Hughes has gone direct to life for his themes and he has embodied its ironies and vagous harmonies in his verse. He has not consulted life of 1890 as observed and recorded by Theodore Dreiser and Rudyard Kipling; he has caught life in its current incandescence as it roars and blazes in the bosoms of the new race of American blacks. Six lines of his are painted on a six-foot sign in the lobby of the Harlem Y.M.C.A. and this is no mere coincidence. It is one of the indications that this pagan poet is fast becoming a religious force. By this expression I do not mean he has invented a novel way to chant halleluiahs to a Jewish Jehovah, a standardized Christ and a Central Islip Holy Ghost. I mean that in giving concrete and definite expression to the incoherent feelings and impulses of his people he is functioning as a unifying spiritual agent. This is the chief work of the artist—this and to crystallize the beauty of his people in stone or verse or enduring drama and so leave behind impressive tombstones when the civilization of which he is a part has trod the road to dusty death.

As no man can read vivid and thoughtful literature without showing the effects of it, there are places, here and there, where his verse faintly smells like the Public Library, as—

> He did a lazy sway . . .
> He did a lazy sway . . .

which suggests the rhythm of the Chinese Nightingale, or "To the Black Beloved," with its subdued elegance which somehow carried the mind back to the Song of Solomon. But these reminders of book lore, faint as they are, are few and far between. What we usually hear is the shuffle of happy feet as in:—

> Me an' ma baby's
> Got two mo' ways,
> Two mo' ways to do de buck!

Or Bessie Smith's robust contralto moaning a seductive ululation like:—

> My man's done left me,
> Chile, he's gone away.
> My good man's left me,
> Babe, he's gone away.
> Now the cryin' blues
> Haunts me night and day.

In "Cross" he takes his theme from the bio-sociological riot of the Aframerican's background and the first line, which establishes its rhythm, comes straight from the guts of 133rd Street, which cries out against the restraints of the Ten Commandments and the factory system in the Rabelaisian couplet beginning

"My old man is a man like this."

It almost tempts one to write him a personal letter demanding something inspired by that other jewel of levity, the quatrain which opens:

"I wish I had ten thousand bricks."

And Hughes, the craftsman, is quite as deft as Hughes the artist is original. His poems which at first sound as simple as the theme of Beethoven's Sixth Symphony on closer examination reveal a good deal of the complexity of that master's music. As an example, I point to "Midnight Nan at Leroy's." You will travel a long day's journey before you find another contemporary poem in which the fundamental poignancy and superficial gayety of life are so effectively blended. Note how skillfully he employs paired iambics to make the Charleston rhythm dance blithely down the surface of the poem while an excess of short feet and weak vowels form an undertow which establishes a final melancholy mood. I can think of no poet since Poe capable of weaving such and intricate tapestry antithetical feelings.

Hughes is not a solitary figure, of course; there are at least two other poets producing work quite as authentic. But I know of no other poet who keeps in such close contact with life in its molten state or who is as capable of getting expression out of gaseous feelings without waiting for them to cool off. If he doesn't stop to mark time now he will certainly grow into a spiritual force of major significance.

PORGY

Porgy, *written by DuBose Heyward, is reviewed here by Theophilus Lewis for the March 1926 issue.*

I have never been to Africa and unless God is kinder to me in the future than He has ever been in the past the chances are I shall never be lucky enough to go there. Still, the moment I clapped my eyes on Rene Maran's fine portrait of Batouala I at once recognized the man as a spiritual cousin of mine. His keen appreciation of the delights of lassitude, his ability to make meditation an engrossing and mellow diversion and his reluctance to dally with work unless it promised some immediate ministration to the wants of the soul or body were mental traits I had no trouble identifying as my own. I have also discovered the same habits of mind lurking in the skull of every black man I have ever heard airing his thoughts. Then there were the numerous little luxuries of the flesh friend Batouala used to revel in. I have never seen a Negro sweating in a glory hole who did not indulge in them as naturally as he breathed. The shrewd humor of his eyes, the aggressively sensual expression of his mouth and the strong, rancid smell of his arm-pits—so different from the stale, sourish odor of Caucasian bodies—are still green in my memory. A dozen times a day I see men in Lenox Avenue who could pass for his brother.

In Porgy, the central character of DuBose Heyward's novel of the same name, I recognize no such familiar nor convincing figure. Porgy, Mr. Heyward says, is a member of a tribe of uncivilized niggers inhabiting the Charleston waterfront. Mr. Heyward, himself a member of one of the white clans that rule the country, claims he has been in constant contact with the subordinate blacks since childhood, fraternizing with them to an extent, and observing the most intimate details of their customs and conduct. Which prolonged and sympathetic study, the book implies, has enabled him to create darkies in the image of Dean Pickens, Marcus Garvey and Shimmy Sam. I fail to see the resemblance.

Although I was born and brought up in Baltimore and have never been any further south than Washington, I am, my mother's side, descended from North Carolina nomads, a disappearing people who once roamed the territory contiguous to that Mr. Heyward declares is the home of the Catfish Alley folk. I lived my first eighteen years among the wild niggers of Tyson Street, Rutter Street and Dallas Street, after which, obeying the nomadic instincts inherited from my parents (my father was a rover from Kansas), I wandered northward, sojourning for more or less prolonged periods among the barbarous blacks of Buffalo, Toledo and Cleveland. I am so familiar with the savages of St. Antoine Street and 133rd Street, I consider myself an authority on their customs and modes of thought. Now it is the unanimous opinion of anthropologists that all the black tribes of North America sprang from the same parent stock, and although presenting superficial differences of speech and appearance, are still closely related to each other. With the dictum of science backing up the experience of my personal pilgrimages I conclude that if Porgy were a genuine Negro, I ought to be able to detect some trace of kinship between him and myself; or, failing that, I should, at least, be able to identify him with some of the bellhops I have hustled handbags with. Which is not the case. I find Porgy every whit as strange to me as Al Jolson or Florian Slappy.

Mr. Heyward's failure to make a convincing character of Porgy is not due to any lack of competence as an artist. Still less is it due to a lack of sympathy with his subject. What hamstrings him is the same thing that will inevitably frustrate the genius of any artist who undertakes to interpret alien character in its lighter moods. In tragedy, the essentials of which lie too deep in human emotions to be affected by race differences, the artist can tackle the job of portraying foreign character with a fair chance of success; his only limitations being those of his ability as a craftsman. But a race is not distinguished by the basic feelings it shares with all humanity; it is distinguished by the peculiar qualities it alone possesses. That is to say it is distinguished by the hereditary habits of life it has developed along with the physical distinction which mark it off from all other races. As the special qualities of a race are not created but developed along with the race itself their formulæ can never be known. It follows that they can never be fully comprehended. They can only be expressed. As all art is expression and expression inevitably comes from within the artist attempting to interpret foreign character pretty soon runs afoul of idioms of feeling he finds himself unable to translate. This is a trying situation and you can hardly blame the artist for getting out of it by substituting his own feelings for the alien feelings which baffle him. The result, however, is usually as happy as attempting to fit one's teeth in the sockets of another man's jaw bone.

Maran was able to make Batouala a virile and convincing character because he had shared the major part of his biological background, and so became privy to numerous little nuances of living and untranslatable thoughts handed down by their common ancestors. Mr. Heyward and Porgy possessed no such common fund of hereditary notions. Many of their ideas were no more interchangeable than their beards. Confronted with the task of interpreting a type of character to a great extent unintelligible to him, Mr. Heyward resorted to a ruse which marks him as an exceptionally resourceful young man. He lifted an Irish peasant bodily from John Bull's Other Island, blacked up his face, twisted his legs, altered his dialect and presented him to the world as a plausible denizen of the Charleston black belt.

As the prevailing intellectual superstition runs to the effect that every Negro chauffeur possesses histrionic gifts beside which the talents of the whole Barrymore family dwindle into insignificance, Porgy was at once acclaimed as a creative masterwork. The emancipated young crackers who hold most of the strategic points on the literary pages greeted it with a roar of hosannas as deafening as the ovation their fathers gave the Clansman. Thus does hokum succeed hokum and the angels rest assured of their ration of mirth.

Now this legend of the Negro being a consummate actor who is perpetually doing his stuff in the presence of white men, while it may be an amusing conceit, has no esthetic value whatsoever; nor is it of any assistance in clarifying what we call "The Negro Problem". So far as my knowledge goes—and it is probably more extensive than that of the intellectuals who accept the legend as the key to Negro character—this whimsy first occurred to Bernard Shaw one afternoon when he was trying to think of wise cracks to write about one of Dion Boucicault's saccharine melodramas. Later on he developed the theme and inserted it into one of his own plays and still later further elaborated on it and built an entire play around it. Hence, it naturally became one of the fundamental dogmas of his solution of the

Irish question. No doubt it is just as germane to the Negro problem as it is to the Irish question. It is no less relevant to the Jewish question. I have seen many an isolated Nordic, overawed by a mob of wrathful shines, conceal his habitual arrogance and eat humble pie. For it is just as natural for the ruck of men to cry "Kamrad!" in the face of superior and hostile odds as it is for a poodle to wag his tail when he gets cornered by a bull dog.

Perhaps I have given Porgy much more space than its importance deserves. But, really, something's got to be done about this thing. Otherwise the declining Eden Philpottses and Thomas Dixons will be succeeded by hordes of Striblings and Heywards, the latter sympathetic and well-meaning fellows, no doubt, but no more capable of interpreting Negro character than I am capable of interpreting Chinese character.

As for Porgy as a story, aside from its false picture of Negro life, it is not so bad. Although its people are simply Shavian manikins blacked up and the description of the storm as a malevolent brute is a device filched from Conrad—the Lord only knows who *he* borrowed it from—there is a certain wistfulness woven in the tale which gives it a novel and seductive charm. As long as folks, even as you and I, like to hear of lilies sprouting through the slime and hardened hearts waxing warm and tender, as long as we are moved by tales of women watching by the sea for ships that never come back; above all, as long as men with a way with words are able to invest any kind of story with the pathos and mellifluence of a sad love lyric, books like Porgy, in spite of their fundamental hollowness, will be read with enjoyment and put away for a second reading.

ALL GOD'S CHILLUN' STILL GOT WINGS

In a brief historical overview, Theophilus Lewis explains the impact the theater has had on attitudes about African-American life. This essay was published in November 1926.

Times sure do change. Ten years ago being a Negro in New York was just one long spell of hard luck. When the industrious Ethiopian left home in the morning to earn his daily bread and room rent it was the way of wisdom to start out with a prayer in his heart and a sharp blade in his pocket; for if he accidentally stepped on a white man's foot in the subway crush he would have to do some fast slashing to keep from being lynched by the populace before the police arrived. If he failed to escape the enraged citizenry and run himself lost before the uniformed posse reached the scene he was a poor boy. The gendarmes would begin manhandling him where the plain people had left off and after they had broken their nightsticks and busted their blackjacks on his skull the magistrate would sentence him to three months on the island for assaulting New York.

Even if he reached the scene of his toil in safety life was far from being one sweet song. When lunch time came the chances were he would have to walk no less than six blocks before he could find a restaurateur willing to give him some stew and chicory in exchange for his quarter. When he came out of the eating place he would immediately be pounced upon by anywhere from two to ten of his compatriots who wanted to know if they really served colored people in that place or if he had only been in there to deliver something. They all knew from experience that hardly any clean looking restaurant would serve a Negro. But that was not an infallible rule as a majority of the dirty ones would also decline to sell an Aframerican a meal. In fact it was possible for a timid Negro to starve to death with plenty of money in his pocket.

When his hours of labor were ended and the time for pleasure came the black New Yorker's problems were by no means simplified. Many saloons would refuse his patronage and only the shabbier and less attractive ladies of the streets would consider his trade. If he craved spiritual entertainment in the form of theatrical divertissement the only way he could get any closer to the stage than the second balcony was to have the district attorney intercede for him at the box office. If he went to the theater alone he would have to park his posterior in a top gallery seat or remain on the sidewalk.

The portrayal of Negro character in the arts was a consummate idealization of the general attitude toward the concrete Negro in the street. In poetry he was the theme of Eden Philpotts' comminatory lyrics of lechery while in fiction the Rev. Thomas Dixon presented him as a rapist and the Hon. Octavius Roy Cohen presented him as an idiot. The official attitude of the theater was adequately expressed in that masterpiece of the screen, "The Birth of a Nation," which pictured the Negro as being endowed with all the attributes of Satan except his courage.

But those days are gone forever. About five years ago that discerning scholar and intrepid publicist, Eugene O'Neill, discovered that Negroes are the offspring of the Almighty and that under their B.V.D.'s and camisoles they conceal irredescent wings. He argued his case in public and proved it, and as a consequence the public attitude toward the Aframerican changed almost overnight. Now Negroes are physically safe in any part of town from Hell's Kitchen to Cannon Street, they can eat in most any restaurant where the scale of prices is not too steep, and it is being rumored that even the managers of Loew's theaters are considering admitting colored people to the orchestra floor without an argument after January 1st, 1938.

Although Mr. O'Neill established the theory of the celestial origin of black folks without assistance his view has subsequently been concurred in by no less than twenty distinguished scholars and scientists, among them, to name only a few, are Professors Odum and Johnson, Dr. Carl Van Vechten, Dr. David Belasco, Professors Jackson and White (Newman Ivey), Dr. DuBose Heyward and Dr. Paul Green. Each of these savants, working independently, has contributed valuable data to Mr. O'Neill's theory and each of them has labored to disseminate it through the public prints at prevailing space rates.

The latest convert to the theory is Prof. Jim Tulley, who assisted by

Mr. Frank Dazey, sets forth the result of his researches in a monograph entitled "Black Boy." The book is not yet off the press but in the interim Mr. Horace Liveright, the well known educator, is presenting the substance of the manuscript to the non-reading public in the form of a morality play which is being shown at the Comedy Theater every week day night and Wednesday and Saturday afternoons.

As theatrical entertainment "Black Boy" is livelier and more interesting than either "Lulu Belle" or "All God's Chillun' Got Wings" and it contains better acting. It is the task of Paul Robeson to act the central role and I doubt if any actor ever had a harder job. The way the play is written all the white characters are first cousins of the Devil while the leading colored character is compounded of the holiness of Simon, the Cyrenian, the spaciousness of Cyrano de Bergerac and the innocence of Little Eva. To give this blend of airy nothings the appearance of a substantial human being requires nothing less than a touch of histrionic genius and fortunately Robeson has it. There isn't a moment when he can afford to ease up, for the part contains at least half a dozen pitfalls where to couple the lines with a look or an inflection a bit too guileless would cause the character to slip off into the fearful abyss of sweetness and light. Robeson maintains the true tempo all the way, playing the part with effervescence and color without once suggesting the fantastic or flamboyant. His work alone invests the flimsy role with dignity and charm.

It is rather unfortunate, but Robeson's work as an actor almost nullifies Prof. Tully's work as a scientist. Complete harmony of collaboration between the two, of course, is not possible. As a scientist, Prof. Tully aims to have Black Boy demonstrate the soundness of a thesis; but once the type leaves his hands and is committed to those of Mr. Robeson, the latter, as an artist, must do his best to convert the wisp of scientific theory into a plausible colored Elk. In Mr. Liveright's morality Mr. Robeson's work unquestionably surpasses that of Prof. Tully. But there is ample consolation for Prof. Tully in the knowledge that when the book appears and his theory is stated in dispassionate print he will have all the better of it.

Next to Black Boy the most difficult part in the play is that of Irene, a near white yes-woman. This character furnished the key to Prof. Tully's thesis. She is about nine-tenths white and nine-tenths bad, and the trend of the play compels one to feel that only the touch of the tar brush gives her what little virtue she has. The role is intrusted to Edith Warren who handles it very neatly and smoothly except in the scene in which she is browbeaten into doublecrossing her lover. In that scene she fails to rise to an adequate heat of emotion, but before and after that she is good enough.

The other characters are conventional morality types, and as the actors to whom they are assigned appear to be skilled workers rather than artists they are presented just as they were written. I rather prefer their finished technique to Mr. Robeson's lavish artistry. After all I stand to gain socially and economically by the success of Prof. Tully's theory, and it won't do to have realists like Mr. Robeson bringing seraphic creatures like Black Boy down to earth. If Prof. Tully will write about three more moralities of this sort and cast them with the right kind of uninspired, plugging actors it will go a long way toward making it possible for a Negro to order a bowl of soup in even one of Child's restaurants without being crowned with a cuspidor.

THE BUSINESS SIDE OF THE LITTLE THEATRE

Little theater organizations, like other spiritual movements, usually start out in a white heat of enthusiasm. The members are full of zeal and they swear eternal allegiance to the cause and predict great things for the future. If the movement has been adequately advertised the first performance usually draws a sizable audience. But invariably the acting fails to run as smooth as it appeared at the final rehearsals. Either the curtain hangs and spoils a scene or some important piece of property is discovered to be missing at a crucial moment or some member of the cast gets nervous and makes a miscue. As a result of these gaucheries the second performance draws a smaller audience than the first one.

The decrease of public interest is followed by a waning of zeal on the part of the members of the organization. The less enthusiastic members begin to skip rehearsals, making it difficult to cast the pieces selected for the next performance. Perhaps it becomes necessary to postpone the next performance, and when that happens the interest of the public, already on the decline, disappears altogether. This is the way four out of five amateur theaters fail.

When the earnest members of the group get together to discuss the situation they usually trace the cause of their failure to the uninspired acting and the inferior quality of the plays they were compelled to present, lamenting the fact that their number did not contain a dramatist like Synge or O'Neill or at least one actor with a bit of the genius of Gilpin. They are likely to forget, or, rather, overlook the fact that the

Theater Guild achieved its phenomenal success without the assistance of an O'Neill and the Pasadena Little Theater, the Chapel Hill Players and the Dallas Little Theater each established itself in its community without the help of a Synge.

Besides the organizations just mentioned the list of little theaters which have won success without the boon of either dramatic or histrionic genius could be lengthened until it included upward of a score. In fact no exceptional talent is required to establish a little theater in any community where there is a spiritual demand for one. But it must not be taken for granted that a spiritual demand for a little theater, plus a willingness to cater to that demand on the part of a group of actors, is alone sufficient to insure the success of the movement.

The ideal of the little theater should be to serve the community by giving it the kind of entertainment the commercial stage will not provide because it is not profitable enough. But no community, no more than an individual, desires an incompetent servant. The first duty of the managers of an amateur theater is to prepare themselves to serve the community efficiently, and the best preliminary step toward that end, perhaps, is for the organization to plan to turn professional as fast as circumstances permit. To turn professional, of course, does not necessarily mean to turn commercial.

A discerning group will very quickly discover that impressive acting is the first step toward winning popular support. The recognition of this fact will bring the group face to face with a problem that must be dealt with intelligently and absolutely without sentiment. Few people think so, perhaps, but to become proficient in acting requires as much study and preparation as are needed to become proficient in the practice of medicine. The organization will have to choose between hiring professional actors to play all important roles and putting the more talented of its own members on a pay basis while they devote themselves to intensive training and frequent rehearsals. As it is easier to hire an actor than train one the former course is usually adopted. It will be recalled how the Provincetown Theater called in Gilpin, an outside professional, to play Brutus Jones, and Robeson, another outside professional, to interpret the leading part in All God's Chillun' Got Wings. Either way the question is decided it means an expenditure of money and raises the problem of how to obtain it. Unless the organization contains a few cool business heads in addition to the members with ability to act or write this is the point where the theater will go under.

There are various ways of dealing with this problem successfully, of course, but I think the plan outlined in the concluding paragraphs of this article will be found serviceable by any Negro little theater which has not already worked out a better solution for itself.

Regardless of the attitude of the other members of the group the persons intrusted with the business management of the organization should regard the little theater as a commodity for which they must find a market. It ought to be obvious from the outset that they cannot sell their commodity to the community as a whole. A part of the public will be found to be opposed to the theater on principle while another section is satisfied with the offerings of the local vaudeville house, and a third contingent is disinterested in the theater as a vehicle of entertainment. For a theater with limited or no funds to attempt to win an audience from the entire community on the merits of its ideals is as ridiculous as a bond salesman looking for customers among day laborers.

The first appeal of the little theaters should be made to those members of the community who are so dissatisfied with the commercial theater that they are willing to contribute toward subsidizing a movement to bring the stage up to the level of the community's culture and spiritual life.

REFLECTIONS OF AN ALLEGED
DRAMATIC CRITIC

In the following essay, published in June 1927, Theophilus Lewis discusses the musical satire Gay Harlem. *He responds to criticism that the play was a "medley of loose morals."*

WHAT THE THEATRE IS SUPPOSED TO DO

Among those who visited the Lafayette seeking diversion the last time Irvin Miller fetched his musical satire, "Gay Harlem," to town was Mr. Edgar Grey, the intensely interesting staff writer of the *Amsterdam News.* Unlike the majority of colored musical shows, which are compounded of sheer imbecility sugar-coated with music and dancing, "Gay Harlem" was an intelligent and highly entertaining lampoon of the more picaresque phases of life as it is lived in this community of rooming houses and hot-dog stands. The revue poked a good deal of ribald fun at the journalistic corruption and high pressure gold digging which exists in this and other big cities, and when the girls came out to dance they showed the audience everything they had except their little belly buttons and two or three other articles. Whereupon Mr. Grey, with a shocked and horrified expression on his face, rushed out in the street and, metaphorically at least, yelled for the cops to stop the show.

The following week Mr. Grey published a brief bill of particulars in which he explained in detail why he objected to the performance. Now Mr. Grey is undeniably an astute observer of life and if anybody doubts it I refer the doubter to his discerning articles on social conditions in Harlem which have been appearing in the *Amsterdam News.* But while he observes life in general with a cool and penetrating eye his criticism of "Gay Harlem" reveals a decidedly puerile conception of the nature and function of the theatre. "Gay Harlem," Mr. Grey complained, was a medley of loose morals and lasciviousness blended with a wanton display of female flesh. That is quite true, as no one who saw the revue can deny; but it was precisely those qualities which made it a valuable contribution to the contemporary theatre. When Mr. Grey contradicts this he places himself in opposition to the greatest authority on the theatre the world has ever known.

The function of the stage, says Shakespeare, is "to hold, as it were, the mirror up to nature; to show virtue her own feature, scorn her own image, and the very age and body of the time his form and pressure." Now swindling and gold digging are everyday occurences in the modern world and journalistic knavery is certainly no rare phenomenon. To prove the first, one has only to read the daily run of police court news and it was only recently that the Associated Press was accused of attempting to build up war sentiment by forging "news" which was nothing more than a libel on the Mexican people. If one demands an example of degraded journalism closer to our own life I point to Chandler Owen's expose of the amazing corruption of the *Chicago Whip*, and Mr. Grey himself claims that a certain Harlem newspaper man was once on the payroll of a night club. Does Mr. Grey believe that an editor who will prostitute his profession for money where a man is concerned, will refuse to let a woman pay off in love? And when Mr. Miller reflects this condition on the stage, with a touch of mordant humor, is he not holding the mirror up to life?

Another phase of modern life is reflected in the prevailing tendency of theatrical producers to require chorus girls to parade the stage in their birthday garments. For whether we like it or not feminine modesty, or what we used to call modesty, has virtually disappeared from women's daily conduct. Not so long ago a woman whose garter snapped while she was walking down the street would ring the nearest doorbell and whisper her predicament to the housewife who came to the door. Then she would retire to the bathroom and lock the door before making the necessary repairs, and when she returned to the street again she would glare belligerently at every man she met in the next five blocks. Nowadays a damsel who feels that her underthings are not just right steps out to the curbstone and blows a police whistle so that a sizable audience will be on hand when she flaps her dress up around her waist and proceeds to arrange her thingumbob. Nudity on the stage is not the cause of this decline of modesty but only one of many reflections of it.

Mr. Grey, like the sincere reformer he is, did not stop with stating his objections to the revue as it was; he made his criticism "construc- tive" by suggesting alternative themes which Mr. Miller could have employed to keep "Gay Harlem" sweet and pure, or at least sanitary. Instead of selecting his material from the dives of the underworld, Mr. Grey declared, the author should have sought his subjects in the home life of Harlem. This suggestion has a good deal of merit in it, but, in passing, one might remark that what usually goes on in the Harlem home is not gay but tragic.

It is sad to say, perhaps, but the modern home, like every other phase of modern life, is in a state of flux and retains precious little of its former stability and serenity. The home of Mr. Grey's youth—the home which by day was the scene of placid domesticity, with the housewife busy canning preserves, darning socks and getting the chil- dren off to school, and by night the haven of the tired husband who smoked his pipe and read his newspaper while his wife crochetted doilies and his son read Oliver Optic's stories, and his daughter played Lead Kindly Light on the piano—that tranquil and romantic home does not exist any more. Instead, the modern so-called home is—well, you can read what it is in Mr. Grey's newspaper. According to an end- less succession of news items a close-up of the typical home today would be pretty likely to reveal the daughter and her sweetie petting in the parlor, the son and his cutie necking in the dining room, a bur- glar somewhere in the house making off with the family jewelry and the star boarder in the housewife's bedroom making off with the fam- ily honor. As for the head of the house, it's a ten-to-one shot that he would be found in some night club telling a sixteen-year-old vamp his wife didn't understand him.

This is a pretty fair picture of the modern home at its best. At its worst—Let us again turn to the public prints for enlightenment. The same week Mr. Grey's article in question appeared his paper carried a story of a man being indicted for tampering with his daughter's virtue, or, at any rate, her sex; and the preceding issue published a report that in one week no less than four men had been tossed in the bastile for de- priving six-year-old girls of their innocence. Not long previous to that the *New Masses* featured an article which disclosed the surprising prevalence of incest in Brooklyn. These practices, because of their very nature and the intimate contact required for their preparation and performance, cannot be carried on in public. They require privacy for their accomplishment and the most private of all places is the home, and the evidence shows that is precisely where most of them occur. For the sake of whatever illusions still exist about the sanctity of the home, let us be thankful that Mr. Miller gathered his material for satire elsewhere.

If Mr. Grey will consider "Gay Harlem" in the light of colored theatrical history of the past fifteen years, I believe he will agree with me that it is the most significant contribution to the Negro theatre since Leubrie Hill's "Darktown Follies." It means far more to our cultural advance than an occasional musical comedy downtown or an occasional dramatic actor in a bogus "Negro" play on Broadway. The Miller revue was a definite effort to get away from the ghost theme, the black man Friday theme and the yardbird theme. It is true that most Negroes, like most Caucasians and Chinese, are afraid of ghosts, but in our crowded urban tenements they seldom see them; perhaps some Negroes have been stranded on desert islands but it is not typical of our experience; perhaps, too, some Negroes are addicted to stealing chickens or anything else that isn't nailed down, but such nocturnal marauders have never been numerous enough to be made the main subject of travesty. Still colored musical shows, including Mr. Miller's own in the past, have depended on those themes almost exclusively to produce their comical effects. And for just that reason most of them have been entertainment fit only for imbeciles.

When Mr. Miller turns away from grotesqueries and bufooneries, which never had any real existence except in the minds of inferior white men and inferior Negroes who imitated them, and attempts to make the stage reflect the foibles and libertinage of our age he is bringing the theater into some sensible relationship with life. In other words, he is holding the mirror up to nature. A looking glass does not make a man ugly; it only reflects the ugliness the man already has. When a man is displeased with the reflection he sees in the mirror he does not throw the mirror away. He purges his body and alters his diet and applies cosmetics to his skin. On the other hand, if he is pleased with his appearance he will do nothing but look in the glass as often as he can. It is the same way with the theatre. If we do not like the social ugliness we see on the stage the remedy is not to close the theatre or bawl the actors out, but to change our way of living. When people pack a theatre every night, it is a sign that they like the social behavior they see reflected there. When they cease to like it they will stay away from the theatre and the producer will alter his entertainment to suit the changed taste of the public.

It is encouraging to note that "Gay Harlem" played to packed houses. If the piece had not drawn well the chances are that Mr. Miller, like the sensible theatrical business man he is, would have discarded it and gone back to the old graveyard comedy. But with heavy audiences clamoring to see the piece every night, he ought to be encouraged to try his hand with other revues of the same kind. If he will only get rid of burnt cork now he will bring the stage even closer to life as it actually is. Then it will be only a step to a still higher form of theatrical entertainment—the authentic portrayal of Negro character through the medium of drama.

MY RED RAG

Theophilus Lewis reviews two plays by Paul Green: The Field God *and* In Abraham's Bosom. *This essay was published in January 1928.*

The Paul Green menace increases. He has conquered the experimental theatres and consolidated his successes behind him and now his vanguard has established contact with Broadway. It is an event I am sorry to see for Mr. Green looms as an evil geni threatening the development of Negro drama. The man, I am convinced, is a third rater at best, whose growing popularity is the result of the efficient ballyhooing of Barrett H. Clark combined with the fact that his more conspicuous successes were won with plays of Negro life. Now the general run of white people are absolutely ignorant of Negro life and white critics appear to cherish wild and antinomian ideas about it. This ignorance on the part of both critics and public enables an incompetent playwright to get away with murder by the simple expedient of calling his gaucheries "Negro" plays, provided he writes about sordidness in a sentimental way and winds up his stories with a sad ending.

Now any playwright in a conspicuous place will be imitated by younger writers struggling for a hearing. It makes no difference whether his high place is the reward of merit or merely the result of persistent advertising. If Paul Green's reputation as a first rate playwright stands embryo colored authors will follow his example and we will have no end of plays imitating Paul Green's imitations of Eugene O'Neill. Already certain intellectuals and actors who played in "Abraham's Bosom" are forming a kind of Paul Green cult and already I discern his influence on the offerings of budding Negro writers. Since Negro drama is my religion just now and since I consider Mr. Green's popularity inimical to its healthy growth it requires no gift of second sight to understand why his works affect me in just about the same way a socialist flag soothes a gentleman Guernsey.

I pick up his latest volume, a McBride book containing two plays, The Field God and In Abraham's Bosom, hoping to find something wrong with it. Happily, I am not disappointed. "In Abraham's Bosom," of course, is what I said it was when I reviewed its Provincetown performance. It is two plays of The Lonesome Road series spliced together and disguised with a few extra scenes and characters. It is entirely without genuine emotional appeal and was able to hold the boards only so long as it was propped up by the Provincetown subscription list. When it moved to Broadway, where a play must at least be interesting in order to make the grade, it fizzled out in short order.

"The Field God" is a somewhat better play that barely manages to achieve mediocrity. In this play Mr. Green deals with familiar material—the life of rustic poor whites. Its best features are the vital and sturdy dialogue which enliven the early and middle scenes and its photographic duplication of the land and its fauna, but this, I hasten to add, is not drama but atmosphere. In character drawing and action, the essentials of drama, the play falls as flat as a mushroom. The characters are mere puppets and the action is entirely arbitrary.

One of Mr. Green's quaint notions is that suffering alone constitutes tragedy. This is not true. Tragedy, in its dramatic sense, is the misfortune that befalls a man as an unescapable result of his efforts to better his condition or preserve his virtue. As conspicuous examples I point to Macbeth, Hamlet, The Wild Duck and The Emperor Jones. Most of the calamities which occur in "The Field God" happen independently of the beliefs and conduct of the characters. Hence the play as a whole is artificial, illogical and unconvincing.

Although the book is no great shakes as literature it is little less than a marvel of the bookmaker's art. Next to The Lonesome Road, it has the most gorgeous cover I have ever seen. Doubtless the publishers felt that they ought to give the purchaser some value for his money.

PART FOUR

ESSAYS

COLORED AUTHORS AND THEIR CONTRIBUTIONS TO THE WORLD'S LITERATURE

In the following essay, Irene M. Gaines presents a compelling discussion of the contributions of African descendants to world literature from the fifteenth century to the 1920s. This essay was published in November 1923.

The evening was very dreary. The rain beat a dismal tatoo on the window pane. Just how long I had been studying my literature lesson I cannot tell, but my eyelids grew very heavy and I could not resist the wooing of Morpheus.

Suddenly I seemed to be standing before a dream palace. A waning sun cast its rays of elfin gold on the wide marble stairs. Lifting my eyes to the inscription over the entrance I saw the words: The World's Literature Building.

Traversing the brilliantly lighted hallway, I stood on the threshold of a spacious, high vaulted room opening into similar ones beyond. I was greeted by a group of friendly persons who volunteered to escort me through this wonderful building. The first room that we visited was Historians' Hall.

In this interesting apartment there were magnificent paintings of the world's great historians. I was surprised by seeing so many black faces. Who are those distinguished looking black men wearing turbans? I asked. The first was Mohaman Koti, an eminent Negro writer born in the year A.D. 1460, in a little Sudanese village. His life and works date from the third quarter of the 15th century to the year 1560. His most celebrated work, *Fatassi*, is a history of the kingdoms of Ganata, Songhai, and the city of Timbuctoo, the queen of the Sudan.

The second painting was that of Ahmen Baba, called, "the unique Pearl of his time." This great man was born in Arawan, Africa, a city of the Sudan, in the year 1556. He is the author of twenty known books, dealing with philosophy, law, ethics, traditions, theology, rhetoric and astronomy. His text books were used in such noted universities as those of Fez, Tunis, Sankore, and Cairo. M. DuBois, a celebrated French scholar and African traveler, was so impressed with the writings and scholarship of the Sudanese Negroes, that he spoke of them in these words of praise:

> The learning and scholarship of the Sudanese Blacks were genuine and so thorough that during their sojourn in foreign universities they astounded the most learned men of Islam by their erudition. That these Negroes were on the level with the Arabian savants, their teachers, is proved by the fact that they were installed as professors in Morocco and Cairo.

By the 16th century these black scholars became so learned that they were regarded as dangerous and it was this that brought upon them the Moorish exile in Morocco. While there our distinguished author, Ahmen Baba, taught rhetoric, law and theology. His decisions in the courts were regarded as final. After some years he was allowed to return to his beloved country where he died in 1627. Among his works we find an astronomical treatise written in verse. *Miraz*, a work written by Baba while in exile, is a wonderful description of the erudition of the Negraic peoples residing in the very heart of Africa. By this work the attention of Morocco and the whole of northern Africa was called to the culture and scholarship of the Sudan Negro. On account of *El Ibitihadj*, his large biographical dictionary of the Mussulman doctors of the Malekite sect (completed in 1596), it has been possible to reconstruct the intellectual past of Timbuctoo, showing the culture and civilization of the Negro race in the Sudan, Africa. For this reason the name of Ahmen Baba should be held in pious memory by every lover of the race. His great, great, grandchildren are now living in Timbuctoo, near the mosque of Sankore.

Passing on I came to the painting of Abderraham es Sadi, another African scholar, whose best works were written in the first quarter of the 17th century. He wrote *Tarik e Soudan*, a history of the Sudan, and is the greatest work on the Sudan in existence. It forms, with the exception of the holy writings, the favorite volume of the Negro savants throughout central Africa, and is known to the furthest extremity of western Africa from the shores of the Niger to the borders of Lake Chad. The whole work is a collection of active morals and is the most charming of its kind; for fables, marvels and miracles are agreeably intermingled with real events.

One enjoys, says a French critic, from its pages the delicate repasts offered by Homer, Herodotus and Froissard, and it is for this reason that the *Tarik* is called the chief work of Sudanese literature.

Adjoining Historians' Hall was another spacious room in which there were thousands of books. Glancing through the catalogue I came across many other Negro historians. There was John Sarbar, author of *Fanti Customary Laws,* written near the close of the 19th century, and said to be the most authoritative work on native laws and customs. The author, an educated native of the Gold Coast, West Africa, tells understandingly and truly every phase of the customary laws of his people. This valuable work has done as much, if not more, than any other to place the African and his institutions before the world in something like their true light and condition.

Casely Hayford is another one of the great native African writers living in west Africa, who is making some valuable contributions to the literature of Africa and the world. His *Institutions of the Gold Coast, Native Constitutions,* and *Ethiopia Unbound* have made the Negroes of Africa and the world his debtors.

Perhaps there is no continent and no people held in such little esteem through ignorance of their true life, culture and character as Africa and its races, and against whom there is so much unfounded prejudice. That the African race has for centuries been producing its own authors to interpret Africa and her people to the nations of the earth, ought to be an inspiration to Negroes and mankind everywhere. By his wide acquaintance with native life and conditions, his great command of literary form and style, Hayford may well be mentioned with Sarbar whose literary prominence recalls the fadeless fame of Koti, Baba and Sadi who gave the heart of Africa to the highest form of literature more than three centuries ago.

There was the great Dr. Edward Wilmot Blyden; this great writer died an old man in 1912, in the little British colony of Sierra Leone. His writings began with the last quarter of the 19th century. Among his most prominent works we find: *Christianity, Islam and the Negro Race; The Koran in Africa; West Africa before Europe; Liberia's Offering,* and *Monrovia to Palestine.* Such scholarly productions were his that they have been translated from English into French, German, Italian and Arabic. Besides these publications Dr. Blyden has written numerous essays and pamphlets on different subjects touching the welfare of African peoples and the government of them by European colonial powers. For years he has been recognized as the foremost authority on west Africa; and has done more than any other thinker and writer to modify and soften the attitude of white Europe in its government and control of black Africa. Familiar with French, German, Arabic and a number of native tongues, and with a literary style that is fascinating, forceful and unique, this noted writer will ever be remembered as among the first and foremost scholars on Africa; besides he was for years Secretary of State of Liberia, Envoy Extraordinary and Minister Plenipotentiary to the Court of St. James, Special Enjoy to the republic of France and Director of Mohamudan education in Sierra Leone.

And W. S. Scarborough, former President of Wilberforce University, a most scholarly gentleman, has contributed several text books. His Greek grammars have been used in Harvard, Yale and other colleges in the United States and are recognized as being among the best text books written on this subject.

There was William A. Sinclair's *Aftermath of Slavery,* a record of the progress of the colored citizens in the United States since the Civil War. This book, written in 1905, has wide reading by the American public and has done much to correct the views of people in this country and abroad, concerning the character and progress of the American Negro. The press and literary critics have justly paid tribute to its merits. For some time Mr. Sinclair was Secretary and Treasurer of Howard University, and has taken a prominent part in the advance movements in behalf of the race. He now resides in Philadelphia.

George W. Williams, of Ohio. Here I find two large and splendid volumes written in 1888 on *The History of the Negro Troops in the War of the Rebellion.* The author of these publications had begun another upon the *History of the Negro of the World,* when in the midst of his literary task he suddenly died. He was a member of the Ohio legislature for some years; and his history of the Negro is perhaps the best history ever written of the colored people in the United States. His style is warm, vivid and glowing and replete with copies of documents from original sources, exhaustive of every phase of his subject. Without a dissenting voice he is the premier historian of the American Negro. It would be difficult to find words that would praise too highly the literary and substantial character of his works.

And now turning to the name of Kelly Miller, I was very much interested in the high quality and character of his works. As Dean of the college department of Howard University for some years he has held a unique position in the education of colored people. He is preeminently a controversial thinker. In the many great questions before the country in which white prejudiced writers sought to defame the character and ability of the Negro race, they have found in the pen of this race thinker, a power that has been unable to be subdued. One after another he dashed off in brilliant form and style, *Roosevelt and the Negro; Appeal to Reason; Forty Years of Negro Education; The Ultimate Race Problem; The Political Capacity of the Negro; Social Equality,* and other pamphlets similar in character and surpassed himself in a splendid collection of high-class essays dealing with the multiform phases of the race problem; and we had in 1905 his great work, *Race Adjustment,* to be followed by his *From Servitude to Service.* The Cleveland Plain Dealer says of him:

Prof. Miller shows himself a master of an incisive style and a keen logician. (Of him the New York Post remarks: Admirable for calmness and temper, thoroughness and skill.)

Dr. Booker T. Washington, regarded by Andrew Carnegie as one of the foremost men of this age, was president and founder of the great industrial Institute of Tuskegee, the greatest institution of its kind in the world. He sprang into prominence in 1890 by what is known as his Atlanta speech, in which he pleads for peace between the races and urged them to unite for the common good in all matters industrial, remaining separate socially. He was the trusted advisor on Southern matters of two presidents, wined and dined by Princes and crowned heads of Europe and accepted by the authorities as the leader of the American Negro. He was an advocate of the gospel of work and so careful a publication as *The Independent,* after his speech on Abraham Lincoln, pronounced him the most forceful speaker living. He was more than an orator, organizer, educator. He was a great writer. His first great book in 1901 was *Up from Slavery,* in which he told to the world his inspiring story of his struggle from the humblest state of the slave to a coveted place among the foremost men of his day and time. He was wont to address his students at Tuskegee in Sunday evening talks, and in a splendid volume he gathered them together in his book entitled *Character,* in which he emphasized the growth of habit and the priceless possession of good character. He is the author of other books, *The Life of Frederick Douglass, My Experience, The Future of the America Negro, Sowing and Reaping, Tuskegee and Its People,* and *The Negro in Business.* With a clear and forceful style and an abundance of practical facts he has impressed this country and the world. It is said that his *Up from Slavery* has been translated into more foreign languages than any other work by an American Negro. The lustre of his life, fame and works sheds glory upon the whole Negro race.

George Washington Ellis, investigator, writer and statesman, served the United States government as Secretary of the American Legation to the Republic of Liberia. While in Liberia he studied the social conditions of Africa, collecting folk-lore stories and African proverbs, and contributed to leading magazines and newspapers on African problems and questions, in Europe and America. Mr. Ellis was a contributing editor to the *Journal of Race Development,* of Clark University, is the author of *Liberia in the Political Psychology of West Africa; Islam as a Factor in West African Culture; Dynamic Factors in the Liberian Situation; Negro Culture in West Africa; The Leopard's Claw; Negro Achievements in Social Progress,* and other subjects. Of his *Negro Culture in West Africa,* the Neale Publishing Company has this to say:

> Undoubtedly, this volume is among the more important contributions to the literature of the Negro race to be published, from whatever angle it is viewed. For eight years, while Secretary of the American Legation to Liberia, this Negro studied social conditions in Africa, collected folk-lore stories and proverbs, took photographs of Negroes at their occupations, and during their social intercourse. In this volume are specimen stories written in Vai tongue, with translations of them. The author was well equipped when he undertook this work.

Prof. Frederick Starr, of the University of Chicago, in his introduction to *Negro Culture in West Africa,* said of Mr. Ellis:

> He was a faithful and competent official, giving good service. He has been useful to Liberia since his return and his thoughtful and valuable articles regarding Liberian conditions and affairs have done much to keep alive American interest regarding the only republic in Africa. During the period of his service in Africa, Mr. Ellis found time and occasion to pursue the studies, the results of which are here represented. Consuls and diplomatic officers have exceptional opportunities to enrich our knowledge of other lands and peoples. Many such officials—British, French, German, Russian—have made important contributions of that sort. American officials who have done so are surprisingly few. Mr. Ellis sets an example that is worthy of wide imitation.

Mr. Ellis is the third colored man to make conspicuous contributions to the knowledge of conditions and peoples in the Liberian region. Neither Blyden nor Crummell have gone quite into the field which Mr. Ellis enters. As a scientific investigation, as a contribution to social problems, as a basis for political action, his book has a definite mission.

Mr. Ellis for his distinguished services rendered Liberia was decorated by that government, Knight Commander of the Order of African Redemption. Mr. Ellis completed his life's work in Chicago in November, 1919. He seemed to be a special envoy and literary ambassador extraordinary, sent to earth by Dame Nature in behalf of the great movements of democracy, inter-racial concord and cooperation. For, as is the custom of such high and special missions, he took his leave as soon as his work was done. Among his papers and documents that he left he has a message for the South and the white races of the world.

Passing from this room we entered *Fiction Hall,* a room just as spacious and more beautiful. This room was crowded with great figures and I wondered if they were visitors like myself; but they looked so much at home, though some were very antique. My guides told me that these were the authors themselves. Naturally I looked for the colored faces—and I found them.

There was a very distinguished gentlemen who came up and said to me in French, "Good evening, Miss" (Bon Soir, Mademoiselle), and then I knew him—we all know him, the greatest of all colored novelists, Alexandre Dumas, born in France in the first half of the 19th century, author of the world renowned *Count of Monte Cristo,* its sequel, *Edmund Dantes; Three Guardsmen; Twenty Years After; The Man in the Iron Mask; The Bastille; The Queen's Necklace; La Tulipe Noire,* and many other notable works that have interested and delighted the world of letters. Some critics place him at the head of the world's novel writers in style, the development and portrayal of characters. His influence for good has been world wide and he has immortalized the Negro in tales of romance and fiction. His name recalls to our minds the great and immortal novelists, Defoe and Dickens of England, Victor Hugo, of France, Harriet Beecher Stowe, of America, Alexandre Pushkin, of Russia, and Cervantes, of Spain.

Another distinguished looking gentlemen whom I recognized at once was W. E. Burghardt DuBois, an American Negro, who for the last fifteen years has been writing some of the world's best compositions. This author has done much to influence the giving of higher education to the Negro boy and girl. His works have caused the world to discuss anew the Negro problem. His renowned book, *Souls of Black Folk,* has been read by millions and entitled him to a permanent place among the fiction writers of the globe. With a charm and felicity of style he has disclosed the inner feelings and emotions of the American black people under the peculiar and embarrassing environment of the American social and political conditions. He is also the author of a recognized and standard work on *The Negro Slave Trade;* and is regarded as one of the most brilliant men ever graduated from Harvard University. From the press there has been issued more recently the *Quest of the Silver Fleece,* reviewed by William Stanley Braithwaite, another brilliant writer of our race. I fancy I see in his hands a picture of a young Negro boy and girl standing in a cotton field and I recall Bless Ahlyn and Zora in their quest of the silver fleece. This was followed by his historical sketch, *The Negro,* issued from the University Press of Cambridge. This little volume, together with his newest work, *Darkwater,* have brought new lustre and fame to the author and will be read with increasing interest and enthusiasm by thousands of black and white, throughout the world. He is the editor of *The Crisis,* a national Negro publication creating and moulding sentiment everywhere for equality and justice to Negro peoples. We might justly say of him what Shakespeare said of Brutus:

> He was mild and gentle and the elements so mixed in him that all nature might stand up and say, "this is a man."

Of the world's great Negroes of this present era we think with pride and delight of DuBois as a scholar and American race champion; of Blyden as a linguist and champion of the African Negro; of Kelly Miller as the thinker and race controversialist, and of Washington as the practical organizer and leader of men.

Sliding doors opened into Poets' Hall. This was the most beautiful of all. Here I also found the little African girl, Phyllis, who in 1871 was sold in a Boston slave market to a very cultured and loving woman, Mrs. John Wheatley, who grew to love little Phyllis dearly and trained her in the fine arts. There were many beautiful poems written from the depths of her pure young heart between the years of 1763 and 1784. The poem addressed to Gen. George Washington brought to her a lovely letter of thanks from the father of our country. Her translation of one of Ovid's stories was widely published in Europe. It was she who said:

T'was mercy brought me from my pagan land
And taught my benighted soul to understand
That there's a God—that there's a Saviour too;
Once I redemption neither sought nor knew.

My guide told me that the next brown, aristocratic personage who greeted me was Alexander Sergeivitch Pushkin, a Russian poet of splendid family. His great grandfather was the distinguished Negro General Hannibal of Peter the Great. This illustrious poet was born at Moscow, May 26th, 1799, and educated at the Imperial lyceum of Tsarskoe Selo, where he acquired a reputation for his liberal opinions. In 1817 he entered the service of the government, and soon became one of the most prominent figures in fashionable society. In 1820 he published his romantic poem of *Ruslan and Liudmila,* which met with flattering reception from the public. The incidents are laid in the legendary times of Vladimir, the Russian Charlemagne. During the next five years Pushkin gave to the world his *Plennik Kavkaskoi* (Prisoner of the Caucasus), which narrates the escape of a young Russian from a Circassian horde by the help of a Circassian maid; and his *Fountain of Bakhtchiserai,* in 1824, a poem of singular beauty and interest. These were followed by *Tzigani* (The Gypsies), a picture of a wild gypsy life in Bessarabia, and *Evgenii Onaegin,* a humorously sarcastic description of Russian society, after the fashion of Byron's *Beppo.* In 1829 he published his narrative poem, *Pultava,* and about the same time he wrote a dramatic poem entitled *Boris Godunow,* one of the best of all his works. He has to his credit the fact that he was the founder of the realistic school in Russian fiction, antedating the English masters of the same school. He is rated as the finest poet that Russia has produced. His countrymen call him the "Russian Byron"; however, it is claimed that he excels the latter in vigor of imagery and impassioned sentiment.

Next, I found a young man, very young, who had written poems since his childhood until his pathetic death in 1906, the beloved poet of the American Negro, Paul Laurence Dunbar. He is to us as Robert Burns singing to the Scotch among the hills of his native land. He wrote many poems on the lowly life of his people. He wrote of their sorrows and their joys and the common walks of their daily life and gave them in permanent literary form to the reading world. Most of his poems are in dialect. They are compiled in several volumes, among them, *Lyrics of Lowly Life, Lyrics of Love and Laughter, Lyrics of the Hearthside,* and others of equal merit. It was he who expressed life so poetically and incisively:

A crust of bread and a corner to sleep in,
A minute to laugh and an hour to weep in;
A pint of joy and a peck of trouble,
And never a laugh but the moans come double;
And that is Life.

A crust and a corner that love makes precious
With the smiles to warm and the tears to refresh us
And joy seems sweeter when care comes after
And a moan is the finest of foils for laughter;
And that is Life.

It would be difficult to find in the whole range of literature lines more immortally beautiful than these from the soul of this Negro poet:

An angel robed in spotless white
Stooped down to kiss the sleeping night;
Night woke to blush; the Sprite was gone:
Man saw the blush and called it Dawn.

When I left the World's Literature Building my heart was joyful and filled with exceeding gladness.

May our authors ever write and our poets ever sing, and in the end may they be heard way out upon the uplifted plains of the future in one grand sweet strain:

Bring forth the royal diadem
And crown Him Lord of all.

THE BLACK CITY

When Eric Walrond published this essay in January 1924, there were 185,000 blacks living in Harlem. Walrond offers a resplendent description of Harlem, the village he called "the seething spot of the darker races in the world."

I

North of 125th Street and glowing at the foot of Spuyten Duyvil is the sweltering city of Harlem, the "Black Belt" of Greater New York. With Negroes residing on San Juan Hill, on the East Side, in Greenwich Village, Harlem, undoubtedly, is the seething spot of the darker races of the world. As Atlanta, Georgia, is the breeding spot of the American Negro; Chicago, the fulfillment of his industrial hopes; Washington, the intellectual capital of his world; so is Harlem, with its 185,000 beings, the melting pot of the darker races. Here one is able to distinguish the blending of prodigal sons and daughters of Africa and Polynesia and the sun-drenched shores of the Caribbean; of peasant folk from Georgia and Alabama and the marsh lands of Florida and Louisiana. Here is banker and statesman, editor and politician, poet and scholar, scientist and laborer. Here is a world of song and color and emotion. Of life and beauty and majestic somnolence.

It is a sociological *el dorado*. With its rise, its struggles, its beginnings; its loves, its hates, its visionings, its tossings on the crest of the storming white sea; its orgies, its gluttonies; its restraints, its passivities; its spiritual yearnings—it is beautiful. On its bosom is the omnipresent symbol of oneness, of ethnologic oneness. Of solidarity! Hence its striving, its desperate striving, after a pigmentational purity, of distinctiveness of beauty. It is neither white nor black.

It is a city of dualities. Yonder, as the sun shoots its slanting rays across the doorstep of a realtor or banker or capitalist there is a noble son of Africa Redeemed on whose crown it shines. Well groomed, he is monocled or sprayed with a leaf of violet. By way of a boutonniere he sports a white or crimson aster—and in he goes. It is the beginning of his day as merchant or realtor or whatever he is.... Towards sunset, as his pale-faced prototype resigns himself to supper or home or cabaret or adoring wife or chorus girl he is seen, is this black son, this time in denim or gold-braided toga, on his way to that thing that puts bread in his and his wife's and his children's mouths, and steels that silver-like spot glowing at the bottom of him, so that day in and day out he doggedly goes on, striving, conquering, upbuilding.

It is the beginning of his day as a domestic.

II

It is a city of paradoxes. You go to the neighborhood theatre and there is a play of Negro life. It is sharp, true, poignant. In awe you open your mouth at the beauty, the majesty, the sheer Russian-like reality of it. Grateful, the house asks for the author, the creator, the playwright. He is dragged forward; there is an outburst of applause—emotion unleashed. Modestly bowing the young man is slowly enveloped in the descending shadows—and the crowd is no more.

Wonderful! You go home; on a roseate bed you sleep, dream, remember things. In the morning you get up. Slipping into a dressing robe you go down in answer to the postman's shrilling whistle. Out of eyes painted with mist you go and take the letter, take the letter from the postman. Wholly by accident you raise your eyes and find, find yourself looking at—the playwright!

It is a city of paradoxes. Along the avenue you are strolling. It is dusk. Harlem at dusk—is exotic. Music. Song. Laughter. The street is full of people—dark, brown, crimson, pomegranate. Crystal clear is the light that shines in their eyes. It is different, is the light that shines in these black people's eyes. It is a light mirroring the emancipation of a people and still you feel that they are not quite emancipated. It is the light of an unregenerate.

As I say, you are walking along the avenue. There is a commotion. No, it is not really a commotion. Only a gathering together of folk. "Step this way, ladies and gentlemen ... step this way.... There you are. ... Now this Coofu medicine is compounded from the best African herbs ..." East Fourteenth Street. Nassau Street. The Jewish ghetto.

Glimpses of them whirl by you. Not of the Barnum herd, you are tempted to go on, to let the asses gourmandize it. Seized by a fit of reminiscence you pause. Over the heads of the mob you see, not the bushy, black-haired head of the Hindu "fakir," the Ph.D. of Oxford and Cambridge (in reality the blatant son of the acacia soil of Constant Springs, Jamaica, still basking in the shadows of dialectical oppression); not the boomeranging Congo oil magnate; nor the Jew invader with his white, ivory white cheeks, hungry, Christ-like features, and flowing rabbinical beard. Instead you see a black man, of noble bearing, of intellectual poise, of undefiled English, a university man, selling at 900 per cent profit a beastly concoction that even white barbarians do not hesitate to gobble up.

And there is a reason, a mighty reason, for this, for the conversion, for the triumph of this black charlatan; a reason that goes up into the very warp and woof of American life. Imagine it—think, think about it sometime.

III

It is a house of assignation, a white man's house of assignation, is this black city. It is voluptuously accessible to him. Before cabarets and restaurants, cabarets and restaurants that black folk cannot go into, he stops, draws up his limousine, takes his lady, bathed in shining silk, out; squeezes through the molting, unminding folk, tips the black pyramidal *major domo,* and skips up to the scarlet draped seraglio. Here is white morality, white bestiality, for the Negroes to murmur and shake their bronzing cauliflower heads at.

It is wise, is this black city.

ART AND PROPAGANDA

William Pickens makes the case that art and propaganda are generally en-twined. He denounces those who claim that propaganda must not exist in art. He published this essay in April 1924.

What we are going to say now will make us a Philistine to some of the "artists," and to all of the near-artists. But a little *thinking* will do even an artist some good.

The artists, and especially the near-artists, are now-a-days far over-doing the idea that Art and Propaganda cannot be done in the same book, or same work of any kind. "There must be no propaganda in a work of art."—They forget that that statement is simply one of the dogmas of art, a convenient reduction of a certain principle,—but that, like all other dogmas, even the dogmas of religion, it is not and cannot be one hundred per cent true.

Have not the artists and the "artists" ever reflected that, just like the religionists, they never offer any inductive proof of this dogma, but they simply *declare* it? And for the simple reason that *data* would over-throw the dogma.

It would be much nearer the truth to say this: *Art and Propaganda always do exist side by side;* for in fact propaganda is the subsoil out of which all art has grown,—religious, ethical, racial or class propaganda. *But* (and here's what the near-artists stumble over) *it is the function of art to so conceal the propaganda as to make it more palatable to the average recipient, while yet not destroying its effect.*

Different arts vary in this purpose element: not every poem, not every lyric, has any general purpose, but practically every story has. And even the little poem, while minus a general purpose in propaganda, may have a direct personal reference or aim toward some individual.

"Uncle Tom's Cabin" can lay some claims to art,—and yet it was the last word in propaganda. Dickens was certainly a literary artist, and about all he wrote was propaganda. And were not all Italian art, and most of the music of the world, done in the cause of religion? The *Art* element will outlast the propaganda element, of course; for if a thing is a good work of art, it will still be a good work of art after the propaganda cause has passed. Who can say today that Phidias had no powerful purpose in his work? Plato certainly had.

The real artist says truly that art must not be confounded with propaganda, and the near-artist gets "literal" and repeats that the propaganda must not exist at all. There is plenty of propaganda without art, but at least mighty little worthy art without propaganda,—for propaganda is the *raison d'etre* of the greatest arts. As a physic is concealed under the sugar-coating, so is propaganda best concealed under art. It then meets less resistance. People are better persuaded when they don't realize that they are being persuaded. They resent the unconcealed and bald implication that they *need to be persuaded*.

And now we come to one literary art which is practically one hundred per cent propaganda—The Art of *Oratory*. You may get away with it, when you say that a picture is painted or a verse written, for the sake of the picture or the verse, but you will hardly have the nerve to claim that a great speech was ever made *for the sake of the speech*. A man may sing a song or play the violin to hear himself, but he will never make a great oration to hear himself talk. Just imagine a fellow speaking over two thousand years ago on the Macedonian question, or speaking today on the Tariff, just to see how many fine phrases he could spin! The poorest specimens of speeches are certainly those made for their own sake and sound. Demosthenes, Cicero, Frederick Douglass, Robert G. Ingersoll,—these are first magnitudes in all the firmament of speech,—and yet they never opened their mouths except in propaganda.—*Oratory*—one of the greatest arts of all time,—among all men,—is all propaganda. But the real orator is so much of an artist that, under the spell of his art, the listener forgets the propaganda, while he "gets" it.

Therefore, Mr. Near-Artist, the truth is perhaps something like this: The origin of art is propaganda, but many of the fine arts have risen far above mere propaganda. Hardly any art, however, is as purposeless as a bird's song. The bird (but not men) may sing indeed just to get the song out of its throat, and it may sing although only the solitude listens. It sings best, however, to its mate. But men are not birds, they are purposeful beings, and their greatest efforts are inspired by purpose. And there is no difference between purpose and propaganda, unless we beg the question by narrowing the idea of propaganda to some *necessarily sordid* meaning.

We can have no quarrel with a purpose, if it is tastily done up in the proper dress of art.

OLD SCHOOL OF NEGRO "CRITICS"

HARD ON PAUL LAURENCE DUNBAR

*In the following piece, Thomas Millard Henry writes that only a few peo-
ple have "lived on earth with finer poetic genius than that which burned in
Paul Laurence Dunbar." Henry notes that there are some who have not
given Dunbar the praise he so aptly deserves—particularly certain gentlemen "who sit in judgment seats for* The Crisis." *This essay was published in October 1924.*

For years I have searched in vain over the contents of *The Crisis* for
words of praise for our beloved poet and short-story writer, Paul Laurence Dunbar. Other Negro publications have given him many
sketches of praise; his poetry has been favorably quoted in the *Outlook,*
and in the *Christian Science Monitor;* there is an upstanding, if brief, review of his merits in the *Encyclopedia Britannica;* but, *The Crisis* (also the
New Encyclopedia), has disparaged him, on divers occasions, and in two
considerable articles has endeavored to strip him of that glory which
the remainder of the world accords to him.

It is true that some of his work was slovenly done; but what worthwhile poet has done all perfect work? Homer is said to have nodded,
and Shakespeare's fire sometimes waned. Many are of the opinion that
clever verse makers have kept the law more strictly than the great
poets did. These are times when polished numbers must come home
though all else fails. One bearing the infirmity as deep-set as Keats did
is hard pushed nowadays. Dunbar knew what many have failed to recognize when he wrote about "The Man Who Fails."

This land is as far from being a friend to poets as it is to being a
friend to grace. White America has not produced a single first rate
poet. The clouds look more discouraging than ever for them now. Po-
etizing has become a mere chasing on verbal wings of phantasmagoria.
The magical whirling of realities that used to constitute great poetry
is now considered by poetic "fans" to belong to the province of prose.

Few men have lived on earth with a finer poetic genius than that which burned in Paul Laurence Dunbar. The best articles that I ever read about him were eulogies that he more than deserved. Mr. William Dean Howells wrote the most substantial review that I have found on his poetry; but, it was not good enough. Although used for an "Introduction" to "Lyrics of Lowly Life," Mr. Howells admitted that it was written before the poems therein had been read. Consequently, "Ione," the masterpiece; "Ere Sleep Comes Down to Soothe the Weary Eyes," one of the rarest odes in the English tongue; and many quatrains and short poems universally quoted and appreciated, have never received noteworthy attention, at least, not from the American press.

The three gentlemen who sit in the judgment seats for *The Crisis* at present, are Dr. Du Bois, Mr. Braithwaite, and Mr. James Weldon Johnson. Each of them have interesting parts. Dr. Du Bois has enough of the Sociologist in him to mar the poet that his disciples see in him, and too much of the singer in him for a good scientist. Mr. Braithwaite has written some very pretty dreams; but, they interest no one but a few bookworms. And Mr. Johnson, by the help of the race question has put thoughts in his verse that appeal to present day antagonists. Any polished student might gain that kind of eminence. None of these gentlemen have that irresistible pulsating vitality in their works which the bard of Dayton shows, and with which song can move mountains. On the other hand, Dunbar in the forenoon of his short days, has done a work that is comparable in no little respect with that of Omar Khayyam's, or with Shakespeare's, or with Homer's. The sweet compelling music of his lyre captivated all America in the dark days that trailed after the reconstruction period; yet, like the mythical bards of Greece, he made the crude masses laugh and dance and aspire. The shadows of the wilderness were oriented by his fire. His objective singing, too, was in line with that African, smiling, good humor which passes understanding. His fine humor wrought miracles and caused the most supercilious white folk on earth to treat him to their good offices and white service. Meanwhile, some envious authors on his side of the color line seized and made capital from unlogical rumors that associated his fine works with the fierce travesties on Negroes so popular on the American stage. Perhaps these attacks deceived many credulous minds, and increased the book sales of these satellites. Mr. James Weldon Johnson caught the idea and left such a masterpiece as "Ione" out of his anthology. And Mr. Johnson is a Southerner, too, even though he may secretly credit his little bloom to his West Indian lineage. The two other gentlemen on the judgment seat hail from unsympathetic New

England. None of these minds contained the warm Southern sympathies of Dunbar or Booker Washington.

Our critical ability is now beginning to show marked progress. Southern Negroes of the literary mould have recently compelled not only local, but even universal attention. What is quite new about them is that sagacity which can recognize worth quite independent of creeds, politics, or sheepskins. When the flaming pens of Messrs. Randolph, Owen, Pickens, Schuyler, Lewis and others, raised their sweet chant in behalf of the black South, the world paused, observed, and decided that the dark veil over the American Negroes' soul was again to be rent in twain.

When those poets whose centenaries were celebrated here during the first decade of the twentieth century got reviewed, their best works were invariably examined to make their individual achievements interesting. Not so with this school of critics now in control of *The Crisis*. We find even the noted anthologist squatting behind such sweeping statements as follows: "No agitated vision of prophecy burn and surge in his poems." It offends us when we find him dismissing the poetry of Dunbar with such generalizations as this. If the disparagements of this pseudo-critic of poetry were accompanied by selections from the poet's best poems he might not have been in such jeopardy under scrutiny. Negro writers are so slightly advanced as a moral force that all such ignominious attacks on noble characters have been to a sad degree unchallenged. It has up to now danced on as easily as "rolling off of a log." And yet the country is peppered with Negroes who hold degrees for their classical attainments.

Were we to read Dunbar more and discuss him less, we should find ourselves pausing over some of his lines in spite of his tender years. In "The Right to Die," for instance, we read:

> "Men court not death
> When there are still some sweets in life to taste."

Our souls would feed on the epigrammatic quality in "Right's Security":

> "Right arms and armors, too, that man
> Who will not compromise with wrong;
> Though single, he must face the throng,
> And wage the battle hard and long."

I should like to select, some day his poems like "Love's Draft." Love, rather than political economy, is the foundation of great poetry:

> "The draft of love was cool and sweet
> You gave me in the cup,
> But, ah, love's fire is keen and fleet,
> And I am burning up.
> Unless the tears I shed for you
> Shall quench this burning flame,
> It will consume me through and through,
> And leave but ash—a name."

Dunbar has written over fifty poems of the same mood, and in similar diction, and yet when Negroes pride themselves in quoting or alluding to the poets, they build bridges across his mighty nose.

On the other hand what intelligent people should be ashamed of Dunbar's dialect poems. Here is "The Delinquent":

> Goo-by, Jinks, I got to hump,
> Got to mek dis pony jump;
> See dat sun a-goin' down
> 'N me a-foolin' hyeah in town!
>   Git up, Suke—go long!
>
> Guess Mirandy 'll think I's tight,
> Me not home an' comin' on night.
> What's dat stan' in' by de fence?
> Pshaw! why don't I learn some sense?
>   Git up Suke—go long!
>
> Guess I spent down dah at Jinks'
> Mos' a dollah fur de drinks.
> Bless yo'r soul, you see dat star?
> Lawd, but won't Mirandy rar?
>   Git up Suke—go long!
>
> Got de close-stick in huh han'
> Dat look funny, goodness lan'
> Sakes alibe, but she look glum!
> Hyeah, Mirandy, hyeah I come!
>   Git up Suke—go long!

We were about to close our protest without mentioning the comparison made between Dunbar and Claude McKay. In Mr. Braithwaite's article mentioned above, it was further stated that Mr. Claude McKay was potentially superior to Dunbar. Mr. McKay's work stands far above the work done by other poets of this republic in our day. In this golden period of new poetry, men and women become experts in the saddle of Pegasus as rapidly as house painters are produced. Mr. McKay's poems have more blood and thunder in them than any other Negro's verse, and it is rather natural for a Jamaica poet to have that turn of mind, but the anathema in his lines will not get him further than humor and satire have taken the Ohioan up towards the sun. I do not doubt, however, that by enjoying a longer poetic career than Dunbar did, the West Indian will reach him in some particular.

PROPAGANDA IN THE THEATRE

In this essay, published in October 1924, playwright Willis Richardson argues that drama is one of the best instruments for getting a message, particularly the cause of black Americans, to the public.

The stage, the screen, the press, the pulpit, and, in fact, every instrument that has the ear and eye of the public, has been used at one time or the other, and very effectively, in the interests of propaganda. Such photoplays as "Civilization," used to get election results, and "The Birth of a Nation," used for creating anti-Negro feeling, have had their day and served their petty purposes. Many other screen productions of less fame have done their part in arousing the enthusiasm or creating the feeling their authors and producers wanted them to create; but since this paper is to deal with the spoken drama, we shall here let the records of the silent drama rest.

In dealing with the spoken drama one does not have to think very long to become aware that this is one of the very best means of getting an idea before the public. A propaganda play is a play written for the purpose of waging war against certain evils existing among the people, in order to cause those people who are in sympathy with the play's purpose to be up and doing, and in order to gain the sympathy of those people who have seldom, or never, thought upon the subject. To cut the description down, a propaganda play is a play written for some purpose other than the entertainment of an audience.

Bernard Shaw, who is the most important person in the drama at the present time, is, with the possible exception of Eugene Brieux, the drama's leading propagandist. Since Shaw's writing of "Widowers' Houses" and "Mrs. Warren's Profession," propaganda in the theatre has been very much alive. In "Widowers' Houses" he strikes a mighty blow at greedy landlordism, at the same time pointing to the fact that the young man and woman of property are slaves to their wealth. "Mrs. Warren's Profession" is a harsh criticism of the system which compels a single woman to choose between the two evils of working for starvation wages and selling herself.

Eugene Brieux, that other great propagandist of the theatre, has given us play after play, each of which has been a masterly criticism of some evil in our present system. "The Red Robe" and "Damaged Goods" are the best known of these plays. "Damaged Goods" is known to the general public because of the public's curious desire to see the Frenchman lay bare the evils of venereal diseases. His masterpiece, "The Robe," is not so well known. Here Brieux shows all the greed of the judges for greater power, and their unfair methods of gaining the influence which gives such power.

Maxim Gorki surely had a deeper reason for writing "The Lower Depths" than simply the depiction of the characters of poverty-stricken Russians. He wanted to show the "smug citizens," as he called them, how the other half lived, so that perhaps they might question the wherefore and why of their less fortunate brother's condition.

Gerhart Hauptmann's "Weavers" is another forceful document against capitalistic greed. Although the claim is that the play is unsuitable for stage presentation, it still ranks as the masterpiece of the greatest writer in Germany at the present time.

Arnold Bennett, in one of his works for the theatre, "What the Public Wants," takes his scene to one of the "Five Towns" and presents us with a play flaying yellow journalism.

James B. Fagan, with a theme similar to Bennett's and with material better chosen and more universal than that used by the author of the "Five Towns," gives us a better play in "The Earth," a play which stands out as the everlasting enemy of the nefarious newspaper article.

When I recalled the two last mentioned plays I thought it would be an excellent thing if some of us who have the ability to write in the drama would write a few plays against the yellow journalism in America which arouses prejudice against us, which promotes riots, which in the guise of friendship strikes at us from every angle and raises a mountain of obstacles in the pathway of our progress.

No sane person would doubt for a moment that the condition of the Negro race in America ought to be changed; and as long as the powers that be refuse to enforce the laws, there is nothing to be done but bring the matter before the public mind for the purpose of changing the opinion of the people. For years those who have been interested in the making of this change have worked upon public opinion with nearly every available method from the prayer meeting to the indignation meeting. How much service either of these methods has rendered, I leave to the judgment of others; but the stage is one medium which has not been used to any extent.

When Miss Grimke wrote "Rachel" we thought we had a good beginning of propaganda plays, but the idea seems to have ended there save in the case of the small but earnest efforts of Mrs. Carrie Clifford in Washington and other energetic little people like her in many cities. Mrs. Clifford's little plays have been far from masterpieces, as she readily acknowledges, but they have been something; and if those like her in other cities would follow her example on a gradually increasing scale we should soon have a powerful medium for propaganda. How much might have been gained if such a beginning as "Rachel" had been followed by three or four such plays each year? I wonder if people do not go to the theatre with more unprejudiced minds than they sit down to read a newspaper or magazine. Anyone who reads these paragraphs can easily see that I am not one of those who believe that a propaganda play is no play at all, and the plays of many of the leading playwrights in the world to-day are excellent refutations of any who hold such a strict opinion.

With propaganda plays I think wonders may be done for the cause of the Negro. On the stage his desire and need for social equality (without which there is no other equality), for equality before the law, equality of opportunity and all his other desires may be shown. Every phase and condition of life may be depicted from that of Maeterlinck's old man sitting quietly in the lamp light to that which Swinburne describes when he sings of

> "*Fierce midnights and famishing morrows*
> *And the loves that complete and control*
> *All the joys of the flesh, all the sorrows*
> *that wear out the soul.*"

The lives and problems of the educated with their perfect language and manners may be shown as well as the lives and problems of the less fortunate who still use the dialect. To many of you educated and cultured among us who,

> "*While in your pride ye contemplate*
> *Your talents, power, and wisdom.*"

may object to the use of dialect on the stage, I say, that neither fifty years nor a thousand years from slavery is sufficiently long to enable a man to completely forget his mother tongue. We know nothing of the language our African ancestors spoke; we have learned the English language, but the dialect of the slave days is still the mother tongue of the American Negro.

So, to be able to sit in your stall at the theatre and witness the interesting things in the lives of your kinsmen, no matter what may be their condition of life, speech or manners, passing before you on the stage, ought to be a source of great pleasure to each and every one of you.

SAME OLD BLUES

Theophilus Lewis writes here that African Americans should not simply conclude that the road to a career in classic drama is difficult, but that blacks should produce their own black dramas for black audiences. Lewis published this essay in January 1925.

When Benjamin Brawley says the Theatre is a field "peculiarly adapted to the ability of the Negro race," he doubtless expresses the prevailing opinion of Aframerican savants and simpletons. If their talk is sincere plenty of white folks hold the same view. Mr. Brawley still has the bulk of opinion on his side when he concludes that "*enough has been done* so far to show that both Negro effort in the classic drama and the serious portrayal of Negro life on the stage are worthy of respectful consideration." The italics are mine.

Perhaps Mr. Brawley is right; however, I propose to conduct an inquiry into just what has been done. As first witness for the prosecution I call to the stand Dr. W.E.B. Du Bois. In "The Gift of Black Folk," Dr. Du Bois says Ira Aldridge, who died in 1867, "had practically no successor until Charles Gilpin triumphed in 'The Emperor Jones' during the season 1920–21." It turns out then that the race possessing special talents for the theatre gave the theatre just two first rate actors in fifty-three years.

Now marked ability for success in an art is almost always found in association with avidity for its practice and observation. Example: Negroes unquestionably excel in the popular art of dancing, and they not only seize every opportunity to indulge in social dancing, but great swarms of them are eager to do it professionally, and a great many make a living at it. Negro theatre audiences seem never to tire of fast hoofing. It seems to me the Negro's aptitude for the stricter theatre arts, so generally taken for granted, ought to manifest itself in a similar urge for expression. In which case we would find in most of the urban black belts groups of professional and amateur actors more or less continuously presenting some form of the drama before appreciative if not discriminating audiences. Then there would be some foundation for the assertion that the theatre is a field "peculiarly adapted to the ability of the Negro race."

Let us hear from J. A. Jackson what the facts are. From statistics prepared by Mr. Jackson for the *Negro Year Book*, 1921–22, I learn that there was at that time not a single theatre in the United States solely devoted to the production of serious drama by or for Aframericans. Three theatres, "The Attucks," Norfolk; "The Dunbar," Philadelphia, and "The Lafayette," Harlem, were presenting a serious drama now and then, but most of the time they were given over to vaudeville and motion pictures. Translated into economic terms, there is not enough money in the Negro's craving and genius for the legitimate theatre arts to make it profitable to devote three stages exclusively to their satisfaction and expression.

Quite as damaging to his own theory is Mr. Brawley's chapter on the Stage in his *Negro in Literature and Art.* Mr. Brawley covers the whole field of the race's contribution to the American theatre in less than seven pages, and quite half the content of the chapter is devoted to movements inspired by white folks and the kudos of white writers. In his *Gift of Black Folk,* Dr. Du Bois begins to tell of the black folks' gift to the theatre on page 309. On page 312 he concludes all he has to say and passes on to painting. Like Mr. Brawley, he uses a great deal of filler from Caucasian pens. Thus, either conned historically, or observed from the point of view of contemporary importance, the Negro's concrete contribution to the Theatre provides an extremely flimsy support for the presumption of his peculiar fitness for distinction on the stage.

The causes of the anaemic condition of the Negro Theatre (a term of convenience) can be readily disclosed by a brief examination of its philosophy. Not that anybody has ever formulated a definite set of principles for its guidance and interpretation. But a fairly coherent unwritten code of attitude and action has been expressed by its development as well as by its apologists.

The first postulate of this philosophy is admirably, if unconsciously, implied in this quotation from *The Gift of Black Folk.* "Charles Gilpin," says the author, "got his first chance on the legitimate stage by playing the part of Curtis in Drinkwater's "Abraham Lincoln." The important point here is not the misstatement of fact but the author's attitude of mind. He implies, unconsciously I hope, that the legitimate stage is synonymous with the white stage, a presumption the white theatre has never claimed for itself. The term "legitimate stage," as employed by white writers, means the stage devoted to the serious portrayal of character (note, I do not say the portrayal of serious characters), barring, perhaps, the work of stock companies. When Gilpin appeared in "The Old Man's Boy"—this was before the organization of the stock company which later became the Lafayette players—he was playing in legitimate drama. The play was shoddy and short-lived, of course; but so are dozens of plays that open up on Broadway each season. Certainly Dr. Du Bois would not deny a play by a white author a place on the legitimate stage merely because it had a run of only three nights. Still, in the mind of this foremost Negro scholar, a Negro actor has not played a legitimate role unless he has played it on Broadway.

And this attitude has been assumed by practically the whole body of Negroes with theatrical aspirations. The goal to be won was a chance to play on Broadway. One way to get on Broadway, apparently the easiest way, was to excel in the things being done on Broadway. This the Negro Theatre set itself to do. Hence that most useful factotum who has appeared early in the history of almost every other group or national theater, the actor-dramatist, striving to express the group character and problems esthetically, has never been evolved by the Negro Theatre. In his stead the Negro Theatre has produced the actor-showsmith who sought his material, not in Negro life, but on the Caucasian stage.

Now let us briefly examine the Negro showsmith's major reference work, the American stage. In 1822, says William Winter, Edwin Forrest acted a part which had never before been presented on any stage, that of an American Negro. The play, of course, was a farce. Shortly after this, according to Arthur Hornblow's "History of the Theatre in America," "The entertaining abilities of the despised slave were recognized and the white actor began to realize he could *make money by imitating* the black man." My italics. It is said that Thomas D. Rice, regarded as the founder and father of "Ethiopian" minstrelsy, probably drew more money to the treasury of the Bowery Theatre than any other American performer of his times. There you have it. White actors making a vogue of presenting Negro imbecilities in a way that appealed to the inferiority complexes of their audiences. For you can rest assured that the crowds who were regaled by the antics of Jim Crow consisted of the fathers and mothers of the hordes who now flock to gape at "White Cargo" while "Roseanne" gathers dust on the shelves of the book shops.

It was to this vogue that the builders of colored musical comedies and revues went to school. The basis of these shows is their humor. And this humor, you will find by running through the entire gamut of them, is the bastard offspring of Lew Dockstader out of a cracker shoe drummer's joke about a coon chicken thief. What genuine Negro humor these shows contain creeps in furtively and remains unemphasized, as if in fear of being ruled out altogether, while such bogus stuff as showing a darky scared to death of something becomes an obligatory scene.

Perhaps the reason why the Negro Theatre has practically no body of even mediocre drama is because the white American Theatre, which the Aframerican actor-writer so sedulously imitates, has not provided it with a sufficient number of working models, either in the form of plays or characters. Until very recently, the only type of colored character presented on the white stage in serious drama was old Uncle Zeke with a misery in his kidney. Now while a scary black man and a feeder are all the framework you need for a musical comedy, Uncle Zeke, on account of that pain in his back, is not able to hold up the weight of a drama, or even a farce, by himself. As the Negro Pineros never thought of going direct to life for characters, there was nothing for the higher type of colored actor to do but run an elevator while waiting for some white playwright to bring out a play with a darky butler in it. Either that, or, like Ira Aldridge, go abroad and try his hand at Shakespeare.

One group of Negro actors, the Lafayette Players, solved the problem presented by a paucity of Aframerican drama in another fashion. They organized a stock company and began to present cast-off Broadway melodramas. This company has held together about ten years now, during which time they have developed or helped to develop a number of highly competent actors and at least one first rate actor, Charles Gilpin. For that they deserve credit. Still, one is inclined to censure them for not doing something to encourage Negro drama. Couldn't they, for example, afford to pay F. H. Wilson twenty dollars a week on the condition that he write two plays a year for them? Couldn't they encourage some member of their own company to do it, if they want to keep the money in the organization? Or do they really think "The Wicked House of David" is worthy of their talents?

These suggestions, I believe, are an adequate answer to such wails as this by Mr. Brawley: "In no other field has the Negro with artistic aspirations found the road so hard as in that of the classic drama." Instead of crying for white folks to give them a chance on the "legitimate" stage, let Negroes turn their attention to producing Negro drama for Negro audiences. Is it a matter of money? Well, here is a feasible plan to meet that difficulty. Let the five most civilized churches in New York, after they have sent their pastors to Europe, contribute a hundred dollars each a month to the support of a company of players headed by Paul Robeson or Charles Gilpin, and make the endowment conditional on every fourth play presented by the company being the work of a Negro playwright. Downing, Wilson, and Dora Cole have manuscripts which could be used to start off with. If this scheme, or some similar scheme, cannot be made to work in the intellectual capital of black America, then the increasing swarms of college educated preachers, school teachers, doctors and university alumni are really coal heavers in culture, without a sufficient esthetic urge to create and sustain a racial theatre. If the thing succeeds, then the presumption of the Negro's aptitude for the theatre arts, which is now an article of faith, will begin to bear some resemblance to a fact.

Again glancing backward over the history of the Negro theatre in America, one is astonished by the almost total absence of indigenous little theatre movements. Practically every one of these movements worth being taken seriously has been inspired by white people. The most vigorous, as well as the most ambitious of these attempts to found a real Negro theatre, is the present effort being made by Mrs. Ann Wolter and her associates. Mrs. Wolter seems to be the type of woman not easily discouraged and her work appears to have in it some of the qualities that make for permanency.

Mrs. Wolter's predecessors in this field, I suspect, were rather credulous souls who were taken in by the extravagant claims of Negro propagandists. None of them seemed to be partial to hard work. They quickly grew weary and laid down the burden, and when they did, the movements they inspired languished and waned moribund. The principal result of the movement fostered by Mrs. Hapgood in 1917, and in the more recent movement started by Mr. Raymond O'Neil, was to bring to light a number of talented actors, in the persons of Opal Cooper, Blanche Deas, Sidney Kirkpatrick, Laura Bowman, Evelyn Preer and Edna Thomas. Mr. O'Neil also unearthed a farce which is the best piece of dramatic writing I have known to come from a Negro pen. It is on the accomplishments of these movements, and on the careers of such men as Aldridge and Gilpin that Negro orators and writers base their claims of racial aptitude for the stage. I fail to see the point. According to the way I reason, Paul Robeson's superlative work in "All God's Chillun Got Wings" does not establish the fact of racial genius for the theatre. It merely proves that Robeson is a mighty fine actor.

AN ACTOR'S WANDERINGS AND HOPES

Paul Robeson wrote the following essay in January 1925. In it, he notes that many blacks boast that America's only original cultural products are African-American in origin. He opines, too, that black drama and its interpretation must be considered an African-American cultural asset.

About 1915, from a rather secluded spot in New Jersey—Somerville to be exact—I read of the interesting debut of Negroes upon the serious dramatic stage of America. Of the four plays by Ridgely Torrence, one, "Simon the Cyrenian," was of unusual interest. Just a short time before, I, as the "Pastor's" son and Sunday School superintendent, had talked at great length about just that man and had pointed out many obvious lessons. Some five years later, after being literally dragged into rehearsal by Mrs. Dora Cole Norman, the honored president and very fine directress of the Colored Players' Guild, I thrust my 215-pound frame upon the small stage of the Y.W.C.A. in the role of that same Simon. At the end, I was congratulated and greatly encouraged by Mr. Torrence, Mr. K. McGowan, Mrs. Hapgood and others, but the "Law" called, and in the mazes of various John Does vs. Richard Roes, I soon forgot my stage experience.

Fate, however, was still conspiring to draw me away from the learned profession, and in the middle of the year I was offered a part in Miss M. Hoyt Wiborg's "Taboo," a play of "Voodooism." After a short run here, "Taboo" was taken to England, where I had the privilege of playing all summer with Mrs. Patrick Campbell. A most interesting experience this, and I received more encouragement from this noted actress.

Coming back I worked for a time in a law office—still the old urge—then came "Emperor Jones" and "All God's Chillun Got Wings." I managed to get in two weeks of "Roseanne"—which I enjoyed immensely. A very fine play I think—and if ever it is revived there awaits a marvelous "Roseanne" in Rose McClendon. Now I'm back again to "Brutus Jones" the "Emperor," and perfectly happy. It's been most thrilling—this acting. So much so, that I'm going to keep on trying to do it.

What are the opportunities? Just what I will make them. As I have met people in various circles I find they are pulling for me. Especially my friends at the Provincetown. I honestly feel that my future depends mostly upon myself. My courage in fighting over the rough places that are bound to come—my eagerness to work and learn—my constant realization that I have always a few steps more to go—perhaps never realizing the desired perfection—but plugging away.

I've heard this cry of "the chance" all of my life. But I've heard of Aldridge and seen Burleigh, Hayes, Gilpin and Williams. In the field of musical comedy I've seen Sissle and Blake, Miller and Lyles, and now Florence Mills, who, I believe, is in a class by herself. So I have plenty of hope.

True—plays are not easy to get, but they come from most unexpected sources. Before they appeared, who saw an "Emperor Jones" and "All God's Chillun Got Wings"—a "Roseanne." And there is an "Othello" when I am ready. And if I reach the continent, which I hope to do some day, I may play any role.

I am unable to comprehend whether they be Negro or otherwise. Perhaps that may come to pass in America. Of course, it is all uncertain. But, tell me, pray, what is life?

One of the great measures of a people is its culture, its artistic stature. Above all things, we boast that the only true artistic contributions of America are Negro in origin. We boast of the culture of ancient Africa. Surely in any discussion of art or culture, music, the drama and its interpretation must be included. So today Roland Hayes is infinitely more of a racial asset than many who "talk" at great length. Thousands of people hear him, see him, are moved by him, and are brought to a clearer understanding of human values. If I can do something of a like nature, I shall be happy. I shall be happy. My early experiences give me much hope.

We who start on this rather untrodden way need all the support and encouragement we can possibly get. I approach the future in a happy and rather adventuresome spirit. For it is within my power to make this unknown trail a somewhat beaten path.

THE BLACK AND TAN CABARET–
AMERICA'S MOST DEMOCRATIC
INSTITUTION

*Chandler Owen, in a cogent discussion in the following essay, character-
izes the cabaret as a place where race, color prejudice, and even caste prejudice are virtually a nonissue. This essay was published in February
1925.*

The object of life is happiness—the gratification of desire. Neither
money nor education is an end in itself. Both simply serve as means to
still further ends. Among all classes, rich and poor, educated or ignorant, the appeal of a prize fight, a football or baseball game, an automobile or horse race is far stronger and more fascinating than the
appeal of the school. Education in any true sense of the word must be
compulsory since pupils would rather play than study. The returns are
too indirect and distant for the young mind to foresee. Even grown-ups
respond most readily to the "call of the wild." To read the box holders
of the Kentucky Derby, an Indianapolis Speedway, or of a Dempsey-
Carpenter fight is like scanning the Who's Who of America. The
Harvard-Yale game and the World Series Baseball Contest attract all
America—cultured and uncultured.

Moreover, the basic pleasures release the true self more than the so-
called more highly (?) developed intellectual and alleged cultural en-
joyments. At a full dress feature ball, an honorary dinner, a memorial
service, Metropolitan Opera box party, people are on their "dignity."
They are formal affairs, and formal is just another term for unnatural.
In other words, people are pretending, putting on, feigning, counter-
feiting, appearing to be what *they ain't.* Under such circumstances we
observe human beings shamming and concealing, hiding their true
selves. Not so with a black and tan cabaret. It is here that we see white
and colored people mix freely. They dance together not only in the
sense of both races being on the floor at the same time, but in the still

more poignant and significant sense of white and colored people dancing as respective partners. Nor can it be said that Negroes are pushing
themselves on the white people. Just the reverse; the white people are
pushing themselves among the colored. There are plenty of other
cabarets in the white sections, but none so popular as these marooned
in the Negro districts.

Why?

Is it because white people like the Negro music? No. Negro orchestras play in the "lily-white" cabarets, too. Is it because cabarets are
lewd and vulgar? This is old stuff. The modern cabaret of New York
and Chicago is conducted with almost the decorum of a supervised
dance hall in California. No shimmying is allowed. The dancers are
not permitted to go to sleep on the floor with cheeks natural pillows as
at many private house parties. The entertainment is not unlike a high
class vaudeville; in many instances it is a revue of twenty-five or thirty
people, racy, vivacious dancing and thrilling music.

Are the people who attend the cabaret of low moral caliber? Hardly.
We go, and large numbers of other respectable people go occasionally.
Opera stars go, business men and women, artists, professional men, just
the plain everyday forgotten man of whom the late Prof. Summers of
Yale said "the forgotten man who sometimes prays, but he always
pays."

But is the cabaret democratic? All classes of people go there, rich
and poor, learned and ignorant, white and colored, prominent and unknown. Besides, they get along. There is no fighting, no hostility, no
suspicion, no discrimination. All pay alike and receive alike.

To illustrate. There was a terrible race riot in Chicago in 1919. Civil
government collapsed; the Church fell down on the job; the school
shrunk away; social service agencies recoiled in their shell; publicists
either succumbed to the hysteria or closed their otherwise vigilant
eyes; the good church people hied away to their holes of holiness. On
either side the races barricaded themselves for a fight to the death. The
dykes were opened and the dark waters rushed in. There was a back-
wash in civilization. For a while the great metropolitan city of Chicago
harked back to savagery—to the jackal and hyena era when nearly
every man of the white race was at his colored brother's throat. The
break down in racial brotherhood was well nigh complete except for
the black and tan cabarets. Here white and colored men and women
still drank, ate, sang and danced together. Smiling faces, light hearts,
undulating couples in poetry of motion conspired with syncopated
music to convert the hell and death from *without* to a little paradise

within. Such an accomplishment renders the cabaret an institution at once social and democratic. It also reveals the unveneered American, white and black, as true human beings, kindly, tolerant, fraternal, able and anxious to get along, and able to get along together, if they can just be left alone and freed from the views of vicious Ku Kluxers who are making a business of race hate.

Again, these black and tan cabarets establish the desire of the races to mix and to mingle. They show that there is lurking ever a prurient longing for the prohibited association between the races which should be a matter of personal choice. These cabarets portray even the vanished prejudice of white men lest a Negro man should brush against a white woman. They show as Emerson would say that "every human heart is human; every human heart is big with truth." They prove that the white race is taking the initiative in seeking out the Negro; that in the social equality equation the Negro is the sought, rather than the seeking factor. They prove that there is no sex line in the seeking since both white men and white women attend—attend not only with their own racial mates but with opposite race mates.

The Sunset cabaret of Chicago, Connie's Inn and Happy Rhone's of New York are high types of cabarets in which a person may go without fear of physical or moral contamination. Cabarets, like other institutions, are good or bad according to the use to which they are put: No sane person would condemn houses because some houses are used for prostitution and dope joints. Nor would he destroy the act of writing because some people use it for forgery. To do so would be as illogical as prohibiting the manufacture of automobiles because Leopold and Loeb kidnapped and murdered the little Franks boy in a Willys Knight car.

Fundamentally the cabaret is a place where people abandon their cant and hypocrisy just as they do in going on a hike, a picnic, or a hunting trip. They get close to earth where human nature is more nearly uniform. The little barracks of hypocrisy and the prison bars of prejudice are temporarily at least torn down, and people act like natural, plain human beings—kind, cordial, friendly, gentle—bringing with them what Walt Whitman called "a new roughness and a new gladness."

True democracy should teach not only how to tolerate each other but how races and people can understand, adapt themselves to and like each other. Especially necessary is this in the realm of pleasure seeking. Here snobbery runs riot—racial and class. For instance white persons will work *all* day side by side with Negroes in factory, mill and office, and then contend that, *in the evening,* they cannot sit together in restaurant, theatre or public conveyance. This too, in spite of the ridiculous time aspects, since white persons will work eight hours or more with Negroes, yet complain about eating a meal together twenty minutes, riding on a car five or ten, or sitting in a show from two to three hours. The reason for this is because a person who is securing pleasure is supposed to be at leisure. He is aping the leisure class. This raises the question of caste. And if white and colored are having the same kind of amusement, at the same time and place, it suggests equality of social class or caste, and its further and inevitable implication of equality of race.

But the cabaret has broken down even this caste, snobbery and discrimination, so deeply imbedded in recreation and amusement. It has broken it not only inter-racially but intra-racially since even all classes of white people congregate here—and congregate voluntarily. The black and tan cabaret is peculiarly fitted for this, since the disintegration of caste which starts on the race question quickly expresses itself as between different social groups inside the white race. The white man of affluence and prestige says, "If I can meet, mix and mingle with colored people then I can afford to be tolerant with poor whites." The poor white says (the lower ever aping the higher): "If rich white people of influence and prominence can associate with Negroes, I too, can certainly afford to." And the Negro who invariably hates the poor whites (his chief competitors) says (also aping his superior rich whites): "If rich white people can afford to associate with these poor whites, then, I, a Negro, will condescend to do likewise."

The result is a tread toward the norm, toward common understanding through general contact. All learn with Shakespeare:

If you tickle us we laugh; if you prick us we bleed.

Does anyone know of a more democratic institution in America than the "black and tan cabaret"?

Survey of Negro Literature,

1760-1926

In the following essay, Thomas L. G. Oxley presents his judgment of nearly three centuries of African-American literature. Oxley notes that the development and growth of black literature is a phenomenon that is unprecedented in all history. This essay was published in January 1927.

This article is not intended to be a comprehensive survey of Negro literature, for it is only a prolegomena to that increasing storehouse of literature produced by colored writers. Negro literature has attained such a remarkable standard of excellence that it would be difficult to analyze all the works written by colored men and women. The growth of Negro literature is unparalleled in all history. And this is one of the many significant proofs that the Negro advances socially, educationally and otherwise; and it is more striking when one notes although handicapped in nearly every way imaginable, he still clings to the proverbial motto: "Forward and up!"

The history of Negro literature must claim our full attention in a special degree. It is intensely national as well as American. In fact, it is more American than anything else. In producing such remarkable literary works the black man enriches and beautifies American literature; he even adds culture, giving to it a sort of a veneered finish. The high humanity of its content, its naturalness and sincerity are the characteristic manner of Negro literature. The writings of the black race is one of the most interesting to-day. It is not only rich in distinguished writers but these writers have a marked Negro individuality, and for these reasons we are surely justified in claiming a national literature for the race over which nations have ridden rough-shodden. Hardly any literature equals the Negro in producing the spiritual struggles of men, of a race oppressed for centuries.... The literature of the Negro is saturated with new color; it expands, it breathes, it arrests; it becomes infinitely more plentiful in motives, observations, ideas. It is the soul of black folk that understands the finite as well as the infinite phases of life.

Negro poetry begins where almost all poetry begins—in the rude ceremonial of a primitive people placating an unknown and dreaded world. The poetry of the first American Negro poet was first expressed in the dialect language several hundred years ago. In this language he voiced the sentiments of his heart and soul in wonderful, poignant expressions. Who have not enjoyed reading the dialect verses of the slaves? Who have not found some beauty in the dulcifluous spirituals of the slaves, passion-souled slaves? Beauty is the word for spiritual. At times the Negro sings with a broken heart; at another instant he tunes his lyre and forgets the world and its cares.

Truly, no branch of Negro literature can boast of the same degree of originality, naturalness and philosophical axioms as its dialect poetry. It may be said that the birth of American Negro poetry was first voiced in the spirituals. Although religion found a ready and eloquent expression in some of the spirituals, denunciation of social abuses were quite as numerous, whilst they were frequently more remarkable from a literary point of view. To know the Negro then, we must know his literature. The spirituals of the Negro, plenty of which is still preserved in the people, are wonderfully rich and full of the deepest interest. No nation possesses such an astonishing wealth of traditions, tales, and lyric folk-songs—some of them of the greatest spiritual beauty—and such a rich cycle of archaic epic songs as the Negro does. . . .

After the Civil War Negro literature acquired an idiosyncrasy of its own. The disappearance of the hypothetical primitive dialect productions of the slaves may have deprived us of some curious specimens of early art. But what has come down to us are examples of the Negro's creative ability as a poet. One need only to examine their spirituals or folk-lore. The folk-lore of the American Negro is rich in all qualities, giving to life itself a new aspect. And it is the only folk-lore of America.

The first poet of the American Negro, who was he? Jupiter Hammon was the first American Negro to publish a book of poetry. His poems are all religious; they are crude and methodless. His first poem: *An Evening Thought* bears the date of 1760. Hammon was a slave belonging to Mr. Lloyd of Queen's Village, Long Island. In 1778 he wrote *An Address to Miss Phillis Wheatley, Ethiopian Poetess,* and in 1782, *A Winter Piece: Being A Serious Exhortation, With A Call to the Unconverted.* With *An Evening Thought* entered the American Negro into American literature. The birth and death of Hammon are unknown.

Nine years after the publication of Hammon's first poems came Phillis Wheatley, the little slave girl who was brought to America a slave among slaves. She was born in Africa about 1753 and was brought to America in 1761, between seven and eight years of age. She was purchased by John Wheatley a well-to-do tailor in Boston. She was taught to read and write by her mistress and Mary Wheatley and was treated like a member of the family. In 1773 she accompanied John Wheatley to London. While in London she was cordially entertained by the Countess of Huntingdon and was presented with a volume of Milton's poems by the Lord Mayor of London. In the midst of her popularity she was suddenly recalled from England by the illness of her benefactoress. In 1773 there appeared in London the first and best edition of her poems: *Poems on Miscellaneous Subjects: Religious and Moral, By Phillis Wheatley of Boston, In New England.* In 1775 she addressed a poem *To His Excellency, General Washington,* then stationed at Cambridge. Reverend J. Lathrop said in a letter dated Boston, August 14, 1775: "Yes, Sir, the famous Negro Phillis, is a servant of Mrs. Lathrop's mother. She is indeed a singular genius. Mrs. Lathrop taught her to read, and by seeing others use the pen, she learned to write; she early discovered a turn for poetry, and being indulged to read and furnish her mind, she does now, and will, if she still lives, make a considerable figure in the poetical way. She is now in London with Lady Huntingdon, and . . . I hope her going to England may do her no hurt."

Phillis Wheatley was a singular genius indeed; she was a girl genius and she never sounds a native note. She kept close to the white man's ideas. She wrote the white man's poetry—the poetry of Gray and Pope. She wrote nothing of her picturesque Africa, nor sounded a note against the vile institution of servile oppression under which her people groaned. Her heart gave her lips no lyric music, nor sonnets to laud the Nubian skin of her people. After the death of her mistress the home was broken up, and Phillis soon accepted an offer of marriage from a young Negro called Doctor Peters and who was sometimes a lawyer. Her three children died at an early age. She died on the 5th of December, 1784. . . . Phillis Wheatley was highly religious and sincere. She deserves a far more greater respect than America has accorded her. She was the first American Negro woman to show any remarkable literary perfection.

George Moses Horton ranks third in giving his name to American Negro literature. In 1829, George Moses Horton of North Carolina published a book entitled: *Poems By A Slave,* and in 1845 appeared *Poetical Works.* Horton taught himself to read and write; there is a current story that the poet was in the habit of picking up pieces of paper hoping to find verses written on them. His first book of poems was published before he was able to write. His friends hoped that enough copies could be sold to secure the freedom of the poet, but the publisher's note to a second edition, in 1837, states that the money obtained from the first impression were insufficient to obtain his manumission papers.

Mrs. Francis Ellen Watkins Harper wrote in the same period as Horton. Mrs. Harper was born in Baltimore, Maryland, in 1825. She was educated by her uncle, the Reverend William Watkins, who taught a school for free colored children in Baltimore. In 1851 she removed to Little York, Pennsylvania and in 1854 she began her career as a public lecturer against the institution of slavery. In 1860 she was married to Fenton Harper of Cincinnati. *Poems on Miscellaneous Subjects* appeared in 1854 prefaced by William Lloyd Garrison. More than 10,000 copies of her books were sold. Mrs. Hemans, Longfellow, and Whittier were her models. Mrs. Harper's poetry is beauty: it is also authentic drama, true, poignant, striking into the depths of humanity. She wrote life, not about life. Her grace is elegant; her style far from being burdensome. Throughout her work one finds scintillal gems which adds beauty to her subject. Her verse is smooth and sonorous, often a little too smooth and sonorous. She shows at times a pathos that grips the heart because she was herself deeply moved. For novel *Iola Leroy, or Shadows Uplifted* is remarkable for its conciseness and truth. She was a splendid forger of aphorisms. Mrs. Harper died February 22, 1911.

Two great figures stand apart, singularly alike in many ways—James Madison Bell and Alberry A. Whitman. Bell was an antislavery orator and a friend of the immortal John Brown of Harper's Ferry fame. Bell was born at Gallipolis, Ohio, in 1826. In 1842 his family removed to Cincinnati where he learned the plasterer's trade. He pursued his trade by day and studied at night, and attended school for a short time: 1854 found him in Canada where he was busily engaged in the activities of the Underground Railroad. In 1860 he returned to the United States, and in the middle of the same year removed to California. Five years later he removed to Toledo, Ohio.

Bell was a powerful and ferverent writer. Self-educated he gained an access to the wisdom of books. He uttered and the air became songful with wisdom; he wrote and his words congeal into exemplars of classicism. Of the Emersonian philosophy he surely was! His poems are terse and are elicitated with sporadical aphorisms. His phrasing is exuberant; there is often a metallic quality bordering on brassiness.

There is a willful flambuoyancy in his impetuous periods. Bell wrote in standard English and Byron was his model.

Alberry A. Whitman, Bell's contemporary, was born in Kentucky shortly after the Civil War. He was a slave. He graduated from Wilberforce University and later became its financial agent. He began life as a Methodist minister. In 1877 a collection of his poems entitled *Not A Man and Yet A Man* appeared. In 1884 he published his longest and most ambitious poem: *Twasinta's Seminoles, or The Rape of Florida.* Whitman, like Bell, wrote in standard English. His poems are long and has romantic charms: a wealth of beauty and imaginery exists throughout his poems. They are of tragic tales of love and romance. The beauty of the south adds charms to their exquisite naturalness. The consciousness of his power is in every line, the characters though they are so lifelike and spontaneous in their action, fall into line and group themselves like puppets at the waving of the magician's hand. In 1901 Whitman published *An Idyl of the South.* He died several years ago.

It is necessary to mention the names of a few outstanding Negro writers who published books during this period. Charles L. Reason *Freedom* (1847), a poem of 168 lines possesses both imagination and dignity. Its central idea is based upon historic struggles of various peoples and concludes with a prayer for freedom in America. Even at this time Negro literature was in its adolescent stage; it had not yet attained its nebulous maturity. Ten years previous the progress made in literature by the American colored writer was microscopical. In 1859 Northrup published *Twenty Years A Slave.* This is a very interesting autobiography recording the sufferings of the author and his people and his final triumphs in life. There is no literary value to his work; the only significant thing about it is its truthfulness and brevity of style. William Wells Brown published some years after *Rising Son and Black Man,* a book remarkable for its style, history and comprehensiveness. He pictures the ancient glory of the black man and paints in bright colors the coruscation of the Negro's tomorrow. There is nothing esoterically evasive about his style. Bishop Payne published *Recollections of Seventy Years,* a work covering his activities in the ministerial field. His style is not trite, not commonplace. *Men of Mark,* a compendium compiled by Reverend William J. Simmons, is a most factual encyclopedia recording the achievements of black men in American life. George Williams published a *History of the Negro Race In America.* Williams was a prolific writer; he knew his subject well. Like Wells Brown, he endeavored to record the Negro in American history. Thomas T. Fortune published *Black and White,* a book of a little over 200 pages. It deplores the situation between the two races south and citations of statistical reports are numerous. He also published a volume of his poems. Other representative works are: *Morning Glories* by Mrs. Josephine Heard; *Negro Melodies* by Rev. Marshall Taylor; and *The Work of the Afro-American Woman* by Mrs. Gertrude N. Mossell.

At the close of the nineteenth century dozens of Negro writers published small fugitive volumes of prose and poetry. This may be called the second renaissance of Negro literature. The significance of these works can not be overestimated. It was the period when the Negro entered more seriously into the world of self-criticism and self-consciousness. It is not the sensitivity of the writer that makes him an artist, but this added to his transmutation of it into a form that acquires esthetic significance. The writings of several of these authors were unpolished and crude; they were devoid of form and system. And we could not expect that Negroes recently emancipated from centuries of the most dehumanizing slavery should be capable of producing great literature.... Even at this period the writings of the white man were in some instances imperfect and methodless. But these unfinished, unveneered products of the colored writers eventually formed the nucleus of the Negroes literature.

With the dawn of a new century, the Negro writer was to create for himself a higher and nobler place on the pedestal of fame. He was to become a great factor in the empire of American literature. He advances steadily, oftentimes without recognition but with ambition and hope. In this era Paul Laurence Dunbar appeared like a bright star from out of the West. Paul Laurence Dunbar was born in Dayton, Ohio, June 27, 1872. His father escaped from slavery, made his home for sometime in Canada, and returned to the United States to bear arms in a Massachusetts regiment in the Civil War. Dunbar was schooled at Dayton and graduated from the Dayton High School in 1891. After graduation he secured a position as elevator operator. He was brought before the attention of the public in 1892, when he delivered in verse the address of welcome at the Dayton meeting of the "Western Association of Writers." In the same year he published his first book of poems entitled: *Oak and Ivy.* William Dean Howells in his Introduction to *Majors and Minors* (1896) hailed him as "the first instance of an American Negro who had innate distinction in literature" and "the only man of pure African blood and of American civilization to feel the Negro life aesthetically and express it lyrically." In 1897 Dunbar went to England and upon his return to America published, *Lyrics of Lowly Life.* Some of his other works are: *The Uncalled; The Love of Laundry; Lyrics of the Hearthside; Lyrics of Love and Laughter; Lyrics of Sunshine and Shadow;* and numerous other short stories and poems. In 1916 Dodd, Mead and Company published *The Complete Poems of Paul Laurence Dunbar.* Dunbar died in Dayton, Ohio, February 9, 1906.

Paul Laurence Dunbar stands out as the foremost Negro interpreter of Negro life. The real Dunbar, the merry or sad, is to be found only in his poems, and by them alone can we judge justly of his greatness as a poet. He may be rightly called the father of American Negro poetry. In truth, Dunbar is a reality as Burns and Riley are realities. Of verse he was the absolute sovereign, the indefatigable forger of rhythms, the magical equilibrist, the constantly fortunate manipulator of rhyme. He gave wings to qualities, a human heart to the inanimate, and expressed no idea without metaphor. . . . All tones are his, especially a tone of inexorable majesty and solemnity. Paul Laurence Dunbar created the modern poetic language: he freed it from dead hyperbolisms and false solemnity; he brought it closer to the living language of the people, and gave it sincerity, dignity, flexibility and vigor. . . . Who shall express thy charms oh! Dunbar?

Negro literature lost in Paul Laurence Dunbar a writer disconcertingly original, of exuberant and apparently universal talent, whose influence upon his contemporaries and successors, has altogether been fruitful, and has at all events been penetrating.

The name of Booker Taliaferro Washington is universally known. Booker Taliaferro Washington was born on a plantation near Hale's Ford, Franklin county, Virginia, in 1859. In 1872, "by walking, begging rides both in wagons and in the cars" he traveled 500 miles to the Hampton (Virginia) Normal and Agricultural Institute, where he remained three years, working as janitor for his board and education, and graduated in 1875. He was the founder of the Tuskegee Normal and Industrial Institute . . . Harvard conferred upon him the honorary degree of A.M. in 1896 and Dartmouth that of L.L.D. in 1901.

Among his publications are a remarkable autobiography entitled *Up From Slavery.* Other notable productions are *The Future of the American Negro* (1889); *Sowing and Reaping* (1900); *Character Building* (1902); *Working With the Hands* (1904); *Tuskegee and Its People* (1905); *Putting the Most Into Life* (1906); *Life of Frederick Douglass* (1907); *The Negro in Business* (1907); and *The Story of the Negro* (1909).

Up From Slavery is a wonderful piece of work. It is one of the enigmas in Negro literature. Washington's style is simple and comprehensive and pleasing. He was a hard, conscientious worker, a finished craftsman who turned out a great volume of copy. *Up From Slavery* is an intelligible and convincing autobiography and one that is destined to live in history and furnish an inspiration for present and future generation. It takes no sides, it does not argue, it is cheerful and is best noted for its syntomy of style, which may be called a luminous serenity. It is the soul of a man yearning for intellectual freedom; it is a human document.

William E. Burghardt Du Bois was born at Great Barrington, Massachusetts, 1868. He received his education at Fisk University, Harvard University and the University of Berlin. He is the author of *The Souls of Black Folk; Dark Water,* and numerous other books. He is Editor of *The Crisis.* Dr. Du Bois is too poetic to be logical. As a sociologist he is preeminent. But his mind is too poetical to make him a profound and logical philosopher. He writes with a style intensely original and beautiful. What a wonderful writer he is! And of such an interesting personality! Dr. Du Bois is sometimes too personal, sometimes of the esoterical type. But after all these are no faults at all. Well, what of it? A man's defects are organically related to his virtues; take out the one and lo, you often discover that you have extricated the other. But what are such objections as these when weighed against the singing beauty that Du Bois has woven into his exquisite books? His works are admirable for their charms; he is a stylist of rare ability; he possesses a brilliant wit and is a fertile coiner of sparkling epigrams. Du Bois understands the passions of the Negro. He feels their heart beats. His pleasure in these souls, black souls, is his pleasure in life—a paradoxical, ironical, mystical intoxication.

Dr. Kelly Miller is a professor of sociology in Howard University. He is the author of several prose works. Dr. Miller is probably one of the soundest analytical thinkers and philosophers of the Negro race. There is something of the poet too in him. His lines have a beauty that derives from something more animate than a lexicographer's lair. He is the author of *Out of the House of Bondage,* and several other books of merit.

James Weldon Johnson was born at Jacksonville, Florida, 1871. He was schooled at Atlanta University and at Columbia University. He was for seven years U. S. Consul in Venezuela and Nicaragua. Authorship: *The Autobiography of an Ex-Colored Man,* and *Fifty-Years and Other Poems.* He is the secretary of the National Association for the Advancement of Colored People. Mr. Johnson is not a poet of the inner soul; he is a poet of the intellect, but he has produced some excellent compositions. His best poem *Fifty Years* has grace and freshness and a distinguished simplicity lend to this apparently spontaneous composition greater vitality than is to be found in any of his other poems.

George Reginald Margetson was born in St. Kitts, British West Indies, in 1877. He was educated at the Moravian school in St. Kitts. In 1897 he came to America. He is the author of *Songs of Life; The Fledgling Bard and the Poetry Society;* and *England in the West Indies.* Mr. Margetson is the only poet of color to develop perfectly the sonnet form. They are of beauty and sing always abundantly for the ear. His poetry is of velvet and the dusk; of bronze and granite, flashing light. Among the writers of this generation who have enriched or at least variegated the garden of Negro poetry with exotics, Margetson has cultivated some rare plants of poetry. It is to be deplored that his works are not more familiarly known to the general public. He has woven a magic web of mists and shadows until each of his poems becomes "an idyll made of shadows there afar in distant forests." They may be likened to a grey shadowland, a mountain mist, often lifting to reveal fair regions of noble verse, or crystallizing into exquisite single lines, now limpsidly clear as running water, now gleaming as a sunglint through the mist. His ferventness is puerile. . . .

Claude McKay is pre-eminently the poet of Negro soul. Mr. McKay was born in Jamaica, B. W. I., in 1889. He received his early education from his brother, and served for some time as a member of the Kingston Constabulary force. In 1912 he came to America and was a student of agriculture at the Kansas State College. Authorship: *Songs of Jamaica, Spring in New Hampshire* and *Harlem Shadows.*

Life is sparkling in his songs, ballads, and verbal paintings; there is often pain and sadness and a longing for unmitigated freedom in his melodies; at times he is bitter, full of indignation and stinging mockery, fire and thunder. His satire is heavy and effective. He is clever and original. His poems are sharply lyrical; he sings no anemic beauties; his beauty is born of pain; often, indeed, it is pain set to music, or rather pain transmuted into music.

Joseph Seaman Cotter, Charles B. Johnson, Georgia D. Johnson, Jessie R. Fauset, Leslie P. Hill, Walter E. Hawkins, Fenton Johnson, J. A. Rogers, William Pickens, Charles S. Johnson, Langston Hughes, and dozens of others are writers possessing a remarkable scope of originality and power.

Walter F. White, who is the assistant secretary of the National Association for the Advancement of Colored People, published a remarkable book in 1925. *Fire in the Flint* is an artistic criterion; it is a miniature masterpiece of psychological fiction. Mr. White is the Lochinvar come out of the West. And his mount is a thoroughbred. *Fire in the Flint* is a novel of passion and power and hatred, of a haunting cantical beauty, of the South's cruelty to the Negro. It has brought music and glamour, without sacrificing an iota of the crude biological realities. Sociology and psychology are blended into Mr. White's first novel. It is an appealing work of fine fabric and deep sentiment.

Countee Cullen is a young poet of remarkable ability. He was born in New York a little over twenty-two years ago. His poems have appeared in various white and Negro periodicals. Mr. Cullen is a prolific writer. He possesses a marvelous power of imagination and is among the greatest Negro poets of today. His poems are of exotic imagery, flaring with color and passion of life, pagan joy and daring imagination. Mr. Cullen is a young poet. He has not yet reached his embryonic maturity. It is folly to say that Mr. Cullen is the leader of Negro poets. He wants two qualities essential to great poetry—truth and humanity. I say this because there are critics who speak of him as though he were Isaiah. He, like Johnson, is a poet of the intellect. No critic should single out a writer as being primarily in the field of literature. Art must be judged by its own perfection rather than by persons defining standards to judge the compositions of a writer. Art is beauty which becomes, not a sort of emotional titillation or intellectual obsequiousness but a something essential at the heart of things that has been disassociated from its temporary, transient trappings and presented in its eternal aspect. Art is best judged by its inner experience, by its authenticity and aesthetic qualities. Negro literature is today expanding more rapidly than ever. The present century has witnessed what must certainly be considered a remarkable phenomenon—the resuscitation of the language, style and literature of the Negro. The Negro race has the broadest comedies and the deepest tragedies. He blends his passion with these two elements. . . . The role of great Negro writers of color is endless. There are some persons who are skeptically inclined to believe that the American black man has not produced anything great in the world of literature. Let them remember that in order to form any adequate judgment as to the greatness of the Negro in the empire of literature, they should first study his works. In the dawn of another few years we may see already emerging more native qualities of finish, directness, composition, measure, chastened emotion—with an added sensitiveness and suppleness, and a greater intimacy.

WHO IS THE NEW NEGRO, AND WHY?

J. A. Rogers, in the following essay, characterizes the "New Negro" as a courageous, often defiant, individual filled with race pride. On the contrary, the "Old Negro" is a complacent worshiper of white culture and white standards of beauty. This essay was published in March 1927.

One hears much these days about the New Negro. Who is he, and who knows him? In slavery times there was a type of Negro, who worshipped his master and his family. He was a tattle-tale also, and whenever he saw one of his fellow-slaves do anything, he ran to the master, for which he would be rewarded with a ham knuckle, or a suit of old clothes. The betrayers of Nat Turner and John Brown were Negroes. The first person killed by John Brown was Hayward Shepard, a Negro.

This type was also made a slave-driver, then he became a tyrant of tyrants. When he became a slave-holder, as many did, he was even more exacting than the whites. When the Civil War broke out, this dog-like creature stayed at home protecting his master's family and property while the master was fighting to keep him enslaved, or he joined the ranks of the Confederacy. Benjamin Tillman later introduced a bill, to make these black Confederates and slaveholders "white," a quite unnecessary step, internally.

On the other hand there was a type of slave—stubborn, rebellious, liberty-loving—who, like Nat Turner and Denmark Vesey, kept his master awake at nights, worrying lest they should rise up, massacre him and his family, plunder the plantation and take to the woods, as was so often the case, particularly in Hayti, Jamaica and Guiana.

The Old Negro is the present-day type of the first; the New of the second. Faces, like styles, may change but the human nature underneath remains practically unchanged.

One may recognize the difference between Old and New in their bearing. The former, respecting color more than qualification, is apologetic when dealing with white people. He acts as if he were always in the way, as if he had no right to be on earth. One can hear the clank of the slave's chain in all that he says and does.

The New is erect, manly, bold; if necessary, defiant. He apologizes to no one for his existence, feeling deep in his inner being that he has just as much right to be on earth and in all public places as anyone else. He looks the whole world searchingly in the eye, fearing or worshipping nothing nor no one. Self-possessed, he makes himself at home wherever circumstances place him. In a word, he respects himself, first of all.

The Old Negro, on the other hand, worships the white man, because of his absence of pigment. He is like the old colored mammy, who seeing the Minister from Hayti at a social function in Washington was horrified that a black man should be associating on terms of equality with white people, many of whom were his inferiors.

The Old Negro has a contempt for his own people, and in speaking of them he uses the same terms of contempt that his spiritual predecessors did. Shut your eyes when he speaks, and you'll hear a cracker talking.

The New Negro wastes no time worrying about his color. He realizes that a human being if he is to be visible at all must have a coloring of some sort, hence to him, one shade of coloring is the equal of every other. If light-complexioned he does not deem himself better than his darker brother.

The Old Negro when insulted, grins and apologizes; the New either ignores it or acts in a way to make his manliness felt. The Old submitted supinely to massacre as in the New York and Philadelphia riots, and the Palestine, Springfield and East St. Louis ones. The New arms himself and prepares to exact as many lives as possible, as in Washington, Chicago, Longview, Houston, Brownsville. All of which makes it clear that the possession of a college degree or of polish and refinement does not necessarily make a New Negro. Also he may be old or young. Manliness is a quality that inheres in the very fibre of one's being—a quality that like wine, improves with age.

The New Negro would rather lose his tongue than betray his people in their struggle for freedom and equality. Should any amelioration come to him because of superior talent, it turns to gall in his mouth when he remembers the sufferings of the rest of his people.

The Old, hat in hand, is always begging white people, a sort of glorified cripple with a can. Because of this he always has two different messages, one which he gives to white people, the other to colored ones. He is a living lie.

The New Negro supports movements conducted by his own people, because he realizes that these are the only ones that are ever going to speak out frankly and forcefully on his grievances. White persons, in such matters as economics, religion, politics, range all the way from the rabid radical to the rank conservative. So far as race is concerned, however, the vast majority is but of one complexion—the conservative, hence organizations supported by them for Negroes, have at bottom, the same Nordic goal, that is keeping the Negro "in his place," or at best a little lower than the angels. The New Negro realizes that the finest work, the real work for the advancement of the group will have to be done by its own members. It's an old saying: The man that pays the piper calls the tune.

The Old Negro is too thankful for small mercies; he believes that the employer does him a favor by hiring *him*. He is always praising enemies of the race like Cole Blease or Tillman or Vardaman, because of some trifling sop given by these individuals to some isolated group or person, while doing all they can to keep back the group, as a whole. The New Negro, on the other hand, is satisfied with no concessions or patronage of any sort. He wants neither more nor less than his rights as a man and a citizen. And this difference between the Old and the New enters into their respective attitudes toward the times in which they are living. While the New Negro prepares to live, to live vigorously, and dangerously, if necessary, to make the whole weight of this presence felt while he moves on this earth; the Old prepares to die, and go to a heaven where he will at least be a white man in complexion. "Wash me," he sings, "and I shall be whiter than snow." He tries to get a corner on religion, and sinks his money in churches, which brings no returns and are shut four-fifths of the week. He is as priest-ridden as the Italians of the Middle Ages, and enjoys it. The New on the other hand, invests his money in homes and factories. He tries to get a corner on business and education that will fit him to compete successfully with the whites, while the Old is singing psalms and repeating like parrots the religious nonsense that the enslavers of his forefathers used also to enslave their primitive minds.

The Old Negro is chiefly interested in what Abraham, Moses, David, Jehosaphat and other fictitious and semi-fictitious creatures of a barbarous tribe did in Palestine thousands of years ago. So far as his thinking is concerned he is a walking mummy. The New Negro relegates all these things to their proper, infinitesimal place in the scheme of things, and is interested most of all in life as it stirs around him. He jettisons Matthew for Marx; David for Darwin, and prefers Douglass to Lincoln. He studies economics instead of wasting his time with epistles.

The New Negro joins unions either of his own, or forces the whites to take him in, and once in never rests until he gets fairplay. He realizes that if white men have to create unions in order to get justice from white men like themselves, then this step is even more necessary for Negroes. The Old Negro, on the other hand, is an individualist. He pulls off to himself and begs the employer for work, thus paving the way for his being used, not as a union, but as an individual, to break strikes.

The Old Negro, once having reached what he believes to be the top of the ladder, spends a great deal of his time kicking off other climbers. He wants to rule the roost alone, to be greatest in the kingdom of heaven, while the New Negro, remembering his own hard struggle, is eager to give other aspirants a helping hand, even though the newcomer gives promise of eclipsing him. In other words, he is a good sport. He is, further, not afraid of contradiction, and does not believe he is an oracle on what will solve this so-called race problem. He is ever eager for new information.

The Old Negro falls glibly for all the agencies used by white friends to sidetrack the mind of the Negro group from its real problems such as over-stressing of Negro art, spirituals, piffling poetry, jazz, cabaret life, and the puffing into prominence of mediocre Negroes. The New Negro again relegates these to their proper place. He realizes that the race question is almost solely an economic one, and is satisfied with nothing less than equal opportunity for employment with equal wages. He sees that in all those things that make for the benefit of the nation, as a whole, there is no color discrimination. That is, as in paying taxes, no one asks his color; it is only in getting a return that there is discrimination. In short that in all those things that make for the white man's benefit, he is a white man, but in those that make for his, he is only a Negro.

The Old Negro is also more interested in "high-yallers," football, boxing, handball, in mastering the intricacies of the black bottom and the Charleston, in making signs in "frats" and lodges and splitting hairs about points of order in such places, in parading in gaudy uniforms, and in slicking his hair than in doing something vital towards getting himself and his group out of the rut of semi-slavery. Improving his mind by reading good books and acquiring a knowledge of the history of his racial group, is to the Old Negro, a real pain.

The Old Negro protests that he does not want social equality; the New, seeing that this is but another phrase for social justice, demands it. No social inequality for him. He feels that the first and foremost of all duties is to seek freedom, hence he has a perfect right to take any step, however violent, to rid himself of tyranny. With Thomas Jefferson he repeats: "Resistance to tyranny is obedience to God." Like the five colored immortals, Anderson, Copeland, Green, Leary and Newby, who joined John Brown in his raid on Harper's Ferry, he stands ever ready to head or to join any movement that will strike for freedom.

The New Negro is not afraid of such bogey labels as rebel, atheist pagan, infidel, Socialist, Red, heathen, radical, realizing that what they really connote is "thinker." He will be anything else but a sheep.

And where is this New Negro of whom we have been hearing so much? Is he an ideal or a reality? This much is evident, that many who have been making a noise like New Negroes have proved to be but asses in lion's skins. When a lion appeared they took to the woods.

The Failure of Negro Leadership

Chandler Owen discusses what he believes to be the failed policies of con-
temporary black leaders W.E.B. Du Bois, James Weldon Johnson,
Archibald Grimke, Robert Russa Moton, and others. He points to the ambi-
guity in Du Bois's position on segregation, black leadership's antilabor
stance, and the naïveté of their belief that the participation of black men
in World War I would reduce racial prejudice. This essay was published
in January 1918.

The Negro leaders have failed. It is hard to admit. Race-pride revolts against it. But the remedy lies in recognizing the condition and setting out to remedy it.

Negro leaders like Dr. W.E.B. Du Bois, Kelly Miller, William Pickens, Archibald Grimke, James W. Johnson, Robert Russa Moton, Fred R. Moore, Wm. H. Lewis and Chas. W. Anderson are a discredit to Negroes and the laughing stock among whites.

We have no ill-feeling toward these men. Many of them have held out the best light (or the least poor) for the race during the last ten or twenty years. We have admired them and we recognize their full merit and worth. We do not now impugn the motives of most of them. We impeach their methods. We do not hold that reality actuates them. But we bring against them the worst indictment of the modern world—ignorance—ignorance of the methods by which to achieve the ends aimed at.

Let us take Dr. Du Bois, for example. He has done some good work in stimulating the formation of the National Association for the Advancement of Colored People. He has persistently and consistently stood for the abolition of disfranchisement, discrimination and Jim Crowism. He has fought to secure larger measure of support for institutions of higher education and to increase public and high school facilities for Negroes. As a general principle he has opposed segregation.

Lynch law he has condemned directly. He fortunately supported woman suffrage though his reasons therefore were not sound and sufficient.

Still Dr. Du Bois has frequently urged the adoption of many measures which defeat his very purposes and aims. To illustrate: He opposes, we believe sincerely, segregation. Yet he was among the first to advocate a Jim Crow training camp for Negroes and he has been a repeated supporter of Jim Crow Y.M.C.A.'s. Some shadow of practicality might be urged in support of the Y.M.C.A. measure as the lesser of two evils, but the Jim Crow camp is indefensible—military duty not being a benefit, but a burden, shunned and rejected from early history by those who could escape from its hideous clutches and its grim tentacles.

Lynch law, Dr. Du Bois condemns directly, but he has seldom, if ever, shown a grasp of its true causes and the probable remedy. One has not seen where the Doctor ever recognized the necessity of the Negroes getting into labor unions in the South as a means of eliminating the Negro as a scab, allaying thereby the ill-feeling against him by the working white man, while at the same time, limiting and controling the supply of labor, which would increase the demand for labor both white and black. Moreover, this would be the strongest blow which peonage could be dealt.

Instead, however, we see Dr. Du Bois and all the other Negro editors and leaders herald in big headlines, "Negroes Break Strike!" As though that were something to exult in. And they preach a gospel of hate of labor unions in criminal ignorance of the trend of the modern working world, when they should be explaining to Negroes the necessity of allying themselves with the workers' motive power and weapon—the Labor Union and the Strike.

Another evidence of the almost criminal incompetence and cringing compromise of the whole array of Negro leaders named in the beginning of this article is their recent endeavor to raise funds for the families of the colored men conscripted into the Army and Navy. A string of names of "so-called big Negroes" have given their endorsement and consent to the scheme.

Now a very elementary examination will reveal the farce of attempting to give any wholesome and fundamental relief to those families by the petty charitable scheme which they have adopted.

There are approximately one hundred thousand Negroes in the army. The smallest amount which might be considered as relief to a family in these days would be one dollar a day. One dollar a day to 100,000 families would be $100,000 per day or three million dollars per month. The impossibility of ever touching the surface of this problem by any hit and miss petty charity should have suggested itself to men like Du Bois, Pickens, Kelly Miller and James W. Johnson, who must have had some study of elementary economics. And nothing more plausible and sound could be conceived of than that the government should take the matter in hand and handle it efficiently and scientifically. Yet not one of these "big Negro leaders" dares mention this either from ignorance or from lack of courage.

Again, we hear Prof. Wm. Pickens, Du Bois and Kelly Miller talking in superlative sureness of how the Negroes' participation in this war will remove race prejudice. Since when has the subject race come out of a war with its rights and privileges accorded for such participation? Leaving out the question of color entirely where is the history to support this spurious promise? Did not the Negro fight in the Revolutionary War with Crispus Attucks dying first (which is not important nor material), and come out to be a miserable chattel slave in this country for nearly one hundred years after? Did not the Negro only *incidentally* secure freedom from physical slavery in the Civil War, only to have peonage fastened upon him almost immediately thereafter, becoming the victim of Ku Klux Klanism, oppression and unspeakable cruelty which were directly perpetrated by the South and condoned by the North. Did not the Negro take part in the Spanish-American War only to be discharged without honors and without a hearing by the president who rose into political prestige and power upon their valor in that war? And have not race prejudice and race hate grown in this country since 1898? The same story must be told of Ireland. She has always helped England in her wars, but she has remained under the feet of the English oppressor for the last eight hundred years.

Professor Du Bois, Kelly Miller and William Pickens, this stuff you are giving out is sheer "clap-trap." It is repelled by the modern Negro student of economics and political science. It is offensive and repulsive.

But when you are known to be the leading Negro professors, it makes us ashamed to consider what men like Professor Charles A. Beard, Scott Nearing, Overstreet, Albert Bushnell Hart and E.R.A. Seligman must think when they read these pigmy opinions and this puerile, credulous interpretation of history from men who are supposed to have given their lives to the study of science, but who are little short of mental manikins and intellectual lilliputians.

Truly the Negro leaders have failed. Most of them are too old to be reformed, which means "re-educated." The hope of the race rests in new leaders with a more thorough grasp of scientific education, and a calm but uncompromising courage.

Du Bois on Revolution

In the following essay, Chandler Owen offers his own explanation of revolution, which is sharply at variance with that of W.E.B. Du Bois. Owen published this essay in September 1921.

In the August *Crisis,* Dr. W.E.B. Du Bois, speaking editorially, writes an article entitled "The Class Struggle" which reads in part:

"The N.A.A.C.P. has been accused of not being a "revolutionary" body. This is quite true. We do not believe in revolution. We expect revolutionary changes in many parts of this life and this world, but we expect these changes to come mainly through reason, human sympathy and the education of children, and not by murder. We know that there have been times when organized murder seemed the only way out of wrong, but we believe those times have been very few, the cost of the remedy excessive, the results as terrible as beneficent, and we gravely doubt if in the future there will be any real recurrent necessity for such upheaval."

For sheer cheap demagogy, for tawdry scholarship, for fragmentary thinking, for sham cerebration and shoddy mentality—this expression could hardly be surpassed. It is on par with the demagogy of the South in dealing with the Negro to pretend that revolution implies human murder. It is worthy of the discredited old Russian emigres in referring to all phases of the Soviet government. It ranks with the forged Sisson papers which were used to disparage the Bolsheviki.

For the benefit of the public we shall now give to our readers an explanation of revolution. By revolution recognized thinkers and scholars mean the change from one system to another and the substitution of the new system for the old. For instance, the change from the geocentric to the heliocentric theory was a revolution in astronomy. Nobody was murdered, but the sun was thereafter considered the center of the universe, instead of the earth. All astronomical thinkers know what an advance this new and correct conception was and is.

In biology the theory of evolution superseded the theory of divine creation. It constituted a revolution when by its thorough exposition Charles Darwin gave to the world the scientific view of unified rather than multiple origin of species.

In chemistry, the atomic theory revolutionized all chemical opinion. Molecules still remained; elements were not assassinated, and the early chemists were not murdered. Nevertheless a striking impetus was given to the development of chemical thought; the early chemical authorities were not murdered; nor did it prevent the still newer advances to the electronic theory of matter.

John Stuart Mill, Adam Smith and Herbert Spencer were staunch philosophers, economists and sociologists of the *laissez faire* school; they believed in the gospel of competition. A revolution in economics and sociology took place with the coming of August Comte, Lester Ward, Richard Ely, Ross, and other economists and sociologists of the school of social control. As against the competition theory of the older group the newer group of economists and sociologists counterposed the higher concept of co-operation. The old group stood for competitive war; the new group for co-operative peace. It was a gigantic revolution in economic and social thought, still we did not learn of the murder of Herbert Spencer, John Stuart Mill and Adam Smith by Ward, Comte or Ely.

In history for centuries the great man theory of interpretation prevailed. Along came the new school of historians with the ideological interpretation of history, showing how world ideas and conceptions determined the course of events. Later another revolution followed, on the surging currents of whose oceanic thought came the materialistic interpretation of history, sometimes dubbed the economic interpretation of history. This group showed the significance of physical environment,—wealth, food, land, trade, commerce, trade routes, and spheres of influence. Yet it might surprise Dr. Du Bois to know that Simon Patten, E.R.A. Seligman, Harvey Robinson, Chas. A. Beard and none of the materialistic historians now living have ever murdered the group of historians of the ideological and the great many theory schools of thought. And even we, who combine all the schools as contributory causes, have no idea whatever of murdering any of the authors of the early schools.

Revolution has gone on steadily in social systems. Savagery, bar-

barism and cannibalism were followed by a revolution which brought on slavery. Slavery, while bad, was a great advance on the previous systems. It was the system by which man passed from savagery to civilization without being annihilated. Another revolution brought on feudalism—less inhuman and more desirable than slavery. A third revolution gave to the world capitalism. Here was a revolution produced by another revolution—the industrial revolution. From hand made products the world went to machine made products as the result of new inventions and discoveries—the invention of labor saving machinery. This was the great revolution of the 19th century. Strictly speaking, it was the revolution from manufacture to machinofacture,—from the hand made article to the machine made article.

To-day we are upon the threshold of a new revolution—the revolution from capitalism to socialism. With it may come the shedding of blood just as the revolution from slavery to capitalism in the United States was accompanied by the mass murder of the Civil War of 1861. Whatever the condition of the transition, the labor and Socialist movement is making every effort for peace. It is engaged in constant education, agitation, organization. It endorses and brooks no violence. No responsible leader, no convention, no responsible group supports any cheap tawdry, petty force tactics. Not even the I.W.W., Dr. Du Bois!

Du Bois after making a veritably superficial scholar of himself on the revolution argument proceeds to make himself more ridiculous in trying to rule out the Negro from the proletariat class. His reason is that we are not a part of the white proletariat because we are not recognized by that proletariat to any great extent. This is about as asinine as saying we are not human beings or men because in the South we are largely not so recognized. Is manhood dependent upon recognition? Is proletariat a product of recognition or is it a state of economic position of human beings? Is a Negro not a Negro when not so recognized? Is he a capitalist if the white proletariat does not recognize him as a laborer? As a superficial sociologist and economist Dr. Du Bois still holds his place. Besides, he shows a crass ignorance of the whole labor problem. Of 32 million white workers in the United States, only 4 million are organized. The 4 million constitute the organized proletariat to which Du Bois refers. Are the other 28 million white workers not members of the working class because they are not organized?

Or let us take another illustration. There are 100 thousand Negro members of the National Association for the Advancement of Colored People. There are ten and a half million Negroes in the United States. Are the 100,000 members to class the great bulk *as not Negroes,* or some such silly balderdash merely because they are not yet organized in the movement?

The next point is also badly reasoned. The Negro race is divided into laborers and capitalists, and their capitalists are of varied shades of opinion just as you find among the whites. Occasionally you discover a liberal and broad scholar among them, now and then public spirited, but on the whole narrow, visionless and reactionary. They charge the highest prices, give the lowest quality, gouge the poor tenants even more heartlessly than the white landlords, not because they are worse naturally, but because they can exploit a fallacious race pride which is little more than a bid for the many to fill the coffers of the few.

Our white professional classes, too, are sons and daughters of laborers at some time in their development.

As to Negroes moving into tenement houses in New York, there is nothing relevant in this whole argument. He says the Negroes moved into Harlem because the white capitalists could get sky high rents—that Negroes would have been mobbed had they gone into quarters where white laborers lived. The answer to this is most properly that the Negroes did live and live now surrounded by white laborers. Again, it is not true of all the laborers. Besides, the white laborers are living in white capitalists' houses also. Neither lives where he wants to but where he must. Nor does the history of this country support the effete and forceless argument of Du Bois. In nearly every section of the country it has been the white capitalist who has fought most vigorously for segregation because of his property values. Witness the present bombing of Negro homes instigated by the Kenwood and Hyde Park Property Owners Association of Chicago. These gentlemen constitute the real estate capitalists who are mobbing and bombing Negroes who attempt to buy property. The Chicago Federation of Labor on the contrary, has frequently protested against it.

The third argument of Du Bois which reveals his much over rated mentality is the confusing of capital and capitalism in his article. He says the Negro would have made a big mistake to fight the $5,000,000 capital paid on his real estate from 1915 to 1920. What has that to do with the control of the means of production and exchange by a few individuals? We do not fight capital such as the factory, the mill, the machine, money, the mine. We do not desire to burn up or sink the land beneath the sea. Nor would we injure (or murder, to use the Doctor's inappropriate language) the capitalist as a person. We do, however, propose to destroy capitalism—that is, the control of the machinery of production and exchange by the limited few for their private profit and benefit. Under Socialism we shall run factories, mills and mines. Food will have to be eaten, clothes worn, houses lived in, persons and property carried, messages transmitted, work done. But this will be done not merely for the benefit of a few Rockefellers, Morgans, Schwabs and Carnegies, but for the teeming and toiling millions who today produce food which they cannot eat, make clothes which they cannot wear, build houses which they cannot live in.

In concluding, Du Bois reflects on what might happen in a way to ventilate an ignorance which, if he understood political science, he would have stated not with such an air of novelty and original discovery. He continues:

"The main danger and the central question of the capitalistic development through which the Negro American group is forced to go is the question of the ultimate *control of the capital which they must raise and use. If this capital is going to be controlled by a few men for their own benefit, then we are destined to suffer from our own capitalists exactly what we are suffering from white capitalists today.* And while this is not a pleasant prospect, it is certainly no worse than the present actuality. If, on the other hand, because of our more democratic organization and our widespread inter-class sympathy we can introduce a more democratic control, taking advantage of what the white world is itself doing to introduce industrial democracy, then we may not only escape our present economic slavery but even guide and lead a distrait economic world."

Why, the control of the capital is the only issue! Nobody but a fool wants to destroy it. It is not necessary for [the Negro] to suffer all the evils of exploitation by Negro capitalists when he can now adopt the more democratic co-operative methods. And the Negro of New York, in particular, has had enough experience with Negro landlords to be perfectly sure that he is in every respect the equal if not the superior of the white landlord in the exploitation of Negro tenants.

Rest assured, Dr. Du Bois, you are not getting by as easily these days with your scholarship laurels as in the old days when you were the literary philosophic lion. Persons in your own group like John Haynes Holmes, Mary W. Ovington, J. W. Johnson, R. W. Bagnall, Herbert J. Seligman, Osward G. Villard and others laugh at this discussion of revolution, the proletariat, capital and Negro capital. Unless you convalesce rather rapidly, we shall have to call out the first aid to doctor your philosophy, unless as a doctor of philosophy you can doctor your own.

A VOICE FROM THE DEAD!

The New York Age was the oldest of New York's black papers at the time this essay was written by Chandler Owens in April 1922. Fred R. Moore was the owner and editor of the Age. In the following, Owens assails Moore and his newspaper for supporting a system that is moribund and most likely obsolete.

We have been travelling for two and half months; we have gone nearly eight thousand miles. Part of our business has been the surveying and ascertaining of newsstands where Negro literature is sold. We have frequently seen the Chicago Defender, the Negro World, the Crisis, the MESSENGER, the California Eagle and the Chicago Whip. But without exaggeration, we went nearly six thousand miles before we saw one New York Age. It was delivered at a home in Spokane, Washington, just before our leaving for St. Paul, Minnesota. As we glimpsed it, we remarked: "That's the first Age we've seen since leaving New York!" "Won't you tell us," we said to the subscriber, "why you read the Age?" To which the subscriber immediately replied: "There's nothing in it except the editorials of James Weldon Johnson!" We asserted whole heartedly: That was all the stronger reason why we wondered at not being able to find it over the long trip before, because we had repeatedly tried to get it for James Weldon Johnson's contributions.

It was well that we got just this issue since it had an editorial referring to Chandler Owen in the West. Mr. Owen is physically, intellectually and socially *alive*. He is *awake* to every new issue. The Age is *dead*: walking around, no doubt, to save the undertaker's expenses.

Throughout all ages death has been the mortal enemy to life. There is nothing surprising, therefore, that the editor of the New York Age should hate the editor of the New York MESSENGER.

The greater part of the Age editorial is cheap, petty and mendacious—so palpably false that we pass it over as not being entitled to a decorous answer. One part of the editorial, however, reads: "He cannot be accused of any constructive accomplishment in business or politics."

Let us see something about this. Let us go right into the field of journalism and test this.

First, in 1919, after his release from the army, within a period of six months from June to November, together with his chief associate, A. Philip Randolph, he drove up the circulation of the MESSENGER Magazine to twenty-six thousand copies per month. The following increases took place: June, 10,000, July, 15,000; August, 18,000; September, 21,000; October, 25,000; November, 26,000. In Los Angeles alone, one agent, Jothar Nishida reached the 5,000 mark; W. H. Tibbs of Chicago 3,000; Charles H. Thomas of Philadelphia, 2,500; W. H. Scarville of Pittsburg, 1,500; William S. Nelson of Washington, D. C., 3,500; Louis Silver of Detroit, 800; Raymer's Old Book Store of Seattle, 500; Perry Murphy of Seattle, 400; Tutt's Barber Shop of Seattle, 500; Thomas L. Dabney of Richmond, Va., 500; Frank Worthy of Atlanta, Georgia, 400; Clifford Williams of Boston, 500; E. K. Thumm of Pittsburg, 300; Charles Mooney's newsstand at 135th Street and Lenox Avenue, New York City, 545; and numerous agents who took 50, 100, 150 and 200. In short, the MESSENGER was the first 15 cent publication put out among Negroes. (The *Crisis* was then selling at ten cents.) Despite its higher price, despite the fact it was denied second-class mail privileges nearly three years—and was the only Negro publication in the United States denied such privileges!—despite all of these handicaps it reached (what we believe to be an accurate statement) *the largest circulation of any Negro publication in the United States,* except the Chicago *Defender* and the New York *Crisis.* [We do not know the *Negro World* circulation, but we have an analytical statement that its circulation was 20,000.] If any publication has an honest-to-goodness circulation which is greater, of which it will present genuine proof like unto ours, a full statement of its exception will be made in the MESSENGER, following submission of its proof.

So much for the business accomplishment of Messrs. Owen and Randolph. What about their social and education achievement? If we were writing this for the editor of the *Age,* it would be like "casting pearls before swine," for when dealing with the *Age* editor, the reader must keep in mind one whose presumption is only exceeded by his ignorance.

Nevertheless, for the benefit of our readers, take note of the following.

(1) The MESSENGER has been able to carry basic and new information to thousands of white and colored readers—*it being reasonably certain that this publication has more white readers than all the other Negro publications in America combined.*

(2) It has reached a very high literary standard as shown by the comments upon the back of this issue. In addition to that evidence, it has been for three years in Princeton, Harvard, Radcliffe, two copies in the Library of Congress, the 42nd Street and 5th Avenue, New York Public Library. Besides it is being read by several leading white professors of English, economics, sociology, political science and history, along with some of the most distinguished publicists in the United States, England, France and Germany.

In a 27 page review of the Negro publications in the United States, the Democratic United States Department of Justice, in a report to the United States Senate, said: "The MESSENGER, *the Monthly Magazine published in New York, is by long odds the most able . . . of all the Negro publications.*"

The same report, as we recall, stated that the "New York *Age* was among the '*better behaved*' *of the Negro publications.*" This terminology will not be understood by most of our white readers nor by some of our northern Negro readers. The southern Negroes will not miss the point, though. *Better behaved* is the Southern term for a "*good nigger,*" that is, one who will take orders from the white bosses against the interests of the Negro.

(3) The MESSENGER was the first publication among Negroes to recognize the Negro problem as fundamentally a labor problem. Pursuant thereto Mr. Randolph and Mr. Owen assembled most of the progressive labor leaders of New York in a conference upon the admission of Negroes into all unions upon absolutely equal terms with the whites. This policy has been widely accepted and many such unions refer to the editors of the MESSENGER upon all questions affecting the race. The general confidence in them can be seen from the following list of persons and organizations who have assisted, endorsed or praised the MESSENGER. (Most of the following have assisted.)

District Council No. 9 of New York City, Brotherhood of
    Painters, Decorators and Paper Hangers of America. Affiliated
    with A. F. of L. and National Building Trades Council.
The General Board of the Amalgamated Clothing Workers of
    America.

The General Board of the International Ladies' Garment Workers of America. Affiliated with the A. F. of L.

The Marine Transport Workers of Philadelphia, Local No. 8.

Micrometer Lodge, Machinists No. 1, A.M.W.A.

General Board United Cloth Hat and Cap Makers of North America.

International Journeymen Bakers' and Confectioners' Union of America.

International Federation of Workers in Restaurant, Hotel and Catering Industry.

Local 25, Ladies' Waist Makers' Union, I.L.G.W.

General Board International Fur Workers' Union, A. F. of L.

Lumber Workers' Industrial Union of Canada.

New York Joint Board of A. C. W. of A.

New York Joint Board of Cloak, Skirt and Reefer Makers' Union.

New York Joint Board of Fur Workers' Union.

New York Joint Board of United Cloth Hat and Cap Makers.

Fancy Leather Goods Workers' Union.

White Goods Workers' Union.

Millinery Ladies' Straw Hat Union.

New York Joint Board, Vest Makers' Union, A. C. W. of A.

Cleaners' and Dyers' Union.

New York Cutters' Union, A. C. W. of A.

Chicago Joint Board, A. C. W. of A.

Children's Dress Makers' Union of New York.

Joint Board of Pants Makers' A. C. W. of A.

The Forward Association.

The Workmen's Circle Convention.

The Rand School of Social Science.

The New York Printers' Pressmen's Union, Local No. 51, A. F. of L.

The New York Jewelry Workers' Union of A. F. of L.

Local No. 261, Painters' Union of New York.

Butcher Workers' Union.

Co-operative League of America.

United Cloth Hat and Cap Makers' No. 6 of Philadelphia, Pa.

Seattle International Workers' Defense.

United Hebrew Trades.

The New York Call.

The New York Jewish Daily Forward.

The Advance of A. C. W. of A.

The Justice of I.L.G.W.

Of this list special mention should be made of the New York Joint Board of the Amalgamated Clothing Workers of America, the International Ladies' Garment Workers' New York Joint Board of Cloak Makers and the Workmen's Circle which gave $500 each to the MESSENGER work last year. Also should be recorded the Marine Transport Workers of Philadelphia which contributed $1,200 last year and purchased for its members 3,600 copies. The New York Jewish Daily *Forward* donated $450, the New York District Painters' Council $300 worth of subscriptions, and a number of unions which responded with $50, $100 and $25, respectively. (P. S.—The MESSENGER has no large individual contributors.)

While the New York *Age* was around looking for political pie, two-by-four jobs for hat-in-hand Negro leaders, A. Philip Randolph and Chandler Owen were securing jobs and increases in wages for thousands of Negro girls and men—jobs which paid through unionization of Negroes, all the way from $30 per week to $60 per week.

(4) Chandler Owen and A. Philip Randolph within the last six months, have addressed many of the largest labor councils and unions in the United States. They have done as much to create good racial relations on a basis of equality as any two men in the United States.

The *Age,* through the Moton influence, has stood for race harmony, but on a basis of caste. The white man was to be master and the Negro a slave. The lamb and lion were to lie down together, but the lamb was to be in the lion's belly. The MESSENGER editors do not accept this kind of racial harmony.

(5) Messrs Randolph and Owen have also considerable constructive accomplishment in politics.

In assembling a group of writers and thinkers like W. A. Domingo, George Frazier Miller and William N. Colson, they got together not only the ablest array of scholars on any Negro publication in the world, but they competed on all fours with the very best white publications.

Again, they secured men of definite political convictions who were not vacillating for a little slush from year to year like some of the reactionary editors. For instance, in 1917, when the Fusionists had a two million dollar chest or slush fund, their candidate was John Purroy Mitchel, a *Democrat.* The Republican nominee was William M. Bennett. The editor of the *Age* was not a supporter of Mr. Bennett, the Republican candidate that year. *Instead, he went the way of the slush, with Mr. Mitchell, a great friend of Benjamin Tillman of South Carolina, the Democratic Mayor who kept the Birth of the Nation upon New York screens, who spoke at the Confederate Flag Celebration in Charleston, S. C., right in the middle of the campaign while Fred Moore of the New York Age was supporting him!*

All of the MESSENGER editors and contributors were on the side of progress in politics that year as they have been the years after. They have resisted all efforts at corruption—*even though it would be eminently profitable for them to yield* to such groups as the Mitchell Slush Fund group of 1917!

Another thing constructive in politics which has to be accorded Chandler Owen and his associates. They have raised New York from the liquorterian leadership which the *Age* has supported for years. When we began our work in New York, most of the political leaders could be found, as a rule, in Mattheny's Saloon, 135th Street and 7th Avenue, New York, drinking liquor and smoking cigars. No campaign, except a beer and sandwich campaign, was made. Not so any longer. Last year we forced the Democrats and Republicans to attempt some kind of educational campaign for about six or eight weeks prior to the election—all over the Negro section of New York.

And all five of these men represent just what they preach—George Frazier Miller, W. A. Domingo, William N. Colson, A. Philip Randolph and Chandler Owen! Not one of them is a liquorterian or tobacco worm! Not one of them tries to look important with a cigar in his mouth and make this practice do duty for thought.

In brief, Messrs. Randolph and Owen have brought education into Negro politics in contradistinction to the ignoramuses like the Honorable Fred Moore who, of course, brought *what they had.*

They raised it from the bar room where all questions were formerly settled by most of the breed supported by the *Age.*

They have created also a large following all over this country of independent, high-souled, intelligent, courageous Negro men and women, young and old, rich and poor, who are tired of the *political* and *intellectualless* pabulum formerly fed them by the New York *Age* editor. This following is rapidly on the increase and bids fair within a few years to retire such political and journalistic fossils as the *Age* editor to that oblivion and obscurity from which they ought never to emerge!

Finally, we can not close without reciting the following story. There is an erroneous belief that asafetida destroys or keeps away disease. So an old Southern father put on his little bag. And there is hardly anything which smells more offensive than asafetida. But as if to add worse to worse, the old man went out, was caught in the rain and got wet. And if there is anything which smells worse than asafetida, it is wet asafetida. Later on the old man came in the house to get dry. He sat down before the fireplace with the children assembled around. And if there is anything which smells worse than wet asafetida, it is wet asafetida hot. Consequently when the fumes of this hot, wet asafetida began to permeate the room, all at once the old man's little girl rose, rushed to her mother crying "Mamma, papa's dead and don't know it."

So it is with the New York *Age* and its editor. He is dead and doesn't know it. The system of society he and the *Age* support are moribund, obsolescent, if not obsolete. Mr. Owen represents a new order of society and, therefore, cannot be persona grata to the old, reactionary, fossilized leadership of the *Age*.

BLACK MAMMIES

The Daughters of the Confederacy asked Congress to grant them permission to erect a statue in the nation's capital in memory of black mammies. Chandler Owen, in the following essay, attacks the Daughters of the Confederacy, who desired to honor "those wonderful" days when black mammies cleaned, cooked, nursed white babies, and essentially made life easy for white women who were the heirs to the Confederacy. This essay was published in March 1923.

One writer has said: "*The existence of monuments is justified on but two grounds—as works of art and that for which they stand.*" We do not agree with his first proposition. We do not believe a mere work of art justifies a monument. We think that a monument ought to be erected to some idea or ideal and that that ideal should be portrayed through a work of art. In other words, art should be made the hand-maiden of truth and justice.

To illustrate: At the present time the Ku Klux Klan is planning to erect in Atlanta a monument which will probably be one of the greatest works of art in America. They have secured the services of sculptors of world-wide reputation. Yet the monument they erect will necessarily be condemned by the sober opinion of the present and the future, on account of the vicious principles which the statue will be designed to commemorate.

The Daughters of the Confederacy (Jefferson Davis Chapter No. 1650) have asked Congress to grant them permission to erect a statue in Washington in memory of the "Black Mammies." They want to bring back memories of the slave days when *black mammies* toiled in the cotton fields, cleaned the houses, cared for the children, nursed them at their bosoms. They want to bring back what (to them) Bert Williams would call "*those wonderful days*"—days when the pay for Negro Labor was the "cruel lash of arrogant idleness upon the naked back of patient 'toil'." They want a memorial of the Southern white's good times gone. To the Southern bourbons these memories are like the photo of a choice and fond friend who had passed away. Though we cannot bring back the friend, we may often look upon and kiss the picture.

Now we don't want any "mammy" statues anywhere. We want the children of this generation to abhor and forget those days when the white madam had leisure and the black mammy had labor—when the white lady loitered and the black mistress toiled. We want to orient ourselves—turn our faces from the dark and discouraging past, and direct it toward a bright and hopeful future.

In fact, people erect monuments for things of which they are fond, and in order to perpetuate the ideas for the future. And that is just what these Daughters of the Confederacy are doing. The "black mammies" made it *soft* for them and they made it *hard* for the "black mammies." They are justified in wanting the "black mammies" to return, but we Negroes are justified in fighting to say that these "black mammies" will be like Poe's Raven—"*never more.*" What one person desires to memorialize, another person may want to forget. For instance: you will not find in Alabama, Florida or Georgia, the statues of Grant or Lincoln; nor will you find in Boston the statues of Jeff Davis, Stonewall Jackson or Robert E. Lee. It would be quite impossible to find in Paris a statue of Hindenburg or Ludendorff, nor would you find in Berlin a monument erected to Foch or Sir Douglas Haig. Why? Because in these respective cases the persons referred to had used their power to injure their opponents.

The writer favors having some statues and monuments erected in this country. We favor one erected to the 200,000 Negro soldiers who fought to wipe out slavery and to unfurl the flag of freedom and let it float like a cloud over this land. We favor a statue to these men who helped to save the Union, who indeed were a great factor in crushing out the iniquitous viper—slavery—which vitiated the entire American atmosphere with its venomous and poisonous breath. We favor a monument to the runaway slaves who had the courage to dash for freedom.

We favor erecting a monument to the New Negro, who is carving a new monument in the hearts of our people. We favor the erection of a monument to the Negroes of Washington, Chicago, Longview, Texas, Knoxville, Tenn., Tulsa, Okla., and Philadelphia, who rose in their might and said to the authorities: "*If you cannot protect us, we will protect ourselves—if you cannot uphold the law, we will maintain constituted authority.*" We favor erecting a monument to the Negro artists and poets, the Negro inventors and discoverers, the Negro scholars and thinkers, who have gone without food, clothing and shelter, in order to lay upon the altar of progress the Negro's meed of achievement. We favor a monument to the Negro women who have risen above insult, assault, debauchery, prostitution and abuse, *to which these unfortunate "black mammies" were subjected.* Yes, we favor erecting a monument to these women, who have almost wiped out this chasm of caste, who have broken the cordon of chains and are now trying to throw them off.

Let this "mammy" statue go. Let it fade away. Let it be buried in that blissful oblivion to which the brave sons of this nation have consigned it; and when it rises again, let its white shaft point like a lofty mountain peak to a *New Negro mother,* no longer a *"white man's woman,"* no longer the sex-enslaved *"black mammy"* of Dixie—but the apotheosis of triumphant Negro womanhood!

SOCIALISM THE NEGROES' HOPE

Dismayed that African Americans do not see the benefit in adopting socialism as a philosophy, W. A. Domingo outlines the reasons why such a doctrine holds hope for the future of black Americans. He published this essay in July 1919.

It is a regrettable and disconcerting anomaly that, despite their situation as the economic, political and social door mat of the world, Negroes do not embrace the philosophy of socialism, and in greater numbers than they now do. It is an anomaly because it is reasonable to expect those who are lowest down to be the ones who would most quickly comprehend the need for a change in their status and welcome any doctrine which holds forth any hope of human elevation. In matters of religion they respond and react logically and naturally enough, for to them, the religion of Christ, the lowly Nazarene, brings definite assurance of surcease from earthly pains and the hope of celestial readjustment of mundane equalities. Their acceptance of the Christian religion with its present day emphasis upon an after-life enjoyment of the good things denied them on the earth is conclusive proof of their dissatisfaction with their present lot, and is an earnest of their susceptibility to Socialism, which intends to do for human beings what Christianity promises to do for them in less material regions.

That they and all oppressed dark peoples will be the greatest beneficiaries in a socialist world has not been sufficiently emphasized by Socialist propaganda among Negroes.

Perhaps this is not clearly understood, but a little examination of the facts will prove this to be the case.

Throughout the world Negroes occupy a position of absolute inferiority to the white race. This is true whether they are black Frenchmen, black Englishmen, black Belgians or black Americans.

As between themselves and the masses of white proletarians their lives are more circumscribed, their ambitions more limited and their opportunities for the enjoyment of liberty and happiness more restricted. White workingmen of England who are Socialists are immeasurably the political and social superiors of the average Negro in the West Indies or Africa; white workingmen of France, who are Socialists are unquestionably the political and social superiors of Senegalese and Madagascan Negroes; white workingmen of the United States who are Socialists are indisputably the social and political superiors of the millions of Negroes below the Mason and Dixon line; yet despite their relative and absolute superiority these white workers are fighting for a world freed from oppression and exploitation, whilst Negroes who are oppressed cling to past and present economic ideals with the desperation of a drowning man.

Socialism as an economic doctrine is merely the pure Christianity preached by Jesus, and practiced by the early Christians adapted to the more complex conditions of modern life. It makes no distinction as to race, nationality or creed, but like Jesus it says "Come unto me all ye who are weary and heavy laden and I will give you rest." It is to procure that rest that millions of oppressed peoples are flocking to the scarlet banner of international Socialism.

So far, although having greater need for its equalizing principles than white workingmen, Negroes have been slow to realize what has already dawned upon nearly every other oppressed people: That Socialism is their only hope.

The 384,000,000 natives of India groaning under the exploitation of the handful of English manufacturers, merchants and officials who profit out of their labor are turning from Lloyd George and the capitalistic Liberal Party to Robert Smillie, the Socialist and the Independent Labor Party. The 4,000,000 Irish who suffer national strangulation at the hands of British industrialists and militarists have turned to the Socialists of England for relief besides becoming Socialists themselves. The Egyptians who are of Negro admixture being convinced that their only hope for freedom from British exploitation is in international Socialism are uniting forces with British Socialists and organized labor. In fact, every oppressed group of the world is today turning from Clemenceau, Lloyd George and Wilson to the citadel of Socialism, Moscow. In this they are all in advance of Western Negroes with the exception of little groups in the United States and a relatively well-organized group in the Island of Trinidad, British West Indies.

Because of ignorant and unscrupulous leadership, Negroes are influenced to give their support to those institutions which oppress them, but if they would only do a little independent thinking without the aid of preacher, politician or press they would quickly realize that the very men like Thomas Dixon, author of "The Clansman," Senators Hoke Smith of Georgia and Overman of North Carolina, who are fighting Socialism or as they maliciously call it Bolshevism, are the same men who exhaust every unfair means to villify, oppress and oppose Negroes. If anything should commend Socialism to Negroes, nothing can do so more eloquently than the attitude and opinions of its most influential opponents toward people who are not white.

On the other hand, the foremost exponents of Socialism in Europe and America are characterized by the broadness of their vision towards all oppressed humanity. It was the Socialist Vendervelde of Belgium, who protested against the Congo atrocities practiced upon Negroes; it was the late Keir Hardie and Philip Snowdon of England, who condemned British rule in Egypt; and in the United States it was the Socialist, Eugene V. Debs, who refused to speak in Southern halls from which Negroes were excluded. Today, it is the revolutionary Socialist, Lenin, who analyzed the infamous League of Nations and exposed its true character; it is he as leader of the Communist Congress at Moscow, who sent out the proclamation: "Slaves of the colonies in Africa and Asia! The hour of proletarian dictatorship in Europe will be the hour of your release!"

"If We Must Die"

In the following editorial, W. A. Domingo discusses a new spirit flourishing among African Americans. President Woodrow Wilson had insisted upon "force, unstinted force" to win the First World War. Domingo writes that African Americans adopted Wilson's method to protect themselves, their families, their properties from mob violence. Domingo calls this spirit a reflex of the war. Quoting the poet Claude McKay, he writes: "Like men we'll face the murderous, cowardly pack. Pressed to the wall, dying, but— fighting back!" This editorial was published in September 1919.

America won the war that was alleged to be fought for the purpose of making the world safe for democracy, but in the light of recent happenings in Washington, the Capital city, and Chicago, it would seem as though the United States is not a part of the world. In order to win the war President Wilson employed "force, unstinted force," and those who expect to bring any similar desirable termination to a just cause can do no less than follow the splendid example set them by the reputed spokesman of humanity. That the lesson did not take long to penetrate the minds of Negroes is demonstrated by the change that has taken place in their demeanor and tactics. No longer are Negroes willing to be shot down or hunted from place to place like wild beasts; no longer will they flee from their homes and leave their property to the tender mercies of the howling and cowardly mob. They have changed, and now they intend to give men's account of themselves. If death is to be their portion, New Negroes are determined to make their dying a costly investment for all concerned. If they must die they are determined that they shall not travel through the valley of the shadow of death alone, but that some of their oppressors shall be their companions.

This new spirit is but a reflex of the great war, and it is largely due to the insistent and vigorous agitation carried on by younger men of the race. The demand is uncompromisingly made for either liberty or death, and since death is likely to be a two-edged sword it will be to the advantage of those in a position to do so to give the race its long-denied liberty.

The new spirit animating Negroes is not confined to the United States, where it is most acutely manifested, but is simmering beneath the surface in every country where the race is oppressed. The Washington and Chicago outbreaks should be regarded as symptoms of a great pandemic, and the Negroes as courageous surgeons who performed the necessary though painful operation. That the remedy is efficacious is beyond question. It has brought results, for as a consequence the eyes of the entire world are focused upon the racial situation in the United States. The world knows now that the New Negroes are determined to observe the primal law of self-preservation whenever civil laws break down; to assist the authorities to preserve order and prevent themselves and families from being murdered in cold blood. Surely, no one can sincerely object to this new and laudable determination. Justification for this course is not lacking, for it is the white man's own Bible that says "Those who live by the sword shall perish by the sword," and since white men believe in force, Negroes who have mimicked them for nearly three centuries must copy them in that respect. Since fire must be fought with hell fire, and diamond alone can cut diamond, Negroes realize that force alone is an effective medium to counteract force. Counter irritants are useful in curing diseases, and Negroes are being driven by their white fellow citizens to investigate the curative values inherent in mass action, revolvers and other lethal devices when applied to social diseases.

The New Negro has arrived with stiffened back bone, dauntless manhood, defiant eye, steady hand and a will of iron. His creed is admirably summed up in the poem of Claude McKay, the black Jamaican poet, who is carving out for himself a niche in the Hall of Fame:

IF WE MUST DIE

If we must die, let it not be like hogs
Hunted and penned in an inglorious spot,
While round us bark the mad and hungry dogs,
Making their mock at our accursed lot.
If we must die, oh, let us nobly die,
So that our precious blood may not be shed
In vain; then even the monsters we defy
Shall be constrained to honor us, though dead!

Oh, kinsmen! We must meet the common foe!
Though far outnumbered, let us still be brave,
And for their thousand blows deal one deathblow!
What though before us lies the open grave?
Like men we'll face the murderous, cowardly pack,
Pressed to the wall, dying, but fighting back!

THE NEGRO IN POLITICS

A. Philip Randolph discusses the history of African Americans in politics and addresses current political trends. Promoting the Socialist Party, he expresses little hope for his race under the existing political systems. This essay was published in July 1919.

The Negro has had a pathetic and unpromising history in American politics.

His eventful and hapless career began under the shadows of the institution of slavery, from which he had just emerged. He was played upon by two forces, viz., the open opposition from his former masters, on the one hand, and the fraud and deception of the white carpet-baggers, who swarmed South, like vultures, to pray upon his ignorance and credulity.

RECONSTRUCTION PERIOD

We have but to take a glimpse into the history of the Reconstruction period, to witness his tragical fight, wrought by a paradoxial combination of his Northern Republican friends and his Southern Democratic enemies.

During this period the Negro was a political football between his former slave masters and Northern political adventurers. The economic basis of this contest was the power to tax: to float bonds; to award franchises: in short, to gain control over the financial resources of the newly organized States. These were big stakes for which to contend. Hence, the carpet-baggers used the enfranchised Negro to assist them in securing control over the Southern State governments and the Southern politicians fought the Negro viciously to prevent this Carpet-bagger-Negro political ascendency.

This period of storm and stress gave birth to two significant social organizations, the Union of Loyal League of Negroes and the Ku Klux Klan, which attempted to protect the political interests of the Negroes and Southern whites, respectively.

They only served, however, to engender bitterness: to breed and to foster suspicion and hate between the races, which resulted in lawlessness, crime and general social anarchy. These too, were natural, political and social consequences of the Reconstruction policy. The inordinate lust for power, overwhelming ambition to rule, the instinct to secure an advantage, impels individuals and social groups to adopt the policy of force, the policy of fraud, or the method of education: whichever policy is available, and is recognized as likely to secure the more permanent results.

Such were the political vicissitudes of the Negro in the South. The Ku Klux Klan and the tissue ballot were social and political inventions of intimidation to discourage the Negroes' participation in politics. The Thirteenth, Fourteenth and Fifteenth Amendments to the Federal Constitution, the Federal army and the Carpet-Baggers were designed to protect the Negroes' suffrage, in order that the Negro might entrench, reenforce and fortify the Republican party's control over Congress. The lessons of this period had been hard, bitter and disappointing to the Negro. The army, the arm of protection of the Federal Government, had been withdrawn. The Negro office holders and their Republican supporters had been hurled from power. The Reconstruction legislation had been emasculated from the statute books. The Southern States had begun a systematic and organized campaign of nullification of the freedom and enfranchisement of the Negro. In fact, the Negro had been reduced to serfdom. And in 1876, the last vestige of Reconstruction governments had disappeared. And it cannot be maintained by the sober and dispassionate historian that the Negro had legislated and administered the State governments wisely and well. As he had ignorantly fought with and tilled the fields for his former masters to maintain slavery, he had also voted to strengthen his Republican political masters, to dominate the government, only to be forsaken, neglected, naked to his enemies. No Negro, with a genius for leadership, had arisen in this period. So much for our Reconstruction history.

SUBSEQUENT POLITICAL COURSE

What has been the subsequent political course of the Negro?

The complete scheme of the Negroes' disfranchisement was in process of development in the South. The South had resented and ignored the fourteenth amendment which had demanded a reduction in representation in Congress, if the Negroes' suffrage was restricted. Intermittant cries against this political brigandage were heard but finally subsided. The South continued to weave a fabric of law, the "Grandfather clauses," which gave legal sanction to an already general custom of Negro disfranchisement. The Republican Party, pretended friend and defender, had assented. Yet the Negro remained a Republican. Why? First, the Reconstruction legislation of the Republican party had forged the "Solid South." The Solid South was dominated by the Democratic Party. The Democratic Party had striven to maintain slavery. It had been the father of the "Fugitive Slave Law," the nullification of the Missouri Compromise of 1820, and Chief Justice Taney had handed down the famous Dred Scott's decision, which gave constitutional sanction to the extension of slavery into new territory.

On the other hand, the Republican Party had been the party of the North, the refuge of the fugitive slave, the home of the abolitionists, Wendell Philips, Garrison, Lovejoy and Sumner was in power when freedom came. It had used the Negro as an office holder and continued to distribute political crumbs in the form of collectors of internal revenue, deputy collectors, registrars of the Treasury, Ministers to Hayti, Liberia and such places, that required no legislative ability, no intelligent understanding of the methods, objects and principles of government. In truth, the Negro office-holders were mainly of the "rubber stamp" variety. But it was sufficient that the Republican Party had awarded jobs, to secure the indiscriminating and unquestioning devotion of the Negro. Thus, the Negro became as staunch a Republican as the Irish a Democrat. It was considered race treason for a Negro to profess any other political faith.

Here and there an eccentric Negro had claimed to be a Democrat, but his claim was considered lightly. It is true that in New York City a tiny fraction of Negroes had bolted the Republican ranks and joined Tammany Hall, seeking political jobs.

There had also arisen among the Negroes a political scism, namely a belief in the virtue of dividing the vote. In support of this political heresy, it was maintained that by dividing the vote the Negro would be able to secure the good will of both parties: it was further maintained that it would create fear in the Republican Party which would result in its giving the Negro a fairer consideration, and that the Negro would be sure of political preferment, regardless of which party was in power. And in 1912 and in 1916 a few Negro leaders had professed sympathy for Woodrow Wilson as the Democratic presidential nominee.

The formation of the Progressive Party of 1912, had marked another important rift in the Negro Republican voters. The love for Roosevelt, the expectation of jobs and the general dissatisfaction with President Taft's attitude towards Negro job-holders in the South, had produced this alienation.

In the mayoralty election of New York City in 1917, occurred another change in the Negroes' political course. This change resulted in 25 per cent of the Negroes voting the Socialist ticket. This vote, too, it might be observed, was achieved despite the fact that heretofore there had been no Socialist vote among Negroes of New York State.

These movements have had their leaders. Who were they and what did they stand for?

TYPES OF NEGRO POLITICAL LEADERS EVOLVED

During the Reconstruction period the Negro leaders were unschooled, credulous, gullible. They had been led by the Republican agents from the North, the carpet-baggers.

Ex-Governor Pinchback, Lynch, Moses, etc., had been accomplices of the most shameless raids upon the funds of the States' destructive legislation and issuance of spurious, inflamed paper.

In Congress White and Bruce had done one thing, they had been loyal to the Republican Party. During the long years from the passing of Negro representatives in Congress, no Negro of large vision and intelligent grasp of the forces in politics had arisen.

Booker T. Washington had become prominent in the industrial development of the Negro, but had counselled the "let alone policy."

Bishop Walters, W.E.B. Du Bois, James Monroe Trotter and Rev. James Milton Waldron—Negroes of national standing and prominence—had turned Democratic. Their object was to make the Republican Party repentant. These men had a vision of the rise of a Radical Negro; they had recognized the failure of the Republican Party; they had not caught the message of Socialism and they were still ruled by the belief that the test of the political progress of the Negroes was the number of jobs he held. They had not realized that out of

12,000,000 Negroes but a tiny fraction could become job-holders. The value of workmen's compensation legislation, widows' pensions, social insurance legislation, measures reducing the cost of living, shortening hours of toil and increasing the wages of the masses, had escaped them.

In the Republican Party, Charles W. Anderson, Ralph Tyler, W. T. Vernon and W. H. Lewis are figures of national proportions. These are men of the old school who make much over what they style as "playing the game of politics," which in other words simply means getting next to "campaign slush funds" and landing a rubber stamp job. Their positions rest upon their ability to echo the will of the masters through flamboyant oratory and their unquestioning obedience to the Republican machine.

Even the generous student of politics cannot accord to them any fundamental understanding of the relation between politics and the business of getting a living, the social purpose and economic basis of modern legislation and the scientific methods of administrative government.

They with the ward-heeler-politician identify their personal prosperity with that of the race and insist that their holding of a government job is an unmistakable sign of the Negroes' political progress.

Negro leaders, generally, have been creatures of the Republican or Democratic parties, which hold them in leash and prevent them from initiating anything fundamental in the interest of the Negroes. This brings us to the consideration of the appointment policy.

INFLUENCE OF THE APPOINTMENT POLICY

Aptly and truly too, has it been said that the "power over a man's subsistence is the power over his will" or expressed more popularly "he who pays the fiddler will call the tune."

Since Negro leaders have been the appointees of the Republican and Democratic bosses it is but natural that they would obey the voice of their masters. And the Republican and Democratic bosses are servants of the employing or capitalist class which thrives upon low wages and high prices, the ignorance and degradation of the workers of which 12 per cent are Negroes.

This principal, however, of appointing members of the servant class to positions in the government or to places of race leadership, has been uniformly adopted by the ruling class in all parts of the world. The social experience is that a member of an oppressed class, invested with power by the master-class becomes the brutal oppressor and exploiter of his class. Note the vicious class of foremen, headwaiters, who are recruited from the working class.

Great Britain employs 250,000 natives of India to hold in subjection 300,000,000. She has also applied this same rule in Ireland and successfully exploited these peoples for 800 years.

Hence, it is apparent that the Negro leaders, the hirelings of the Republican and Democratic bosses who are in turn the agents of anti-labor forces, are the worst enemies of the race.

THE GROWTH OF THE MOVEMENT FOR NEGRO ELECTIVE REPRESENTATION

The movement is conceived in the idea that those whom the people elect will represent them. But, in the light of the history of government, it cannot logically be maintained that all persons elected by the people will represent the people. For instance, during the Reconstruction period the Negro office-holders and legislators, represented the carpet-baggers and not the people. Today, all legislators are elected by the people but the people suffer most from poverty and ignorance, hence it cannot be maintained that the present government represents the people, if by representation we mean the enactment of legislation for the relief of human suffering and the improvement of social conditions. The people elect but the capitalists select.

There are three main conditions to a representative's representing those by whom he is elected. First, his chief interests must be identical with those by whom he is elected; second, he must be the member of a party organization which is controlled by his constituents; and, third, he must be sufficiently intelligent to understand his class interests.

To illustrate: If a real estate owner is elected to the legislature from a district composed largely of working people, his tenants: his chief interests would lie with the members of his class—the real estate owners and in opposition to those who elected him—the tenant-class. If a measure was raised to abolish the "law of dispossess," who would wonder as to how the real estate owners would vote, despite the fact, the measure would be palpably in the interests of those whom he was presumed to represent.

Again, suppose the representative's chief interests are identical with those of his constituents, and is also the member of a political organization which is controlled by forces which are opposed to the chief interests of his district. Is it not plain as to how he would vote? The history of politics is clear on this point. The lack of regularity would result in his political death. Note the fate of Ex-Governor Sulzer of New York, who opposed the Tammany machine which created him. Note Roosevelt's plight who bolted the Republican machine in 1912.

Lastly, given that the two foregoing conditions are satisfied, if the representative was not sufficiently intelligent he might be used as the most effective opponent of his own and his constituent's interests.

Thus, it is apparent that the election of a Negro by Negroes, is not enough and does not guarantee Negroes, of whom 99 per cent are working people, that their chief interests, as working people, will be represented.

Just as the election of a woman, by women does not guarantee that their chief interests will be represented.

Witness Jeannette Rankin, woman representative from Montana, lining up with the Republican and Democratic parties in unquestioning support of the capitalists, despite the fact, women and their children are the chief sufferers from long hours and low wages in factories and mines.

Witness the election of the Negro Assemblyman, E. A. Johnson, from the 21st Assembly District of New York City. Introducing a bill to permit children of the tender age of 12 when they are out of school to be exploited at work. Note, too, that he cited as his main reason for his bill, the recent exodus of Negroes from the South and the likelihood of idle Negro children getting into mischief in the streets of New York. This bill was condemned by the educators and union leaders, on the ground that children are in need of play and recreation as much as they are in need of book learning. Work stunts the bodies and arrests the mental growth of children.

Here, two facts are evident: first, that the Assemblyman was ignorant of the fundamental recreational and educational needs of children; second, that he is part of the Republican machine, which represents the factories and canneries interests which make millions out of child labor. Here then is the clear case of a Negro being the father of a measure, from which Negro children will be the chief sufferers, being as they are in more need of education and wholesome recreation.

However, I might observe that I am simply predicting of the Negro representatives what is true of all white representatives of the capitalists parties, Republican and Democratic.

Will the entrance of Negro women into politics change the general tenor of things? My answer is no. The history of women in public affairs, black and white, warrant me in taking this position. Their traditions, education and environment, are similar to those of the men and they may be expected to follow the same course of political thinking. They will also be influenced by their male companions.

However, I might observe here, that Negro women, especially may profit from the political blunders of Negro men. It is admitted by both white and black that the Negro men have made a mess of politics. It is further admitted that, during his entire political career, he has been nothing else but a Republican, so that the logical deduction is that, to follow in the course of the Negro men is to make similar mess of politics.

THE RISE OF POLITICAL RADICALISM AMONG NEGROES

The political Radicalism of the Negro has been marked by three definite movements: First, the entrance of the Negro into the Democratic Party; second, the transition to the elective idea of representation; third, and the most fundamental and significant of all is, the change from the old parties to Socialism.

The last of these changes has been the result of the rise of a new type of leaders. The old Negro leaders have had the intent to serve the interests of the Negroes, but they have lacked the knowledge as to how they could best serve them. And it is recognized today that the possession of an intent to do good without the knowledge, is more fatal than the possession of knowledge without the intent. To illustrate: History attests that during the early Christian era, Marcus Aurelius was the most savage persecutor of the Christians, yet he was one of the most upright of men and it is maintained that he persecuted them on the ground that he was saving them from the consequences of their folly. His intent was to do good. Even Protestant historians accord to those who maintained the Spanish Inquisition, honest intentions, while they murdered, massacred and outraged the heretics of their day. The suppression of free speech, the freedom of the press and the lynching of Negroes and I. W. W. are based upon the intent to subserve the country's interests. The system which produces these conditions, determines the social consequences of the policies, adopted by both good and bad men. Thus, it is apparent that an individual's power to do social and personal mischief is, in proportion to the intensity of his belief in the rightness of his act and the absence of knowledge as to its social consequences. An ignorant man may take Bicloride of mercury for quinine; the result is death, though his intent and desire was to live.

THE FUTURE OF THE NEGRO IN AMERICAN POLITICS

Thus it is obvious that the hope of the Negro lies, first in the development of Negro leaders with the knowledge of the science of government and economics, scientific history and sociology; and second, in the relegation to the political scrap heap, those Negro leaders whose only qualifications are the desire to lead and the intent to do good.

The old Negro leaders have been factors in producing and perpetuating a patent contradiction in American politics: the alliance of a race of poverty, the Negro, with a party of wealth, the Republican Party.

The Republican Party has been the instrumentality in American politics of abolishing agricultural feudalism of the South for the establishment of industrial capitalism of the North. Industrial slavery has been substituted for human slavery.

But how is the Negro to know which party to support? Before answering this question may I observe that a party is a body of individuals who agree upon a political program and who strive to gain control of the government in order to secure its adoption. Its campaigns are made possible by a fund created by those persons who desire the adoption of its program. It is natural and plain, then that those who supply the funds will control and direct the party.

Now, it is a fact of common knowledge that the Republican and Democratic parties receive their campaign funds from Rockefeller, Morgan, Schwab, Shonts, Ryan, Armour and other capitalists. It is also a fact of common knowledge, that the chief interests of these capitalists are: to make large profits by employing cheap labor and selling their goods at high prices to the public.

Thus, since the chief interests of the workers are more wages, less work, cheaper food, clothing and shelter, it is apparent that their chief interests are opposed to those of their employers—the capitalists which are represented by the Republican and Democratic parties.

Now, since almost all Negroes are workers, live on wages and suffer from the high cost of food, clothing and shelter, it is obvious that the Republican and Democratic parties are opposed to their interests.

But since neither the Republican and Democratic parties represent the Negroes' interests, the question logically arises as to which party in American politics does?

I maintain that since the Socialist Party is supported financially by working men and working women, and since its platform is a demand for the abolition of this class struggle between the employer and the worker, by taking over and democratically managing the sources and machinery of wealth production and exchange, to be operated for social service and not for private profits; and further, since the Socialist Party has always, both in the United States and Europe, opposed all forms of race prejudice, that the Negro should no longer look upon voting the Republican ticket, as accepting the lesser of two evils, but that it is politically, economically, historically and socially logical and sound for him to reject both evils, the Republican and Democratic parties and select a positive good—Socialism.

The Negro, like any other class, should support that party which represents his chief interests. Who could imagine a brewer or saloon-keeper supporting the Prohibition party?

It is like an undertaker seeking the adoption of a law, if possible, to abolish death.

Such is not less ludicrous, however, than that of a Negro, living in virtual poverty, children without education, wife driven to the kitchen or wash-tub: continually dispossessed on account of high rents, eating poor food on account of high cost of food, working 10, 12 and 14 hours a day, and sometimes compelled to become sycophant and clownish for a favor, a "tip," supporting the party of Rockefeller, the party of his employer, whose chief interests are to overwork and underpay him. Let us abolish these contradictions and support our logical party—the Socialist Party.

Reply to Marcus Garvey

Marcus Garvey, president of the Universal Negro Improvement Associa-
tion (U.N.I.A.), had been arraigned in the seventh district court for mail
fraud at the time of this essay. Garvey had published an editorial in his
newspaper, The World, *denouncing* The Messenger *by calling it a*
merely sporadically published journal and challenging the leaders of The
Messenger *who criticize him to prove their own ability. In the following*
reply to Garvey, published in August 1922, A. Philip Randolph asks, "Why
is it the stock and trade of crooks to call others crooks who condemn them?"

In the July 8th issue of the *Negro World* under the caption "Marcus Garvey asks Malicious Negroes Who Criticize Him to Prove Their Ability," the Honorable Marcus Garvey assails the Editors of the *Messenger,*
purporting to answer an editorial which appeared in the June issue,
comparing the Black Star Line to the failures of the True Reformers
and the Metropolitan Realty Company.

In his characteristic demagogic fashion, he proceeds to answer the
above named editorial by alleging that the *Messenger* is irregularly published. Suppose it were. What has that got to do with the truth or falsity of the charge? Is the Black Star Line failure not a disgrace to
Negroes similar to the True Reformers and the Metropolitan Mer-
cantile Realty Company? That is the question. A counter charge does
not answer or settle the question. Even a child can see that, to say nothing of a grown-up. Counter accusation of the accuser by the accused
does not excuse or vindicate the accused.

But back to the alleged irregularly published *Messenger.* If Mr. Marcus Garvey will consult the files of the Congressional, 42nd Street,
Harvard or Princeton Universities' Libraries, he will find that the
monthly appearance of the *Messenger* since the United States Government ceased interference with it something over a year ago, has been
as regular as the succession of day and night. It might not be amiss to
say, in this connection, that the *Messenger* is the first and only Negro
publication in America ever to be denied the mails. The *Negro World*
was sufficiently time serving to merit and secure the approval of the

virulent Negro haters during a war period when the Negro was being called upon to sacrifice his blood and treasure for a country which was at the same time lynching and burning him. The *Messenger,* on the contrary, was militant, uncompromising and bitter in its denunciation of the hypocritical policies of the Government toward the Negro, for which it was denied second-class mailing privileges which imposed an unprecedentedly heavy burden of expense on it, entailing a cost of thousands of dollars of which the *Negro World* was free. Of course, the Garvey paper is not bothered about the lynching of Negroes in America! He wanted to deport them to Africa, hence, he had no trouble. Despite this difficult situation, however, the *Messenger* grew in power and circulation which is a verifiable question of fact and not of a piece with the inflated membership of the U.N.I.A. and the circulation of the *Negro World.*

But a word more about the subject of irregularity. How simple and stupid of Brother Garvey to conjure up this Banquo's Ghost to plague and haunt his every step! There is that joke of the maritime world—the Black Star Line. What about its irregularity? Who is there so base, so shorn of every vestige of probity and character as to jeopard his good name and interests upon the irregularity of this non-sailing, line-less ship line? If it isn't an unkind and embarrassing question for this self-elected, self-styled Provisional President of the African continent, I should like to inquire as to where that Black Star Line is, anyhow? Is it on top of, or under the water? Are the ships sailing or being assailed by the courts? Nor are these questions put in a satirical spirit; for persons of unquestioned honor give currency to the statement that the "Kanawha" is rotting away in disuse, that the "Shady-Side" is still in the shades of libels and dilapidation, and, of course, the "Phylis Wheatley" resides in the Honorable Marcus' imagination. So far as the "Yarmouth" is concerned, the *Nauticus,* a journal of shipping and investments, in its issue of Dec. 10, 1921, settles the question as to its whereabouts. It states that on December 2, the United States Marshal sold, at auction, the "Yarmouth" to Frederick Townsend, for the almost unbelieveably insignificant sum of $1,625, or for $143,375 less than what the great business genius Brother Marcus paid for it. Did you get that? Impossible? It would seem so, wouldn't it? But not so. It's a matter of record. Consult the *Nauticus* of Dec. 10, 1921 for yourself. *This is running through the cold cash of the poor simps with a vengeance.* And yet this half-wit, low grade moron, whose insufferable presumption is only exceeded by his abysmal ignorance, has the cheek and brass to mention the business affairs of others. If he had never attempted to do business of any kind, he would have much better grace and ground for speaking on the subject than his scandulous, disgraceful and childish business record warrants. Far better and safer for Brother Garvey to observe the rule: "that it were better to keep silent and be considered a fool or a crook than to speak and remove all doubt." But no, the conscienceless braggart and egotist that he is, he would like the cuttlefish, muddy the waters by misrepresenting others, hide his own dirty deeds of business disgraces in order to escape detection, to foil his prosecutors.

The white Ku Klux Kleagle's Black Ku Klux Eagle thinks that by resorting to the time-worn trick of condemning others for the things he is doing himself, he will avert suspicion from himself. But that will never carry. The smoke screen is too transparent. Telling what the accused has or has not done does not prove that the defendant, the accused, is innocent of the charge. Either a charge is true or false, and it must be refuted upon a basis of fact and truth. There is no other alternative.

Does Garvey employ the direct, honest and intelligent method of meeting the indictment of the editors of the *Messenger?* Dear readers, judge for yourself. Listen to this. Says he: "Before Owen and Randolph can speak of the failure of any business and the incompetency of any individual to do business they should first prove their success and their competency to handle business." Think of such downright inanity and silly tommy-rot. In other words, a person must be a thief in order to have the right to criticise and apprehend a thief. A critic of acting or of the drama is not required necessarily to be an actor or a dramatist. A person may be the reviewer of books without being an author of books. A patient may know when his pain is relieved without being a doctor. Few economists are business men, yet they formulate the rules, laws and principles of business. Intelligent business men such as Morgan and Rockefeller employ economists to formulate, direct and guide their business policies. They don't rely upon the hit and miss method of guess, conjecture and mother-wit. That period of catch-as-catch-can economic action has passed with everybody with a grain of common sense, except the Honorable Black Kluxer. Thus, it ought to be apparent that the right to criticize work is not contingent upon the ability to do that form of work or upon the fact of having done it. Hence, it is the sheerest idle prattle and an evidence of dishonesty and guilt for Garvey to retort to persons who charge him with shamelessly mishandling the Black Star Line that they are not pilots or captains, that they have owned and operated no ship lines, and, consequently, are not justified in criticizing him! Of course, he, naturally, would wish that to be so. It is the stock and trade of crooks to call others crooks who condemn them. *It is always to the interest of a man with a false stone to impeach the knowledge and honor of a lapidary.* That is the only way he can defraud the public. By lying about Owen's and Randolph's business ability. Garvey thinks that he will be able to divert attention from his own appalling business ignorance and tricks. But he has another thought coming.

Listen to this grandiose balderdash and burlesque on business. Speaking of what *he* has done, with emphasis on "he," if you please—he says that he has established the greatest Negro paper—the *Negro World.* That is a lie. The *Chicago Defender* is, by long odds, the greatest Negro paper in the world. Every honest, intelligent Negro knows that. What sort of a newspaper is the *Negro World,* anyway, which devotes its front page, the news page of every modern, civilized, recognized newspaper in newspaperdom, to the wild vaporings, imbecile puerilities and arrant nonsense, of a consummate ignoramus? But what's claiming the greatest Negro newspaper in the world, or the greatest anything in the world, to this Supreme and Exalted Ruler of the Annanias fraternity?

On his erratic rampage of mendacity and bigoted, groundless braggadocio, he beats the air, waving his big, fat hands furiously, and yaps: "We find established to the credit of the Negro a line of steam ships known as the Black Star Line, which has sent out two of its ships on the high seas and has registered the Negro as a competitor in maritime affairs." Is that so? And to the credit of the Negro! Can you beat that for unmitigated, arrogant asininity. Let us hear what Judge Jacob Panken thinks of this great miracle of business success.

Marcus Garvey, who was arraigned in the Seventh District Court upon charges of fraud, admitted that the $600,000 invested in the Black Star Line by poor, hard working Negroes had been practically wiped out, that the "Yarmouth" cost $145,000 and lost $300,000 on its first trip, that the "Maceo" was purchased for $65,000 and had lost $76,000 on its maiden voyage.

Justice Panken, in addressing his remarks to Garvey said: "It seems to me that you have been preying upon the gullibility of your own people, having kept no proper accounts of the money received for investment, being an organization of high finance in which the officers received outrageously high salaries and were permitted to have exhorbitant expense accounts for pleasure jaunts throughout the country. I advise these "dupes" who have contributed to these organizations to go into court and ask for the appointment of a receiver. You should have taken this $600,000 and built a hospital for colored people in this city instead of purchasing a few old boats. There is a form of paranoia which manifests itself in believing oneself to be a great man."

What has happened here is not so bad from the point of view of Marcus Garvey as it is from the damage done to the confidence of colored people. The editors of the *Messenger* warned Garvey and the people that what has happened would surely come to pass.

Still the Imperial Black "Blizzard" says that the Black Star Line is a credit to the Negro. By the same token of reasoning, one may be justified in concluding that the True Reformers' collapse, the Metropolitan failure were credits to the Negro.

Would any sane white man maintain that the financial adventurers, Charles Ponzi of Boston and young Bischoff of Chicago, who wasted millions of innocent white people's money in visionary, airy schemes *not much sounder than Garvey's,* were a credit to the white people? No, not by a long shot. They pay their respects to them through the prison bars, and credit them with an involuntary vacation from the community of civilized, respectable, law-abiding citizens, such as is likely to be tendered to Garvey. Still one might well doubt whether their sins against the people are as great as Garvey's.

He says further that the ships are on the high seas. Where, may I ask? Either Brother Marcus is blind or he thinks that the public is blind. It is a matter of common knowledge that the old, rickety, rotten ships of the Black Star Line can hardly stay on top of the water in port, to say nothing about withstanding the waves of the high seas. So unseaworthy was the "Yarmouth," when it ventured out from port, bootlegging, in calm weather, that the New York white press described it as a "Booze ship," reeling and rocking as it was like a drunken old sot. This is what he styles as a competitor in maritime affairs. Indeed, it is to laugh. A competitor! Think of it! A shaky "booze ship line" competing with the great British, French, Italian and American steamship lines! No doubt it is competing as the braying of a jackass competes with the roaring of a lion, as an ox-cart competes with a steam engine, as an infant competes with a man! It is competition of a sort which none but a fool would claim!

However, on he goes like a mad man making specious, foolish, irresponsible statements about what he has done.

"*We find enterprises, namely, grocery stores, restaurants, laundries, tailoring and dress making establishments* established at different points of the country in the name of the Universal Negro Improvement Association," sputters Hizzoner. Well, grant that it is true, what of it?

What good are they to the members of the U.N.I.A. or anybody else? These two-by-four, dirty, dingy, mismanaged dumps, misnamed enterprises, are a liability, instead of an asset. They are a disgrace instead of a credit. They are rat holes in which to dump money. Nobody but an idiot would mention them as an achievement. Upon seeing his inability longer to inveigle the dupes, on account of Government prosecution for fraud, to dump their dollars into the Black Star Line Sea, he got together these business jokers to serve as flypaper to ensnare the unsuspecting, ignorant and gullible. When the well-meaning, but misguided delegates come to the convention, His Noble and Imperial Highness can point to these picayune junk shacks as the achievements of a mighty business wizard. "See what I have done; see what we have got! Down with the traitors and agitators who point out my faults! Down with all Negro leaders but me! Hurrah! for the Ku Klux Klan! Up with Kleagle Clark! Up with Marcus Garvey!" will be the effusive ejaculation of this Black Don Quixote. Add to this the ceaseless band-playing, the waving of the red, black and green flag of the African Empire, the imperial parade, the flaunting of the habiliments of the Black Cross Nurses and the Black African Legion, the Court Reception, the knighting of the "insane," and the perpetual flow of hot-air which is the supreme function of His Honor, the Black Infernal "Blizzard,"— and the mesmerized fanatics are supposed to cough up, each and every one of them, from one to a 100 bucks for the African Redemption Fund, the revival of the Black Star Line, the Factories' Corporation, the Liberian Loan, the Convention Fund, and whatever other scheme happens to crop up in his imagination which might serve to skin the people. It might be interesting to add that these so-called enterprises seldom last more than a few months before they fail like the biggest of all his schemes, the Black Star Line. But as fast as one fails, he starts a new one, ever alert to have something into which the people can waste their moneys.

But in order to justify this saturnalia of waste and reckless extravagance, he observes that: "We find this organization giving employment to thousands of Negro men and women." Yes, that's true. But are they paid? From the number of suits for wages filed in the Seventh and Third District Courts, it would appear that employment is all that he gives them. The only way he keeps work going is by getting new employees to work from week to week.

And at the climax of his grotesque and imposing claims, he settles down in a sort of satisfied imperiousness. Says he: "Now if Marcus Garvey has done these things, is Marcus Garvey a success or a failure?" Yes, Brother Marcus you have been both a success and a failure! How, you ask? Well, you have succeeded in wasting more of the Negroes' money than any other Negro. You have succeeded in beginning more impossible schemes than any other Negro. You have succeeded in making the Negro the laughing stock of the world. So much for your success. Now as to your failure: *You have failed to succeed in anything except failures!*

Now you ask what have Owen and Randolph done?

Before pointing out what Owen and Randolph have done, I shall indicate briefly what Owen and Randolph have not done.

First, they have not made away with $600,000 of the people's money on any worthless ships.

Second, they have not been indicted for defrauding the people, white or black, by the United States Government.

Third, they have not initiated any wild-cat bunco games for skinning the public, incorporating them in Delaware, a state that will incorporate anything, however fantastic.

Fourth, they have not been relieving ignorant Negroes of their hard-earned cash to establish millinery shops and grocery stores that they knew could not succeed.

Fifth, they haven't been carrying on any propaganda to divide the American and West Indian Negroes, the black and mulatto Negroes.

Sixth, they haven't conjured up any fantastic projects for conquering Africa as a means of taking in the uninitiated.

Seventh, they have never organized any non-going Black Star Lines and been compelled to suspend them because of Government indictment for fraud.

Eighth, they have never accused a Negro of being a white man to suit demagogic ends, when they knew it was a lie.

Ninth, they have never lied about men of public affairs and been compelled to retract upon pain of being locked up in jail. Everybody remembers the Assistant District Attorney Kilroe case and Marcus Garvey.

Tenth, they have never held any secret interview with the Ku Klux Klan, surrendering the rights of the Negro to a criminal, murderous gang of cut-throats and mid-night assassins. They have never advised the Negro to stop fighting those who are lynching, burning and trying to sterilize Negro men. They have never opposed and denounced as rabid race baiters all white men at one time, only to shift to the support of that most conscienceless mob of Negro phobists—the Ku Klux Klan.

Eleventh, they have never advised Negroes to go where they couldn't or didn't ever plan to go—Africa.

So much for what Owen and Randolph have not done. Not a bad record this, though negative. But I am not going to answer Mr. Garvey with mere negation.

Now about what Owen and Randolph have done.

First, they have established a great journal of scientific opinion, fearless, able and uncompromising. Witness the survey of the United States Department of Justice in its report on radicalism in the Negro press: "The *Messenger* is by long odds the most able and the most dangerous of all the Negro publications." How is that Brother Marcus? Some publication, eh? The *Negro World* was fully considered in its report when it made this statement on the *Messenger.*

Second, we established the first publication among Negroes to advocate the principles of organized labor. Unionism gets more wages for workers. Don't you think Negroes need more wages? Ask your own underpaid employees! Wages buy food, clothing and shelter. Without wages, Negroes who are chiefly workers, cannot live. Hence, he who fights for more wages for the Negro, fights for more life for the Negro. This is no mean achievement, is it Brother Marcus? At least, *intelligent people,* white and black, think it a great achievement.

Third, Owen and Randolph have spoken to hundreds of thousands of white and black workers in the unions from Coast to Coast, insisting upon the Negro workers' right upon a basis of equality, discussing every aspect of the Negro problem to white workers who, heretofore, have been ignorant of same.

Fourth, they are the first and only Negroes to present the Negro workers' question to the European workers, radicals and liberals.

Fifth, Owen and Randolph were the first to organize the Radical Movement among Negroes in America. They organized the first Socialist Branch in a Negro community which white and black Socialists attend. The People's Educational Forum, the greatest Negro Forum in the United States, grew out of this radical work.

The Garvey Movement could only have begun in New York City where the field had been prepared by Owen and Randolph for the reception of new ideas, presented through the vehicle of radicalism. It is well known that Garvey began his propaganda in harmony with the *Messenger*'s principles in order to get a hearing. He shifted his propaganda after he got a foot-hold. It is a verifiable fact that Brother Marcus got his first knowledge of the African problem from a program drawn up by the writer and presented at a conference, held at the late Madam C. J. Walker's home, Irvington-on-the-Hudson, out of which grew the "International League of Darker Peoples." Mr. Garvey was there and participated in the conference. During the pre-peace conference, Owen and Randolph were the theoretical exponents of achieving the goal of "Africa for the Africans" through the instrumentality of a league of darker peoples, re-enforced by an alliance with the white radical, liberal and labor movements of the world.

So much was this recognized that Mr. Garvey capitalized the reputation of the writer by selecting him as a representative of the U.N.I.A. to the Peace Conference. Needless to say that I never went. The money collected was used as the money has been used that was collected for the Black Star Line. It is also a matter of record, that the first big mass meeting ever held by the U.N.I.A. was held under the pretext of sending the writer to the Peace Conference. The writer didn't know then that Mr. Garvey was untrustworthy. Garvey claims to have sent some one to the conference. No legitimate reporter at the conference took note of his presence.

Seventh, Owen and Randolph organized the first Negro movement with a sound economic program.—The Friends of Negro Freedom. It's founders include the ablest Negro thinkers and men of public integrity which is in striking contrast with the U.N.I.A., which does not include a single reputable scholar and honorable public figure. This is their record of achievement which I submit before the high tribunal of Negro public and world opinion. In conclusion, Mr. Garvey attempts to get an alibi for his business miscarriage by saying: "Marcus Garvey does not hold himself up to be the doer of the impossible. Marcus Garvey is not a navigator; he is not a marine engineer; he is not even a good sailor, therefore, the individual who would criticize Marcus Garvey for a ship of the Black Star Line not making a success at sea is a fool, because no head of any steamship company can guarantee what will be the action of the captain of one of his ships when he clears port." Such is his excuse for the dismal and miserable failure of the Black Star Line. If he was ignorant of the shipping business, why did he go in it?

Pointing out that he is not a captain or an engineer or a sailor is not sufficient. The owners and managers of steamship lines are not supposed to be sailors. Still they are morally and legally responsible for the business of the steam ship lines, including losses by sea and otherwise. Hedley, the president of the Subway, is not a motorman, but he is responsible for the business condition of and accidents on the Subway. This is too obvious to need debate. All honest and intelligent business men recognize and accept the responsibility of the principal for the acts of their agents.

Mr. Garvey further states in his lamentation upon the farce and mess he has made of everything he has touched: "What can Marcus Garvey do if men are employed to do their work and they prove to be dishonest and dishonorable in the performance of that work?" So Brother Marcus admits that he has failed. Very well! What about your pompous ravings on your so called achievements? A great leader is supposed to know how to pick men. It is the chief function of a leader. But you admit that it is beyond you. Then why don't you be honest and stop misleading ignorant Negroes, wasting their money and making them the butt of ridicule and raillery? If your own stricken conscience does not lead you to stop, I assure you that the aroused and awakened, militant, intelligent Negro masses will see to it that you and all that you stand for will be driven from the American soil.

THE WEST INDIES: THEIR POLITICAL, SOCIAL, AND ECONOMIC CONDITION

J. A. Rogers, a native of the West Indies, had traveled for six years across America by the time he wrote this essay. In the following, he explains the political, social, and economic history of European colonialism in the New World, particularly in the West Indies, and how that oppressive system affects contemporary life in the islands. This essay was published in three issues: October, November, and December 1922. These three parts, together, comprise his third book.

Considerable light will be thrown on the present political, social and economic status of the British West Indies, at the outset by pointing out the following: first the purpose of the earliest Europeans who visited them; second, that Negro slavery existed in all of the islands; and third, that present conditions are very likely to be an evolution of the above-named facts.

PURPOSE OF THE EARLIEST EUROPEANS

In the colonization of the New World there was a distinct difference between the type of European who came to the region north of the Rio Grande and the one that went to all that region south of it. The former came to settle; he was the victim of religious and political persecution; the latter came to plunder. Like burglars, the sole aim of the Europeans of the second type, was to get all the wealth they could lay their hands on in the shortest time and scuttle home to live at ease. The result was that the natives were ruthlessly butchered, and their civilization quickly swept out of existence. The planting of crops was out of the question with these Europeans.

NEGRO SLAVERY

To replace the Indians, who were nearly all exterminated, Negroes were introduced. Slavery began in the West Indies more than a century earlier than in the United States and was abolished in the British Islands in 1838, twenty-seven years earlier than in the United States.

POPULATION

The population of the British West Indies including British Guiana is approximately two million, three hundred and fifty thousand, about half a million less than that of Cuba. Of the forty-five islands or so that comprise the group, Jamaica with 4,209 square miles and a population of 858,118 is the largest. Trinidad, next in size, is 1,863 square miles and has 312,803 inhabitants. The vast bulk of the population are full-blooded Negroes; from twenty to twenty-five per cent are mulattoes, while the whites number about 40,000 or less than two per cent. A third of the population of Trinidad, and nearly half of that of British Guiana, are Hindus. Jamaica has about five thousand Chinese, eighteen thousand Hindus, and a sprinkling of Syrians. Antigua and St. Kitts have a considerable number of Portuguese. Dominica and St. Vincent still have a hundred and fifty of the aboriginal Indians. In short almost every race and nationality under the sun can be found in the British West Indies.

POLITICS

All of the islands, except the Bahamas and Barbados, which have a measure of self-government, are Crown Colonies, that is to say, the control of affairs that are really vital, lies in the hands of the Secretary of State for the Colonies, who sends officials from Downing Street as governors. Jamaica is said to have representative government but this will be found to be merely a euphuism, as in really vital matters the representatives of the people have no real power. The chief legislative body of that island is composed of fifteen government officials and fourteen members elected by the people, with the governor as president of the Council. The fifteen officials are directly and indirectly appointed by the Crown, and vote always as directed by the Governor. These officials, except in rarest instances, are all white and from the British Isles. The elected representatives, as will be seen, are always outvoted by a permanent majority of one. To defeat or to pass any measure the Governor has but to declare it "a matter of paramount importance," and bring up his battery of officials. He, himself, has a casting vote.

In Barbados the government consists of a Governor, a legislative council of nine members appointed by the Crown, and a house of assembly elected annually by less than two thousand voters. The executive council consists of the governor and any number of officials the Governor thinks fit, together with one member of the legislative council and four members of the assembly named by the Governor. The latter body introduces all money votes, prepares the estimates, and initiates all government measures. Barbadoes is empowered to refuse a Governor it would not like, but, as with Jamaica, the Crown controls in vital affairs. Trinidad is a Crown Colony pure and simple, the people having almost no voice in the control of their own affairs.

Unlike Martinique, which sends representatives to the French Chamber of Deputies and the Senate, no British West Indian goes to the British Parliament. The West Indian, with all his patriotism, thus has no means of influencing British imperial policy. His only method of redress is by petition or memorial. For the first time in the history of Jamaica, a dark mulatto, Rev. A. A. Barclay, has been appointed a member of the local privy council.

In minor domestic affairs there are lesser houses, like the State legislatures in the United States. In these the peoples of nearly all the islands are permitted their own way. The Governor, however, is permitted to dissolve them when he sees fit and appoint a Commission to administer affairs.

THE VOTE

In the West Indies there is no manhood suffrage as in the United States. To vote one must pay taxes. In Jamaica one must have or hold property on which he pays not less than ten shillings (normally two dollars and a half) a year; or must have personal property on which he pays seven dollars and a half a year; or must receive a salary of not less than two hundred and fifty dollars a year. The result is to disqualify the greater part of those of voting age. Many of the peasantry own their land, but the land tax is twenty-five cents on every fifty dollars' worth. Many also rent land for which they pay five dollars an acre per annum. Most of the taxation, as will be shown later, is indirect.

The high financial qualifications for eligibility to the Legislative Council, and other assemblies, effectually bar black men from these places.

The salary qualification would seem absurdly low, but the low wages, as will also be shown later, makes it excessive. In 1921 there were only 42,267 Jamaicans qualified to vote, about one in every 200. In Barbados matters are even worse. Barbados is a sugar country, and like most sugar countries the land is in the hands of a few. Barbados presents, possibly, the most perfect example of a landless proletariat anywhere in the world. There are less than two thousand voters in Barbados. The census of 1913 gives 1886. In Trinidad, where Hindus constitute a third of the population the percentage of voters is even less. As in parts of Mississippi and North Carolina, where Negroes are not permitted to vote, the total polling strength for the election of important offices does not exceed twenty in many districts in the West Indies.

Very little interest is taken in elections, except in the larger towns like Bridgetown and Kingston. Elections are usually uncontested. When contested the number of voters at the polls rarely exceed one-sixth of the voting strength. In short, the black population is pretty thoroughly disfranchised. The difference between the disfranchisement in the Southern States and that in the West Indies is solely that in the latter place the process is more politic. The government of the British West Indies, like other British Colonies where colored peoples predominate, may accurately be called a Caucasian oligarchy.

SOCIAL CONDITIONS

As was said, the first Europeans who went to the West Indies were adventurers. Having thoroughly plundered the Indians, many of them next started to exploit the soil. Establishing sugar and tobacco plantations, they then left them to overseers, and returned home to live on the monies from them. Because of this there was at all times a great preponderance of first, Indians, and then Negroes, over the whites. Massacres of the whites in all the islands, British, French, Spanish, or Dutch, were numerous. The Maroons, or runaway Negroes, of Haiti, Cuba, Guiana and Jamaica, wiped out settlement after settlement. Slave revolts were common. The whites now resorted to strategy to make their position safe. A mixed population had grown up in the islands. These, the whites erected into a superior caste over the blacks to serve as a buffer between them and the blacks with the result that throughout the West Indies there exists at the present time an officially and unofficially recognized color line between the mulattoes and the full-blooded blacks.

Everyone in the West Indies, except Asiatics, belongs to one of three divisions. The first in importance is the whites, which includes the near whites, or white-by-law, as they are called. Many classed as Negroes in the United States would be counted as white in the West Indies. The second is the colored, or those whose white blood exceeds the black. The lowest in the scale are those with a preponderance of Negro blood. How the distinction between colored and black is determined it is difficult to tell. By some subtle process of judging, now of hair, now of color, one is immediately placed in his proper group at sight. The census reports of the different islands all give populations as belonging to one of three groups. The Asiatics are generally regarded by the blacks as being inferior to them.

As W. P. Livingston, author of "Black Jamaica" puts it, society in the West Indies is like a pyramid; "the whites constitute the apex; the colored, the middle courses; and the masses, or Negroes, the broad base." In other words, the whites are seated on the shoulders of the colored, who in turn are seated on those of the blacks.

Many visitors to the West Indies, like the late Ella Wheeler Wilcox, Prof. Royce, W.E.B. Du Bois, and Robert R. Moton, give the impression that there is no color line there. Such also is the proud boast of many West Indians in the United States. This view is very superficial, and far from being correct.

The difference between the United States and the West Indies as regards color differences is merely the difference between an active volcano and an inactive one, or between a visible disease and a secret one, which, while leaving the victim in apparent good health is undermining his constitution, just as effectively.

The color question is little agitated because the black peasantry, as a mass, are extraordinarily, almost preternaturally, good-natured. Intensely religious and patriotic, they accept their inferior position and regard the mulattoes as superior. They voluntarily segregate themselves as in street cars and urban churches. The mixed bloods, in their turn, having a left-handed association with the whites, are content with their superior position over the blacks. They also look up to the whites, and permit them, with their vastly inferior numbers to stay at the top. The color question will then be seen to be merely dormant and as having all the potentialities it manifests in the United States. But let the mass of struggling blacks be once aroused to a sense of their great injustice, let them once feel that they are the equal of the mixed-bloods, and there would be the devil to pay. Now and then one may catch fierce glimpses of the revolt that slumbers deep in the sub-conscious minds of the blacks, when pushed too far, they raise the cry of "color for color."

Again, let the number of whites be suddenly increased, as in Cuba and the West Indian whites would no longer be forced to maintain their left-handed alliance with the mulattoes. They would very likely declare, as in the U.S. and Cuba, that one drop of Negro blood makes a Negro. In that event the mulattoes would then throw in their lot with the blacks in the U. S. Patriotic West Indians will assert that race discrimination as it exists in the United States would not be permitted on British soil. One has, however, but to point to South Africa.

In 1865 the blacks in a corner of the island of Jamaica revolted because of oppressive taxation and injustice in the courts under Paul Bogle and a mulatto named George William Gordon. They killed twenty-one whites and near-whites. The blacks were punished with such ferocity and brutality that they have been intimidated ever since. Four hundred and thirty-nine were killed, six hundred men, women and children were scourged, and over a thousand of their homes burnt to the ground. "We shot the niggers like the blackbirds off the trees," said an English soldier in a letter.

There is no color question in the West Indies simply and solely because the black peasantry accepts exploitation passively.

Two other factors that aid in keeping the color question dormant are education and emigration. These will be dealt with later.

EDUCATION

The nature of West Indian education was given as one of the causes for the chronic economic depression. Education in all of the islands and British Guiana is of a metaphysical and most impractical nature. The objective is purely classical.

The first stress is laid on loyalty to the king, who is worshipped in an equal breath with God. Titles are regarded with bated breath. A Sir So-and-So or a Lord That is worshipped as the savage worships his lesser gods. With the West Indian patriotism is a fetish, a fact that undisguised race prejudice in the United States serves to strengthen.

The second defect is that most of the schools are denominational, that is, each religious body, as the Anglicans, Baptists, Methodists, Presbyterians and Roman Catholics who generally predominate in the order named, maintains its own schools. In Barbados the Anglican

Church is endowed by the government. Great stress is laid on religion in the schools. A great part of the time is used in studying the exploits and achievements of the ancient Jews. The subjects taught have little relation to life as lived there. Most of it is pro-British propaganda. And of course, as in all oppressed countries great stress is laid on the ethical in the instruction of the peasant.

The Under-Secretary of State for the Colonies, Major Wood, recently made a tour of the islands, with a view to bettering conditions. His report to Parliament was published in the Jamaica *Daily Gleaner,* July 4, 1922, and following dates. He has suggested that Handwork, Agriculture, Domestic Economy, Hygiene and Practical Nature Study be taught in the elementary grades, which is the stage at which West Indian education usually stops. The teachers also complained to Major Wood about the denominational system and "of the employment of the clergy who had often no educational experience as sub-inspectors of schools."

Prior to emancipation there was no education of any sort for the blacks. Later there was introduced a system of school fees of from six to twelve cents a week. Most of the peasantry were too poor to pay this. All of the islands now have free schools and education is compulsory on some of them as Jamaica and Trinidad. Purely elementary subjects are taught. All education beyond that is expensive, and beyond the reach of the lower middle classes. There are no free high schools, as in the United States. The West Indian has perhaps not a hundredth part of the educational opportunity of the Northern Negro in the United States. Something less than one in 20,000 West Indians are college graduates. The following from the report of the Under-Secretary, already mentioned, will throw some light on the situation: "As in England, so in the West Indies, the elementary school curriculum shows a tendency to be too elaborate. . . . A good deal was said in the various colonies about compulsory education. . . . Compulsory education cannot be extended to areas more than two or three miles from a school and of such areas there are many. It must be remembered in this connection that in most of the colonies—more than half in some colonies over 70 per cent of the children are illegitimate and that parental control and parental responsibility are unenforceable. In Trinidad, which is about the best colony as regards attendance, 56 per cent of the total number of children are at school.

"As regards curriculum and text books, dependence upon English models and English publications, is the rule. There is so much local history, so much of interest in the local natural history that it should be easy to produce a "West Indian Reader."

Nearly all of the teachers of the elementary schools are colored and black males. Their salary is very small ranging from three hundred to seven hundred dollars a year, the latter amount in rare instances. This salary depends upon the average attendance. In Grenada the teacher is paid according to the marks his school made at the last inspection. The teachers of Trinidad are the best paid.

Schools are examined annually by inspectors, who formerly were all white men from the British Isles. Within recent years a few colored and black inspectors have been appointed.

There are a few scholarships to universities in the British Isles and to local colleges. The principal colleges are Queens College in Trinidad, Mico College Barbados. George Washington received a part of his in Jamaica and Harrison and Codington College in education in Barbados.

BARBADOS AND ITS INTELLECTUAL STATUS

The most intellectually advanced of the islands is Barbados. Barbados was settled after the manner of the American colonies; the settlers came largely to avoid persecution. This island has produced many distinguished men. All of its chief justices have been natives, among them being Sir R. B. Clarke, Sir C. Tucker, Sir W. H. Greaves and Sir W. C. Reeves, who was colored. Sir R. C. Piggott, a native, became Attorney-General of England. The intellectual advance of Barbados may be due to the severe struggle for existence on that island.

MEAN WHITES OR "RED-LEG JOHNNIES"

A characteristic feature of Barbados are the poor whites who live chiefly in the northern part. They are descendants of once leading families; of the militiamen who guarded the slaves; or of white ex-slaves. Many royalists, divines and English gentlemen were sold there as slaves in the 16th and 17th centuries. The price was 1,500 pounds of sugar each. Massachusetts also found a market for Quakers there.

Color prejudice with these poor whites is a religion. They have all the blind, unreasoning hate manifested by "the poor white trash" in the United States toward the colored American. They are bloodless in appearance and very thin. They go barefooted and the sun has given a brick color to their legs, hence the term "Red-leg Johnnies." A writer has described them as "having eyes inflamed and in a chronic blood-shot condition with huge freckles on their brick-colored faces, and sun-dried feet and hands, mailed with horn-like scales."

In parts of Jamaica there are also poor whites of no higher social status than the black peasantry, who look down upon and call them "white labor."

While the Negro thrives in hot and cold countries alike, the white man invariably degenerates in the tropics, unless he is in an administrative or other exploiting position. When forced to live in the tropics, and under the same conditions as Negroes, he invariably sinks lower than the Negroes.

BARBADOS IS CALLED "LITTLE ENGLAND"

Barbados is called "Little England." The island is tidiness itself. Someone has likened it to a well-kept tennis-court. Other West Indians are inclined to be jealous of the Barbadians because of their superior intelligence and sharpness.

The joke is told that when England declared war against the Boers, Barbados at once called to London: "Go to it England. Barbados is behind you." The flee backing the mastodon.

EMIGRATION

As was pointed out emigration is one of the causes for the inactivity of the color question. Every year large numbers of the most progressive and educated spirits leave for Panama, Costa Rica, Guatemala, Cuba, Nicaragua, South America, the United States and Canada, because of inability to find work. The islands being agricultural and with no scientific agriculture to engage their higher talents, they must either do laborer's work at an absurdly low wage and loss of caste or join the scramble for the few clerical positions. The departure of these discontented spirits acts in the nature of a safety valve or there would probably be a revolt worse than that of 1865.

There are about 50,000 British West Indians in Cuba, 28,000 in Costa Rica; 65,000 in Panama, and 60,000 in the United States.

It has been asserted that many West Indians leave because they object to manual labor. Abroad, as in the United States, there is hardly

any other field open to them. The difference is that abroad they receive many times more pay than they would get at home. How emigration affects the social progress of the islands will clearly be seen.

RESULT OF EMIGRATION

One result of emigration is that the population of nearly all the islands is decreasing. According to the 1891 census, Barbados had a population of 182,306. In 1911 it had 171,893, a loss of 10,423. In 1919 the deaths exceeded the births by 675, a phenomenal case in any country, but easily explained when one understands the severe struggle for existence. The land as was said is in the hands of a few.

Barbados is perhaps the most thickly populated integral spot on earth. In 1891 it had 1096 people to the square mile; in 1914, 1033. Prewar Belgium comes next with 600. Grenada and Nevis are also thickly populated, having 500 and 400, respectively, to the square mile.

In Jamaica, while the increase of births over deaths in the years between 1911 and 1921 was approximately 125,000, the census for 1921 showed an increase of only 27,735 in the same period.

West Indian laborers have contributed greatly to the development of Costa Rica and Panama. They built up the banana industry in Central America, the railroad in Ecuador, and built the Panama Canal. Many of the leading doctors, lawyers, preachers, writers, and educators among Negroes in the United States are from the British West Indies. The first Negro to publish a newspaper in the United States was John Brown Russworm, a native of Jamaica. Alexander Hamilton, who laid the foundation for the financial greatness of the United States was a West Indian.

WAGES

Previous to the war, the West Indian laborer received from twenty-five to thirty-six cents a day. Women got from eighteen to twenty cents. This has been the rate since emancipation 76 years before.

Work is irregular and laborers leave in large numbers for Cuba and Central America under contract which in many instances is little short of slavery. In those countries they get from a dollar to a dollar and half a day, returning when work is exhausted.

The pay of housemaids is from thirty-six cents to a dollar a week without board. Cooks get from a dollar and a half to two dollars a week

None but the menials are content to do this work. The term "servant" is one of opprobrium, and so is the word bium [*sic*].

Clerical work is also poorly paid in comparison with the United States. Fifteen dollars a week is considered a very good salary. Wages are higher in Trinidad than in any of the other islands.

INDUSTRIAL CONDITIONS

Industries, as was said, are chiefly agricultural. Jamaica produces bananas—about a quarter of the bananas used in the U. S. and England come from Jamaica—sugar, cocoa, cocoanuts, ginger, dyewoods. A valuable by-product of the sugar industry is the well-known Jamaica rum. Prohibition in the United States and the war with Germany caused the islands to lose two of its best customers. During the last few years the demand for rum in Great Britain has fallen off 1,295,433 gallons. Stocks in bond have reached the enormous figure of 11,689,000 proof gallons with no business in sight.

Trinidad exports sugar, cocoa, cocoanuts, copra, petroleum and asphalt. The two last products give Trinidad a reliable income, and makes it the most uniformly prosperous of the islands. Situated at the mouth of the Orinoco, it is also a port of entry and exit for trade in the South American interior. In 1919 Trinidad yielded 64½ million gallons of crude oil. In proportion to its size and population the revenue of Trinidad is nearly three times that of Jamaica.

The chief export of Barbados is sugar. More than half its arable land is given over to sugar cane. Some cotton is grown. Barbados had a whaling industry, now almost dead.

The principal exports of St. Kitts, Nevis, the home of Alexander Hamilton; St. Vincent; Monserrat and Antigua is Sea-island cotton. British Guiana exports sugar and rice.

Dominica, whose principal export is lime, a citrus fruit, similar to the lemon, is another island severely hit by prohibition. In pre-Volstead days great numbers of limes were exported to the United States for use in cocktails and gin-rickeys. Dominica exports citric acid, which is used as a fixative in calico printing, and for use in the Navy, as a preventative of scurvey.

The boom of the sugar industry in the latter part of the war brought a prosperity that carried a great deal of hardship in its train. The sugar industry had been languishing since the Brussels Conference in 1874 when England gave the preference to German and Austrian sugar over

that of her colonies in the West Indies. The result was that most of the estates were either in ruin, or their machinery in bad shape. Then came the boom. The banks made great loans, machinery was installed at the time when it was abnormally expensive, and the industry was getting on its legs once more when the price of sugar tumbled downwards, leaving the planters with their crop and no market for it. The price of sugar is now $62½ a ton. The producers insist that they cannot make it pay under $75.

The possible competition of beet sugar from countries like Czecho-Slovakia and Germany with their depreciated exchange makes the situation still worse for the British West Indian planters, many of whom, with their estates heavily mortgaged, are thinking of giving up sugar altogether for other crops.

Another factor against the West Indian planter is that the United States give a preference of about $40 a ton to Porto Rican sugar and $8 to Cuban, thus crowding British West Indian sugar out of the U.S. markets, the best in the world.

Major Wood, in the report already mentioned, in speaking of industrial conditions says:

"During the last year of the war and the two succeeding years, the West Indies enjoyed a brief period of exceptional prosperity. The price of all their products, except limes, rose to abnormal heights, big profits were made, wages and the cost of living generally increased, the revenues of the Colonies expanded, and the Governments seized the opportunity in many cases, of improving the pay of their educational and other services. This period of abnormal prosperity has been succeeded suddenly, and with great violence by a period of acute depression. The revenues are contracting and every Colonial government is finding that it is much easier to increase expenditure in good times than to reduce it in bad times—the same problem in fact which is facing the Government at home. Taxation, which was hardly felt two years ago, is now proving a burden upon industry as a whole, as well as upon all classes of individuals. Though the prices of imported requirements have come down they are not yet down to pre-war level, whereas the prices of the agricultural products have reached pre-war level and in some cases have sunk below it. Nevertheless it would be wrong to paint too black a picture of the economic outlook, whether in the present or the future. Taken as a whole the West Indies are standing the strain. There is little or no unemployment and thanks to the bountiful provision of nature, there is no real physical distress among the poor section of the community. In this connection it should be borne in mind that, except the sugar islands of Barbados, Antigua and St. Kitts, the vast bulk of the population consists of families who have obtained or can obtain sufficient land on which to grow enough to feed themselves.

"The real difficulty is that of the planter or proprietor who has invested in land and its equipment during the boom period immediately following the war.

"Credit which was given freely by the banks, during the boom period is now drastically restricted."

CONSTITUTIONAL AND TRADE REFORMS

Major Wood has made most liberal recommendations to Parliament for the betterment of conditions. Among them are a lowering of the import duties: a minimum preference of $18.75 a ton in the British markets in favor of West Indian sugar; and a greater measure of representative government in all of the islands. In Jamaica, for instance, he recommends that the elected members should be placed in a permanent majority, and that the governor have a reserve power to be used only in extreme emergency.

He adds: "Several reasons combine to make it likely that the common demand for a measure of representative government will in the long run prove irresistible. The wave of democratic sentiment has been powerfully stimulated by the war. Education is rapidly spreading and tending to produce a colored and black intelligenzia, of which the members are quick to absorb elements of knowledge requisite for entry into learned professions, and return from travels abroad with minds emancipated and enlarged ready to devote time and energy to propaganda among their own people."

LOCAL RACE PROBLEMS

Both Jamaica and Trinidad have local race problems. The former with the Chinese and the Hindus; the latter with the Hindus.

After emancipation the slaveholders seeking the cheapest possible labor, imported East Indians. They were indentured for five years and paid twenty-four cents a nine-hour day. The Jamaican laborer got 36 cents. These East Indians were virtually slaves. The indenture system has ceased.

The question of the Chinese is more aggravated. About 5,000 in number, they have cornered the small retail grocery trade in pretty much the same way the Jews and the Greeks have cornered Negro business in the United States. With their superior trading instincts the Chinese merchants are driving out the Jamaican ones. They grow fat where others fail. The governor in Council, July 5, 1922, said: "The Government was fully resolute that the time had come when the Chinese settlement should not be allowed to increase in size." A literacy test will be used in an endeavor to keep them out. Emigrants to the island will be called upon to read and explain any fifty given words in the English language.

In Trinidad and British Guiana, East Indians constitute 33 and 42 per cent of the population, respectively. They are the backbone of agriculture. According to the report of Major Wood they complain of discrimination in the schools, and of having no voice in political affairs.

In Antigua and St. Kitts, the Portuguese have cornered the retail business, as the Chinese in Jamaica.

ANNEXATION TO THE UNITED STATES

This is a topic that provokes great bitterness in the West Indies. The mere thought of annexation is regarded with horror. In 1860, when during a period of unusual depression, it was seriously suggested that the islands be given over to the United States, the people were near the point of rebellion. In 1907, when an American admiral landed in Kingston to relieve the earthquake sufferers, he was very coldly received, and in the sharp diplomatic correspondence that ensued the governor was recalled. American visitors are received with that courtesy native to all classes in the islands, particularly as the former have money to spend. But annexation they do not want.

The case of Cuba and Haiti has but served to aggravate this decision. In Cuba before the war of 1898, Negroes had equal rights. Intermarriage was common. They took an equal part in the war of liberation. Many of the most famous leaders, as Antonio Maceo, were Negroes. American intervention awoke color prejudice. This resulted in a rising of the Cuban Army of Liberation, in which Estenoz and over five thousand of his followers were slain. Race prejudice is an American disease, and like the Wandering Jew; the American spreads it wherever he goes. Annexation would mean an influx of Americans, who would at once side with the native whites and establish an aggressive white despotism. The near-whites, colored, and blacks would then be thrown together, and violence would undoubtedly result. The question as it stands is: "Which is preferable? Peaceful exploitation of the blacks by the whites, near whites and colored, or violent exploitation of the near-white, colored and blacks by the whites?"

On the other hand the economic condition of the islands would be undoubtedly improved by annexation, something like that of the West Indian immigrant to the United States who, although he sufferers more sharply from color prejudice, lives much better than at home.

Cuba and Porto Rico have benefited enormously from American intervention. In 1899 the total exports of Porto Rico was $10,156,541. Under American rule it leaped in 1919 to $150,811,449. During the same period imports have increased from nine to ninety million dollars. Cuba has shown a similar phenomenal increase. In both Cuba and Porto Rico exports now exceed imports; while in the British West Indies the opposite is true except in Trinidad. Both these countries have the advantage of American capital and they have enjoyed the greatest prosperity of their entire history under American control.

Proximity makes the United States the logical market for West Indian goods, and the logical protector of the islands.

POLITICAL ATTITUDE OF BRITISH WEST INDIANS IN U.S.

The census of 1920 gives 73,803 foreign-born Negroes in the United States. The majority, say about 60,000, are British West Indians, the most of whom live in New York City.

Comparatively few West Indians become American citizens. Coming to the United States with a strong British bias and hatred of American color prejudice, they see the Negro Americans possessing few rights that they, the West Indians, cannot get. Indeed, a certain preference is given them particularly outside of New York, the more so if they have a smattering of French or Spanish. They see that even a newly landed immigrant, who is white, is accorded privileges that are withheld from the Negro America, and that late enemies in the last war, though they had each slain a thousand Americans, and made a thousand widows and orphans, have opportunities that are denied a Negro American veteran though he had saved an army division from destruction. Consequently they are inclined to look down upon the value of American citizenship, while their pride takes refuge in their British birth. But it is precisely because of this that the West Indian should draw closer to the American Negro, it is precisely because of this that a feeling of common humanity should prompt him to aid the American Negro in his long fight for liberty.

The facts to be taken into consideration are that the West Indians came here almost solely because of the pressure of conditions at home, and they have found relief; that as long as they are here they are virtually American Negroes, being indistinguishable from them except by their accent; and that they will in all probability stay here for the remainder of their lives.

At the present time the Negro in New York is greatly handicapped in the fight for his rights because of the large percentage of West Indians who cannot vote. New York has the largest Negro population in the United States, yet in political strength it is behind Chicago with nearly forty thousand less Negroes.

The destiny of the West Indian Negro and the American brother, as is also that of the white American, appears to be firmly linked. To the far-visioned and humane it will seem no different whether the battle against color hate and economic injustice be fought in the West Indies or in the United States.

ECONOMICS AND POLITICS

George S. Schuyler cogently assesses economic realities for the masses within the framework of American politics. This essay was published in March 1923.

The methods of supplying the needs of life and the relationship between individuals, growing out of the associations required for this production of the vital necessities, form the basis upon which are built up the laws, customs, morals and theology of any human group.

When the means of supplying human needs in any group are owned and controlled by a certain section or class within it; that class becomes dominant for the simple reason that they have the power of life and death over the masses because of this ownership and control. All must bow to the owning class, for all must eat, sleep, and clothe their bodies. For this arrangement of things to continue, it must be considered just by the masses whose toil accumulates wealth for the owning class.

This work of keeping the great majority loyal to the owning-class philosophy is entrusted to the judiciary, pedagogues, politicians and theologians. These gentlemen also require food, clothing and shelter, so, for fear these vital necessities may be withdrawn, they are bulwarks of loyalty to the owners. These intellectual custodians of the owning-class philosophy constitute the mercenary ruling-class of every nation. In press, pulpit, school, legislature and court they diligently labor to instill into the minds of the masses a proper loyalty to things-as-they-are. Any adverse criticism of the prevailing philosophy is considered heretical, immoral, unethical and seditious. Social and economic pressure, aided by the police power of the state is generally sufficient to keep the number of dissenters at a safe minimum. A certain amount of criticism and reformism is allowed when the dominance of the owning-class and their intellectual police is firmly established, but the lid of repression is clamped down when any crisis impends. Then liberals, reformers, labor "leaders," professional agitators and revolutionists either join the reaction, go to jail, or hibernate until the country is again safe for dissenters.

As Korzybski points out in his "Manhood of Humanity," the development of the mass mentality moves in arithmetical progression, viz.: 2, 4, 6, 8, 10, 12, 14, 16: while the development of industry moves in geometrical progression, viz.: 2, 4, 8, 16, 32, 64, 128, 256. Hence, new relationships between individuals associated in industry are continually being formed, which necessitates synchronical changes in the social structure. As Van Loon puts it, in his "Story of Mankind," "the 20th century man in an automobile has the mind of a 16th century tradesman." So it is not surprising to find that in every nation the social structure of jurisprudence, morals, ethics and theology is more or less out of plumb with the industrial foundation. As this condition of affairs becomes more and more pronounced, greater becomes the unrest, dissatisfaction, spirit of revolt, poverty, crime and degradation.

The necessity for change is first felt among the members of the group most intimately associated with industry, and first to be effected by changes due to new industrial methods, new inventions, adverse climatical conditions, opening or closing of markets. This discontent is given voice and organized by agitators, intellectual heretics descended by desertion or ousting from the ruling class, or political retainers of the owning-class.

Any change beneficial to the majority of the working class is violently opposed, by the owning-class through their intellectual phonographs, because it involves a sacrifice. A mild reform here, a conciliatory gesture there, are the extent of their concessions, unless a great danger, such as war, makes prudent the casting of a more meaty bone to the mob.

Within the owning-class, however, are various sections with slightly different economic interests who struggle for power to enact legislation favorable to them. For this purpose two or more rival political organizations are supplied with the pecuniary sinews of political conflict. In the United States the two dominant firms of political brokers are Republican and Democratic parties. Here as elsewhere, "He who pays the fiddler calls the tune."

The masses, drugged by the mental opiates administered to them from every side, are the pawns in the political contest for privilege. They are swayed hither and yon by the political herdsmen whose bait consists of bogus "issues" designed to play upon the fears, prejudices, ignorance and superstitions of the discontented mob. Since the radical organizations with an intelligent program make only appeals to reason, their slow growth is easily understood. These political "issues" are merely "red herrings" drawn across the path of proletarian discontent to divert them from the source of their troubles—the incompatibility of the industrial and social structures due to the form of ownership in vogue. For further convenience and confusion these campaign "issues" are condensed into slogans subject to numerous interpretations, such as: "Full Dinner Pail," "He kept us out of war," "A World safe for Democracy," "White Supremacy," "America First," "The Yellow Peril," and "Back to Normalcy."

Editorial writers on the kept press, with tongues in cheeks, take opposite sides with long kindergarten editorials; custodians of the "hire" education contribute solemn lectures and magazine articles; political henchmen "explain" the "issues" with straight faces; ignorant workers vociferously exchange expletives and fisticuffs over this or that "good" man.

After election, costumes and scenery are stored within reach, lights extinguished, and the political cowboys, who were elevated to office by reason of having corralled the most votes, proceed with the prosaic business of "delivering the goods" for their respective machines until nearly time for the next perennial farce. The wage-slaves return to their toil, and hopefully await the relief "their" man promised. This failing, of course, to materialize, the discontent again rises. The masses feverishly await another opportunity to vote out one representative of business and vote in another.

Midsummer comes. The political mummers haul out costumes, scenery and lights to rehearse the next farce. The capitalist-owned machine bosses select a double cast of characters from among the "faithful" and adopt appropriate slogans. The electorate nominates the "honest" and "good" men from among the "faithful," and the yearly farce is repeated.

What has been the result of this policy for workers and owners? A few figures on the distribution of wealth give the answer:

Two per cent of the population owns 65 per cent of the national wealth of the United States; 33 per cent of the population owns 30 per cent of the national wealth of the United States; 65 per cent of the population owns 5 per cent of the national wealth of the United States.

Nearly ten millions are illiterate, while the majority are morons.

The bourgeoisie and their intellectual and political gendarmerie are trying to maintain a rickety social structure on a rapidly moving industrial foundation for which a new structure of social concepts is absolutely necessary to insure a measure of justice to those who do the world's work.

These capitalist-owned political parties can no more represent the workers than a group of undertakers could represent an organization spreading knowledge of the attainment of immortality. They have never represented the white workers. How then can they be expected to represent the black workers. At least 98 per cent of the Negroes are workers.

By throwing their votes into one or the other of these political hoppers, the Negro worker may obtain a few soft jobs for subservient, hat-in-hand "deserving" leaders, but the masses cannot benefit except at the owners' expense. The interests of the two groups are diametrically opposed. The workers want more wages, lower living costs, steady employment, and a shorter working day. The owners cannot satisfy these desires, even if they wanted to, without depleting their bankrolls. They have rarely, if ever, shown evidence of such beneficence.

Only by economic organization much similar to that of the owners, can the workers combat the evils confronting them. It is ofttimes better policy for the owners to grant concessions than to attempt to fight powerful labor unions. In order to safeguard these concessions from vicious legislation and biased court rulings, it is necessary that a pronounced effort be made to place in legislatures and courts, representatives possessed of the working class viewpoint. This political side of the main economic struggle must be carried on by a group of politicians owned and controlled by organized labor. "He who pays the fiddler calls the tune." Rewarding "friends" and punishing "enemies" has proven futile for the workers in the past. What is sauce for the goose is sauce for the gander: a course of action capable of satisfying the aspirations of white labor, is also good for black labor. The great issue in the United States is not, "Black or White," but "Robbers or Robbed."

The slight natural aversion to the Negro because of his color, would have long ago vanished, as it has in the greater part of Latin America, through understanding and friendship bred of association. Unfortunately it grew into prejudice of a bitter type through accentuation due to economic competition between slave labor and "free" labor, and increased immeasurably by the propaganda of the slave owners and their intellectual police. In later years Negro migration into Northern industrial centers has engendered a similar hostility between black and white wage labor because of the competition for the inadequate supply of jobs.

The intellectual mercenaries of the owning-class have used this situation to their advantage by playing upon the fears, ignorance and hatreds of both groups of workers to keep them divided and exploited. A house divided against itself cannot stand. The owning-class believe in their class philosophy: they organize economically and politically; they are a freemasonry of economic oligarchs disregarding race, color and creed. The working-class largely have no class philosophy; their few economic organizations are archaic in structure; while their political efforts are largely confined to the long discredited policy of rewarding "friends" and punishing "enemies;" their one or two independent political groups are weak in numbers and dollars; they are easily divided on racial and religious lines.

The white trades unions, unorganized workers, skilled and unskilled, must be brought to a realization of these truths, and the necessity of acting upon them. The same is true of the Negro. Neither can hope to free himself while the other remains in servitude. The inexorable laws of industrial evolution is arraying the classes in our society on the side of exploiter or exploited. On which side the exploited Negro worker should stand politically is quite evident.

The union into a solid phalanx of black and white labor on the economic and political field is not as difficult as some may think. It is only necessary to expose through press, pamphlets and lectures, the falsity, deception and grotesquery of the "obstacles" supplied by the intellectual serfs of the bourgeoisie, which keep the workers divided, and profits only the owning class. This work can only be done by the workers themselves. Those who have banished the owning-class philosophy from their minds and let in the pure, free air of economic truth, must lead the way.

THE BUSINESS SIDE OF A UNIVERSITY

This essay was published in November 1923, when its author, Emmett J. Scott, was secretary-treasurer of Howard University. At that time, Howard University was the largest African-American university in the nation. Scott offers a detailed description of the business side of Howard University, making the point that an effective business system is pivotal to a great university.

Howard University is the largest institution in the world specializing in the collegiate and professional training of colored men and women. The type of scholastic work given in its Junior College, its School of Liberal Arts, and its Schools of Education, Commerce and Finance, Applied Science, including Architecture, Art, Civil Engineering, Mechanical Engineering, Electrical Engineering, etc.; Public Health, Music, Religion, Law and its School of Medicine, including also the Dental and Pharmaceutical Colleges, has won for the University a high and important place in the sisterhood of American colleges and universities.

That Howard University is continuing to fulfill in a large and important way the enviable leadership it has gained among educational institutions in America, specializing in the training of colored youth is evidenced by the new record set by the University this year when three hundred and eleven (311) college and professional degrees were conferred upon graduates of the classes of 1923 by President J. Stanley Durkee at the Fifty-Fourth Annual Commencement Exercises held on the University Campus, Friday, June 8th, 1923.

The business management of a great university, like Howard, entails more than the mere collection of student fees and the disbursing of salaries to members of the faculty and administrative staff. Those who are informed know that few modern institutions of learning can be conducted in so simple a way. Most of them are as highly organized as any commercial business concern, and have to deal with problems equally as intricate and in many cases a bit more difficult.

The business side of Howard University involves the collection of fees from more than 2,000 students, the providing of lodging and board for nearly seven hundred students, the payment of the salaries of a faculty of two hundred or more members and an administrative staff of sixty persons, the investment of trust funds amounting to approximately $400,000, the expenditure of over $40,000 some years for repairs to buildings and improvement of grounds, the expenditure of a government appropriation of some $283,000 (1923–24, for instance, not counting an additional $157,500 authorized, but not yet available), the preparation of publicity regarding the activities of the school for some 200 white and colored newspapers, and, in co-operation with the President, the presentation of its claims for support to the philanthropic public. The Secretary-Treasurer is the Business Manager of the University.

The assets of Howard University as of June 30, 1922, amounted to $2,134,940.98. With a budget calling for the expenditure of nearly $500,000 a year, it seems but fair to say that Howard University as a business concern comprises the widest range of activities engaged in by any institution specializing in the training of colored youth, or, perhaps that of any commercial concern among colored people. Indeed, it compares favorably with leading white institutions as well.

Howard University operates under a budget system covering a fiscal year running from July 1st to June 30th. The budget of expenditure for a year is prepared and submitted to the Board of Trustees of the University for approval. The monies to cover the expenditure under the budget are secured from student fees and such Congressional appropriations as may be granted, and such donations for current expenses as may be given the University by its Alumni and friends.

In the collection of fees from the more than two thousand students attending Howard University a great amount of clerical work is required. In addition to the fourteen persons regularly employed in the Secretary-Treasurer's office, for the collection of fees, there is also need for the assistance of some additional six to eight persons during the quarterly registration periods. The matter of collecting student fees is more intricate than would appear to a casual visitor. In this connection correspondence is required to be had between the University and the parents of the students and between the University and the students themselves. In addition to this, since the World War the University has had a large number of students who are securing training under the Veterans' Bureau of the Government and the work in connection with the payment of tuition and other fees from the Government for these men devolves upon the business office of the University. This is also true of the men who are given aid by the Government while securing military training in the R.O.T.C. Unit at Howard University. During the past year the equipment turned over to the University for the men of the R.O.T.C. Unit amounted to approximately $40,000, for which the Secretary-Treasurer is bonded. The responsibility for this equipment falls upon the University business office.

The providing of lodging and board for 700 students is a business problem in itself. There are three dormitories for students operated by the University which house these 700 or more students. All of the problems of housekeeping are involved in the conduct of the student dormitories. Matrons must be provided to see that proper decorum is observed. Janitors must be employed. Provision must be made for the furnishing of linen and other housekeeping needs.

Howard operates a dining hall which accommodates 525 students. This new dining hall was erected (1921–23) at a cost of $201,000. It was designed by members of the University Department of Architecture. All of the expenditures involved in the erection of the dining hall building were made through the business office of Howard University. There is employed in the dining hall department a staff of sixty odd persons including the head of the department, assistant to the head of the department, cooks, waiters, janitors, and other helpers. This department is operated under the direct supervision of the business office of the University, all supplies and materials being purchased through that office.

A modern printing office is operated by Howard University. The management of this printing office is under the supervision of the Secretary-Treasurer of the University. He must see that proper employees are provided. He is in charge of the purchase of such supplies as are necessary in the publication of the several University periodicals and for the vast amount of printed matter required by the various departments of the University. There are regularly employed in the University Printing Office a staff of six to ten persons.

An important function of the business office of Howard University is the proper investment of the trust funds amounting approximately to $400,000. From time to time the investments in which portions of these funds are placed mature and it becomes necessary to properly reinvest the money. In this connection the University's business receives sundry applications for first trust loans and other investments and with authority of the Loans and Property Committee of the Board of Trustees accepts such applications as will provide suitable returns on the University's trust funds. The business office in superintending the investment of these funds performs in many respects the functions of a banking institution.

Some years there is expended for repairs to buildings and improvements to grounds some $42,500. The things for which this large amount of money is spent cover the interior and exterior repair of University buildings and care of the University ground, including the outlying properties owned by the University and sundry other items. In the care of the University grounds there is required to be employed some fifteen or more men. The direct oversight of the work of these men falls to the business office of the University. The improvement of the grounds of the University is also a part of the duty of the business office. In keeping with this duty there must be continual study of the grounds so that such improvements as may add to the beauty and convenience may be brought to the attention of the Trustees. As a result of such study during the past few years improvements have been made in the physical beauty of the University grounds by the laying of cement walks, the planting of shrubbery and the preparation of flower beds, the placing of all overhead wires (electric and telephone), in underground conduits, and the installation of standard white way electric light posts.

In order that Howard University may receive proper publicity regarding its activities, the business office has established a press service which supplies news regarding the University to some 200 white and colored newspapers. The providing of such news releases is one of the important extra-activities of the business office. This particular feature of the work of the University business office resembles very much that of a regular established news bureau.

The business office of Howard University serves as purchasing agent for the institution, having supervision of all requisitions for the purchase of supplies and materials of every description. In this connection a competitive system of securing bids in purchasing supplies is followed. Nearly all supplies, of every character, which are needed in connection with the activities engaged in by Howard University are secured through this purchasing department.

As may be generally known, Howard University has for a number of years received appropriations from the Congress of the United States. These appropriations are disbursed through the U. S. Department of the Interior. Each year the claims of the University for aid at the hands of the National Government must be presented to the Congress through the Secretary of the Interior. This in itself is a task not usually expected of the President and the business manager of an educational institution.

In the expenditure of funds under the Department of the Interior the procedure under which that department operates must be followed which makes necessary the employment on the part of the University of two systems of expending funds for University needs: one covering funds of the University, and one covering funds expended for the University by the Government.

Such, in brief, is the story and picture of the business side of a great university. In the business management of an institution like Howard University, there are various interests to be safeguarded, intricate problems to be solved, and divers tasks to be undertaken. It is only by the helpful co-operation of one's co-workers that successful results are secured. No official could wish for a better trained, a more efficient, or a more devoted group of helpers than the one that co-operates with the Secretary-Treasurer of Howard University.

The Hue and Cry about
Howard University

*Novelist Zora Neale Hurston attended Howard University in 1918 and
1919. Here, Hurston writes about a number of issues Howard's students
and faculty face, including questions over the university's white president.
Although Hurston points out some problems confronting the university, by
1921 the institution had a scholastic standing among its graduates comparable to any school in the nation. This essay was published in 1925.*

I went to Howard as a Prep in 1918–19. I had met Mae Miller and she
liked me and urged me to transfer from Morgan to Howard. I still have
her little letter of friendship and encouragement. I value it too. That
was the beginning of a personal and literary friendship that has lasted.

The thrill Hannibal got when he finally crossed the Alps, the feeling of Napoleon when he finally placed upon his head the iron crown
of Constantine, were nothing to the ecstasy I felt when I realized I was
actually a Howardite.

We used to have "sings" in Chapel every Monday during services
and nobody knows how I used to strive to eradicate all pettiness from
my nature so that I might be fit to sing "Alma Mater." We always finished the service with that. I used to indulge in searching introspection
to root out even those little meannesses that put us far below the class
of the magnificent transgressor and leave us merely ridiculous.

It was during the next year (1919) while Howard was not recovered
from the S. A. T. C., that Wienstein came to Howard under government
pay to conduct the singing in the "camp." He had a magnificent tenor
voice, and wore his khaki well. He had worked with Prof. Wesley, also
a tenor, in the war camps of the country and together they had us
singing lustily. We liked it. We sang lots of things: "Long, Long Trail a
Winding," "K-K-Katy," "Roll Jordan Roll," and "Gointer Study War
No Mo' " among other things but we always ended with "Alma Mater."

After Wienstein left, the singing was continued under Wesley. He
used to come out before the faculty on the platform and lead the

singing daily. The President would arise with beaming face and ask us to sing our songs for him.—He said that Negro music began where "white" music left off. We used to respond cheerfully. Then we would select any song from the book we liked. Hymn 245, "God of Our Fathers" and 180, "Immortal Love Forever Full," were our favorites. This went on for weeks and weeks. Spring was approaching.

One day I wrote Dr. Durkee a note and left it on the pulpit as I came into chapel, asking him to read the 91st Psalm. He has a marvelous speaking voice and I could wish nothing better than hearing him read that beautiful piece of prose poetry. He did not read it. I felt snubbed and disappointed, but the next day he began that beautiful one, "The Heavens Declare the Glory of God." The sun shone in mellow tones through the stained windows, tendrils of the ivy vine crept in the open windows and the sparrows chirped incessantly in the midst of their nest building.

The President knew it perfectly and before he was fairly under way he had his audience on the edge of the seats so that the last tones left us still hanging there. And when we realized that he was really through we sank back tremendously moved.

Howard was unutterably beautiful to me that spring. I would give a great deal to call back my Howard illusion of those days.

Every day after that for a month the President read a psalm. It took a long time to reach the 91st, but I did not care. He never looked in the book—I am certain he knows them all by heart. E. H. Sothern in "Hamlet" has nothing on Dr. Durkee reciting the psalms.

I dwell on these seemingly trifling details to give one a picture of Howard before the storm.

A few days later and the first storm broke. A great number of students but not the entire body of students by any means were holding indignation meetings alleging that they had been forced or commanded by the President to sing "Spirituals." He was denounced as a despot, a tyrant, who was dragging us back into slavery.

Though there were spokesmen among the students, various members of the faculty were credited as the real leaders. Among whom were Miss Childers, Mr. Tibbs and Miss Lewis. Some said Miss Childers didn't like the idea of Wesley leading the singing as she used to "raise" all the songs. The papers printed things down in the city and some members of the Senate denounced us as ingrates and accused us of being ashamed of ourselves and our traditions.

The President held a conference with the students one day after Chapel to find out how he had offended. There were speakers for and against the "Spirituals." John Miles, now of Yale Divinity School, was one of the "Pros," Mae Miller and another young lady whose name has slipped me, were "Antis."

The "Pro's" made the usual stand: *(a)* The beauty and workmanship of the songs. *(b)* Only American folk songs. *(c)* Only beauty that came out of slavery. The "Anti's" held: *(a)* They were low and degrading, being the product of slaves and slavery; *(b)* not good grammar; *(c)* they are not sung in white universities.

The thought that any Negro could or would be ashamed of Negro music, had never occurred to Dr. Durkee I am sure, for he seemed pained that he had unwittingly offended and never since has suggested them.

After a few days of bluster this affair died down but not before a perceptible rift had been made in the faculty and student group.

II.

A little later that same year, Senator Smoot arose on the floor of the Senate with a book in hand which he informed the Senators was a highly culpable bolshevistic volume which he had received from the hands of a Howard student. He understood it came from the university library and insinuated that it was in the curriculum. He held forth that a government supported institution that was making bolshevists should be allowed to toddle along without government aid seeing that this was the U. S. and not Red Russia.

Rumors flew thick and fast among the students as to who had engineered the book into the Senator's hands. It is to be remembered that Smoot was head of the Appropriation Committee. Durkee hastened down to the Senate Committee room and explained that the book had been given by the Rand School and it was the policy of the university to accept all gifts. It was neither taught nor recommended. This satisfied the Senator evidently, for finally the appropriation came through. He was denounced by some on the Hill and some off for having cringed before the Senate. He should have informed that body that we could teach what we liked and if the money was withheld we could have the satisfaction of being untrammeled. I even saw a typewritten, unsigned card on the bulletin board on the second floor of the main building to the effect: "It is better to lose $250,000 than our manhood."

After the smoke had cleared away, a young man known to be socialistic, a close friend of mine, left Howard forever. I saw him recently in

New York. He says he has been around the world twice since 1919 but never feels right to go back to any school.

More than one person was accused of having sent that book to Smoot by the student. Some say that a professor in the law school did it, others that a teacher in the department of history, to embarrass the administration. Perhaps it will not be known just who, but anyway, Senator Smoot never drew it from the library.

"The University Luncheonette," run by two law students, Dyett and McGhee, was a place where a great deal of discussion went on, Mr. Dyett being known as the anti-administration man.

About this time the "Contemptible puppy" rumors began to circulate. Students were beginning to see that there was something wrong somewhere. Some faculty members and the Administration were not so "clubby," so to speak, as they might be. There were stories flying about the campus that certain members were giving certain trusted students "tips" on faculty meeting doings.

Dr. Emmett J. Scott had been made secretary-treasurer of the university, succeeding both Cook and Parks in their respective jobs. This, some felt, was unjust and muttered that an attempt was being made to "Tuskegeeize" Howard, Dr. Scott being the first gun fired. There was no one to whom these rumors could be definitely traced, but the students passing along the complaints always claimed faculty sources. For instance a young lady friend of mine stopped me in the upper corridor of main building to tell me that Dr. Durkee should be thrown out. I was astonished and asked her why she thought this.

"Well," she said, "he called Kelly Miller a black dog to his face."

"How did you hear it?"

"A very high member of the faculty—an official told me, and I know he wouldn't lie."

This was the first time I had heard the story, but not the last by any means. I heard it variously repeated. In one story Mr. Miller had been called a "puppy dog;" in another "a black dog," in another a "contemptible puppy." From neither of the principals have I ever heard a syllable on this matter, but whether it is true in any part, it had a tremendous effect upon the students—a Negro professor being called out of his name by a white man—no matter what the provocation, if any.

More and more it came to be so that every official act of the faculty must be subject to student scrutiny. In some way or other Alexander Z. Looby, George Brown and Fred Jordan had a pretty thorough knowledge of what went on in the chamber. But Mr. Looby was President of the Student Council and perhaps had a chance to know things that way.

A great many of us took no stock in the hurly-burly, feeling that we could not as students act in the capacity of the Administration, but a great number were flattered at these rumored confidences. I discount most of it as being untrue—the figment of persons wishing to enhance their own importance in student eyes by appearing as the confident of the faculty. One instance I know to be true.

In political science Mr. Tunnell digressed one day from government in general to government in particular and told the class that Dr. Durkee was a joke; that some one (I forget who) had foisted that fisherman on us and that he was being paid a high salary to raise funds, but he was a failure. He then told us the President's salary was $7,000 per year and his house. He then told us that Emmett J. Scott had been brought on from Tuskegee and paid $5,000 ($4,500 salary, $500 incidentals) to divert the golden stream from that school to Howard but he was a white elephant.

Of course I was surprised at such confidences but so much was being said here and there on the campus that one could expect about anything. It was evident to me now that the faculty (I mean by that term the entire governing-teaching body) was a Spartan youth concealing a fox under its clothes.

Then there was the instance of the famous note on the desk of Senator Smoot written by Professor Kelly Miller. It had to do with the appropriation rules. The Administration was making a tremendous fight for the $500,000 for the Medical school. A number of Senators were doing battle for and against it, but a strong group had pledged themselves to see it through. President Coolidge in his message to Congress had urged that it be given Howard. Dr. Durkee is a Massachusetts man and his Senators had taken the field openly in his behalf. In the midst of this came Prof. Miller's note to Senator Smoot asking him not to ask for the half million dollars for fear of losing the regular appropriation of $267,000, I think it was, and threw the Administration friends into confusion. The daily press of Washington accused the professor of attempting to embarrass the Administration since the President stated that Miller's action was unauthorized. I have never seen an authorized version of the affair from Prof. Miller's pen, and shall therefore suspend judgment until I do. There have been a number of stories pro and con, but so far as open statements are concerned, the affair remains where the press left it.

There are those who hold that Prof. Miller aspires to the presidency of the university. No one can deny the urge to ascend in humanity. If we do we preach stagnation. His ability to bring this about, if it is true, and if so rather to his credit than otherwise, what man is satisfied and his fitness for the job is being hotly debated all over the country at present. Some members of the alumnæ claim that all that has happened at Howard in the way of disturbances is a part of the ladder up which Dean Miller prepares to ascend. The human mind unexpressed being unreadable, all these things pro and con on the subject are still conjectures. Every one who reads or listens knows how often mole hills of trifling incidents are stretched to mountains and given special significance.

On the other hand there are those who contend that Dr. Durkee is an obstruction in the path of Howard's progress. This calls attention to the accomplishments of his administration. His bitterest enemy cannot but admit that more has been done for the advancement of the university under him than in all the other administrations put together. The following are excerpts from "Facts," a pamphlet issued by the university:

By vote of the Trustees, June 4, 1919, the offices of Secretary and Treasurer were combined, and Dr. Emmett J. Scott elected as Secretary-Treasurer. He began his services July 1, 1919.

The office of Registrar was created as a separate position and a Howard alumnus, Dwight O. W. Holmes, was elected to that position, and succeeded by Mr. F. D. Wilkinson, upon the former's appointment as Dean of the School of Education.

Both the offices of Secretary-Treasurer and Registrar have been put by these officers on the most modern administrative basis with extensive rooms on the first floor of the Main Building.

The office of Dean of Men was created, and to it elected Dr. Edward L. Parks, former Treasurer.

The office of Dean of Women was created and to it has been elected Miss Lucy D. Slowe, a Howard alumna, formerly principal of the M Street Junior High School of Washington. Miss Slowe is completing her first year most successfully.

For the academic deans has been created a group of offices on first floor of Main Building, with clerks. The Dean of Men and Dean of Women each have also been given fine offices with clerks.

There is also a University Council, composed of two members of each school of the University, including both undergraduate and graduate schools. The purpose of this Council is for a better understanding between the schools and for a more united purpose. This Council meets three or four times a year.

It has long been felt that an Alumni Secretary was necessary to our greatest success. In June, 1921, the Trustees voted as follows:

"Authority is granted to the President to secure an Alumni Secretary under conditions which will be of best advantage both to the University and to the alumni, paying such salary as shall be needed, money paid not to exceed $1,000 toward the salary of the person employed."

Mr. Norman L. McGhee, College '19, Law '22, a member of the Secretary-Treasurer's office force, is temporarily heading up this movement for closer affiliation with our alumni.

In February, 1920, the Board of Trustees voted as follows:

"One Trustee may be elected each year from a number recommended by the Alumni Association of the University, such Trustee to automatically retire at the expiration of his term of office."

Since the report of the Committee, no vacancies on the Board have occurred. It is interesting to note that eight Alumni of Howard University are now serving as members of the Board of Trustees.

BUILDING AND GROUNDS

New buildings erected: The Greenhouse, erected in 1919, at a cost of $8,000, and the Dining Hall Building with class rooms for the Department of Home Economics, erected in 1921, at a cost of $201,000. Plans are now under way for the new gymnasium and stadium. The General Statement, given below, will show numerous renovations made. Howard Hall, General O. O. Howard's old home, used for so many years as a detention house for incorrigible children, has been reclaimed, the old outbuildings torn away, and the home restored as a dormitory for girls. In the Main Building, a United States post office has been established, thus serving the postal needs of student body and faculty. In the Main Building, also, has been equipped a Rest Room for girls and also one for women teachers and workers. Both were greatly needed.

The items in the General Statement "Improvement of Grounds" includes the following: Reclaiming of the bank overlooking the Reservoir, formerly a dump for cans and a place for burning rubbish; trees on the campus have been treated twice; large flower beds of rare beauty have been placed; plaza and front of Thirkeld Hall made beautiful and splendid concrete walks and steps to Sixth Street provided; fence surrounding the lower half of main campus; unsightly plot of ground on Georgia Avenue changed into a beautiful little park with paths crossing and steps leading up to Sixth Street; surroundings of Howard Hall graded and granolithic walks and steps placed; grounds surrounding School of Music beautified; underground electric lighting system installed with posts and globes like those used in the District of Columbia—this latter one of the biggest improvements.

It also became necessary for the Trustees to appropriate certain amounts out of general funds so as to complete the improvements and repairs mentioned.

A summary of the amounts spent since July 1, 1919, up to the period ending December 30, 1922, follows:

Repairs to sundry buildings, including the Main Building, Science Hall, the Chapel, President's House, Spaulding Hall and various residence properties of the University	$55,487.34
Repairs to Clark and Miner Halls, dormitories for young men and young women	21,625.08
Improvement of grounds	15,896.98
Repairs to Law School Building	15,530.06
Improvements, Library Building	1,388.61
Repairs to Medical and Dental Schools Buildings	13,745.46
Installation New Electric Feeders, thereby making more efficient the heating and lighting facilities of the University	1,246.20
Repairs to Boarding Hall, while in basement of Miner Hall	478.30
Repairs to Manual Arts Building	732.56
	$126,130.59

CURRICULUM

At the close of school year 1918–19, all secondary schools were abolished, leaving a college registration of 1,057. Dire disaster was everywhere prophesied by the following year the college opened with 1,567 college students.

The whole plan of undergraduate work was changed. The four years' college course was divided into two periods of two years each—the first two years named the Junior College, and the second, the Senior Schools. A student entering the undergraduate department will take two years of general college subjects leading to his last two years of specialized work in whatever field he may choose, graduating at the end of four years with his degree from that particular school. The College of Liberal Arts cares for all those students who desire four full years of undergraduate non-professional work.

New courses of study authorized by the Trustees during the present administration:

Architecture
Art
Dramatics
Public Health and Hygiene
Reserve Officers' Training Corps

At the Trustee meeting of June, 1919, the old semester system was abolished. Under that system it took the college three weeks to register its students and get to work in its classes. We are now on the quarter system, and register two thousand students and more in two days at the opening of the year, and in one day for the winter and spring quarters, classes beginning recitations the following day.

The General Education Board required as a basis for its help that all finances of the School of Medicine be taken over by the general administration of the University and be handled in one office. When this was done, the Board pledged the University $250,000 as an endowment to the Medical School, providing the University would raise a like sum. This sum, in cash or pledges, must be raised by July 1, 1923, pledges to be redeemed by July 1, 1926. With such an endowment the Medical School may be kept in Class A. Without this endowment the Medical School will lose its Class A rating. Hence, the necessity for every friend of the School to rally to its support now. To show the remarkable spirit among the student body, the President announces that the student body has pledged $24,843. The Trustees, administration, and faculty have pledged practically $15,000. The total gifts so far (May 21) amount to about $220,000.

During 1920–21 evening classes were established. The attendance for that year was 46. The registration for 1922–23 is 153. So far we have served 104 teachers from the public schools of Washington.

In 1919 the Trustees, on recommendation of the President, adopted a Faculty Salary Scale, toward which the administration should work. The scale is as follows:

Dean	$3,000 to $3,500
Professor	2,500 to 3,000
Associate Professor	2,000 to 2,500
Assistant Professor	1,500 to 2,000
Instructor	750 to 1,500

Over $63,000 have been added to the teachers' salaries alone during this administration. The minimum scale has now been practically reached, and the last two surpassed. Many salaries have been doubled in three years. Average increase of salaries 56 per cent; 26 new teachers have been added.

By recommendation of the President, the Trustees voted that teachers of professorial rank may have the privilege of a sabbatical year of absence on half pay, providing they use that year's leave of absence for advance study in some standard institution of learning, the better to fit themselves for their particular field in teaching.

With the opening of the present administration, 1918–19, total financial income was $220,553.43, of which sum the Federal Government appropriation was $117,937.75.

Our auditors reported for the year 1921–22 a total budget figure of $589,033.87, of which sum the Government appropriation was $363,135.25; $116,000 of the $363,135.25 was appropriated for the New Dining Hall, which has been in use during the school year 1922–23.

We have a School of Public Health and Hygiene with a Director. Under that School comes the Department of Physical Education with a director in charge; also the Department of Military Education with six officers detailed from the United States Army to care for our Reserve Officers' Training Corps. But the Trustees voted to have student managers of the individual teams, such as football, baseball, track, etc., and also invited the alumni to elect three representatives from the alumni as an Advisory Committee who will meet with the staff of the Department of Physical Education concerning all matters of interest in that Department.

With the opening of this administration there was but one department of the University approved by the rating associations of America. The School of Medicine was Class A.

In the autumn of 1921, the Association of Colleges and Preparatory Schools of the Middle States and Maryland after most rigid personal investigation, placed our College of Liberal Arts on the Approved List. This means that now our graduates from such college have the same scholastic standing as graduates from any other first-class school in America.

In the spring of 1922, our Dental College was registered in the New York State Board of Regents, thus giving it the highest rating.

Our College of Pharmacy has just been given the highest rating with the Pharmacy Board of the State of Ohio.

Our School of Law is now applying for admission to the Association of American Law Schools, and we are confident of success.

A careful organization of the students has been approved, and under the title of "Student Council," the students have a very large measure of self-government.

IN THE NAME OF PURITY

American immigration authorities who used morality as a litmus test angered the author of this essay, Wallace Thurman. Here, he argues that it appears that efforts are being made to fundamentalize the United States. He published this essay in March 1926.

I started to entitle this article "The Damn Fool Americans," but decided that a mere damn was too mild, and realizing that if I should happen to make it more emphatic I would be liable to detention in the nearest hoosegow, I discarded the idea. Then, too, I reasoned that all Americans are not to be placed in this category; at least five out of every million are exempt.

The present mood of irritation has been induced in many others besides myself, in fact anyone with an I. Q. registering above that of a moron would react belligerently toward the constant efforts being made to fundamentalise the United States of America. We have had conscientious fundamentalists like Bryan, we have had unscrupulous fundamentalists like Simmons, and now we have deliberate fundamentalists like our Secretary of State, our Secretary of Labor, and their underlings.

The latest gesture on the part of these gentlemen to keep America free from moral blemishes, and to convert it into a sublimated Valhalla is the exclusion of the Countess Cathcart. No more asinine gesture has been made. This surpasses even the Dayton, Tennessee circus, and the exclusions of the Karolyis and Saklatavla. As someone has so aptly phrased it: "If the present regime continues much longer anyone whose countenance does not reflect the sublime contentedness and Christian piety of a Texas yokel will be excluded, to say nothing of people with red hair and tilted noses."

The Countess Cathcart was once upon a time impelled by the call of youth to leave her husband and flee to the wilds of Africa with the Earl of Craven. Eventually they tired of their adventure, the husband of the countess divorced her and named the Earl as co-respondent, while the offending Earl was welcomed back to his family hearth. Thus the incident closed, and thus it would have remained closed had it not been for the official piddling of our addle-headed ninnies in Washington and Ellis Island.

Just why the immigration authorities thought that the Countess could in any way lower the moral standards of America is not quite clear. In the first place the law has been sadly misinterpreted, for neither the Countess nor the Earl were ever convicted of a crime, nor were they even indicted for one; and the law specifically states that the person must be guilty of moral turpitude, meaning this not in the light of one's personal sex behavior, nor in the light of one being supposedly guilty of committing a crime against some European dictator, but in the light of ones being an actual criminal. If being sued for divorce is a crime then 90 per cent of our "pure, white, Nordic, American stock" should be incarcerated immediately. Then, too, the Earl was admitted without question not only once, but twice, and would have remained here undisturbed had not certain persons become inquisitive anent this double standard. Can it be that our governmental authorities are advocates of the "woman must always pay" doctrine, or is it that they feared the Countess might choose to elope with a fatal number of our American husbands?

Seriously, though, such tommyrot should be thoroughly investigated. This sudden alertness is indeed unnatural, and was certainly provoked by other agencies than the mere concern of our immigration authorities about the morals of the Homo Americanus. "Touch my palm with silver, and . . ."

Perhaps the present case may be the means of generating an organized reaction against this drive for a nationwide purity. In the words of a pool hall Johnny: "Who in the hell wants to be pure anyway"; especially, I might add, when purity is measured in terms of hypocrisy. As long as one hides one's supposed impurity, one is according to the standards of our governmental officials, pure. At least that is what I infer from the presented evidence in the Cathcart-Craven case. Had the Countess lied she would have been admitted without further question.

It seems to me that our authorities would at least have something upon the statute books to back them up. In the instance of the Countess Karolyi, a war-time measure prohibiting the admittance of anyone who might preach a doctrine subversive to the best interests of the government of the United States was invoked. This bill was specifically aimed at Bolshevists. The Countess Karolyi is no preacher of Bolshevism nor is she a Communist, and in no way liable to be included under the invoked statute. It so happened that Premier Horthy of Hungary considered Countess Karolyi his own personal enemy so he informed his ambassador to get busy here in the United States since she might influence certain persons against him who were preparing to lend his government some money. The ambassador did get busy, and "Nervous Nellie" Kellogg flew to the rescue, striving to save we susceptible Americans from being innoculated with the deadly germs of Communism.

Thus we are kept pure from ideas and infidelity. Americans must not become cognizant of any doctrines save the existent one, nor must they be contaminated by an adultress. In this nation of prohibition and prostitution one lone woman might incite us all to Bolshevism, and another might incite or excite us all to indulge in promiscuous sex relations, which is the ultimate reduction ad absurdum, the last word in asinine ridiculousness, and should be hahahed into limbo.

This fanatic fervour to reform is also due to the war, I suppose, as is every other deplorable condition now extant since 1914. We Americans sallied forth to make the world safe for democracy, and returned home still seeing phantoms. Consequently we have been pursuing these phantoms ever since, and it has reached such a stage that it seems that the whole nation will evolve into Don Quixotes attacking moral wind-mills.

First the Anti-Saloon League begged enough money to effect prohibition; then the K.K.K. culled enough coin from the pockets of our illiterati to effect racial purity, female chastity, and America for Americans; next the leading fundamentalists of the country began to plea for funds to establish a memorial to William Jennings Bryan in order to carry on that worthy's campaign against science and evolution; now our government authorities are evidently receiving their salaries to give vent to personal judges or to cater to the prejudices of our financial giants. And all in the name of purity.

QUOTH BRIGHAM YOUNG–
THIS IS THE PLACE

Wallace Thurman was a native of Salt Lake City, Utah. Here he relates his opinions on the social, political, and cultural conditions of his home state—a place he can find little to be enthusiastic about. This essay was published in August 1926.

I am fully aware of what Brigham Young had in mind when he uttered the above enthusiastic statement, yet try tho I may the most enthusiastic thing that I can find to say about my home state and its capitol city is that it invariably furnishes me with material for conversation. It does not matter to whom I am talking, whether it be Jew or Gentile, black or white, Baptist or Episcopalian, thief or minister, when the conversation begins to lag I can always casually introduce the fact that I was born in Utah, and immediately become the centre of attraction nonchalantly answering the resultant barrage of questions. I find that I can even play this trick on the same group of persons more than once, for it seems as if they never tire asking—Do Mormons still have more than one wife?—Do they look different from other people?—How many wives did Brigham Young have?—Are there any Negro Mormons?—Can one really stay afloat in the Great Salt Lake without sinking?—and thus they continue ad infinitum, and I might also add—ad nauseam. Nevertheless it is amusing at times, and, as I say, it is for this reason alone that Utah has one warm spot in my rather chilled heart, for whenever I stop to remember the many dull hours I spent there, and the many dull people I spent them with, even that aforementioned warm spot automatically begins to grow cold.

Utah was a wilderness composed of ore laden mountains, fertile valleys, and desert wastes frequented only by trappers and Indians when the Mormons, an outlaw religious sect believing in and practising polygamy, settled there. These Mormons had treked over half of the continent in search of a spot where they could found a settlement, earn their livelihood from the soil, and indulge in their religious peculiarities unmolested by their pernicious brethren in God who insisted that they practise other religious peculiarities. They had been run out of Illinois, they had been run out of Missouri and Kansas and they had forged their way over miles of Nebraska prairie land, miles of Wyoming sage brush hills, and miles of mountain trails before they finally stood on a peak overlooking the beautiful Salt Lake valley, surrounded by the Wasatch range of the Rocky Mountains, and cheered when their intrepid leader, Brigham Young, shouted: This is the place!

Once they had found this suitable site the Mormons, under expert leadership, founded their mundane Zion, named their townsite Salt Lake City after the great inland sea nearby, christened the crooked river that ran around the city's outskirts—the Jordon, cultivated the rich farm lands, carried on a profitable trade with the Indians, began to raise stock, and started the construction of their sacrosanct religious temple and tabernacle, which stand today as monuments to their super-achievement.

Things hummed in the new town. Cattle carts lumbered down rocky mountain trails carrying the big stones that were being used in building the temple. Gold rushers, bound for the coast, stopped and sometimes stayed if they felt like braving the arrogant hostility of the Mormon fathers. Square blocks of land were apportioned off to the various churchmen, who energetically erected primitive homes for themselves and their wives. The great tithing square on the site where the renowned Hotel Utah now stands, teemed with people pouring in from the surrounding countryside to pay their tithes, while the public watering ground, where the Salt Lake City and county building was later built, was crowded with overland wagon trains, and Mormon visitors from nearby settlements, for Zion had soon overflowed and mushroom towns appeared overnight in the immediate vicinity. Zion flourished, Zion grew wealthy, and Zion grew more holy per se.

However all mundane paradises seem subject to an invasion by the devil's forces, and the Mormon Zion was no exception, for the devil's forces soon came in the persons of non-Mormons, derisively called Gentiles. Like most gold seekers of their day (and are gold seekers ever any different?) they wanted only the chance to garner gold—damn how they got it or how they suffered meanwhile. So Zion was invaded, and Zion soon succumbed to a wave of prosperity, progress and prostitution, and the transcontinental railroad, which had its east-west junction near Ogden, was the most telling blow dealt by the Gentiles.

The result was pitiful. Thousands of easterners came pouring in to see whether or not these Mormons really had horns, and finding that they were not so endowed by nature decided to stay and break down the Mormon wall around the natural wealth of the state. The Mormons put up a brave battle while Brigham Young lived, but after his death there was a complete debacle. Utah was finally forced to come into the Union, and for coming in she had to abolish polygamy, and lose her individuality, for from that day on Utah was just another state, peopled by a horde of typical American booboisie with their bourgeoisie overloads, and today Utah is a good example of what Americanization and its attendant spores can accomplish.

I have as yet made no mention of the Negro, and this article is supposed to fit into the series called—"These Colored United States." For the moment I wish to quibble, and assert that there are no Colored United States, *id est*, no state in the Union where the Negro has been an individual or vital factor. As George S. Schuyler is so fond of saying all Aframericans are merely lampblack whites steeped in American culture (?) and standardization. When it comes to such localities as Harlem, the south side black belt of Chicago, the Central Avenue district of Los Angeles, the Seventh Street district in Oakland, the North 24th Street district in Omaha, the Vine Street district in Kansas City, the Beale Street district in Memphis, and similar districts in Atlanta, Charleston, New Orleans, Houston, El Paso, Richmond, Birmingham, et cetera one might write of these as colored cities, for it is there that the Aframerican spirit manifests itself, achieving a certain individuality that is distinguishable from that achieved in similar white districts despite all the fervent protests of Brother Schuyler to the contrary. What I am leading to is this, that to write of "These Colored United States" is to be trying to visualize a phantom, for in state lots the Negro, save in such southern localities where the population is greater than the white and even in these one can only pick out certain communities to dissect, is a negative factor contributing nothing politically, historically, or economically. He only contributes sociological problems.

The above paragraph is rather rash, and perhaps I should temper it somewhat, and confine myself to the north eastern and north western states, for I am not so sure that the Negro has not made some contribution at least economically in the southern states, but neither am I so sure that this has not been swallowed up beyond the point of recognition by the whites who most certainly hold the power. And now I find justification for having such a series of articles even if they are rather far-fetched, for Negroes need to be told of past achievements and present strivings. They need this trite reminder to stir them, and to urge them on to greater achievements. They must develop a race pride, and so they must be told of what they and their foreparents have achieved. I am sorry then that I have to write of the Utah Negro, for there has been and is certainly nothing about him to inspire anyone to do anything save perhaps drink gin with gusto, and develop new technique for the contravention of virginity.

There is little difference between the few Negroes in Utah and their middle class white brethren. The only difference is one of color, and those Aframericans who have been in the state longest have done everything in their power to abolish even this difference. Miscegenation was the common thing for years, and until a state law was passed prohibiting intermarriage the clerks at the county court house were kept busy signing up fair ladies with dusky men. Then when the prohibitive law was passed the roads to Wyoming and Montana were crowded until those commonwealths also passed anti-miscegenation laws. What is more it reached such proportions that even as late as 1915 there was in Salt Lake a club catering only to Negro men and white women, and, when I was last there, which was a year ago, there were three super-bawdy houses that I knew of, where white ladies of joy with itching palms cavorted for the pleasure of black men only.

This situation was of course not peculiar to Utah alone. It was also true of most western states, and the "Manassa" group of the middle-west was far more notorious than any like group Utah has produced. However, this happened only because the population of Utah was considerable less than that of some of her sister states. Statistics will readily prove, I believe, that comparatively speaking the intermixing of races was as great or greater in Utah than in any other western state.

But to get to another point—There were two Negroes in the first overland Mormon train, a man and his wife, (he had only one, for Mormons did not believe that a Negro could ever enter into Heaven as an angel, and that since because of Ham's sin he was to be deprived of full privileges in Heaven, he was not entitled to enjoy the full privileges of a good Mormon on earth), who were servitors to Brigham Young. A little later other vagabond souls, eager to escape the terrors of both the pre and post civil war south, drifted in and remained if they found employment. Then still others were caught in the contemporary westward drift of American population, and entered into the "Bee" state as gamblers, gold-seekers, prostitutes, and home servants. And later, during the ascendancy of the Gentile regime there was quite an influx of

Pullman car porters, dining car men, hotel waiters plus more pimps and prostitutes. This population was for the most part transient, but a few of them accidentally during drunken moments or temporary physical ecstasy settled there and commenced the raising of families, which families are now members of the Utah Negroes' *haute monde*.

Until the war had inspired the northern migration of southern colored people there were few of what is known as respectable Negroes in the whole state. These strived hard to cling together, and they generally did except upon the matter of religion, which I might boldly add herein, has done more to keep the American Negro at variance with himself than any other agency. Some folk were Methodists, some were Baptists. Then some Methodists would turn Baptists, and some Baptists would turn Methodists. Moreover some Methodists and some Baptists, would grow discontented and there would be rumors of a split, and most times these rumors would develop into actualities. At the present time there are three Negro churches in Salt Lake City, which has a population of about 1,800 colored people. Only about 500 of these are of the church going variety, and imagine their strength divided as they are between two Baptist and one Methodist Churches.

Salt Lake City and Ogden have the largest Negro communities, and of these two Salt Lake has the greater population, but one would never believe this after walking thru the streets of the two cities, for one can walk for hours in Salt Lake without meeting a colored person, while in Ogden one will meet any number in the downtown district. This is due to the fact that the Negro population of Salt Lake has not become centralized, and there is no Negro ghetto, while in Ogden almost the entire Negro population is centered around the railroad yards and depot, because almost the entire Negro population of Ogden is engaged in fleecing the transient railroad porters and dining car waiters out of as much money as possible while these men are in the town. The only other place in Utah where there is an appreciable colored settlement is at Sunnyside, in the southern part of the state, where some two or three hundred men are employed in the coke ovens.

In the glorious state of Utah there are no representative Negro institutions of note save the deluxe gambling clubs, and whore houses in Salt Lake and Ogden. The churches are pitiful and impotent. There are no Negro professional men. There are no Negro publications not even a church bulletin. There are no Negro business houses. There are no Negro stores. There are no Negro policemen, no Negro firemen, no Negro politicians, save some petty bondsmen. There are a few Negro mail carriers, and the only Negro mail clerk in the state passes for

Spanish or something else that he isn't in order to keep his position and not be forced to become a pack laden carrier. Most of the Negroes in the state are employed on the railroad as porters and dining car waiters, or else in the local railroad shops, or else earn their livelihood as janitors, hotel waiters, and red caps, thereby enabling themselves to buy property and become representative bourgeoisie.

Negroes are rigorously segregated in theaters, public amusement parks, soda fountains, and eating places. This too seems to be a result of the post world war migration of southern Negroes to the north which was accompanied by a post world war wave of Kluxism and bigotry. The earlier Negro settlers experienced little of these things. They were welcome in any of the public places, but as the Negro population grew, and as the Gentile population grew so did prejudice and racial discrimination until now the only thing that distinguishes Utah from Georgia is that it does not have jim-crow cars. Last year there was even a lynching—the second in the history of the state.

Add to this the general dullness and asininity of the place and the people, and you will understand why a writer (who was also born in Utah) in a recent issue of the *American Mercury* declared that there was not an artist in the entire state, and that if one was to stay there he would soon be liable to incarceration in the insane asylum at Provo, or else buried in one of the numerous Latter Day Saint cemeteries. I was there for a short time last summer, and sought to buy my regular quota of reading matter. I asked for a *New Republic* at every down town newsstand in Salt Lake City, and out of ten stands only one had ever heard of it. I made equally vain searches for *The Nation, The Living Age, The Bookman, The Mercury,* and *The Saturday Review of Literature*. At the only stand that had ever heard of these publications the proprietor advised me to pay him in advance and he would order them for me as he did for a few other of his customers who were crazy enough to read such junk. He capped it all by enquiring whether or not I was a Bolshevist.

Thus is Utah burdened with dull and unprogressive Mormons, with more dull and speciously progressive Gentiles, with still more dull and not even speciously progressive Negroes. Everyone in the state seems to be more or less of a vegetable, self satisfied and complacent. Yet I suppose that Utah is no worse than some of its nearby neighboring states, which being the case the fates were not so unkind after all—I might have been born in Texas, or Georgia, or Tennessee, or Nevada, or Idaho.

WOMAN'S MOST SERIOUS PROBLEM

In an essay that resonates in today's society, Alice Dunbar-Nelson writes about the sociological impact of black women's changing employment patterns upon African Americans generally. This essay was published in February 1927.

E. B. Reuter, in his latest book, "The American Race Problem," makes this comment, "During the past decade there has been a somewhat marked improvement in the economic conditions of the Negroes. This is reflected in the decline of the number of women employed, and in the shift in numbers in different occupations." This statement is followed by a table showing the shift in occupational employment.

From one elevator operator in 1910, the number jumped to 3,073 in 1920. Those engaged in lumber and furniture industries in 1910 were 1,456. In 1920, 4,066. Textile industries jumped from 2,234 to 7,257. On the other hand, chambermaids in 1910 were numbered 14,071, but in 1920 they had declined to 10,443. Untrained nurses from 17,874 to 13,888; cooks from 205,584 to 168,710; laundresses, not in public laundries, from 361,551 to 283,557. On the other hand, cigar and tobacco workers jumped from 10,746 to 21,829, and the teaching profession showed a normal increase from 22,528 to 29,244.

Just what do these figures indicate? That the Negro woman is leaving the industries of home life, cooking, domestic service generally, child nursing, laundry work and going into mills, factories, operation of elevators, clerking, stenography (for in these latter occupations there is an almost 400 per cent. increase). She is doing a higher grade of work, getting better money, commanding better respect from the community because of her higher economic value, and less menial occupation. Domestic service claims her race no longer as its inalienable right. She is earning a salary, not wages.

This sounds fine. For sixty-three years the Negro woman has been a co-worker with the Negro man. Now that she is more than ever working by his side, she feels a thrill of pride in her new economic status.

But—"the ratio of children to women has declined from census to census for both races. The decline has in general been more rapid for the Negro than for the white elements in the population."* In 1850 the number of children under five years of age per 1,000 women from 15 to 44 years of age for Negro women was 741, for white women, 659. In 1920 the Negro birth rate had decreased to 439, the white to 471. While the percentage of children under five years of age had decreased in the case of Negro women from 13.8 in Negro families to 10.9, and in white families from 11.9 to 10.9!

"In spite of the considerable increase in the Negro population and in the increase of the marriage rate, the actual number of Negro children under five years of age was less in 1920 than at any of the previous enumerations."* In 1900 the number of Negro children under five years of age was 1,215,655; in 1910, the number was 1,263,288; in 1920 it was 1,143,699!

And this sharp decline in the face of increased knowledge of the care and feeding of infants; the work of the insurance companies in health, Negro Health Week, public health nurses, clinics, dispensaries, and all the active agencies for the conservation and preservation of health.

One startling fact is apparent. Negro women are exercising birth control in order to preserve their new economic independence. Or, because of poverty of the family, they are compelled to limit their offspring.

The same author, Dr. Reuter, tells us that a recent study showed that fifty-five Negro professors at Howard University had come from families averaging 6.5 children, while the professors themselves had an average of 0.7 children. Some were unmarried, but for each family formed, the average number of children was 1.6. "The birth rate of the cultured classes is apparently only one-third of the masses."

The race is here faced with a startling fact. Our birth rate is declining: our infant mortality is increasing; our normal rate of increase must necessarily be slowing up; our educated and intelligent classes are refusing to have children; our women are going into the kind of work that taxes both physical and mental capacities, which of itself, limits

*E. B. Reuter

fecundity. While white women are beginning to work more away from home, at present, even with the rush of all women into the wage earners class, in New York City alone, seven times as many colored as white women work away from home.

The inevitable disruption of family life necessitated by the woman being a co-wage earner with the man has discouraged the Negro woman from child-bearing. Juvenile delinquents are recruited largely from the motherless home. That is the home that is without the constant care of the mother or head of the house. For a child to arise in the morning after both parents are gone, get itself an indifferent breakfast, go to school uncared for, lunch on a penny's worth of sweets, and return to a cold and cheerless house or apartment to await the return of a jaded and fatigued mother to get supper, is not conducive to sweetness and light in its behavior. Truancy, street walking, petty thievery and gang rowdyism are the natural results of this lack of family life. The Negro woman is awakening to the fact that the contribution she makes to the economic life of the race is too often made at the expense of the lives of the boys and girls of the race—so she is refusing to bring into the world any more potential delinquents.

This is the bald and ungarnished statement of a startling series of facts. The decline in the birth rate of the Negro. The rise in the economic life of the Negro woman. The sharpest peak of the decline—if a decline can be said to have a peak—is in the birth rate of the more cultured and more nearly leisure classes. The slow increase in the national family life, caused by the women workers not having time to make homes in the strictest sense of homemaking. The sharp rise in juvenile delinquency—in the cities, of course, and among the children of women workers. And worst of all because more subtle and insinuating in its flattering connotation of economic freedom, handsome salaries and social prestige—the growing use of married women of the child-bearing age as public school teachers, with the consequent temptation to refrain from child-bearing in order not to interfere with the independent life in the school room.

This is the situation. I would not suggest any remedy, make any criticism, raise any question, nor berate the men and women who are responsible for this crisis. For it is a serious crisis. I would only ask the young and intelligent women to give pause.

The new Negro is the topic most dwelt upon these days by the young folks, whom some call, frequently in derisive envy, the "Intelligentsia." In every race, in every nation and in every clime in every period of history there is always an eager-eyed group of youthful patriots who seriously set themselves to right the wrongs done to their race, or nation or sect or sometimes to art or self-expression. No race or nation can advance without them. Thomas Jefferson was an ardent leader of youthful patriots of his day, and Alexander Hamilton would have been dubbed a leader of the intelligentsia were he living now. They do big things, these young people.

Perhaps they may turn their attention, these race-loving slips of girls and slim ardent youths who make hot-eyed speeches about the freedom of the individual and the rights of the Negro, to the fact that at the rate we are going the Negro will become more and more negligible in the life of the nation. For we must remember that while the Negro constituted 19.3 per cent. of the population in 1790, and 18.9 in 1800, he constitutes only 9.9 per cent. today, and his percentage of increase has steadily dropped from 37.5 in 1810 to 6.3 in 1920.

No race can rise higher than its women is an aphorism that is so trite that it has ceased to be tiresome from its very monotony. If it might be phrased otherwise to catch the attention of the Negro woman, it would be worth while making the effort. No race can be said to be a growing race, whose birth rate is declining, and whose natural rate of increase is dropping sharply. No race will amount to anything economically, no matter how high the wages it collects nor how many commercial enterprises it supports, whose ownership of homes has not kept proportionate pace with its business holdings. Churches, social agencies, schools and Sunday schools cannot do the work of mothers and heads of families. Their best efforts are as cheering and comforting to the soul of a child in comparison with the welcoming smile of the mother when it comes from school as the machine-like warmth of an incubator is to a chick after the downy comfort of a clucking hen. Incubators are an essential for the mass production of chickens, but the training of human souls needs to begin at home in the old-fashioned family life, augmented later, if necessary, in the expensive schools and settlements of the great cities.

Biographical Notes of Contributors

Bagnall, Robert (1864–1943), clergyman and civil-rights worker, was born in Norfolk, Virginia. He was educated at Bishop Payne Divinity School (Virginia) and was ordained an Episcopal priest in 1903. He served pastorates in Pennsylvania, Maryland, and Ohio. In 1921 Bagnall became director of branches for the NAACP. In 1931 he accepted the pastorate of St. Thomas's Episcopal Church in Philadelphia. Bagnall was a man of broad knowledge and possessed great writing and oratory skills. His writings appeared mainly in *The Crisis*.

Bontemps, Arna (1907–1972), poet, librarian, and novelist, was born in Alexandria, Louisiana. At the age of three, he moved with his family to Los Angeles. Educated at San Fernando Academy and Pacific Union College, he moved to Harlem in 1924, where he was soon welcomed into the "Talented Tenth" club, was published, and received awards for poetry from both *Opportunity* and *The Crisis*, and a Rosenwald fellowship for Caribbean travel. Following some career-enhancing collaborations with Countee Cullen, Harold Arlen, and Langston Hughes, he spent his final years as curator of the James Weldon Johnson Memorial Collection of Negro Arts and Letters at Yale University.

Coleman, Anita Scott (1890–1960), poet, short-story writer, and essayist, was born in the city of Guaymas, Mexico. Her father, a Cuban, purchased her mother as a slave. She was educated in the school system in Silver City, New Mexico. She published in *The Crisis, Opportu-*

nity, The Messenger, Flash, and other magazines. Under the pseudonym of Elizabeth Stapleton Stokes, she published a book of poems: *Small Wisdom* (1937).

COLSON, WILLIAM N., essayist, editorial writer, was a contributing editor for *The Messenger* magazine.

CULLEN, COUNTEE (1903–1946), poet, essayist, and educator, was the adopted son of the prominent Harlem minister Reverend Frederick Cullen. Born in Lexington, Kentucky, he attended De Witt Clinton High School in New York City, where he was editor of the school newspaper. Cullen earned his B.A. degree and election to Phi Beta Kappa at New York University and his M.A. in English at Harvard University. His first poetry was published at age fifteen. He received the Witter Bynner Poetry Prize at New York University, the Harmon Foundation Gold Medal Award, *Opportunity* poetry prizes, and, in 1928, the first Guggenheim fellowship awarded to an African American. He taught in the public-school system of New York City.

DOMINGO, W. A. [WILFRID ADOLPHUS] (1889–?), journalist and activist, was born in Jamaica. He came to New York City in 1910. Around 1918, he cofounded the African Blood Brotherhood, a proto-Marxist African-American group. He was among the early members of fellow West Indian Marcus Garvey's Universal Negro Improvement Association (UNIA), and became a founding editor of the organization's official publication, *The Negro World.* By 1919, Domingo had committed himself to socialism. More receptive to *The Messenger*'s socialist views, he joined A. Philip Randolph and Chandler Owen on that magazine's editorial staff in 1919. Fearing that Garvey's extremist philosophy was a threat to socialism among black Americans, he vigoriously attacked Garvey's financial handling of the UNIA in his writings.

DUNBAR-NELSON, ALICE (1875–1935), author, social worker, and poet, studied at Straight College (now Dillard University), New Orleans, Louisiana; the University of Pennsylvania; Cornell University; and the School of Industrial Arts (Philadelphia) before she married the poet Paul Laurence Dunbar in 1898. Dunbar died in 1904. In 1916, she married Robert J. Nelson. Alice Dunbar-Nelson was a probation and parole officer, served as associate editor of the *AME Review* of the African Methodist Episcopal Church, and was editor of the Wilmington, Delaware, *Advocate.* She was also a weekly contributor to the Associated Negro Press. Her books include *Goodness of St. Rocque,* a book of short stories (1899); and two volumes, *Masterpieces of Negro Eloquence* (1914) and *The Dunbar Speaker* (1920).

GAINES, IRENE, was an author, a social worker, and an essayist. She was a contributor to *The Messenger* and lived in New York City.

GRIMKE, ANGELINA WELD (1880–1958), poet, playwright, and teacher, was born in Boston, Massachusetts. The only child of the noted lawyer and government official Archibald H. Grimke, she graduated from the Boston Normal School of Gymnastics (1902). She taught at the well-known Dunbar High School in Washington, D.C., until 1933. Grimke wrote *Rachel,* a three-act play, which was performed in Washington in 1916. She was active in Washington literary circles but became more reclusive during her final years.

GRIMKE, ARCHIBALD (1949–1930), author, lawyer, civil-rights leader, and diplomat, was born in Charleston, South Carolina. He graduated from Lincoln University (Pennsylvania) and Harvard Law School in 1874. He served as president of the American Negro Academy. In 1894 he became the U.S. consul to Santo Domingo. A leading force in the NAACP, he received the organization's prestigious Spingarn Medal in 1919.

HAWKINS, WALTER EVERETTE was the poet for *The Messenger.* He contributed to *The Crisis* and *Opportunity* magazines and lived in New York City.

HENRY, THOMAS MILLARD, poet, short-story writer, and essayist, contributed to *The Messenger.* He lived in New York City.

HUGHES, [JAMES] LANGSTON (1902–1967), poet, playwright, novelist, anthologist, and historian, was born in Joplin, Missouri. His parents separated when he was a child. His maternal grandfather was the abolitionist Charles Langston, who fought with John Brown at Harper's Ferry, and his half-brother was John Mercer Langston, a U.S. congressman from Virginia. While his rearing was rather peripatetic, his literary talents brought him notice in elementary and secondary schools. As a merchant seaman, Hughes saw much of the world but was "discovered" by poet Vachel Lindsay as a "busboy poet" in Washington, D.C. Having dropped out of college at Columbia, he returned to Lincoln University with the financial assistance of Amy Spingarn, wife of the NAACP board chairman J. E. Spingarn. His touching and lyrical poetry won him notice from both jazz and literary patrons, but he began to lose favor when he chose voluntary exile for a time in Cuba, Russia, and Spain. He later collaborated with Arna Bontemps on anthologies and children's works and funded theater groups in Harlem, Chicago, and Los Angeles.

HURSTON, ZORA NEALE (1907?–1960), short-story writer, playwright, and novelist, was born in Eatonville, Florida. Studying under famed anthropologist Franz Boas, she received a B.A. degree from Barnard College. She wrote three novels, *Jonah's Gourd Vine* (1934), *Their Eyes Are Watching God* (1948), and *Seraph on the Suwanee* (1948). Her autobiography, *Dust Tracks on the Road*, was published in 1943.

IMES, NELLA LARSEN (1893–1963), novelist and nurse, was born in Chicago, Illinois. She attended Fisk University and graduated from the prestigious Lincoln Hospital Training School for Nurses (New York City) in 1915. In 1930 she became the first African American to receive the prestigious Guggenheim Award. Her two novels, *Quicksand* (1928) and *Passing* (1929), were widely acclaimed.

JOHNSON, GEORGIA DOUGLAS (1886–1966), poet, essayist, and educator, was educated at Oberlin Conservatory of Music and Atlanta University, where she met and married her husband, Henry Lincoln Johnson. They settled in Washington, D.C., where she was employed by the federal government and he became a prominent figure in the Republican party. Georgia Douglas Johnson was a founder of "The First Nighters," a literary club whose membership included Mary Miller, Angelina Weld Grimke, Alain Locke, Jean Toomer, Richard Bruce Nugent, James Weldon Johnson, W.E.B. Du Bois, Jessie Fauset, and Langston Hughes. She was the first African-American woman to be widely recognized as a poet in the early twentieth century, received considerable acclaim as a poet and teacher, and won a first prize in an *Opportunity* contest for one of her plays.

JOHNSON, HELENE (1907–1995), one of the youngest of the Harlem Renaissance poets, was born in Boston, Massachusetts. She attended Boston University and Columbia University. Her poem "The Road" appeared in Alain Locke's critically acclaimed volume *The New Negro*. Her other poems were published in *Opportunity, Vanity Fair,* and *Fire!!* Johnson disappeared from Harlem shortly before the literary movement ended.

JOHNSON, S. MILLER (1900–?), poet and short-story writer, was born in Calhoun County, Arkansas. He received a B.A. degree from Hampton Institute (Virginia).

LEWIS, THEOPHILUS (1891–?), drama critic, essayist, short-story writer, was born in Baltimore, Maryland. He moved to New York shortly before World War I. In 1922 he became the drama critic for *The Messenger*. Mainly self-educated, Lewis became the most qualified black drama critic in New York.

MCKAY, CLAUDE (1889–1948), author and poet, was born in Jamaica. His initial training was in agriculture at the Tuskegee Institute, from which he later transferred to Kansas State College. Upon his arrival in New York City, he entered the bohemian and revolutionary lifestyle in Greenwich Village. His first American poetry was published under the pseudonym Eli Edwards. In 1919, McKay moved to London, where he read the works of Marx and Lenin and joined the staff of the Communist newspaper *The Worker's Dreadnought*. Disenchanted with America's race relations, with Marcus Garvey's Universal Negro Improvement Association (UNIA), and with editorial politics at the *Liberator,* where he had become editor, he traveled to France and North Africa, where he wrote many of his prize-winning works. Making an exception of James Weldon Johnson, McKay sharply criticized many senior notables of the Harlem Renaissance.

MOORE, WILLIAM, received his training in the New York City public schools, the College of the City of New York, and Columbia University. Moore was well known in literary circles in New York and Chicago.

NUGENT, R. BRUCE (1906–1989), poet, essayist, illustrator, was born in Washington, D.C., where he attended public schools. His poems were published in Countee Cullen's *Caroling Dusk* anthology. His illustrations appeared in *Fire!!, Harlem,* and other journals of the time.

OWEN, CHANDLER (1889–1967), socialist, civil-rights activist, journalist, political speech writer, was born in Warrenton, North Carolina. He graduated from Virginia Union University in 1913 and attended Columbia University. In 1917 he founded, with A. Philip Randolph, *The Messenger* magazine. During the Second World War, he worked for the Anti-Defamation League and B'nai B'rith. From 1945 to his death he wrote speeches for numerous political candidates.

OXLEY, THOMAS L. G., poet and essayist, was a contributor to *The Messenger*. He was a well-known poet in Boston literary circles.

PICKENS, WILLIAM (1881–1954), educator, college dean, civil-rights worker, and government worker, was born in Anderson County, South

Carolina. He received his B.A. from Talladega College (Talladega, Alabama) in 1902. He received a second B.A. from Yale University in 1904, where he was elected to Phi Beta Kappa. He earned his M.A. from Fisk University in 1908. He taught at Talladega College and Wiley College (Marshall, Texas), and he served as dean of Morgan College from 1915 to 1920. He then served as field secretary for the NAACP for twenty-two years. He left the NAACP in 1942 to work for the U.S. Treasury Department, where he remained until 1950. He published his autobiography, *Bursting Bonds,* in 1923.

RANDOLPH, A. [ASA] PHILIP (1889–1979), socialist, labor leader, and civil-rights activist, was born in Crescent City, Florida. Randolph moved to New York after high school. He worked at a series of odd jobs before he cofounded a socialist weekly, *The Messenger,* in 1917. In 1925 he founded the Brotherhood of Sleeping Car Porters (BSCP), and a decade later the union successfully negotiated a collective bargaining agreement with the Pullman Palace Car Company. In 1957 he was elected vice president of the AFL-CIO. His socialism toned down, he was a prominent organizer of the 1963 March on Washington. Randolph founded the A. Philip Randolph Institute in New York City, which is dedicated to education and job training.

RICHARDSON, WILLIS (1889–1977), playwright and essayist, was born in Wilmington, North Carolina, and reared in Washington, D.C. He studied at Dunbar High School. Among those who encouraged and inspired him were his teacher and aspiring playwright Mary Burill, author Angelina Grimke, and W.E.B. Du Bois. From 1910 to 1955, he supported himself as a clerk at the U.S. Bureau of Engraving. His play *Chip Woman's Fortune* opened on Broadway in May 1923. The Howard Players staged his *Mortgaged* in 1924. Other relevant works include *Plays and Pageants of Negro Life* (1930) and *Negro History in Thirteen Plays* (1935).

ROBESON, PAUL (1898–1976), lawyer, actor, singer, activist, was born in Princeton, New Jersey. He graduated from Rutgers University (New Brunswick, New Jersey) in 1919, and received a law degree from Columbia University (New York). Robeson starred in Eugene O'Neill's Broadway revival of *The Emperor Jones* in 1925. Three years later, he appeared in *Porgy* and *Show Boat.* Making racial history, Robeson starred as Othello at New York's Shubert Theatre. He was an international success as a singer, blending folk music of the world with spirituals, popular music, and other classical songs.

ROGERS, J. A. [JOEL AUGUSTUS] (1880–1966), writer and historian, was born in Negril, Jamaica. After arriving in the United States in 1906, he began to write fiction and history. His writings include *Man and Superman* (1917) and *The World's Greatest Men of African Descent* (1931).

SCHUYLER, GEORGE SAMUEL (1895–1977), novelist, journalist, activist, was born in Providence, Rhode Island. He was educated in the public schools of Syracuse, New York. Schuyler joined the army in 1912. Serving with the 25th U.S. Infantry Regiment, he rose to the rank of first lieutenant. After his seven-year army stint, he eventually settled in New York. From 1923 to 1928, he was a member of the editorial staff of *The Messenger*. During this time, he also contributed a weekly column to the *Pittsburgh Courier*. Schuyler's most well-known book, *Black No More* (1931), expressed his discontent with such Harlem Renaissance personalities as Langston Hughes and Zora Neale Hurston.

SCOTT, EMMETT J. [JAY] (1873–1957), college administrator and author, was born in Houston, Texas. He received an M.A. degree from Wiley College (Marshall, Texas) in 1901. In 1897 he became secretary to Booker T. Washington. He left Tuskegee in 1919 to become the secretary-treasurer and business manager of Howard University. He authored *Tuskegee and Its People* (1910) and *The American Negro in the World War* (1916).

THURMAN, WALLACE [H.] (1902–1934), novelist, poet, dramatist, was born in Salt Lake City, Utah. He attended the University of Utah (1919–1920). After enrolling at the University of Southern California, he met fellow writer Arna Bontemps. In 1924 he founded *The Outlet*. The journal folded in 1925, and he moved to New York City. He worked for several publications, including *The Looking Glass, The Messenger*, and *The World Tomorrow*. In 1927 he started the magazine *Fire!!*

WALROND, ERIC D. (1898–1956), short-story writer, was born in Georgetown, Guyana. He moved to New York in 1918 and later attended City College and Columbia University. After serving as a staff member of Marcus Garvey's newspaper, *The Negro World*, Walrond joined the staff of *Opportunity* as business manager from 1925 to 1927. He left America for England in 1928 to write a novel about the Panama Canal. For the next twenty-eight years he would remain in England without ever publishing.

WEST, DOROTHY (1908–1998), short-story writer and novelist, was born in Boston, Massachusetts. She attended Boston University and Columbia University. "The Typewriter," a short story, was published in *Opportunity* when she was eighteen years old.

BIBLIOGRAPHY

Anderson, Jervis. *A. Philip Randolph: A Portrait.* New York: Harcourt Brace Jovanovich, 1972.

Aptheker, Herbert, ed. *A Documentary History of the Negro People in the United States, 1910–1932,* vol. 3. Secaucus, N.J.: Citadel Press, 1977.

Bontemps, Arna, ed. *The Harlem Renaissance Remembered.* New York: Dodd Mead, 1972.

Cruse, Harold. *The Crisis of the Negro Intellectual: A Historical Analysis of the Failure of Black Leadership.* New York: Quill, 1984.

Du Bois, W.E.B. *The Autobiography of W.E.B. Du Bois.* New York: International Publishers, 1968.

Gates, Henry Louis, Jr., and Nellie Y. McKay, eds. *The Norton Anthology of African American Literature.* New York: W.W. Norton, 1996.

Hemenway, Robert. *Zora Neale Hurston: A Literary Biography.* Urbana: University of Illinois Press, 1977.

Huggins, Nathan Irvin. *Black Odyssey: The Afro-American Ordeal in Slavery.* New York: Vintage Books, 1979.

———. *Harlem Renaissance.* New York: Oxford University Press, 1971.

Johnson, James Weldon. *Black Manhattan.* New York: Alfred A. Knopf, 1930.

———. *Negro Americans, What Now?* New York: The Viking Press, 1934.

Lewis, David Levering. *When Harlem Was in Vogue.* New York: Oxford University Press, 1981.

———. *W.E.B. Du Bois, A Biography of a Race: 1868–1919.* New York: Henry Holt & Company, 1993.

———, ed. *The Portable Harlem Renaissance.* New York: Viking Press, 1981.

Moses, Wilson Jeremiah. *The Golden Age of Black Nationalism.* New York: Oxford University Press, 1978.

National Association for the Advancement of Colored People. *The Crisis* (1910–1931).

Rampersad, Arnold. *The Life of Langston Hughes, Volume I: I, Too, Sing America.* New York: Oxford University Press, 1986.

Singh, Amritjit, William S. Shiver and Stanley Brodwin, eds. *The Harlem Renaissance: Revaluations.* New York: Garland Publishing, 1989.

Watkins, Sylvestre C., ed. *Anthology of American Negro Literature.* New York: Modern Library, 1944.

Wilson, Sondra Kathryn, ed. *The Selected Writings of James Weldon Johnson,* vols. 1 & 2. New York: Oxford University Press, 1995.

ABOUT THE EDITOR

DR. SONDRA KATHRYN WILSON is an associate of Harvard University's W.E.B. Du Bois Institute and executor of James Weldon Johnson's literary properties. Her publications include two volumes of Johnson's writings and *The* Crisis *Reader: Stories, Poetry, and Essays from the N.A.A.C.P.'s* Crisis *Magazine, The* Opportunity *Reader: Stories, Poetry, and Essays from the Urban League's* Opportunity *Magazine,* and *In Search of Democracy: The N.A.A.C.P. Writings of James Weldon Johnson, Walter F. White, and Roy Wilkins.* Her upcoming publications include *Lift Every Voice and Sing: 100 Years, 100 Voices,* edited with Julian Bond.